ARTISTS IN THE ARCHIVE

ARTISTS IN THE ARCHIVE

Creative and Curatorial Engagements with Documents of Art and Performance

Edited by Paul Clarke, Simon Jones, Nick Kaye and Johanna Linsley

Artists in the Archive

Artists in the Archive explores the agency and materiality of the archival document through a stunning collection of critical writings and original artworks. It examines the politics and philosophy behind re-using remains, historicising this artistic practice and considering the breadth of ways in which archival materials inform, inflect and influence new works.

Taking a fresh look at the relationships between insider know-how and outsider knowledge, *Artists in the Archive* opens a vital dialogue between a global range of artists and scholars. It seeks to trouble the distinction between artistic practice and scholarly research, offering disciplinary perspectives from experimental theatre, performance art, choreography and dance, to visual art making, archiving and curating.

PAUL CLARKE is an artist, theatre director, and Lecturer in Performance Studies at the University of Bristol.

SIMON JONES is Professor of Performance at the University of Bristol, a writer and scholar, and founder and co-director of physical theatre company Bodies in Flight.

NICK KAYE is Professor of Performance Studies at the University of Exeter.

JOHANNA LINSLEY is an artist, researcher and producer, a founder of the performance/producing collective I'm With You, and a founding partner of documentary arts centre UnionDocs, Brooklyn, NY.

Introduction: inside and outside the archive

Paul Clarke, Simon Jones, Nick Kaye and Johanna Linsley

To archive is to give place, order and future to the remainder; to consider *things*, including documents, as reiterations to be acted upon; as potential evidence for histories yet to be completed. As the material in this book demonstrates, the archive is never static nor simply pertains to the past. Archives are comprised in their continuing and future enactment and use; in layers of performance. *Artists in the Archive* explores performances and interactivities within and across the boundaries of the archive and its performance, in exchanges between archives, archivists and communities of performance-makers, scholars and audiences where materials of the archive are defined, used, reiterated, brought out-of-context, *done with*. Such practices erode conventional antagonisms between performance and archive, acknowledging that performance remains and recordings disappear, that archives perform and that documents are performative. To this end, this book approaches archival acts as performative in their aesthetic, social and political staging of the remainder and the document; formulating archives as leaky economies of generative and persistent acts in time; exploring traversals in which materials are placed, removed and implicitly returned to the archive in new variations and redefinitions. This focus also reflects a growing interest in curation, performance and performance theory in ways in which performance art history can be conserved, communicated and understood trans-generationally and in how we *do* history through practice. Here, as theoretical framework and cultural practice and product, performance provides models for the use and embodiment of archive and archival material. Elaborating this emphasis on equations between the archive and temporality, performance and performativity, this volume brings together essays, scores, reflections and documentations that interrogate the discreteness of documents and the performance events they construct as their objects; questioning distinctions between acts of performance, documenting, archiving and re-use.

To archive also means to encounter and navigate institutions, which are sites of this practice and which also condition how this practice is legible: how events and things are constructed as potential 'evidence'. Here, archiving means engaging with economies: not just markets but systems of distribution of resources, which provoke questions around waste and conservation, and around the commodification of what remains. There are matters of skill and labour that attend the practice of archiving, including questions about the impact that this work has on the body.
In these regards, *Artists in the Archive* also addresses the definition of the archive found in dialogues between infrastructural and institutional contexts and individual and communal artistic practices. Institutional archives may amplify the dynamics of authority that operate between the recollection of practice, the recovery of the remainder and truth-making. They may trouble the ephemerality of performance by asserting continuations, repetitions, and entanglements of things and events; by valorizing the recurrence (and performance) of origin; and by configuring new acts of performance as *documentary*. It is a process linked also to the politics and aesthetics of commodification and the development of new technologies, in and through which histories of de-materialization and the definition of performance art are re-written, through the contemporary art market and its archives, as the performative production of objects, relics and traces of value and desire. Practices that counter these tendencies include positioning the relic as *score*, incorporating the agency of objects and things into performance, and exploring counter-hegemonic practices of self-archiving that reiterate identities in layered understandings of self and community, history and performance. Here, the remaking, remixing and review—the repetition and rewriting—of performance exposes and extends the archive's generation of new histories, working over the paradoxes of loss, remainder and recurrence that archival acts precipitate.

These approaches to archive draw on the notion in Jacques Derrida's *Archive Fever* that etymologically *arche* is not only 'the commencement', but also 'the commandment' (1998: 2): that the performativity of the archive rules and shapes an artistic discipline or art institution's future, commanding the re-writings and re-makings of the past that history can perform. The archive thus brings the artefact to a place where simultaneously memory is claimed and a future authority asserted; to *acts of ordering* that the future use and performance of artefacts or archives inevitably participates in and extends. So, whereas traditional scholarship invariably appraises archives in relation to historical and art-historical narratives, positioning its documents as *evidence* of past events, this book explores models for the future use of documents in practice-as-research, and the potentialities, effects and implications of such processes. Here, objects, traces and relics are read as potential sources of new knowledge and activity; as affected by and affecting emergent histories. In this context, *Artists in the Archive* also looks at how artists and academics can use and reuse documents of past events to inflect and inspire their own performance practice and discourse: it addresses the relationship of archives to the future of creative practices, exploring the tactics of artists and practitioner-researchers in the archive as models for the future use of documents and potential relationships of the archive to the future of art and performance practice. To this end, this volume also shifts an engagement with the archive from being orientated to the past, to the future of the past.

The tenses of archive

As this emphasis implies, archives and archival material also stand at a juncture of archaeology and historiography. The archive houses and orders artefacts - traces, relics, other modes of 'evidence' —the status (and meaning) of which is liminal, *in potential*. Archival material precedes and disrupts historiographical practice, holding 'information' in excess of narratives yet to be written. This emphasis on *potentialities* also underlies the archive's tie to performance. Archive is of interest to performance precisely because its elements are unresolved, are subject overtly to *acts of ordering*, as 'potential evidence,' as that which is to be read; as *score*: while many archival collections of contemporary material are frequently, in practice, yet to be ordered; remaining preserved, held and unavailable, locked away into their potential; *awaiting an act*. Archival collections consequently order things *towards* a future, are caught in the midst of a process of place-making, of a setting of things in an order:

a distribution of points yet to be joined, to be acted out and realized as histories.

In this book, performance as archive captures this troubling of the narrative place of things, where artefacts are hinges between tenses, disciplines, and potential stories. It is a tendency readily reflected in performance practices defined or invested in the return of actions and events that are ostensibly *of* the past: re-stagings of the remains of earlier works through the generation of new performances that become implicitly archival gestures. Such re-doings have proliferated as a strategy in contemporary art and curatorial practices, along with the prevalence of performance as a medium in gallery and museum contexts: contexts identified with the archive, with collection and preservation. Notable examples from many of such recurrences include Marina Abramović's 'cover' of six iconic performances from the late 1960s and 1970s in *Seven Easy Pieces* (2005), André Lepecki's meticulous reconstruction of Allan Kaprow's 1959 *18 Happenings in 6 Parts* in Munich in 2006, the series of re-stagings of 1960s performance in the Performa Biennial in New York in 2007 and subsequent re-performances of Kaprow's participatory happenings in 2011 at Tate Modern. More recently, the Slought Foundation has published its studies for a re-staging of Dennis Oppenheim's *Protection* (1971) in its original location of the Boston Museum of Fine Arts (Lucia 2016). It is an agenda that extends also to the remaking of work across media, such as Alexandra Prici and Manuel Pelmus' *Public Collection Tate Modern* (2016), in which the artists re-make as performances artworks in other media and held in the Tate collection, including Mark Rothko's *Seagram Murals* (1958–9), Carl Andre's *Equavalent VIII* (1966), but also including Tania Bruguera's performance work, *Tatlin's Whisper #5* (2008). Re-doings have also extended to old and new media, such as Franco and Eva Mattes staging of Abramović and Ulay's *Imponderabilia* (1977/2007), Chris Burden's *Shoot* (1971/2009), Vito Acconci's *Seedbed* (1972/2010) and actions by VALIE EXPORT and Gilbert and George in synthetic Second Life performances (Mattes and Mattes 2016). Such work also frequently erodes conventional distinctions between performance and its documentation, posing questions over what archives may in practice recall. In this context, Rebecca Schneider has critiqued Abramović's *Seven Easy Pieces* as reconstructing performances from their documents in order to document again; naming this practice 'Redocumentment' (Schneider 2009). Rather than performance re-enactments, Abramović enacts or re-does documents, which are used as scripts for performances to camera, to produce new documentation with high production values. It could be argued that some of the works documented in the pages that follow are 'redocumentments', although often of marginalised artworks, not with the intention of reconstructing, or with higher production values to which capital would accrue. These ideas and practices also place under pressure the notions of 're-enactment', 're-staging' and 'repetition'. Rather than calling the examples included in *Artists in the Archive* re-enactments, we use the term enactment as these iterations do not lay claims to reconstruction, reproduction or a desire to restore a past work to full presence, but instead carry forward a certain life-cycle of the work: elements re-contextualized and transformed; acts invoking a knowledge or memory of other events in which they are also formed. Thus, rather than re-enacting 'to fix a work in its singular (originating) possibilization' (Lepecki 2010: 31), whereby performance becomes known and stabilized in its re-documented history, the works engaged with here take up the strategy Lepecki proposes in 'The Body as Archive: Will to Re-enact and the Afterlives of Dances' of treating past works of performance as 'always incomplete'. Lepecki proposes 'turning/returning to' them 'and experimenting with creative means' of activating their latent forces in an attempt 'to unlock, release, and actualize a work's many (virtual) com- and incompossibilities, which the originating instantiation of the work kept in reserve, virtually' (2010: 45).

These continuities between performance, document and archive also have consequences for the idea and practice of performance itself. Where performance acts as a metaphor for the *potentiality* and *acts* to which archive and archiving are deeply linked, so the objects of the performance archive—in their persistence—challenge the dichotomies in which performance and performance art have frequently been defined. The emergent orders, that archives promise, work to trouble the ephemerality of performance by posing questions of continuation, recurrence, repetition and entanglement. In response, this publication also moves beyond the well-rehearsed ontological debates around performance disappearing (Phelan 1993) and performance remaining (Schneider 2011). Instead the texts and artists' pages explore how the apparently stable world of 'things', traces, or remains, and time-based, ephemeral or immaterial performance interact, influence, determine and co-constitute one another. Performance both 'becomes itself through disappearance' (Phelan 1993: 146) *and* remains: it *becomes itself* in a process of disappearance in which 'it' remains entangled in the things by which it is known. In the archive, too, performance cannot be separated from afterlives that continue to circulate and be transmitted in many forms;

body-to-body, through documents, in-and-through practice, re-performance, word-of-mouth and oral history, rumour, embodied memory, and so forth. This emphasis resists the tendency in performance theory to rehearse relationships between performance and matters of loss and death, where performance's ontology in disappearance gains resonance in relationships with mortality, trauma and the rehearsal of irrevocable loss. Such equations are powerfully introduced in Phelan's *Unmarked* (1993) and elaborated explicitly in her essay 'Performance and Death' (1999) as well as writing by Marvin Carlson (2001), Adrian Heathfield (1997) and others. *Artists in the Archive* counters this in its invitation to consider the construction of memory in performance and by the use of objects; and in asking how remains carry traces of the events that produced them.

Here, too, *Artists in the Archive* interrogates practices and discourses reflecting the paradoxical notions of continuity captured by *intangible heritage*: in the persistence of the immaterial; of how cultural continuity is at play in new iterations and inscriptions of performed acts. As Diana Taylor has argued in *The Archive and the Repertoire* (2003), the authors take performance seriously as a means of storing and transmitting knowledge, accepting that performances function 'as vital acts of transfer, transmitting social knowledge, memory, and a sense of identity through reiterated, or what Richard Schechner has called "twice-behaved behavior."' (Taylor 2003: 2–3). The doing of performance history through artists' workshops in archives, exhibitions and performance relates also to what, Elizabeth Freeman writes, 'following the film critic Laura Marks, might be called haptic historiography [...] ways of negotiating with the past and producing historical knowledge through visceral sensations' (2010: 123). There is also a proximity to what Freeman calls 'erotohistoriography', which 'sees the body as a method' and 'uses the body as a tool to effect, figure, or perform' encounters with the past in the present. Freeman concludes that: 'Erotohistoriography admits that contact with historical materials can be precipitated by particular bodily dispositions, and that these connections may elicit bodily responses, or "corporeal sensations," even pleasurable ones, that are themselves a form of understanding' (2010: 95–6). In the artists' pages in this volume, the reader will find propositions or case studies for ways of doing historiography through performance, 'touching history' or 'erotohistoriography'; understanding through doing performance, curating, spectating or viewing. Where previous studies have tended to explore the potentiality of the archive either as carrier of meaning, problematizing agency and historical account, or as a necessary component in the fascination with re-enactment, re-play and revival (see Schneider 2011, Taylor 2003 particularly; also, Borggreen and Gade 2013, Jones and Heathfield 2012), *Artists in the Archive* focuses on the breadth of ways in which archival remains inform, inflect and influence the production of new works, on how artists are incorporating archival material in their creative processes across a range of performance and visual-arts practices. This shifts attention firmly on to the doing of things with performance's material remains, and towards particular encounters with the materiality of such remainders. *Artists in the Archive* thus builds on the interest shown by both artists and scholars in the relationship between the archive and contemporary performance and visual arts. It engages with and moves beyond studies on the re-animation of archives in re-enactment and re-visualization in exhibition to focus on the agency and materiality of the archival document, the role such materials play in artistic process, specifically *the making of new works*.

Traversals

Echoing ways in which practice and use move across the boundaries and order of the archive, in its structure this book is designed to produce open dialogues between artists and scholars exploring a range of relationships between *insider know-how* and *outsider knowledge*, so interrogating and troubling the distinction between artistic practice and scholarly research. *Artists in the Archive* offers a framework of keynote chapters exploring the publication's focus on doing and making with archives, their agency and materiality, set in juxtaposition with clusters of exemplary case studies by artists exploring how archives are active, prompting and intervening in the making of new work. Performance, visual forms and writing by artists are treated as critical practices, whilst criticism and curating are considered in their creative aspects, the resultant exhibition and discursive framings of which transform the remains of art and performance. Case studies are clustered in accordance with affinities and dialogues between actions and processes that REMAKE, RETURN, REVIEW and ARCHIVE. Each practice case study is also represented in a different form on the page, providing a diversity of design intended to extend and reflect upon relationships between analysis and documentation, while laying out a range of models to inspire readers in critical reflections on their own creative engagement with archive. Further to this Introduction, each cluster of case studies is prefaced with a discussion of their practices and themes, as well as introducing the artists and the contexts in which these various documentations, scores and reflections were generated and developed. In its range of contributions, *Artists in the Archive* also traverses diverse practices from experimental theatre, to performance art, choreography and dance, to visual art making, archiving and curating. The geographical and cultural reach of the volume extends beyond Western Europe and the United States, to Asian, Middle Eastern and Eastern European contexts. This multi-perspectival use is intended to address a wide range of scholars and students, as well as artists and arts professionals, across the disciplines of both performance studies and visual art.

The structuring principle of the volume is played out, too, in many individual contributions, where practice traverses the boundaries and purposes of the archive. Rather than emphasize formal interests around the archive and documentation, these critics and artists are concerned with the philosophical implications and resistant politics of re-using the remainders of art and performance: queering archives, intervening in conventional chronologies and fictionalizing art historical narratives; in mining the socio-political potentiality of reiterating past works in the present scene; of working over the impact of critically re-contextualizing significant works from Western art history in other cultural contexts; and in remaking the self and the relationship between contemporary archival technologies and identity.

Introducing a key theme of the volume, Nick Kaye's opening essay, 'Liveness and the entanglement with things,' reads relationships between performance and its material remainders through recent archaeological concepts of 'entanglement' and the co-dependency of humans and things, to challenge the conventional dichotomy of the live event and its dead remains. Focusing on the life-cycle of performance and conceptual art works through the lens of Marina Abramović's celebrated reiterations of earlier performance works in *Seven Easy Pieces* (2005), Kaye considers how the affordances and agency of objects and things have been integral to performance and conceptual art, including Abramović's own practice. It follows that where the materials and objects of performance afford and shape events and processes, so the locus of the 'live' may shift from a present-tense ephemerality always already lost, towards its processual construction over time; and so in relation to things as well as acts. The artists' pages that follow—clustered as REMAKE—interrogate and embody diverse practices that carry forward things and processes from specific performances, towards the new: from the enactment of scores and scripts (Etchells), to the re-imaginings and reconstructions of events and objects (Butcher and Sachsenmaier, Janša, Zhang), to speculations on the dream as documentation (Deacon). Adrian Heathfield's 'The ghost time of transformation' directs an analogous debate towards other reiterations of ephemeral forms, calling on Henri Focillon's 1930s treatise on *The Life Forms in Art* to consider the fluidity and metamorphosis of forms and the affective nature of things. Heathfield's focus is the 2012 exhibition 'Moments. A History of Performance in 10 Acts' at ZKM Karlsruhe, Germany, which comprised performances by ten female artists, whose first iterations were in the 1960s and 1970s. Exemplifying, for Heathfield, curation as a self-questioning mediation, 'Moments' was openly 'assembled, reconfigured and disassembled over a period of 52 days'; a processual approach invested also in the iterations of each of the works re-visioned. In this workshop-style process, Heathfield argues, these enactments were '"returned" through morphological display to conditions of relation, flow, and multiplicity from which they had been extracted'. Observing the interrogation of the institution—and re-staging itself—in the contingent return of Simone Forti's *Face Tunes* (1967), a performance concerned with Forti's sense of 'the tangibility of the invisible,' Heathfield poses questions of the 'here-not here' in which the 'return' of the work and its materials occur, is experienced, and regains critical and political force. In turn, this essay presages practice case studies clustered as RETURN: of the diverse materials of an artists' earlier works (Blast Theory) or the beginnings of works now being unmade (Hixson and Goulish); of the repeated and meaningful absence of work retold (Performance Re-enactment Society); of the archive in performance and as repetition (Pil and Galia Kollectiv). In this section, too, Paul Clarke's contribution explicitly brokers between essay and document to interrogate the temporal practices of 'Performing art history' through the Performance Re-enactment Society's *Group Show* (2012). Drawing on Elizabeth Freeman's concept of 'temporal drag,' Clarke and PRS explore the asynchronous effects of embodying ostensibly absent objects, of performing installations no longer present in transitions to time-based narrative, in partial and palimpsestual recollection; a process whose effects challenge linear art histories and settled taxonomies of practice.

Subsequently, Amelia Jones and Andrew Quick address, in different practices and contexts, artists' use of self-archive as process and source in the making of work. Jones focuses on Nao Bustamente's performative self-display of the traces of identity, and so of 'the human subject as *archival*'; a history of work that Jones associates with Yayoi Kusama, Urs Lüthi, Martha Wilson,

Eleanor Antin, Lynn Hershman Leeson and others. Bustamente's enactment of the self-as-archive through performance engages with live performance, video, installation, talk show and reality TV formats; while in 2015 for her exhibition 'La Soldadera', Jones notes, Bustamente overtly adopted the roles of art historian, archivist and curator to explicitly engage with archive through performance. Jones analyses Bustamente's working over of the 'embodied' and 'textual' archive: her mining of the various media her performances occupy for their capacity to stage or produce the self: her 'queering' of the figure of the trickster; her conflating multiple readings of her performative and actual self. Through these tactics, Bustamente at once enacts her self-as-archive—and in doing so appropriates multiple cultural archives—and plays toward an excess that disrupts the production of these social identities, resulting in a highly politicised confusion of categories. Counterpointing this, Quick elaborates The Wooster Group's self-archiving of their performance history through and in relation to their production of new work. Positioning documentation as a core practice, and a ghost in the machine in the company's generation of performances and creative process, Quick opens the question of how the documentary act generates and inhabits performance; and how simultaneously performance 'affords' the documentary act. It is a dynamic that reflects, again, on the performativity of archive and, as Quick proposes, the nature of performance as a truth-making practice. The artists' pages that follow implicitly speak back to this discussion in practices of REVIEW: in archaeologies of the performing body, through the readings of how the marks, the damage, of earlier performance form mnemonic texts of the flesh (Pearson) and in the revisiting of scenes and processes of performances' production in encounters between 'flesh and text' (Bodies in Flight). REVIEW is also enacted in looking back at processes of authorship, and the 'truth-making' that ties authoring and authority to performance history and the archive, as well as the cross-generational re-doing and repetition of actions that form personal and performance legacies (Templeton, Gmelin).

The final cluster of documents, ARCHIVE, is in juxtaposition with Maaike Bleeker's and Johanna Linsley's contrasting explorations of the limits and stabilities of the archive in performance. For '*9 Beginnings*: sonic theatrical possibilities in the live art archives', Linsley approaches the 'futurity' of the archive through sonic terms: echo, voice, rhythm, amplification; to reframe archive as a site 'of potential and possibility,' a fulcrum between an order representing past events and the indeterminacy of scores and new departures. In doing so, Linsley mines *9 Beginnings*, a performance project by the Chicago-based performance company Every house has a door, made in the reiteration of the beginnings of performance works by others, a process that works to amplify the sense of possibility and potentiality of each replayed point of departure. Here, Linsley emphasises the company's focus on auditory elements that operate at the margin of the archive's conventional things, objects, statements and compositions: ambient sound; sensed vibration; silence; individual and communal 'rhythm'; Roland Barthes' 'idiorrhythmy', where individuals maintain idiosyncrasy while forming the aggregated rhythm of a participating community. Defining the core elements and dynamics of performance as an unfolding dialogic event, these auditory identities evade the archive's conventional order and materiality. Extending the limits of archive and representation toward a sharply political arena, Maaike Bleeker's analysis of Rabih Mroué's thought-images explores themes and questions raised also in the Performance Re-enactment Society's *Group Show*, in which absent works are re-told through an overtly theatrical apparatus. Here, though, via Mroué and Saneh's *Who's Afraid of Representation* (2005) and Mroué and Elias Khoury's *Three Posters* (2000), Bleeker explores the aesthetics and ethics of the theatricalised first person re-telling of early conceptual art and performance art, alongside troubling recollections and allusions to aspirations to martyrdom and acts of terror. Mroué's various performers offer testimonies through which documentation is weighed against diverse modes of knowing; as the 'thought-image' is interrogated as a fabrication of truth and as truth-making, and images are treated as sites where 'conflicts are fought out and negotiations happen'. Reading performance and the testimony and legacy of political events via performance theory and criticism, Bleeker works over the complicated relationships between documentation, archive and aesthetic and political spheres in dispute, observing how the images and things placed in the archive mediate the performance of thought. Where these essays engage with the aesthetic and political limits of the archive, the final cluster of artists' pages that follow present ARCHIVE as a verb, as a practice of performance. These contributions encompass speculations over non-linear practices of archiving where performance becomes a principal methodological tool (Bailey); recollections about that which the archive overlooks or elides and that forms its supplement (O'Connor); the conflation of archiving with aesthetic practice and form (Koh How); and considerations of archive as call to remain, energy, mark, as critical point, as lack, and culture (Hancock and Kelly). In closing the book, Simon Jones' essay 'The future perfect of the archive: re-thinking performance in the age of third nature' looks towards the future of performance and the archive. Here, Jones reads the engaged processes that characterize the performer and performance's *being with* the archive, as producing the archive as a recursive space of *doing* in which there is a lack of reflective distance between archives and the pasts they may be used to invoke. Through reflections on Heidegger, Jones contrasts the experiences of being in the midst of performance's collaborative unfolding of archival and other spaces, with the exhaustive and unedited memory and order promised by the digital archive. It is a reading that drives towards an account of the phenomenal uniqueness of performance, captured here in the resistance of performance practice to the ubiquity of 'the third nature' of humanity, where 'all knowledge will be externalized'.

In *Performing Remains*, Rebecca Schneider describes the archive as an architecture housing archival acts, which constitute and delimit a structure as archive (Schneider 2001). In this reading, ephemeral events of use and re-use, rituals of appraisal, accessioning and arrangement, traditions of conservation and remediation, of searching, researching and reinterpretation challenge the stability of the order whose 'commandment' otherwise faces the future. In her study, *Where is Ana Mandieta? Identity, Performativity and Exile*, Jane Blocker extends this position toward historiography, stating that 'we need a history that does not save in any sense of the word; we need a history that performs' (1999: 134). *Artists in the Archive*, and the artists and writers whose work is compiled here, address 'archive' as something done, rather than the archive as a static place or repository, so arguing for an archive that performs. This archive is a set of processes, rather than a building where documents of art and performance are put away or domiciled. Rather than considering the archive as a structure or proper place, the reader of this book might keep in mind Foucault's definition, from *The Archaeology of Knowledge* (2002), which André Lepecki cites, that an archive is 'a system of transforming simultaneously past, present, and future' (2010: 30). *Artists in the Archive*, of course, even as it seeks to open these debates, and like any academic volume claiming its authority, also makes its own strongly archival gesture and so 'commandment' in Derrida's sense. Nevertheless, we hope that the traversals, in which this book finds its form, counter Schneider's description of the architecture of the archive, in favour of a *making-place* where the document and its boundaries are sufficiently uncertain as to generate unexpected questions and offer conversations for future practices.

References

1999 Blocker, J. *Where is Ana Mandieta? Identity, Performativity and Exile*, Durham NC: Duke University Press.

2013 Borggreen, G. and Gade, R. (eds) *Performing Archives / Archives of Performance*, Chicago: University of Chicago Press.

2001 Carlson, M.A. *The Haunted Stage: The Theatre as Memory Machine*, Ann Arbor: University of Michigan Press.

1998 Derrida, J. *Archive Fever: A Freudian Impression*, Chicago: University of Chicago Press.

2002 Foucault, M. *The Archaeology of Knowledge*, London: Routledge.

2010 Freeman, E. *Time Binds: Queer Temporalities, Queer Histories*, Durham and London: Duke University Press.

1997 Heathfield, A. 'Facing the Other: The Performance Encounter and Death'. In A. Heathfield (ed.) *Shattered Anatomies: Traces of the Body in Performance*, Bristol: Arnolfini Live, n.p.

2012 Jones, A. and Heathfield, A. (eds) *Perform, Repeat, Record: Live Art in History*, Chicago: University of Chicago Press.

2010 Lepecki, A. 'The Body as Archive: Will to Re-enact and the Afterlives of Dances'. *Dance Research Journal*, 42(2): pp28–48.

2016 Lucia, A. *'Study for The Protection Papers: Borders, Boundaries, and Blockades in the Art of Dennis Oppenheim'*. Available online. http://www.andrewlucia.com/works_slought.htm. Accessed 28 May 2016.

2016 Mattes, E. and Mattes F. *Reenactments 2007–10*. Available online. http://0100101110101101.org/reenactments/. Accessed 2 June 2016.

1993 Phelan, P. *Unmarked: The Politics of Performance*, London: Routledge.

1999 'Performance and Death: Ronald Reagan', *Cultural Values*, 3(1): pp100–22.

2001 Schneider, R. 'Performance Remains', *Performance Research*, 6(2): pp100–8.

2009 'Remimesis: Feminism, Theatricality, and Acts of Temporal Drag.' Unpublished conference paper delivered at *Re.Act.Feminism*, cross links e.V. and Akademie der Künste, Berlin, January.

2011 *Performing Remains: Art and War in Times of Theatrical Re-enactment*, London: Routledge.

2003 Taylor, Diana *The Archive and the Repertoire: Performing Cultural Memory in the Americas*, Durham, NC: Duke University Press.

Liveness and the entanglement with things

Nick Kaye

> So-called conceptual art existed only by means of reportage and rumour. If there's no thing, if there's no object, if there's nothing that can be gone back to, the only thing that can be gone back to is reportage or rumour—and rumour could be false.
>
> Vito Acconci 2008

> The only real way to document a performance art piece is to re-perform the piece itself.
>
> Marina Abramović 2007: 11

The widespread re-staging and re-use of the material, documentary and textual remains of live art signals a self-consciously archaeological turn in recent and contemporary performance. Such tactics are now established as integral to the circulation and discourses of performance art. Notable examples from many include Marina Abramović's 'cover' of six iconic performances from the late 1960s and 1970s in *Seven Easy Pieces* at the Guggenheim New York in 2005, André Lepecki's meticulous reconstruction of Allan Kaprow's 1959 *18 Happenings in 6 Parts* in Munich in 2006, as well as numerous simulations and interrogations of past events through new works in old and new media; a turn to which this volume attests.

Such re-doings of performance art in particular not only participate in the writing of a history and a canon, but imply relationships between ephemeral acts and material remains that invite questions over how live art might be re-thought in relation to the things—the objects, texts, images, descriptions or video—it produces, or that persist in the absence of past actions and events. In this debate, recent archaeological thinking and theory can speak directly to the re-use of remains of art and performance, addressing questions not only of relationships between events and materials, but of liveness and ephemerality; presence and persistence. In particular, concepts of 'entanglement,' introduced by the Stanford-based British archaeologist Ian Hodder (2012, 2014) and now elaborated through various archaeological and anthropological contexts, bring into focus post-hoc constructions of liveness that can speak back to the place and nature of experiences of the ephemeral in time-based art, and so to the continuance and transformation of live art works over time.

The equivocal relationships between performance, documentation and material remains that re-staging and re-use often enact are, in fact, also present in the history and practice of performance art. Live and performance art did not emerge in the late 1960s in a linear and consistent trajectory toward the objectless and ephemeral, nor has it been consistently defined in a simple opposition between a live act and its representation. As Acconci's equation between conceptual art and rumour suggests, questions over the specificity of acts to a time and a place and the persistence and construction of work through report in the forms of visual and object remains or relics, are also part of the discourses and practices of performance by artists in the 1960s and early 1970s. If performance can exist by means of rumour, then the conventional opposition between the ephemerality of live art and its material remains becomes uncertain, as works may gain their currency primarily through these remainders. It is an analogous post-hoc construction of performance that is the subject of Phillip Auslander's often-cited essay 'The Performativity of Performance Documentation' (2006). Noting that many actions of this period took place in the absence—or near absence—of a witnessing audience, Auslander emphasises the critical role of photography in the enactment of performance art. Concluding that '*the act of documenting an event as a performance is what constitutes it as such*' (2006: 5, original empahasis) Auslander proposes that the 'audience has no real importance to the performance as an entity whose continued life is through its documentation' (2006: 6–7).

While questioning the place of audience and the 'authenticity' of the live event in defining performance art works, Auslander's thesis nevertheless maintains a strong dialectic and distinction between performance and its record, as documentation either looks back to define an event it records, or performance operates directly in the space of photography or video. Yet for the generation of work of which Acconci's performance was a part, live actions frequently maintained blurred boundaries with the material forms they left behind or on which their circulation and identity depended. Such performance was frequently linked, also, to conceptual art, which was itself developed in critiques and modifications of the conventional material forms of art in steps towards a de-materialization of the object (Lippard 1973). Where conceptual art abuts performance, static modes of 'documentation'—in the form of text, photographs, and installations—have also frequently been bound up in the instantiation and provocation of performances and events to such a degree that they cannot easily be separated from the 'live' work. The contemporary re-performance of ostensibly ephemeral performance art works that emphasised their *situatedness*, similarly poses questions regarding the import of 'liveness' in actions that, sometimes from their inception, existed for their wider or even principal audience in documented forms. Here, archaeological theory and performance history offer challenges to the valorisation of the present-tense as the locus of performance's occurrence, instead implying entanglements of the experience of the live with the remains of performance and posing, in turn, questions over the stability of the archive as source and future record.

Objects of performance art

In her acute analysis of Marina Abramović's staging of presence (Jones 2011), the art historian Amelia Jones records Chris Burden's response regarding permission to re-perform his action, *Trans-fixed* (1974). Abramović had conceived of re-enacting Burden's work as part of *Seven Easy Pieces*, her celebrated re-doing of six iconic works of performance art at the Guggenheim Museum, New York, in 2005. Known primarily through a single image and description of Burden's crucifixion through his palms to the rear of a Volkswagen—and in its full form accompanied by a relic comprising the nails used in the action—this documentation conveys Burden's act through simple factual description and material remains. In its final form, and presented over successive evenings, *Seven Easy Pieces* re-interpreted actions and works by Bruce Nauman, Vito Acconci, VALIE EXPORT, Gina Pane and Joseph Beuys, while on a sixth evening Abramović re-enacted her own action, *Lips of Thomas*, first performed in Austria in 1975.

The series culminated in a new 'living installation' by Abramović, *Entering the Other Side*, for which she states: 'The artist is present, here and now' (Spector et al. 2007: 220), implying that for this last evening the veil of performing through the acts of others fell away. In each 're-doing,' Abramović chose to represent an action, image or fragment of performance derived from documentation, scores or other partial records. Each action was staged from 5pm to midnight on a raised platform in the centre of the Guggenheim atrium,

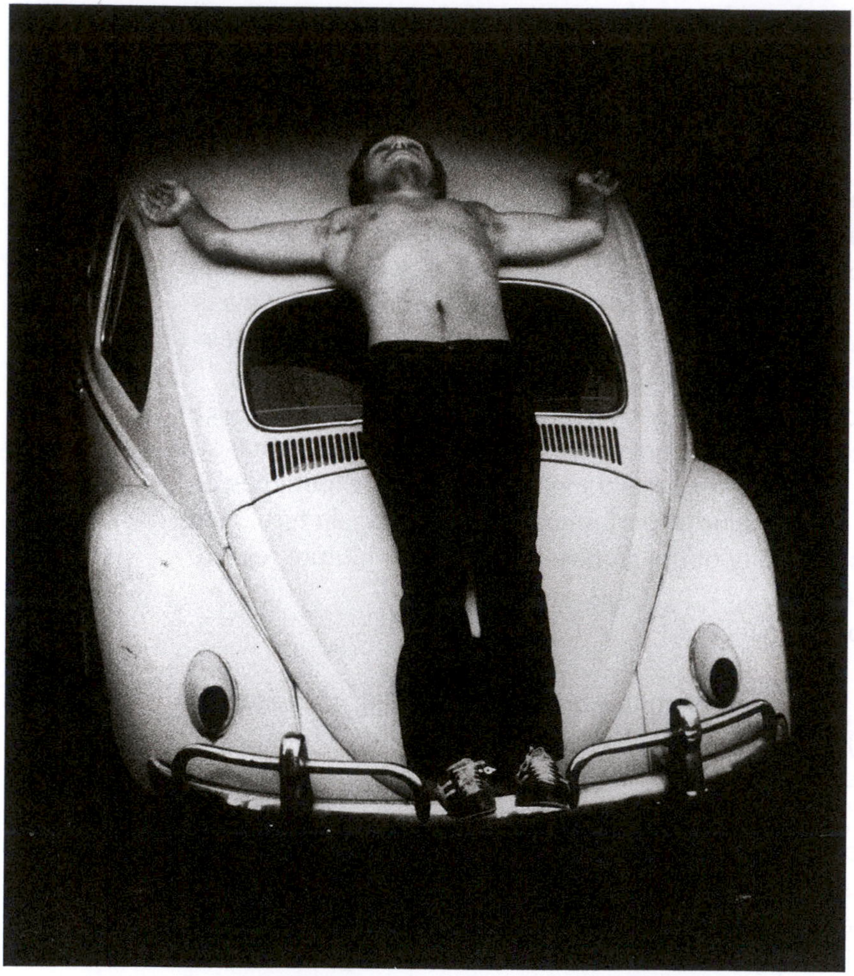

Chris Burden, *Trans-fixed* (1974). Performance. **© Chris Burden. Image courtesy of The Chris Burden Estate and Gagosian.**

Trans-fixed, Venice, California: April 23, 1974

Inside a small garage on Speedway Avenue, I stood on the rear bumper of a Volkswagon. I lay on my back over the rear section of the car, stretching my arms onto the roof of the car. The garage door was opened and the car was pushed half-way out into the Speedway. Screaming for me, the engine was run at full speed for two minutes. After two minutes, the engine was turned off and the car pushed back into the garage. The door was closed.

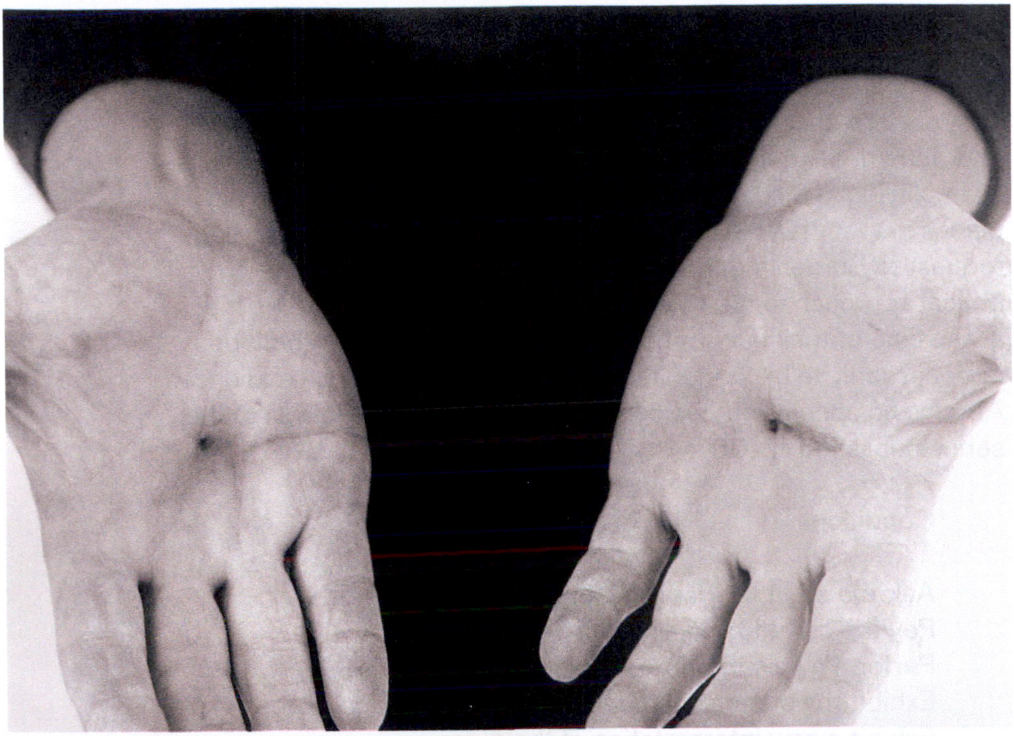

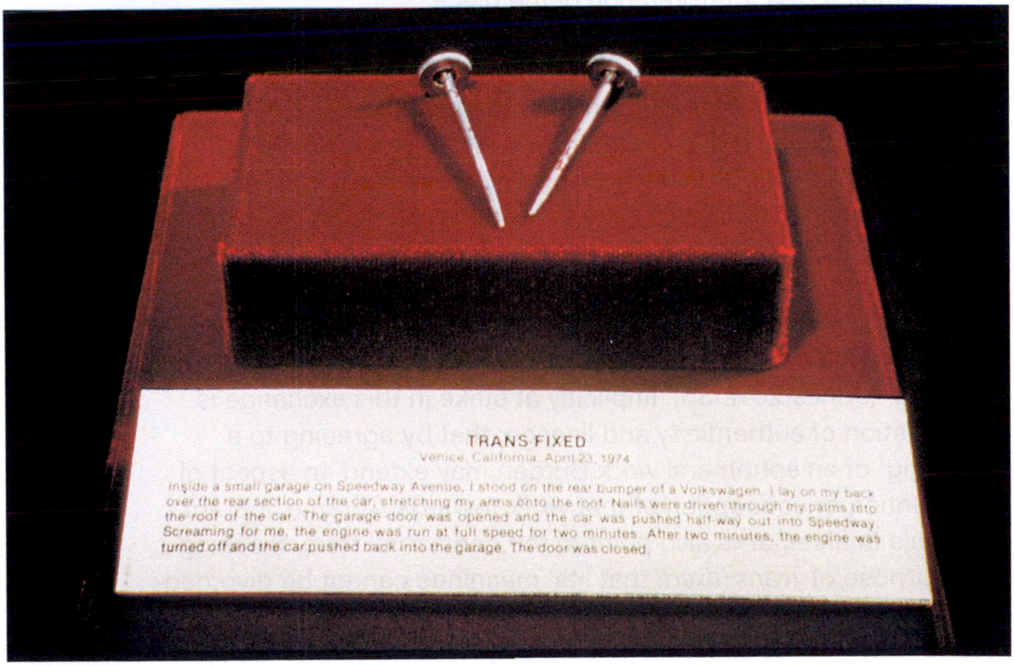

Top: Chris Burden, Relic from *Trans-fixed* (1974). Two nails, 6 ¼ x 6 ¼ x 6 ¾ inches. **© Chris Burden. Image courtesy of The Chris Burden Estate and Gagosian.** Bottom: Chris Burden, *Trans-fixed* (1974). Performance. **© Chris Burden. Image courtesy of The Chris Burden Estate and Gagosian.**

so refracting these past works through her commitment to durational performance and her developing approach to theatrical presentation. For Abramović, *Seven Easy Pieces* served to 'cover' past performances, 'interpreting them as one would a musical score and documenting their realisation' (Spector et al. 2007: 230) while exemplifying 'a model for re-enacting other artists' performance pieces in the future' (Abramović 2007: 10). In these contexts, her request to Burden regarding *Trans-fixed* followed rubrics for an ethical approach to the re-doing of ephemeral performances that at the time of their occurrence were not conceived for repetition or necessarily to be staged directly in the presence of an audience. Abramović specified these conditions in her documentation of the series published in 2007:

> Conditions
>
> Ask the artist for permission
> Pay the artist for copyright
> Perform a new interpretation of the piece
> Exhibit the original material: photographs, video, relics
> Exhibit a new interpretation of the piece
> Abramović 2007: 11

For Abramović, however, Burden's response made it impossible to re-enact *Trans-fixed* in accordance with this framework, in so far as these conditions include the artist's assent and compensation. In a telephone call with Jones, Burden reported his response to Abramović as: 'You don't [legally or morally] need to ask me and you don't need my permission; you can do whatever you want, but now that you are asking me I'm saying no because it's absolutely meaningless for you to do that performance or it has no meaning' (Jones 2011: 35). Implicitly at stake in this exchange is the question of authenticity and lineage; that by agreeing to a 're-doing' of an ephemeral work Burden may extend an aspect of his intention or conception of that work towards Abramović's act. Burden's final remarks also point to the contextual form, meaning and purpose of *Trans-fixed*: that 'its' meanings cannot be divorced from the time of its execution and those which accrue subsequently in relation to that occasion. In contrast, Abramović's conditions emphasise the mortality of performance art, which is explicitly one of the motors of *Seven Easy Pieces*: that performance is defined in original acts, of which subsequent documentation is frequently distorting. In this perspective, the meanings of performance, and performance art in particular, reside in the ephemerality of the live and are lodged in the occasion and form of its execution, the loss of which is then valorized. 'Documentation' is a subsequent and separate matter from the event itself. In conversation with the Guggenheim's curator, Nancy Spector, Abramović responded to Spector's proposition over ephemerality and the problematic of re-doing performance by emphasising precisely this binary relationship between performance and its record:

> NS: Peggy Phelan has written that performance is intrinsically ephemeral and it's the ephemerality of it that gives it its meaning. The idea of re-doing performance is thus a contradiction in terms. I don't know if certain artists believe that, too, that the meaning of their work lies in the fact that it's impossible to revisit it other than through documentation.
>
> MA: But then we come to the point of documentation: many artists don't even take care of documentation either. Much documentation doesn't even represent the piece. Instead, it even goes in the opposite direction and misrepresents the work.
>
> Abramović et al. 2007: 22

Abramović's position purposefully troubles her own practice in *Seven Easy Pieces*, acknowledging the differences in which any documentation is animated. Read after Michael Shanks' work on archaeological thinking and sensibility, *Seven Easy Pieces* is explicitly a work of the 'archaeological imagination' (Shanks 2012); as is the endeavour of artists in the archive in so far as such artists 'work with the remains of the past, acting on and through artefacts' (Shanks 2012: 17–18). It is a sensibility shared by Abramović herself, who has stressed the overtly archaeological nature of her project (Obrist 2010: 65), aligned to the value of performance's ephemerality.

Phelan's celebrated analysis, in *Unmarked: The Politics of Performance* (1993), focuses on the politics of visibility and representation, reflecting on the potential of performance to enact subjectivities and represent identities the visual elides (1993: 1). Seeking to mark 'the limit of the image in the political field of the sexual and racial other' (1993: 2), Phelan then models performance as troubling an economy of the visible in which 'Representation reproduces the Other as the Same' (1993: 3). In its ephemerality and its excess, Phelan suggests, performance, as that which *cannot be reproduced*, offers a political disturbance of representation's self-affirming relationship to the real (1993: 2–3) and a means of speaking in and of subjectivities without 'calling for greater visibility of the hitherto unseen' (1993:1). To this end, Phelan provides a profoundly influential definition of the ontology of performance, the realisation and import of which is aligned to that which 'cannot be reproduced within the ideology of the visible' (1993: 1): its political force and fragility lies in the resistance its ephemerality enacts 'to the laws of the reproductive economy' (1993: 146). In this reading, performance unequivocally realises itself in 'the now':

> Performance's only life is in the present. Performance cannot be saved, recorded, documented, or otherwise participate in the circulation of representations of representations: once it does so, it becomes something other than performance. To the degree that performance attempts to enter the economy of reproduction it betrays and lessens the promise of its own ontology. Performance's being, like the ontology of subjectivity proposed here, becomes itself through disappearance.
> Phelan 1993: 146

The emphasis in Phelan's analysis on ephemerality as the fundamental structure in which performance reveals itself, accords in significant ways with Abramović's articulation of the experience and power of her performance art. It is a valuing of the live and the temporary evident in Abramović's discussion of one of her most well-known and influential works performed during the twelve years of collaboration with her then life and work partner Ulay: *Nightsea Crossing* (1981–7). Realised over 90 days, configured as 22 performances, *Nightsea Crossing* comprised the artists' shared act of sitting, motionless, normally for a period of seven hours in each day, facing each other across a table; occasionally with objects or symbols placed in the designated space, and at times in the presence of other performers or observers (Abramović and Ulay 1985). At the time of its realization in 1983, Abramović emphasised the gradual absorption of the image of sitting into their durational act and the resultant engagement of the viewer-participant over time:

> It's just the presence, the feeling for each of them. The idea of our sitting is that we're present in that moment with the mind and the body. What you see is exactly what is happening. And that is the reality [...] In that moment, when you sit with the body and the mind you manage to make contact with us, because you are taking the reality as it is without any projections. It's like now, it's now.
> Kaye 1996: 184

The works that *Seven Easy Pieces* engages with, however, are often articulated across this apparent dichotomy between performance and its representation, and so between presence and absence, in ways that marshal ephemerality differently. Much of this work explores the affect of performance on objects and images, challenging the absorption of the act into the 'now' of performance—or reconsiders when the 'now' of performance occurs—with implications for concepts and practices of documentation, the re-doing of performance, and the re-use of its material remains.

In this context, too, it is significant that *Seven Easy Pieces* focuses primarily on artwork that although in the lineage of performance art, preceded the widespread use of the term. In the late 1960s, Vito Acconci has recalled, 'We hated the word "performance", because "performance" had a place, and that place by tradition was a theatre' (2001: 353). This concern reflected not only a widespread rejection by artists producing time-based or performance-based work of conventional theatrical apparatus, representation and audience, but the place of these 'real time' actions within eclectic bodies of activity, where individual works frequently combined media, while their development moved rapidly across private actions, photography, texts, video, installation, and hybrid strategies. In this work, 'performance' is frequently defined in challenges to and articulations of the artist's and viewers' engagements with material forms. For Acconci, specifically, such tactics were rooted in his response to minimalism, in which the seemingly mute nature of minimal objects' architectonic and implicitly anthropomorphic forms confronted the viewer with their own time and presence. 'Minimalism', Acconci recalled, 'was the art that made it necessary to recognise the space you were in [...] I had to recognise I was in a certain floor [...] I was in a certain condition, I had a headache, for example. I had a certain history, I had a certain bias' (Acconci 1982). In this context, Acconci's first 'Steps Into Performance (and Out)' (Acconci 1979) captured 'performance' in its disruption of other forms, arising, for example, in an awareness of the time and phenomena of reading, of viewing, or of producing things. In the first of these works, Acconci turned his writing and poetry towards the deployment of self-referential language on the 'page-space' to prompt, shape and interrupt the real time of reading as an analogue to his response to minimalism. Texts such as *Twelve Minutes* (1967), *RE* (1968), and *READ THIS WORD THEN READ THIS WORD* (1969) (Acconci 2006) mark times and acts integral to the reader's awareness of the material space of the page. From this attention to action and time in relation to '"page time," "reading time"' (Acconci 1978), Acconci's activities stepped into schemes for the street or other specific and designated locations where 'There's no audience (or, if there is an audience, terms of "subject" and "object" are reversed)' (Acconci 1979: 28), including *A Situation Using Streets, Walking, Glancing* (1969), *12 Pictures* (1969) and *Following Piece* (1969) as well as the Photo Pieces *Blinks* (1969), *Throw* (1969) and others. Many of these actions produced images, texts, plans or video in Acconci's execution of the activity; the material remains of a once live action that invokes a 'performance' that was never encountered directly. For *Throw* on the afternoon of November 23 1969 Acconci moved down Vandam Street between Greenwich and Hudson, in Manhattan, wielding a camera as if throwing a ball: 'Reach back as if to throw: snap photo 1. Throw and follow through: snap photo 2' (Acconci 2004: 113) The resulting image sequence forms a component part of *Throw*, in which Acconci's act is evoked in lacunae: inferred, tracked but unseen.

For Dennis Oppenheim, whose *Extended Armour* (1971) Abramović had also considered re-doing in *Seven Easy Pieces* (Heathfield 2004: 150), performance provided a means of enmeshing art in 'real-time structures or disciplines' (Oppenheim in Wood 1981: 133). Reflecting this, of the one hundred or so actions Oppenheim himself executed and recorded in video, photographs, installations and descriptions between 1969 and 1973, very few took the form of performances in the presence of more than an incidental audience: specifically, *Extended Armour* (1971) at the Reese Palley Gallery, New York; *Vibration 1* (1971) and *Do-It* (1971) at the A Space, Toronto in May of the same year (Kaye and van Winkle Oppenheim 2016) each of which incorporated the production of video. In Oppenheim's body art, performance drives the production and reception of other material forms; yet these forms are not a second order to the work or 'documentation' that distorts or remakes an act in which the work momentarily inhered. Instead, live actions are integral to strategies that condition the diverse modes of his works' production and reception. Thus Oppenheim emphasised that his actions served 'to activate the periphery of things [...] charges that opened up doors that were not going to be found on the paper that you were presenting the work to' (Oppenheim in Kaye 1996: 63). Oppenheim's performances remain, in this sense, and like Acconci's Activities, *no less present* and *no less available* than at the time of their original execution and distribution, operating instead in a 'liveness' that was always already recollected, yet which alters the conceptual basis of the work, prompting Oppenheim's use of the term 'conceptual/performance' (Kaye and van Winkle Oppenheim 2016: 9).

Most of the works that Abramović finally selected for performance in *Seven Easy Pieces* also operate in relation to such absences, or carry forward uncertainties over what originally occurred. At the time of the series' preparation, EXPORT's unannounced action in a commercial cinema, *Genital Panic: Action Pants*, was subject to rumour and variation in accounts of its location and date, prompting Abramović to comment that 'it was really difficult to determine the facts about the original piece from all the archaeological evidence' (Abramović and Spector 2007: 22). Abramović's subsequent cover comprised a *tableaux vivant* of an image selected from EXPORT's later photo-series, *Action Pants: Genital Panic* (1969),shot in an abandoned cinema (EXPORT 2012: 79) in which EXPORT adopted a series of poses with the addition of a machine gun that was not part of the original performance, the subsequent 'iconic' status of which EXPORT found unhelpful (Fore 2012: 2). In the context of the 2012 exhibition, *VALIE EXPORT. Archiv*, in which the action pants themselves and photo series were shown as 'autonomous works' (EXPORT 2012: 79), EXPORT detailed the original 1968 event:

> It was an *Expanded Cinema* action. Wearing the action pants I walked through the rows of seats then switched the cinema spotlight onto the screen and announced to the audience that what they would normally view on the screen, they could now view in reality [...] My intention was to bring reality into the cinema's reality, into the cinematographic reality of the film theatre.
>
> EXPORT 2012: 79

Others of Abramović's re-doings also provided distillations or condensations of actions, traversing a documentation, variation and continuation of these conceptual works. Beuys' *How To Explain Pictures To A Dead* Hare took place at the opening of the exhibition 'Joseph Beuys ... irgendein Strang' at Galerie Schmela, Dusseldorf, on 26 November 1965, where: 'Beuys spent three hours explaining his art to a dead hare. The gallery was closed to the public, and the performance (although recorded on television) was only visible from the doorway and street window' (Tisdall 1979: 21). Noting that it was Beuys' practice to allow photographers unfettered access to his performances, following which he would select a small number of resonant images to represent an event (Obrist 2010: 67), Abramović focused on the image of Beuys sitting outside the gallery, anointed in gold leaf and honey, cradling the hare; punctuating this action with cycles of Beuys' ritual-like

VALIE EXPORT. Genitalpanik/Hose, 1968/69. Display cabinet 53, installation view „VALIE EXPORT – ARCHIV", Kunsthaus Bregenz, 2012. Photo: Markus Tretter. © VALIE EXPORT/VBK, Vienna, 2011, Kunsthaus Bregenz.

activities. For *The Conditioning, first action of Self-Portraits* (1973), Abramović adopted Gina Pane's original 30-minute action, in which the artist lay 'on a bed-like grill while candles burned just beneath her and she tolerated as long as possible' (Spector et al. 2007: 156), extending this fragment to seven hours. Nauman's 'conceptual performance' *Body Pressure* (1974) provides a set of instructions made available in multiple copies for visitors to enact in the gallery, inviting them to press their body systematically against a constructed installation wall: an arrangement Abramović inverted for her audience, performing the action against a free-standing glass wall staged at the centre of the Guggenheim atrium. For Acconci's *Seedbed* (1972), Abramović occupied a ramp underfoot of her audience, masturbating repeatedly as her commentary and fantasies about the visitors are relayed into a space that they could step in and out of at will. At once the fullest re-enactment of an original scheme for performance, Abramović's *Seedbed* is acutely reconfigured, with echoes of Paul McCarthy and Mike Kelley's gender-reversed re-doings of Acconci's video artworks, *Fresh Acconci* (1995) (McCarthy and Kelley 1995).

Liveness and material remains

Noting a widespread 'return to things' in thinking in the social sciences and humanities (Hodder 2014: 19), Ian Hodder has most recently proposed a turn in archaeology towards 'The Entanglement of Humans and Things' (Hodder 2014), observing that the proposition 'humans and things are relationally produced' (2014: 19) has become established in a variety of disciplines. For Hodder, specifically, the concept of entanglement advances thinking and practices established in the influential propositions of postprocessual or interpretive archaeology, whose definition was led by Hodder in the 1980s in conjunction with Daniel Miller (Miller and Tilley 1984), Michael Shanks and Christopher Tilley (1993), Julian Thomas (1996) and others. Interpretive archaeology challenged the assumptions of the 'new' archaeology emerging in the 1960s that methods based in anthropological science could provide positive (objective) knowledge of the past, unaffected by the context and conditions under which the practices of archaeology take place (Shanks and Hodder 1997). Instead, interpretive archaeology aligned archaeological theory with the social sciences, refocusing on the relationships between material remains of subjects now lost and contemporary archaeologists themselves as social actors. Rather than offering a window to the past, then, archaeology becomes instead 'a material practice in the present, making things (knowledge, narrative, books, reports...) of the material traces of the past' (Shanks and Hodder 1997: 5). Contemporary archaeology is thus a brokering of diverse interests in the construction of narratives over matters—including social relationships and the meaning of things in the past—that were no less multiple and uncertain in their 'own' time. As a result, Shanks and Hodder emphasise 'The interpretive practice that is archaeology is an ongoing process: there is no final and definitive account of the past as it was' (Shanks and Hodder 1997: 5).

Hodder's notion of 'entanglement' extends this thinking toward the dynamics in operation between humans, 'things' (and 'objects') as equal actors within transforming social networks, in which humans are produced in dynamic relations that include their entanglement (and entrapment) with other humans, and with things; just as things are produced in their entanglement (and dependency) on each other (Hodder 2014: 20) and with humans. Entanglement rests also on the agency of things and objects. Hodder thus notes that 'discussions of agency, vibrancy, and vitality of mute things, have converged on some version of the idea that subject and object, mind and matter, human and thing co-constitute each other,' concluding that 'humans and things are relationally produced' (Hodder 2014: 1). Furthermore, 'materials and objects have affordances that are continuous from context to context' (Hodder 2014: 25). It follows that things dynamically and simultaneously enable and constrain, forming 'a sticky entrapment' (Hodder 2014: 25). More recently still, Lindsay Der and Francesca Fernandini have explored entanglement as a model for analysing the cultural construction of historical trajectories, past and anticipated, in 'human-thing relations and the way they develop through time'; as well as dissonant constructions of temporalities, observing that 'time for things [...] is often in contrast with conventional human measures of time' (Der and Fernandini 2016: 19). Our own idea and understanding of the present is similarly entangled in our uses of the material remains of the past, just as our construction of that past is a function of this entanglement.

The hybrid forms and practices associated with 'conceptual/performance' in which actions are encountered in their report or remainder also articulate entanglements between things, objects and events; exploring the capacity of performance to affect the material remains by which it is known. Entanglement is the basis of Acconci's plays between activity and the materiality of the page; of the 'charge' Oppenheim enacts in documentation; it is implied in Burden's use of relics and EXPORT's exhibition of the object *Action Pants: Genital Panic* as an autonomous work.

These material remains assert a sense of agency and meaning: they appear active. Such objects and materials play also with notions of artefact. Defined as objects or things subject to human invention, alteration or use, artefacts provide evidence and act as mnemonics and prompts to actions and purposes. Artefacts frequently garner 'aura,' where, according to Mike Pearson and Michael Shanks in *Theatre/Archaeology*, 'aura refers to the life of things': to the 'sense of associations and evocations that cluster round an object, correspondences and interrelations, engendered by an object' (Pearson and Shanks 2001: 95–6). Beuys thus consistently re-articulated objects and remains from his performances and actions directly as material works: invoking, in meanings and the reports that accrued around them, ritualistic actions and events they never directly described. Some conceptually-based performance, including the California-based conceptual artist Tom Marioni's social art work *The Act of Drinking Beer with Friends is the Highest Form of Art* (1970), are encountered only in such remains. In the first iteration of this event at the Oakland Museum of Art in October 1970, Marioni recalled:

Tom Marioni, *Café Society Beer* (1979). Soft ground etching with engraving, embossing and gold leaf stamping mounted on a bottle of Anchor Stream beer. Published by Crown Point Press and printed by Lilah Toland.

> I invited 21 of my friends to come and drink beer at the museum. And 16 people were there. All of the people were sculptors except for Werner Jepson, the music composer. We got drunk in the museum together and the debris that was left over was exhibited as documentation of that activity—empty beer cans and cigarette butts, just morning after kind of debris.
>
> Marioni in Vergine 2000: 143

Seemingly 'altered' by their use and left to evidence the story or history of an event, Marioni's artefacts extend to *Café Society Beer* (1979), a numbered edition of 800 bottles of Anchor Steam beer, 'In champagne bottles, large enough to be shared with a friend' (Marioni 1979). Such objects act as mnemonic prompts of his continuing private and public variations of his 1970 performance work, currently known as *Beer with Friends* (Kaye 2013), as well as an object-score to future activity—in this case the injunction to open the bottle in company. Other artefactual performance includes Lynn Hershman Leeson's *Roberta Breitmore* (1974–8), comprising 171 objects, images, texts, everyday items, reports and videos that 'document' or evidence the identity and activity of Hershman's fictional persona and alter-ego (Giannachi and Kaye 2011: 40–7) and that include reported events which may or may not have occurred, as well as substitutions and impersonations. Abramović's early controversial action *Rhythm 0* (1974) also engaged directly with the agency of things. Abramović offered her presence for six hours at the Galleria Studio Morra in Naples before 72 objects placed on a table, including a piece of bread, perfume, an apple, wine, a rose, but also scissors, nails, a whip, a pistol and a single bullet. Framed beside the objects are the instructions: 'I am an object. During this time I take full responsibility'. Here, things become invitations and active intermediaries, in the event affording and provoking a series of de-humanizing exchanges:

> At first nothing really happened. The public would come, they would give me roles, they would play with me, kiss me, look at me. And then the public became more and more wild: they cut my neck and drank my blood [...] one person took the pistol, put [in] the bullet, and see if I would with my own hand [pull the trigger].
>
> Abramović 2015

'Altered' by their use, Abramović reported that to her surprise the gallerist retained the objects as original artworks, objecting to the subsequent display of 'substitute' objects at L.A. MOCA in 1998 (Abramović and Spector 2007: 16). Such artefacts, and such artefactual performance, shifts a focus from what is 'lost' and 'documented' to what 'remains' and what is prompted: an emphasis taken up by Abramović herself in the subsequent release of *Rhythm 0* as an edition of three clusters of 72 objects. 'Entanglement', in this context, erodes the conventional dichotomies between the ephemeral live and its remainder: between an un-representable event and the things upon which events depend. 'Liveness' surrounds these artefacts, is carried forward in the stories and associations in which these things gain meaning and remains evident in their potential. Herein lies the shock in encountering the nails as relics of Burden's *Trans-fixed*: they are entangled with Burden's live act.

The experience of the 'present moment' of 'liveness' is also evidently entangled with things in a way that divides the 'now' and experiences of 'the present' and 'presence'. Writing of Abramović's work in 'Artistic Re-Enactments and the Impossibility of Presence,' Amelia Jones points out the inevitable division produced in the 'live', as 'performance, by combining materiality and durationality (its enacting of the body as always already escaping into the past) points to the fact that there is no "presence" as such' (2011: 18). This is a division in the experience of the present tense and the presence of things that phenomenology has also consistently articulated (Giannachi and Kaye 2011: 10–20). *Seven Easy Pieces* is itself overtly articulated as a layered and self-reflexive event whose present tense occurrence, and 'liveness', is entangled in a plurality of *things*: in media, in objects; in multiplying times and encounters. In her first person documentation of the event, Sandra Umathum recounts how:

> By modifying, linking, and superimposing several different 'scores' within the same performance, Abramović finds a wonderful way to question the evolution of our conceptions of a performance that we—like her—did not ourselves experience. And she shows that the genesis of these conceptions always involves different 'scores', eyewitness accounts, as well as photos or film segments.
>
> Umathum 2007: 52–3

The 'liveness' of *Seven Easy Pieces* is shaped by the frisson, the dissonance, the coincidences and gaps between these 'things'; an ephemerality amplified in the multiplying and shifting relationships between media, materials and events in which the performance unfolds.

Underlying this, Abramović's re-doing comprises a re-staging of relics, artefacts and even documents of works that continue to garner meanings. This accumulation and extension of meaning over time is another excess afforded by object-remains; a process *Seven Easy Pieces* further effected as its representations became a powerful means of circulating knowledge of the works in which it is anchored (Jones 2011: 20–1). Critical and theoretical sources of knowledge are equally entangled in the determination of what performance comes to be over time; and so equally in views of what it was. My own accessing of *Seven Easy Pieces* has itself been through extracts from Babette Mangold's extensive and eloquent film documentation, Abramović's accompanying catalogue and the numerous reviews and essays that have followed, rather than the event itself. In turn, the actions *Seven Easy Pieces* replayed have only been available to me through layers of documentation, report, theory, and criticism; sites that in many ways these works are also formed within, and which provided Abramović with the basis of her own interpretations.

Real time and the life cycle of events

It is in the relationship between things and events, too, that *Seven Easy Pieces* brokers relationships between performance traditions and contested meanings of theatricality; a feature of Abramović's work that is frequently overlooked, and that further inflects the relationship between objects and 'real time' processes. In her early performance, Abramović had shared an antagonism towards the theatrical apparatus and recalls declining to document so that work 'would only exist afterwards by word of mouth' (Abramović and Spector 2007: 16). For Abramović, such tactics explicitly privileged the sense of 'real time' inhering in 'the equal duration of the action and the perception' (1998: 20); a dynamic refined over a decade towards *Nightsea Crossing*'s emergent activity and exchange of energy. It is an emphasis aligned also with contemporaneous experimental theatre practice, especially in Eastern Europe. While Abramović has stressed the importance of George Gurdjieff's philosophy and practices to the mind-body disciplines she enacts through performance (Mogutin 2010), Abramović's drive toward 'real-time' performer–viewer encounters also had a theatrical counterpart in the tenets of Jerzy Grotowski's *poor theatre*, which, in seeking to divest performance of anything superfluous to its nature, concentrated on the ephemeral meeting or communion of performer and spectator. It is a process Grotowski influentially described in *Towards a Poor Theatre*, first published in 1968 and in English in 1969:

> By gradually eliminating whatever proved superfluous, we found that theatre can exist without make-up, without autonomic costume and scenography, without a separate performance area (stage), without lighting and sound effects, etc. It cannot exist without the actor-spectator relationship of perceptual, direct, 'live' communion.
>
> Grotowski 1975: 19

The contexts into which Abramović draws her re-staging of early performance art suggest persistent meetings with this essentialist mode of theatre. Indeed, Abramović emphasises how the preparations, privations and committed actions of the performer may produce a profound experience in a symbiotic exchange with audience members, which is a consistent feature of her narratives surrounding her durational performances including *Nightsea Crossing, The House with the Ocean View* (2002) and *The Artist Is Present* (2010). In *Performing Body* (1998), Abramović stresses that 'I could not produce a single work without the presence of the audience, because the audience gave me the energy to be able, through a specific action, to assimilate it and return it, to create a genuine field of energy' (Abramović and Belloni 1998: 18). Many of Abramović's actions and her definition of a system for performer training (Viola and Sileo 2012) can be read as driving towards performance as 'embodied mind' as captured by the performance theorist Erika Fischer-Lichte. Summarised in Fischer-Lichte's analysis of Grotowski's practice and legacy, the means and goal of this 'radical concept of presence' mirrors Abramović's enabling of the viewer's experience of 'Being Present' (Abramović and Ulay 1985):

> Through the performer's presence, the spectator experiences the performer and himself [sic] as embodied mind in a constant process of becoming—he perceives the circulating energy as a transformative and vital energy. This I call the radical concept of presence, written as PRESENCE: PRESENCE means appearing and being perceived as embodied mind; perceiving the PRESENCE of another means to also experience oneself as embodied mind.
>
> Fischer-Lichte 2012: 115

Yet *Seven Easy Pieces* also returns to other, more overtly hybrid theatricalities, with its focus on things and remains, images and documentation. The 'conceptual/performance' of Nauman and Oppenheim, as well as aspects of work by EXPORT, Burden and Acconci, responded to the perceived 'theatricality' of minimalism; a theatricality presciently defined in 1967 by the critic Michael Fried's celebrated assault on post-modernist tactics. In his essay 'Art and Objecthood', Fried argued that the 'literalist' nature of minimal or 'ABC Art' (1968: 116) comprised an attack on the separateness to which modernist painting and sculpture necessarily strove, whereby 'what is to be had from the work is located strictly within [it]' (1968: 118). In contrast, through their anthropomorphic scale and blank architectonic forms, minimal art offered object-interventions into the 'real' (literal) space and time of viewing. In Fried's analysis, by identifying sculpture with conditions that 'virtually by definition, *includes the beholder*' (1968: 125), minimalism entered that which Clement Greenberg had described as 'the condition of non-art' (Fried 1968: 118), forcing attention towards the very situation and prosaic circumstance all art must transcend to realise its identity and value. The emergence of performance—and subsequently performance art—in relation to this concept of 'theatricality' is not intrinsically linked to an act seen by others, but to the intrusion of time, duration, event, and the agency of viewers into the operation of sculpture. The currency of performance art, in this context, has not only been 'liveness' in 'the now'- and so ephemerality and disappearance—but the construction of liveness and its 'meanings' artefactually and discursively, where events permeate and are prompted by objects; where artworks are subject to the passage of time, to multiple agencies, to quotidian time and space. In such sculpture and performance, the event of the work has also been bound up with its 'remains': in encounters with the trace, the relic, the artefact, or, as Acconci himself suggests, with rumour.

In this context, and as the work Abramović re-stages suggests, 'real time' implies not only a moment of unity between action and perception, that Abramović sees as key within her own work (Abramović and Belloni 1998: 20), but also the co-existence of different values and subjective experiences of duration and so a further unruliness and fragmentation over time. The condition of 'theatricality'—after Fried—speaks to this fragmentation: to an artwork's specificity to *situations of viewers*, a feature that other forms of re-stagings have explicitly engaged with. One of these, Silvia Kolbowski's *An Inadequate History of Conceptual Art* (1998–9), has articulated the friable aspects of this generation of performance work. Initially inviting 60 artists to briefly describe a conceptual art work that they had personally encountered between 1965 and 1975, Kolbowski's final video installation incorporated contributions by 22 artists who remain un-named and recount their experience against an unedited close shot of their hands. In this extract, a male voice recounts what is evidently Chris Burden's *Back To You*, performed once only at 112 Green Street, New York, in January 1974 (Burden 2007: 55):

> The artist was in the elevator shaft, and he was going to invite three people to come into the elevator shaft and stick pins in him.
>
> I found that a very strange thing, but I think what was strange was that there were quite a lot of people—I can't remember how many, maybe 50 or 60 people. And I think what struck me about the whole thing was the audience's response [...] I think I saw him lying down, with just his pants on, lying on some kind of table or something [...] It looked a little bit like a kind of execution chamber. I thought this is a very strange kind of thing to look at.
>
> But the people there were sort of festive: it struck me as a little bit like a carnival. I mean people had wine [...]
>
> But the whole thing still has a kind of resonance with me, in terms of why people [...] as a piece of sculpture, the idea of stabbing someone with little pins. I still think it was kind of powerful. Today, imagine someone doing that—it could be deadly, you'd think there could be AIDS, there'd be all kinds of contamination.
>
> Kolbowski 2004: 9

Kolbowski's installation emphasizes not only the definition of conceptual and performance art events in their *afterlife*, but their elaboration through a life cycle of remainder, memory and re-telling: focusing on the ways performance is lodged and made in multiple, situated receptions. Indeed, Burden evidently structured some of his work to erode distinctions between the 'now' of performance and its afterlife, reconfiguring viewers as complicit or even accomplices *subject to* an action they carry forward. For *The Confession* (1974) at the Contemporary Art Centre, Cincinnati, Burden explicitly used personal information so that the performance acted as a catalyst to individuals' relationship with him:

> I invited only those people I had met and talked with since my arrival in Cincinnati, four days earlier. I called each of the 25 people and invited them to come to the Art Centre on Thursday evening at 8.30. The guests were seated around

a monitor when my face appeared on the screen. I began to talk about why I was very unhappy, confessing the most intimate details of my personal life. Faced with the need to make a decision concerning a love triangle, and being unable to act. [...] They sat in complete silence as I exposed myself, imposing on them disturbing knowledge which had to be reconciled with my public image. I talked for about half an hour, until I was unable to continue. The audience left quickly without discussion amongst themselves.

Burden 2007: 58

Performances such as *The Visitation* (1974) and *There Have Been Some Pretty Wild Rumours About Me Lately and I Just Want to Set the Record Straight* (1981) elaborated this strategy in events structured through individual meetings or refusals to document that might result in multiple, fragmentary retellings. From 1970, Acconci had similarly stepped towards the viewer as the psychological space of actions, frequently constructing antagonistic and potentially coercive relationships with his prospective audience: in public intrusions into personal space (*Proximity Piece* [1970]), sexual fantasy (*Seedbed*, [1972]; *Undertone* [1972]), by inviting his own potential blackmail (*Project for Pier* 17 [1971]) and in other site- and temporally-specific investigations of power dynamics, so as to provoke radically diverse encounters.

This extension beyond the event is resonant also to Beuys, whose work places explicit emphasis on the importance of the material remainders of actions. Beuys' images, objects, actions and installations are intertwined through complex systems of allusion, cross-reference and displacement between narrative and symbolic systems; systems which were partly of his own invention, yet rich in allusion to ecologies of ideas, places, animals, and traditions, exemplified by extensive post-hoc performance scores such as that for *24 hours...and in us...under us...landunder...* (1965). A common thread through his work is the notion of materials and objects as 'transmitters' and 'receivers,' exemplified by images, objects and multiples works such as *Earth Telephone* (1973), *Score for Action with Transmitter (Felt) Receiver in the Mountains* (1974) and *Telephone T—R* (1974). Beuys' charismatic performances, which included ritualistic actions as well as lectures and extended discussions, served to reflect upon, charge and articulate these networks of objects and remains, with the intention of drawing viewers into their individual animation of conversation, of thought, toward conceptual processes of forming and so processual acts of 'social sculpture' (Beuys and Tisdall 1979).

The ruling logic of Beuys' work, then, is the overlapping of performance with personal, social and political process that extends beyond any specific event. In this context, Beuys' performances provided concentrated moments focusing on his person—and his reflection of the image and narrative of the shaman—to produce auratically charged future encounters. In his dense, deeply political actions, Beuys enacted condensations of discourses, questions and references around objects charged by their inclusion in these ritualistic performances; remains then left, frequently clustered in vitrines as relics and independent works. Beuys' actions thus remain entangled with objects left behind; incomplete cyphers that pose questions of how meaning may be unveiled in further enactments of process, thought and social sculpture. This elaboration of performance is resonant to contemporary concepts of the artefact and its acquisition of meaning over time. Michael Shanks draws attention to the 'continuity of cycles of interpretation' that form the 'life-cycle' of artefacts (1999: 31) and through which, rather than act as cypher to an 'original' state—a past moment in which the artefact 'had' its place, meaning and purpose—objects accrue meanings through differing states, uses and relationships over time. In this sense, an artefact is comprised simultaneously of the data that forms this life cycle: as clay, as pot, as fragment, as the various dimensions, readings, and meanings it affords. An artefact is thus not singular, but 'as assemblage, is a substantial multiplicity' (Shanks 1999: 30). With Mike Pearson, Shanks concludes: 'We come to an object in relationships with it, through it, perceiving it, referring to it, talking of it, feeling it as something' (Pearson and Shanks 2001: 99). Beuys' discarded objects from performances engage with this life cycle: they carry Beuys' action forward, mnemonically, and in their future effects.

In these contexts, *Seven Easy Pieces* can be seen to rest not only on Abramović's commitment to performance defined in a symbiosis of performer-spectator encounter, but also in negotiations with these other modes of object-based theatricality rooted also in her earlier performances. Harnessing the auratic effect of objects, Abramović and Ulay incorporated artefacts into performances to create specific cultural resonances. Occasions of *Nightsea Crossing* frequently included objects placed on the table between them or on an adjacent wall, including, in different performances, the Indian swastika (gammadion cross), gold found by the artists, a boomerang, a live snake, and others. In *Nightsea Crossing Conjunction* (1983), the performance was shared with the Aboriginal artist Charlie Tararu Tjungurrayi and the Tibetan Lama Ngawang Soepa Lueyar, reflecting the origins of *Nightsea Crossing* in their experiences in the Australian desert and subsequent engagement with cross-cultural memory. For Abramović and Ulay, these performances were evidently influenced by Beuys' allusions to shamanism, deploying objects and actions mnemonically in the context of a meditative act. In 1983, at the time of *Nightsea Crossing Conjunction* in Amsterdam, Ulay recounted that:

> We have been trying to integrate certain symbols into our work. [...] I think the symbols—the material, the colour, the shape, the placement of the symbol, and the approach to the symbol, has to be perfect. Then the symbol will be able to generate power. But only if it is perfect. If it is placed in the right time and the right place, and if the symbol itself consists of a certain kind of material and shape and form and colour. Then it can work.
>
> Kaye 1996: 185

Seven Easy Pieces is a further elaboration of these deeper logics of Abramović's work that operate through theatrical exposures of resonant objects, actions and intense, lived condensations of images. Distilled into partial and fragmentary images—or embodied as self-conscious reversals in the case of *Seedbed*—Abramović's acts offer unruly and excessive recuperations of actions by an extended focus on specific artefacts and the animation of fragmentary material remains. As Lindsay Der and Francesca Fernandini suggest in *Archaeology of Entanglement*, too, 'time for things' is different, or dissonant 'with human measures of time' (2016: 19). It is this difference that *Nightsea Crossing* also plays across and that Abramović plays towards in combining objects and images, as these durational acts seemingly adopt the time of objects, while the staging of things is treated as active and affective. Such dissonances enact the entanglement of durational acts and objects, as the terms of one explicitly play over the other. *Seven Easy Pieces*, then, following *Nightsea Crossing*, rests on entanglements of things with events; presenting a theatre archaeology (Pearson and Shanks 2001) of auratic objects and images through embodied acts; acts in continuation of the life cycle of works defined in their material remains.

Archival acts

The re-enactment of past performances is an implicitly archival act: every new iteration sets its object in a place, subjects it to an order, perhaps even enunciates its meanings for a new audience. Herein lies one of the appeals of re-doing and re-use for artists and curators as they explore the value and lineage of performances now past and new work's place and relationship to emergent and living histories: yet here too lie risks of recuperation and implicit claims to veracity. Hence, perhaps, Chris Burden's misgivings over Abramović's proposed re-enactment. The 'original' act of *Trans-fixed* was never 'in possession' of its meanings, which flowed from its dissemination and representation: its meanings did not coalesce *within* a discrete performance now lost, to which in fact there was no audience, but in its subsequent circulation over time, its *ramifications*. Not only this 'liveness' of *Trans-fixed* to its audience, but the completeness of Burden's work is entangled with the life of these remains. Indeed, the genres of work towards which *Seven Easy Pieces* directs attention often embrace such passages between times, states and objects; even obscuring access to events, or combining actions with an emphasis on the life cycle of *things*. Object-remains from these works often seem *excessive*, rather than documentary: they are auratic and affective. Such live art explores the inter-laced affect of performance and the remains to which it clings. Entanglement describes an analogous and dynamic process, in which the interdependencies and meanings of things and their associated narratives remain in transition; and in which objects are lent agency. For the artist in the archive, using things (objects, scores, images) entangled in the nexus and life cycle of past works—in the multiple acts, images, memories, reports, and discussions in which works continue their definition—this entanglement also qualifies the implicitly archival act. Entanglement works against not only a simple opposition between the live act and its dead material remains, but the very idea of the 'static object' which many conceptual artists specifically rejected (Marioni 2000: 10; Oppenheim in Wood 1981: 137) in favour of the de-stabilising effect of performances, processes and events afforded by things.

2007 Abramović, M. 'Reenactment'. In Nancy Spector, Erika Fischer-Lichte and Sandra Umathum (eds) *Marina Abramović: Seven Easy Pieces*, Milan: Edizioni Charta, pp9–12.

2015 'Marina Abramović on *Rhythm 0*', *Artforum*. Available online. https://www.youtube.com/watch?v=3d30mfVm9ug. Accessed 20 June 2016.

http://www.medienkunstnetz.de/works/rhythm-10-2. Accessed 5 June 2016.

Abramović, M. and Belloni, E.

1998 *Marina Abramović: Performing Body*, Milan: Edizioni Charta s.r.l.

Abramović, M. and Spector, N.

2007 'Marina Abramović interviewed by Nancy Spector'. In Nancy Spector, Erika Fischer-Lichte and Sandra Umathum (eds) *Marina Abramović: Seven Easy Pieces*, Milan: Edizioni Charta, pp13–31.

Abramović, M and Ulay,

1985 *Modus Vivendi*, Eindhoven: Stedelijk van Abbemuseum.

1978 Acconci, V. *Vito Acconci*. Luzern: Kunstmuseum, Luzern, n.p.

1979 'Steps Into Performance (And Out)'. In A.A. Bronson and Peggy Gale (eds) *Performance by Artists*, Toronto: Art Metropole, pp27–40.

1982 *Recorded Documentation by Vito Acconci of the Exhibition and Commissioning for San Diego State University*, San Diego, CA: San Diego State University (audio cassette)

2001 [1989] 'Performance After the Fact'. In Gloria Moure (ed.) *Vito Acconci: Writings, Work, Projects*, Barcelona: Ediciones Polígrafa, pp353–7.

2004 *Diary of a Body: 1969–1973*, Milan: Edizioni Charta.

2006 *Language to Cover a Page*, edited by Craig Dworkin, Cambridge, MA: 2006.

2008 *Vito Acconci in Conversation at the Acconci Studio*. DVD. Philadelphia: Slought Foundation.

2006 Auslander, P. 'The Performativity of Performance Documentation'. *PAJ: A Journal of Performance and Art*, 84: pp1–10.

1979 Beuys, J. and Tisdall, C. 'From a Telephone Conversation'. In Caroline Tisdall (ed.) *Joseph Beuys: The Secret Block for a Secret Person in Ireland*, Oxford: Oxford Museum of Art, n.p.

2007 Burden, C. *Chris Burden*, London: Thames and Hudson.

2016 Der, L. and Fernandini, F 'Introduction'. In Lindsay Der and Francesca Fernandini (eds) *Archaeology of Entanglement*, Walnut Creek, CA: Left Coast Press, pp11–30.

2012 Dziewior, Y (ed.) *VALIE EXPORT: Archiv*, Bregenz: Kunsthauz, Bregenz.

2012 EXPORT, V. 'An Apparently Orderly Affair: VALIE EXPORT speaks to Yilmaz Dziewior about her archive.' In *VALIE EXPORT: Archiv*, edited by Yilmaz Dziewior, Bregenz: Kunsthauz, Bregenz, pp77–96.

2012 Fischer-Lichte, E. 'Appearing as Embodied Mind: Defining a Weak, a Strong and a Radical Concept of Presence'. In Gabriella Giannachi, Nick Kaye and Michael Shanks (eds) *Archaeologies of Presence: Art, Performance and the Persistence of Being*, New York and London: 2012, pp103–18.

2012 Fore, D. 'Art: VALIE EXPORT' *Interview Magazine*, 9 October. Available online. http://www.interviewmagazine.com/art/valie-export. Accessed 31 May 2016.

1968 [1967] Fried, Michael 'Art and Objecthood'. In G. Battcock (ed.) *Minimal Art: A Critical Anthology*, New York: E.P. Dutton, pp116–47.

2011 Giannachi, G. and Kaye, N. *Performing Presence: Between the Live and the Simulated*, Manchester: Manchester University Press.

1975 Grotowski, J. *Towards a Poor Theatre*, London: Methuen and Eyre Methuen.

2004 Heathfield, A. 'Elevating the Public: Marina Abramović in Conversation with Adrian Heathfield'. In Adrian Heathfield (ed.) *Live: Art and Performance*, London and New York: Tate and Routledge, pp144–51.

2012 *Entangled: An Archaeology of the Relationships between Humans and Things*, New Jersey: Wiley-Blackwell.

2014 The Entanglement of Humans and Things: A Long-Term View'. *New Literary History*, 45: pp19–36.

2011 Jones, A. '"The Artist is Present": Artistic Re-Enactments and the Impossibility of Presence'. *TDR: The Drama Review*, 55(1), Spring: pp16–45.

1996 Kaye, N. *Art into Theatre: Performance Interviews and Documents*, London and New York: Routledge.

2013 'One Time Over Another: Tom Marioni's Conceptual Art', *PAJ: A Journal of Performance and Art*, 104: pp26–38.

2016 Kaye, N. and van Winkle Oppenheim, A. *Dennis Oppenheim: Body to Performance*, Milan: Skira.

2004 Kolbowski, S *Silvia Kolbowski:I Inadequate ... Like ... Power*, Köln: Walther König.

1973 Lippard, L. R. (ed.) Six Years: *The Dematerialisation of the Art Object 1966 to 1972*, New York: Praeger.

1979 Marioni, T. *Café Society Beer*, numbered edition of 800, plus artists' proof, San Francisco: Crown Point Press.

2000 Marioni, T. *Writings on Art 1969–1999*, San Francisco: Crown Point Press.

1995 McCarthy, P. and Kelley, M. *Fresh Acconci*. Available online. https://www.youtube.com/watch?v=auFwtrDgRsU. Accessed 2 June 2016.

1984 Miller, D. and Tilley, C. (eds) *Ideology, Power and Prehistory*, Cambridge: Cambridge University Press.

2010 Mogutin, S. 'The Legend of Marina Abramović: Interview and Portraits', *Whitewall Magazine*, Summer. Available online. http://slavamogutin.com/marina-abramovic/. Accessed 20 September 2016.

2010 Obrist, H.U. *Marina Abramović*, Köln: Walther König.

2001 Pearson, M. and Shanks, M. *Theatre / Archaeology*, London and New York: Routledge, 2001.

1993 Phelan, P. *Unmarked: The Politics of Performance*, New York and London: Routledge.

1999 Shanks, M. *Art and the Greek City State*, Cambridge: Cambridge University Press.

2012 *The Archaeological Imagination*, London and New York: Routledge.

1997 Shanks, M. and Hodder, I. 'Processual, Postprocessual and Interpretive Archaeologies'. In Alexandra Alexandri, Victor Buchli, John Carmen and Ian Hodder (eds) *Interpreting Archaeology: Finding Meaning in the Past*, New York and London: Routldge, pp3–29.

1993 Shanks, M. and Tilley, C. *Re-constructing Archaeology: Theory and Practice*, New York and London: Routledge.

2007 Spector, N., Fischer-Lichte E. and Umathum, S. (eds) *Marina Abramović: Seven Easy Pieces*, Milan: Edizioni Charta.

1996 Thomas, J. *Time, Culture and Identity: An Interpretive Archaeology*, New York and London: Routledge.

1993 Tilley, C. (ed.) *Interpretive Archaeology*, Oxford: Berg.

1979 Tisdall, C. *Joseph Beuys*, New York and London: Guggenheim Museum and Thames and Hudson.

2007 Umathum, S. 'Beyond Documentation, or The Adventure of Shared Time and Place. Experiences of a Viewer'. In Nancy Spector, Erika Fischer-Lichte and Sandra Umathum, *Marina Abramović: Seven Easy Pieces*, Milan: Edizioni Charta, pp46–55.

2000 [1974] Vergine, L. *Body Art: The Body as Language*, Milan: Skira

2012 Viola, E. and Sileo, D. *The Abramović Method*, Milan: 24 ORE Cultura.

1981 Wood, S. 'An Interview with Dennis Oppenheim', *Arts*, June: pp133–7.

REMAKE

The *OED* defines the verb REMAKE as to 'Make (something) again or differently'. It is a term that has associations with remakes of Hollywood movies. Slavoj Žižek writes 'Is there a proper way to remake a Hitchcock film?', proposing that there are two approaches to 'the ideal remake'. Firstly he proposes 'an exact frame-by-frame' reconstruction, which takes further 'Gus van Sant's strategy with *Psycho*' and attempts to shoot 'formally the same film' in order to 'achieve the uncanny effect of the double'. He suggests that 'on account of this very sameness' of 'shots, angles, dialogue', 'the difference would have become all the more palpable' (Žižek 2007: 263). Žižek goes on to suggest that 'the second way', which would be preferable to 'direct "homages"', would be to stage in a well-calculated move, one of the alternative scenarios that underlie those actualised by Hitchcock' (2007: 264). For Žižek creation is perceived as a negative gesture of selecting from among multiple virtual versions and thus limiting possibilities. The artists in REMAKE apply both of Žižek's strategies, often in combination: firstly, attempting to reconstruct formally, whilst explicitly staging the process of copying and doing so in order to produce difference rather than sameness; secondly, calculatedly constructing alternative versions in order to make again differently, thus producing gaps between archival source and remake in which reflection can take place.

As Janez Janša notes below, *Monument G*, 'stages the fundamental tension included in every historicization, the tension between history and story, facts and their construction'. In relation to an earlier remake, *Puilija, Papa Pupilo and the Pupilceks—Reconstruction* (2006), Janša writes that the motive for reconstructing was not to 're-experience a performance from the past' but to experience or watch 'our relation to history' in order to question the present, for instance contemporary cultural or ethical positions (Janša 2012: 373). In the case of Etchells' *Untitled: After Violent Incident* (2013), this work attempts to produce sameness in another medium, remediating Bruce Nauman's *Violent Incident* (1986), a twelve channel video installation, through performance. As two performers try to reiterate the loops of Nauman's video recordings live, version control fails and becomes impossible to manage, as human error, physical exhaustion and contingencies find their way in and are documented. *Violent Incident* represents a traumatic domestic event, while drawing on slapstick and clowning. Hal Foster (1996), citing Freud, argues that the subject is compelled to repeat such events 'in actions, in dreams, in images', and similarly, Žižek (1991) writes of 'traumatic encounters' with film or video, which produce a surplus that 'propel[s] us to narrate [them] again and again' (133), to screen or perform them repeatedly.

Robin Deacon's long-term project, *Approximating the Art of Stuart Sherman* (2008–14), around the work of the late American artist Stuart Sherman arose out of a formative encounter, when he saw Sherman perform in 1994, at Cardiff School of Art. Deacon suggests that he has 'a personal investment because of his influence on me' (Deacon 2009). He specifically notes that the small scale of Sherman's work 'really stayed with' him and 'from then on all [his] performances were on little tables', using the tabletop as a stage. Deacon says that he went back to 'actual documents' in order to 'try to do something different with them' (Deacon 2009) and the title of his Sherman series acknowledges that his remakes are approximations of the artist's complex tabletop choreographies of objects. His Sherman project also explores 'the possibility for the preservation of ephemeral artworks through reenactment' (2013), especially in the case of artists whose work has been marginalised by history, left out of the authorized archival or art historical record and not digitised. Perhaps we might think of this as the return of a culturally repressed work and of practices that left an affective trace in Deacon's body.

On their pages, Rosemary Butcher and Stephanie Sachsenmaier write around Butcher's series of choreographic responses to Kaprow's *18 Happenings in 6 Parts* (1959), a work regularly written into art histories as the first happening and the originary event in the emergence of this form. *18 Happenings* is a performance that has now inspired multiple versions, including André Lepecki's redoing for Haus der Künst, München, in 2006, and subsequent iteration for *PERFORMA 07*, New York. Butcher responds to Kaprow's will, permission, explicit wish or direction that this work should be performed again and have a future, but, rather than reconstructing with 'near archaeological accuracy' (Dorment 2010) from the meticulous documents that Kaprow left in the manner of Lepecki's redoing, her cycle of new actualizations are reinventions filtered through contemporary aesthetics. As Sachsenmaier remarks, the impetus for Butcher, who sadly passed away in 2016, was to trace her roots and influences in New York, where she worked with members of Judson Church in the late 1960s and early 70s. In the process of reinventing *18 Happenings*, by 'going back' to Kaprow's archive, she was able to 'move her work on' and to experiment with ways to 'move dance into a visual [art] setting'.

The final artist's pages in this section, by Chinese artist Zhang Huan, shift the focus to sculptural objects that are bodily in form and to materials that carry traces of cultural acts. Zhang Huan began by making performance art in Beijing, then emigrating to the US in 1998. In 2006 he returned to China, and focused on the production of sculptures, often rendered on a monumental scale. Zhang's vast public artworks, such as *Three Legged Buddha* (2010), both reconfigure and monumentalise the remains of Buddhist relics and the minor histories or unauthorised cultural memories they hold. *Rui Lai* (2009) is also a reconstructed Buddhist figure, but in this instance it is the material that is remarkable, as it is partially made of ash from incense and burnt offerings, which were gathered from a local Buddhist temple. This material documents the ritual acts that produced it and for Zhang Huan carries forward traces of the personal feelings, blessings and souls with which it was associated. For him found materials and objects are performative and can have a powerful agency that excites him, makes him sleepless and compels him to rework them.

References

2009 Deacon, R. 'Robin Deacon on Stuart Sherman'. Interview by Rachel-Lois Clapham. Available online. http://www.robindeacon.com/rl_clapham_interview.htm. Accessed 1 March 2017.

2013 Deacon, R. 'Spectacle: A Portrait of Stuart Sherman'. Available online. http://www.robindeacon.com/spectacle_movie.htm. Accessed 1 March 2017.

2010 Dorment, R. 'Allan Kaprow's *18 Happenings in 6 Parts*, Festival Hall, review'. *The Telegraph*, 30 November. Available online. http://www.telegraph.co.uk/culture/art/art-reviews/8170048/Allan-Kaprows-18-Happenings-in-6-Parts-Festival-Hall-review.html. Accessed 2 March 2017.

1996 Foster, H. *The Return of the Real*, Massachusetts: MIT Press.

2012 Janša, J. 'Reconstruction2: On the Reconstructions of Pupilija, Papa Pupilo and the Pupilceks'. In A. Jones and A. Heathfield (eds) Perform, Repeat, Record: Live Art in History, Bristol: Intellect, pp367–83.

1991 Žižek, S. *Looking Awry*, Cambridge, Massachusetts: MIT Press.

2007 'Is There A Proper Way To Remake A Hitchcock Film', In S. Brode (ed.) *J. Grimonprez: Looking for Alfred*, Berlin: Hatje Cantz, pp261–73.

MONUMENT G AS A CALL FOR RECONSTRUCTION

Monument G (1972) directed by Dušan Jovanović, performer Jožica Avbelj. Photo: personal documentation of Jožica Avbelj.

Janez Janša

Upon the attentive reading of the purified text of *Monument G* (from 1972), we find that it practically calls for a reconstruction:

> Do not be surprised at my coming.
> I might only be a trick of your memory.
> [...] Man searches in memories.
> He holds a living being in his hands.
> In a hospice without memory,
> Without a compass or a steering wheel.

When these words are uttered in the reconstruction (2009), this inevitably refers to the lost original.

The reconstruction of *Monument G* (the reconstruction is entitled *Monument G2*), features Jožica Avbelj and Matjaž Jarc, so the original cast, and in addition to them, also Teja Reba and Boštjan Narat, who were both born after *Monument G*. The basic dramaturgical characteristic of the reconstruction is the reference to the original performance, which is very poorly documented (a several-minute recording from a rehearsal and poorly preserved photo material). Avbelj and Reba tackle the reconstruction from two different perspectives: Avbelj with an overall, also bodily memory, Reba on the basis of analysing the procedures we can recognise in the recording of the rehearsal for the original performance. Avbelj carries in her memory a long acting career that filters her view of *Monument G*, Reba approaches from a dancing perspective, with a knowledge of movement and substantially less experience. A complex relationship is established between them of mutual reference and of individual and joint reference to the absent source. In the reconstruction, the words that Avbelj uttered in the original performance function as a commentary of the reconstruction itself:

> It seemed to me that someone stepped out of the monument and followed us.
> [...] Someone lives next to us.
> [...] I do not want to be snuffed for good,
> I will not allow this.
> I suffered when they lit and put me out.
> This is a time of performances.
> Curtains, lights! Dear words!

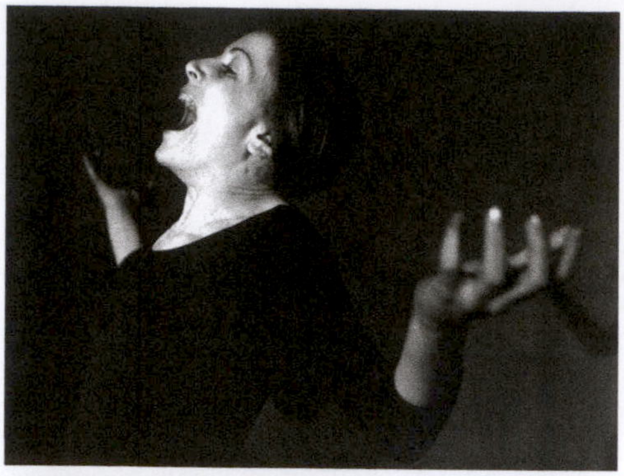

Monument G (1972) directed by Dušan Jovanović, performer Jožica Avbelj. Photo: personal documentation of Jožica Avbelj.

Someone comes and lights me.
Again someone comes and snuffs me.

The only uttered text we added in the reconstruction is composed of quotes from the reviews of the original *Monument G*. Teja Reba speaks it while running on the spot[1]:

Monument G...

is an experiment—Andrej Inkret
is not an experiment—Peter Božič

is a ritual theatre—Borut Trekman
is not a ritual theatre—Veno Taufer

is a new theatre—Muharem Pervić
is not a contemporary theatre—
Marija Vogelnik
is improvised—Borut Trekman
is not improvised—Peter Božič
is a laboratory theatre—Andrej Inkret
is pure theatre—Peter Božič
is a kinetic monologue—Marija Vogelnik
is total theatre—Veno Taufer
is yoga—Dalibor Foretić
is an etude for an actress and various instruments—Borut Trekman
is a concert for an actress—Boško Božović
is a concert for a young body—MES Festival
is contemporary dance—Marija Vogelnik
is physical theatre—Boško Božović
is kinetic theatre—Muharem Pervić
is avantgarde theatre—Veno Taufer

Monument G shows us that, with its thematisation of the past, it created the possibilities that, in the reconstruction, this thematisation refers to the performance itself. Precisely because the historical situation was fictionalised, the final writing on the wall is 'And what if we made it all up?'. *Monument G2* stages the fundamental tension included in every historicisation, the tension between history and story, facts and their construction, between *l'histoire* and *l'histoire*. At the same time, it shows that some performances are predisposed to be reconstructed. It would therefore not be surprising if *Monument G* were reconstructed again in 30 years with three generations on stage.

Notes

1 Running on the spot in the 'Someone Walked the Lonely Road' scene was not recorded. The part performed by Reba was a combination of two runs on the spot from two performances: *The Power of Theatrical Madness* (1984) by Jan Fabre and *Baptism Under Triglav* (1986) by the Scipion Nasice Sisters Theatre. In these scenes, both performances refer to historical sources, in Fabre's performance, they enumerate important theatre performances of the 1960s and 1970s, whereas the Scipions refer directly to Meyerhold's biomechanics. Reba, therefore, does not refer only to the absent original but also to the history of what happened between the original and the reconstructed *Monument G*.

Monument G2 (2009) directed by Janez Janša and Dušan Jovanović, performers Jožica Avbelj and Teja Reba. Photo: Tone Stojko.

UNTITLED (AFTER VIOLENT INCIDENT)

HE'S STANDING ON THE LEFT-HAND SIDE OF THE TABLE AND SHE'S STANDING BY THE CHAIR ON THE RIGHT-HAND SIDE. HE WALKS AROUND TOWARDS HER AND SHE WATCHES, SMILING, AS HE GETS CLOSER. HE ARRIVES AND THEN MAKES A SHOW OF PULLING THE CHAIR OUT, GESTURING FOR HER TO SIT DOWN. SHE STEPS IN AND GOES TO SIT. AS SHE DOES SO, HE PULLS AWAY THE CHAIR, THROWING IT BACK AND ONTO THE GROUND. ATTEMPTING TO SEAT HERSELF ON THE CHAIR THAT HAS NOW BEEN REMOVED, SHE FALLS OVER BACKWARDS. AS SHE TUMBLES, HE MOVES TO PICK UP THE CHAIR, WHICH IS NOW ON THE GROUND, HIS ASS IN THE AIR AS HE BENDS. LYING ON THE GROUND AND RECOVERING FROM HER FALL, SHE TWISTS AND STARTS TO RISE, THEN SEES AND QUICKLY TAKES ADVANTAGE OF HIS PROFFERED ASS, JABBING IT HARD WITH HER FINGER. SURPRISED, HE SPINS TO CONFRONT HER, STEPPING TOWARDS HER. SHE RISES, THEN BACKS OFF A STEP IN REACTION TO HIS ADVANCE. SHE GRABS A GLASS OF WATER FROM THE TABLE AND THROWS IT IN HIS FACE, STOPPING HIM IN HIS TRACKS. HE SLAPS HER IN THE FACE. SHE KNEES HIM IN THE BALLS. HE BENDS DOUBLE, SLUMPING FORWARD TO LEAN ON THE TABLE. BENT OVER IN THIS WAY, HE GRABS A FORK FROM THE TABLE, SPINS, AND AS HE IS RISING, STABS HER IN THE STOMACH. DURING THIS STABBING MANEUVER, SHE GRABS HIS FOREARM AND THERE'S A STRUGGLE IN WHICH SHE TAKES POSSESSION OF THE FORK, USING IT TO STAB HIM HARD IN THE STOMACH. HE COLLAPSES, FALLING OVER BACKWARDS. HE ENDS UP SITTING ON HIS ASS, CLUTCHING HIS STOMACH. SHE TOO COLLAPSES, BENT FORWARD, ON HER KNEES AND CLUTCHING AT HER BELLY.

Tim Etchells

As the title suggests, the video *Untitled (After Violent Incident)* began as a response to Bruce Nauman's seminal multi-channel video installation *Violent Incident* (1986). In Nauman's work a man and a woman are shown across 12 screens in a series of out-of sync takes, enacting and re-enacting a brutal slapstick routine. The effect, a kind of asynchronous cacophonous scratch-mix of the scene, is driven partly by the action of the performers, and partly through the simultaneous presentation, stopping and starting, playback and slowing of multiple takes of the scene over the numerous screens of the installation.

Drawing on aspects of my own practice, especially in respect of duration and performance, *Untitled (After Violent Incident)* meanwhile takes the physical choreography of Nauman's original as a score, playing it out doggedly on one single monitor using two performers, who enact a version of the sequence as a continuous loop, without pause, for a period of one hour. Where Nauman's original installation orchestrates energy from the multiplication and multi-tracking of the scene as video, my interest was in the performative transformation of the action 'in real time' as the performers became more and more exhausted through repetition of the task. Recorded in a single unbroken take by a lone camera on a dolly, which relentlessly circled the action, the trajectory of the camera was also subject to different kinds of decay and change, much of it produced by human error and chance as its circular path repeated again and again, in an effort to keep pace with the action.

Interrogating the differences between the dynamic force produced in editing and video replay, and that produced through extended physical labour and performance, the work also explores the different relations to both the comic and the abject inherent in these two forms of repetition—the one staged via the apparatus of video and media (repetition as replay) and the other staged through the brute force of embodied human labour (repetition as task or compulsion), replete with the psychological burdens of ownership and characterisation that such persistent embodiment might imply. The array of Nauman's video creates a spectacular dispersal of the scene, fragmenting and distressing it, much as one might experience multiple perspectives of an event via any number of video-wall installations in an art context, surveillance centre or TV newsroom. In *Untitled (After Violent Incident)* the scene is not dispersed, but rather focused in one place—a single screen, a single shot and a single pair of performers who take no breaks from their task. Indeed, the investigative return to the object of Nauman's work can be seen, in some ways, as an act of simplification, or de-sophistication, in which the rhetorical structure of multi-screen edit-video is 'reduced' to a singular lo-fi object, a translation that in part mirrors the cultural shift from the 80s multi-screen of shopping-mall video wall and MTV backdrop to the paradigmatic single-unbroken-and-unedited-shot phone-video of the early twenty-first century.

In the installation version of this work presented at 'Version Control' in 2013, I presented the single channel video *Untitled (After Violent Incident)* next to two other elements—the table, chairs, table cloth, flowers and other place-setting of the dinner scene, which occupied the gallery as a kind of stage-set or space of potential action, and, installed beside the monitor bearing the video-loop, a printed text describing the movement at the heart of Nauman's piece, which also serves as the basis for my own choreography. This plain language step-by-step account of the performers' actions is both an after-the-fact breakdown of the sequence—a piece of reportage—and at the same time of course, a virtual staging of the piece as well as a linguistic score from which further versions of the *Violent Incident* could easily be constructed, even without access to Nauman's original. These additional elements of the installation (stage setting and score) are significant in underlining the versional nature of this work and of my approach to the 'found' or 'recovered' material of Nauman's *Violent Incident*—offering, by way of instructional text and concrete location for action, the possibility of further future re-enactments.

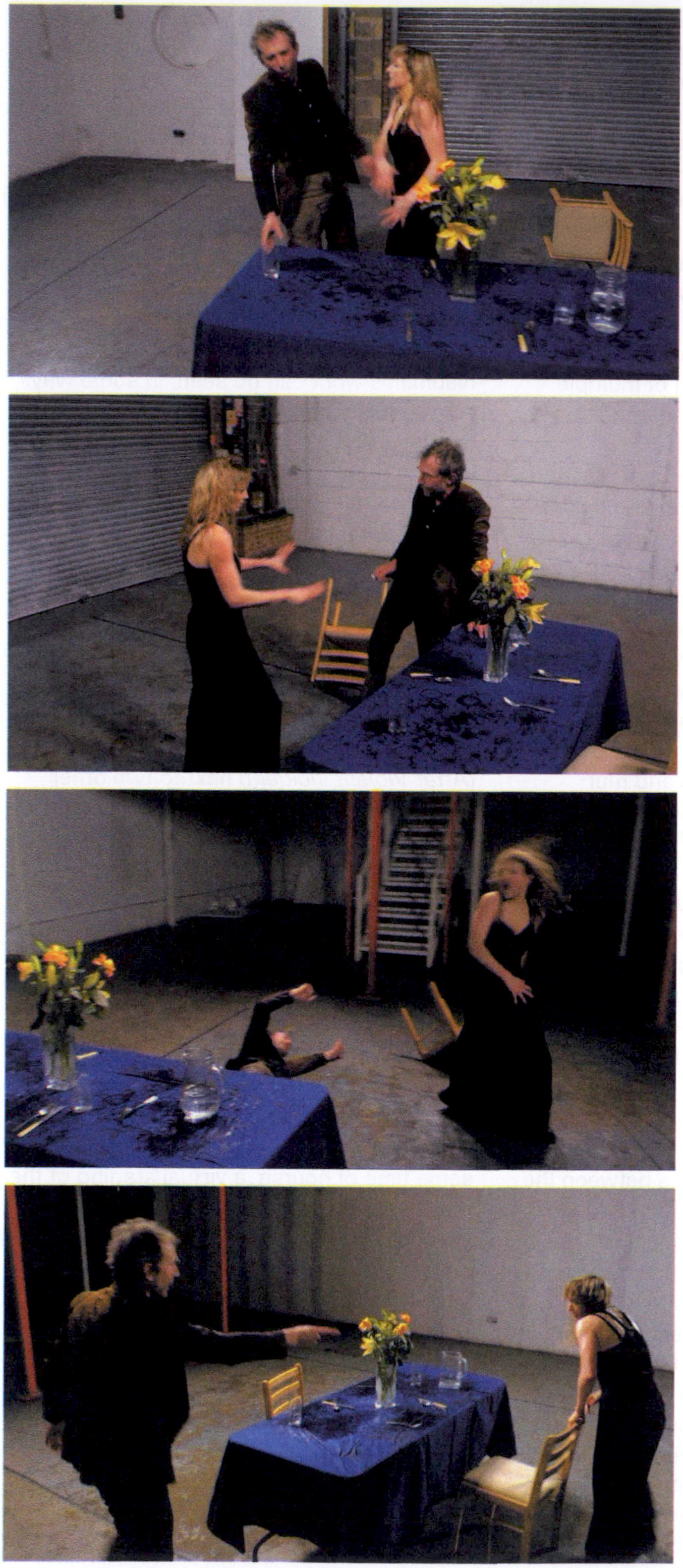

Tim Etchells, *Untitled (after Violent Incident)*. Courtesy of the artist.

STUART SHERMAN'S HAMLET: A CAREFUL MISREADING

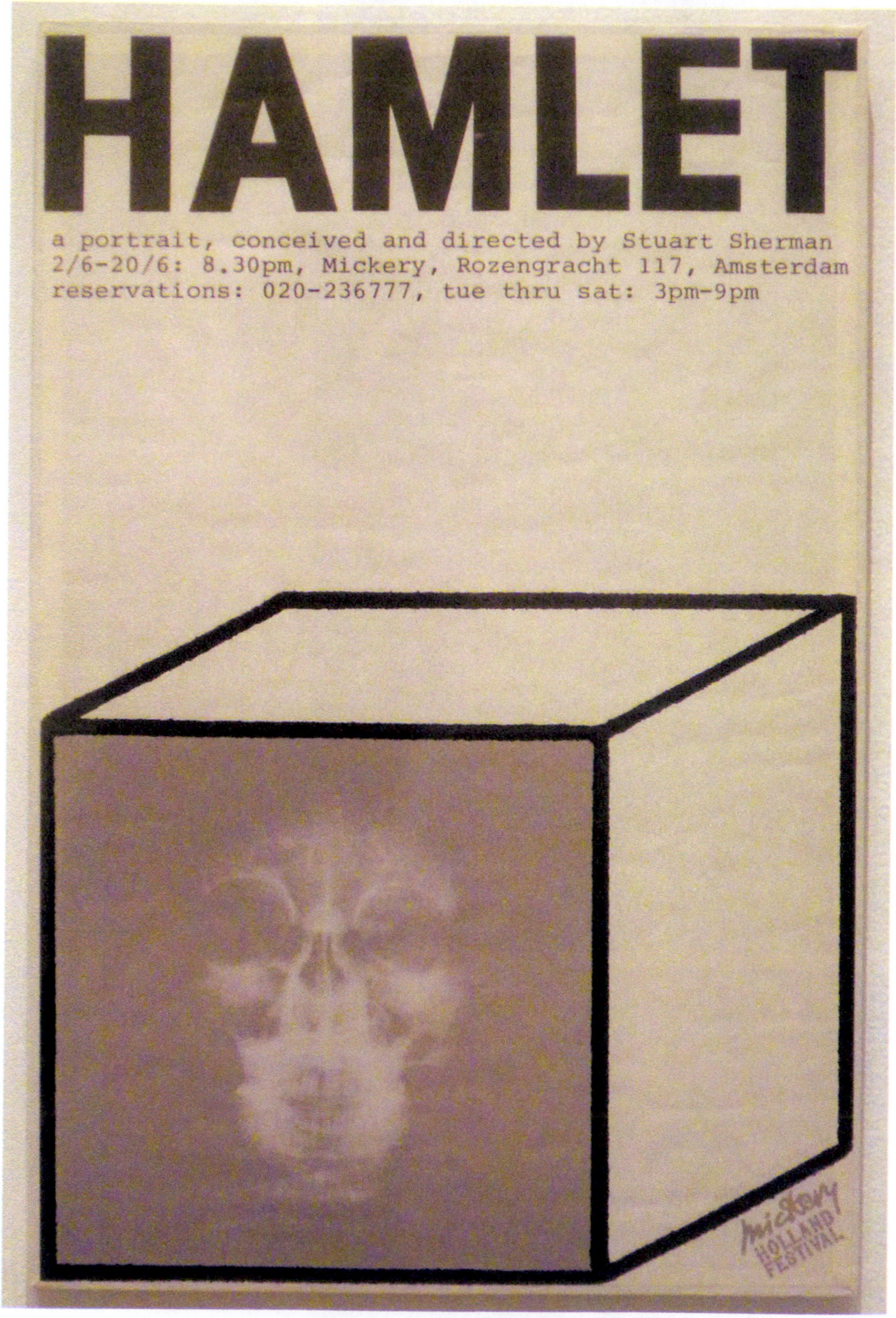

HAMLET
a portrait, conceived and directed by Stuart Sherman
2/6-20/6: 8.30pm, Mickery, Rozengracht 117, Amsterdam
reservations: 020-236777, tue thru sat: 3pm-9pm
mickery
HOLLAND FESTIVAL

Hamlet: A Portrait by Stuart Sherman. Poster reproduced with the permission of the Estate of Stuart Sherman.

Robin Deacon

Between 2008 and 2014, my primary point of focus as an artist was an on-going research project pertaining to the work of the late US artist Stuart Sherman (1945–2001). This included a reenactment of one of Sherman's ensemble works *Stuart Sherman's Hamlet: A Portrait*, first shown as part of the US Radical season at the Chelsea Theatre, London in 2010, with a second version presented as part of the Remake symposium at Arnolfini, Bristol in 2012. In both cases, the working process explored what 'new' might be possible in re-visiting past works with different performers in a contemporary context. In assembling my version of this experimental reading of Shakespeare, video, photographs and textual remnants of the original performance told partial and sometimes contradictory stories that I drew together to create a new approximation of Sherman's original 1980s staging.

As both director and set maker, my role included accounting for the relationship between my remaking of the set and objects and their utilization by re-enacting bodies. I had in my possession a series of materials that mapped out the original piece. One of these was a text entitled 'The Mickery's Production of *Hamlet*', written by Liesbeth Jansen, an assistant on the first 1981 production of Sherman's *Hamlet* at the Mickery, a theatre in Amsterdam. Published in *TDR (The Drama Review)* in 1982, this is something of a blow-by-blow account of the performance, reflecting the observation frequently made that writings about Sherman's work tend towards dry and descriptive list making. However, Jansen's text also served as an indicator of the performance's set design, formed of a complex series of moveable interlocking flats and objects. Setting the scene, she lists the visual characteristics of a series of Styrofoam cubes, a key part of the set:

> Behind the flats [...] is a tower of white cubes, with a small red square on the front side of each. The other sides of the cubes show the following:
>
> Cube No. 1: A photo of Sherman's face, of a cassette recorder and of a hand holding a sword.
>
> Cube No. 2: An x-ray photo of Sherman's face, of a cassette recorder and of a hand holding a sword.
>
> Cube No. 3: The words: 'Hamlet', 'Cassette-recorder', 'Hand', and 'Sword'.
>
> Cube No. 4: A concentric oval, concentric rectangle, and the figure of a sword with the same concentric lines.
>
> Cube No. 5: A black oval, a black rectangle, and a black sword.
>
> The cubes also have a small red door, about three inches square, a small hole in the red square of the same size as the small door, and a black side with pages [from Shakespeare's Hamlet] arranged horizontally.
>
> Jansen 1982

My interest here is in expanding focus from re-enactment as a bodily interpretation of the original performers' activities (the *remaking of actions*) towards the *remaking of objects*, and the significance of this process relative to the subsequent embodied activation. Considering Jansen's descriptions of these objects in their own right led me to question the idea of a re-fabricated set or objects as interchangeable elements in a reenactment, relative to a specific performer's body that is often assumed not to be interchangeable.

My reconstruction of Sherman's *Hamlet* set also relied on visual approximations from video documentation, and in particular, a degraded VHS tape copy documenting the Amsterdam performance in 1981, which ran at about 20 minutes in length. Again, the focus was on aspects of the documentation that did not depict the work in terms of performer action. For instance, the video silently spends the first three and half minutes with a series of still and slow tracking shots of the aforementioned cubes

Stuart Sherman's Hamlet: A Portrait by Robin Deacon. Courtesy of the artist.

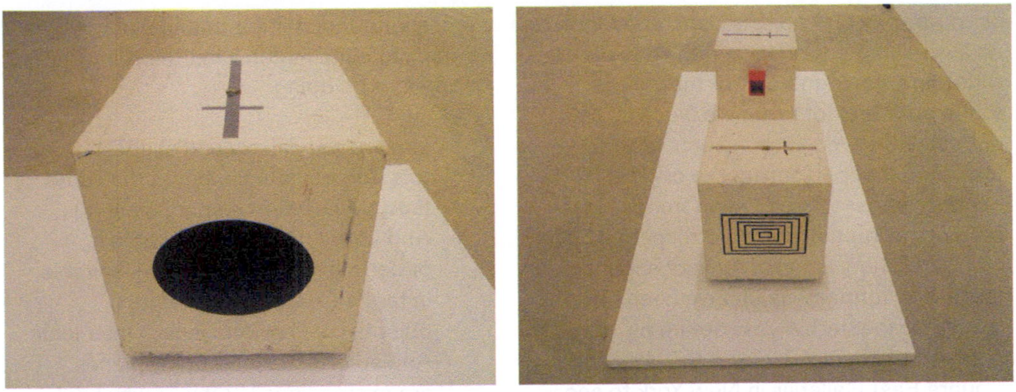

Styrofoam cubes used in *Stuart Sherman's Hamlet*, Washington Square East Galleries, 2009.

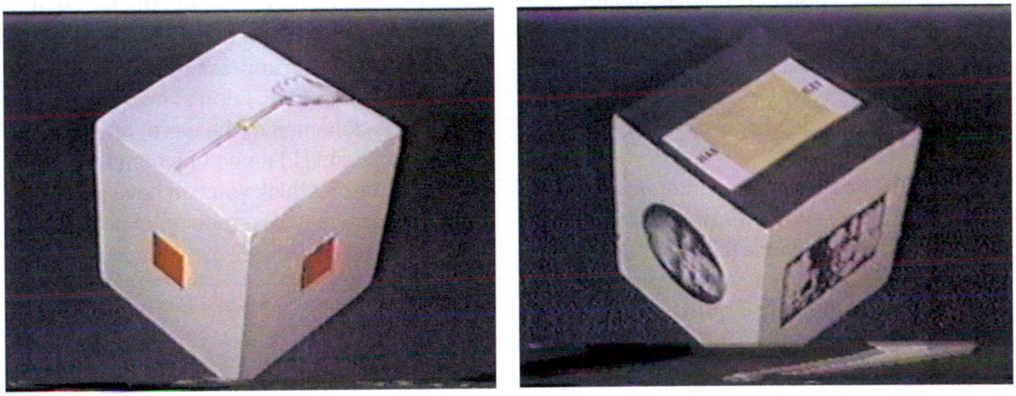

Styrofoam cubes in video documentation of *Stuart Sherman's Hamlet*, 1981. Reproduced with permission of The Estate of Stuart Sherman.

and the remainder of the set. The poor visual quality of this third or fourth generation tape makes the subtle distinctions of signification between the cubes established by Jansen harder to ascertain, but a much clearer sense of the dimensions and solidity of the objects begins to emerge.

Of course, sooner or later (in both Jansen's text and the video documentation), the performers eventually arrive. As they enter the space, flats are wheeled aside and the tower of cubes reconfigured horizontally at the front of the stage:

> After the man and woman have placed the last cube, which is furthest to the right, they walk back to the first one on the left. They pick it up and start tumbling it. Sherman walks to the left plexiglass cube, removes the sword and the cassette recorder and steps behind the tumbling cube. The man and woman stop tumbling it, and hold the cube with the picture of the cassette recorder. The sound of a sword fight is heard. Slowly, he lowers the sword with his outstretched arm until it is horizontal above the cube. He switches off the cassette recorder.
>
> Jansen 1982

How might we engage with the handling and manipulation of the objects described here by Jansen? What haptic concerns arise? Mindful of these objects as *things to be performed with*, they could only be reconstructed with their very particular utility in mind. Therefore, in rehearsal, the significance of physical activation and bodily experience in direct relation to the scenography and objects concerned took on an increasing importance with speculations regarding the 'rightness' of the weight, touch and 'feel' of materials (such as the cubes). However, such aspects of the experience of performing the original piece cannot necessarily be drawn from a videotape or instruction set. In retrospect, I have wondered how *material rules of engagement* for the performers could have been more clearly delineated. A year before my reenactment of Hamlet, I visited the Washington Square East Galleries in New York to see the Stuart Sherman retrospective entitled *Beginningless Thought/Endless Seeing*. In the rear of the gallery were two of the cubes used in Sherman's *Hamlet*. Of course, with the usual prohibitions of touching in the gallery, the one thing I could not do was pick them up.

In 2010 I conducted an interview with Anna Kohler, one of the performers in Sherman's Hamlet in Paris in the early 1980s. She says '...I was totally surprised that to him it was really important that I was a good juggler, and that I was able to juggle his cubes in the show...just so'. Kohler uses the word 'juggle' to describe her interaction with the cube, whereas Jansen writes of the performers 'tumbling' the cube. In semantic terms, tumbling could imply a downward motion, or the image of something falling, whereas the image of the juggler suggests the upward motion of balls tossed into the air, and kept there. Lacking the luxury of time to unravel such complexities during the process of making the reenactment, my own rehearsal notes settled upon 'a mutual rotation of the cube between two performers'.

How might the notion of 'tumbling' or 'juggling' have affected my approach to constructing the cubes? As I now write, a series of further questions emerge suggesting other possibilities for potentially absurd forms of micro management. Did the thickness of the Styrofoam matter? What would have been the implications of a solid or hollow interior for accuracy of the chosen action? In watching the videotape again (and again), it is somehow reassuring that neither 'tumble' nor 'juggle' seems to quite match what the performers appear to be doing.

> I mean, you can try and shape it, to a degree, mold it, but at the same time, you have to respect what it is. And after I make certain choices, or certain choices become inevitable, in terms of actions and certain objects [...] I have to accept their logic. And so in a sense all of my pieces are misreadings [...] this is why I did a piece called *A Careful Misreading*. That once I had accepted the fact that my understanding (it's going to be the essence of an impression) all impressions are partial. I don't know if this is the definition of the word, but an impression [...] it can't be comprehensive. I don't think you can have a comprehensive understanding of anything.
>
> Sherman interviewed by John Matturri, c. 1978. Transcribed by Robin Deacon from cassette recording, quotation reproduced with permission of John Matturri.

References

1982 Jansen, L., 'The Mickery's Production of *Hamlet*', *The Drama Review: TDR*, 26(2): pp125–31.

ROSEMARY BUTCHER: AFTER KAPROW—A VISUAL JOURNEY

Rosemary Butcher and
Stefanie Sachsenmaier

Rosemary Butcher, *After Kaprow—Book of Journeys*. Courtesy of Sam Williams.

In early 2010 British choreographer Rosemary Butcher travelled to the USA in order to trace her own history and influences, in particular investigating her own experience of the Judson Church Movement in the early 1970s when living in New York. As part of this journey she also accessed the archive of American artist Allan Kaprow at the Getty Research Institute in Los Angeles, where she watched several of Kaprow's films. She subsequently agreed to reinvent Kaprow's first Happening entitled *18 Happenings in 6 Parts*, which originally took place at the Reuben Gallery in New York City in 1959.

Butcher's commissioned reinvention was presented in 2010 at the Clore Ballroom of the Royal Festival Hall as part of the exhibition event *Move: Choreographing You*, which explored the connections between dance and visual arts over the previous five decades. It was the only time Butcher took the completed artwork of another artist as a starting point for her own choreographic work. Doing so, as she emphasised in the years following, was a strong challenge to her, since during her research of Kaprow's archive she never quite reached an insight into why Kaprow's performers were doing what they were doing.

Rosemary Butcher, *18 Happenings in 6 Parts* 1959/2010. Courtesy of Rocco Redondo.

The creative process of Butcher's *18 Happenings in 6 Parts 1959/2010* involved looking at many meticulous copies of Kaprow's handwritten scores, photographs and fragments of his published writing. The choreographer searched for connection points between Kaprow's and her own practice and found an interest in Kaprow's preoccupation with the everyday. In particular she explored his concept of 'activities'. The dancers she chose to work with were Ben Ash, Elena Giannotti, Dennis Greenwood and Lauren Potter. Also involved in the project were architect Matthew Butcher and artist Pablo Bronstein who created the set. Artist Edwin Burdis contributed a sound score as well as objects that the dancers used in the live performance. During the actual presentation of the reinvention Butcher herself was present in the performance space, creating and distributing instruction cards, which the dancers picked up and responded to spontaneously as part of a live score of events.

Butcher stated that she experienced a sense of loss of her own aesthetic in this reinvention process, and yet afterwards she felt unable to return to her previous ways of working. Searching for new ways to move her work on, Butcher embarked on a subsequent cycle of works which she called *After Kaprow*. In the two works *After Kaprow—The Silent Room* and *After Kaprow—The Book of Journeys* Butcher retained a sense of the rooms she had encountered in Kaprow's Happening. Aiming for nothing to be 'danced', the developed movement was a response by the dancer

Rosemary Butcher, *After Kaprow—The Silent Room*. Courtesy of Sam Williams.

to specific situations provided by Butcher, focusing on the idea of a woman being alone. In these works she further pursued her research into the concept of activities. Reflecting on the creative process, she stated at the time:

> I'm going back to looking at movement again rather than taking an outside concept and developing an idea through a particular sort of history; this is purely looking at the way a movement is put together and how movement can lead to an activity which gives you information, as opposed to the other way around. This is why the figure is concentrating on very, very simple working activities; that's the point. Some of them lead to wider perspectives, some of them are purely, fundamentally, probably utilitarian.
>
> Butcher in Sachsenmaier: 2012

After Kaprow—The Silent Room was presented in a work-in-progress showing at Bloomberg Gallery London in 2011 with dancer Ana Mira and film work by Sam Williams. In the gallery space there were two projections framing the live work of the dancer—one showing pre-recorded and edited footage of the same gallery, and the other a live video feed of the dancer. In the work Butcher was interested in setting up a landscape that relates to painting, which does not have a performance narrative. Her experiment was to move dance into a visual art setting, to create a moving sculpture, rather than thinking of the work as 'placing a dancer into a gallery'. The work was later performed in a different version at The Place Theatre in London in 2012, with dancers Ana Mira and Rosalie Wahlfrid. *After Kaprow—The Book of Journeys* is a dual screen film created with filmmaker Williams, dancer Mira and composer Jonathan Owen Clark. As a self-contained film, it works with two elements, again involving the idea of rooms: a woman alone is 'looking out', at a world beyond—a conceptually added 'third room', the world outside. There was a sense of time—past, present and future—inherent in the work, in that the actions starting on the first screen (or 'room') were the ending actions in the second, and *vice versa*.

References

2012 Sachsenmaier, S. 'Beyond Allan Kaprow: An Interview with Rosemary Butcher'. *Journal of Dance & Somatic Practices*, 4(2): pp267–81.

Further reading

2016 Butcher R. artist website. Available online. http://rosemarybutcher.com/. Accessed 30 October 2016.

2016 Getty Research Institute website. Available online. https://www.getty.edu/research/. Accessed 14 November 2016.

2016 Hayward Gallery *Move: Choreographing You*, exhibition website. Available online. http://move.southbankcentre.co.uk/microsite/. Accessed 30 October 2016.

2013 Sachsenmaier, S. 'Reinventing the Past: Rosemary Butcher Encounters Allan Kaprow's *18 Happenings in 6 Parts*'. *Choreographic Practices Journal*, 4(2): pp223–44.

SIX QUESTIONS

Q1

The monumental sculpture *Three Legged Bhudda* (2007) was modelled on fragments of bronze Buddha sculptures you encountered on a visit to Tibet in 2005. A series of your works that followed were based on such fragments. What interested you in these objects?

Zhang Huan

Zhang Huan, *Three Legged Buddha* (2010), steel and copper. 339 x 504 x 272 inches (860 x 1280 x 690 cm). Courtesy Zhang Huan Studio.

The inspiration of *Three-legged Buddha* comes from Tibet. I collected a lot of fragments of Buddhist sculptures in Tibet. When I saw these fragments in Lhasa, a mysterious power impressed me. They are embedded with historical traces and religion, just like the limbs of a human being.

It was related to one's life experience: traffic accident may lead to disability, violence may break your head, many lives may be lost in war, families broken by calamity. These fragments make me think about what being human means.

Sculptures such as *Three Legged Buddha* are so pure that they can be understood by different cultures. I focus on the problems that human beings are facing and express them in my own way.

Q2

You have incorporated the ash gathered from the burning of incense at Buddhist temples in Shanghai into many paintings and sculptures, including monumental Buddha sculptures. Why is this material important to you?

ZH

Zhang Huan, *Ru Lai* (2009), ash, steel and wood. 549 x 459 x 340 cm. Courtesy Zhang Huan Studio.

I often go to the temples. In the early years I prayed for myself, then for my family and colleagues working in my studio. Of those devout men and women who go to the temple, some are praying to have a child, some are wishing

Zhang Huan

for the well-being of their family members, some are wishing to recover from illness, some are wishing for luck and success in the new year, some are hoping to get through some difficulty, free themselves from poverty, have success in their work and endeavours. Inside the temple it is a completely different world of hopes. But hospitals are also a world where desperate struggles are made, where we face pain and death. I felt deeply moved when seeing incense ash burned by the prayers. The idea of making artworks with ash came into being.

The artworks are like mirrors. The audiences observe themselves when they watch the artworks. To me, ash is not a material, it conveys the collective soul, collective memory and collective blessings of the Chinese people. Incense ash can bring life back to people but can also terminate lives. The power of incense ash makes me sleepless and sentimental. Everyday I work with numerous souls within incense ash.

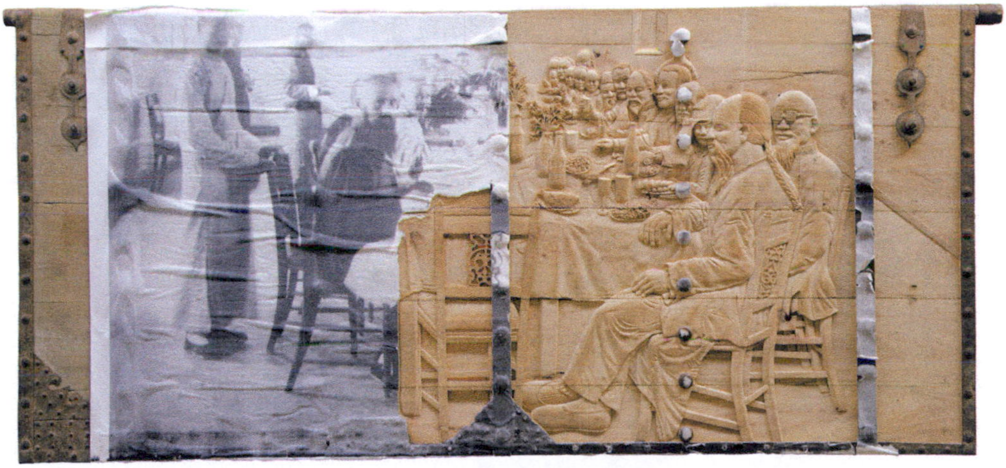

Zhang Huan, *Negotiation* (2008), silkscreen mounted on carved antique wood door 160 x 350 x 20 cm. Courtesy Zhang Huan Studio.

Q3

The Memory Door series combines images of photographs from the 1920s to the 1970s that mark historical events with wooden doors taken from traditional Chinese houses then being demolished in the Shanxi Province. What are the evocations, memories or associations that these reclaimed doors carry for you?

ZH

What I use are mostly abandoned things, such as door panels and incense ash. Farmers sell the old wooden doors and replace them with metal ones. These are unpretentious, close to origin materials.

It is sort of like the peeling back of skin. I call it "memory door". I choose images from old magazines and use silk screen print method to enlarge them. My very first impression seeing the enlarged screen print version compared to the original

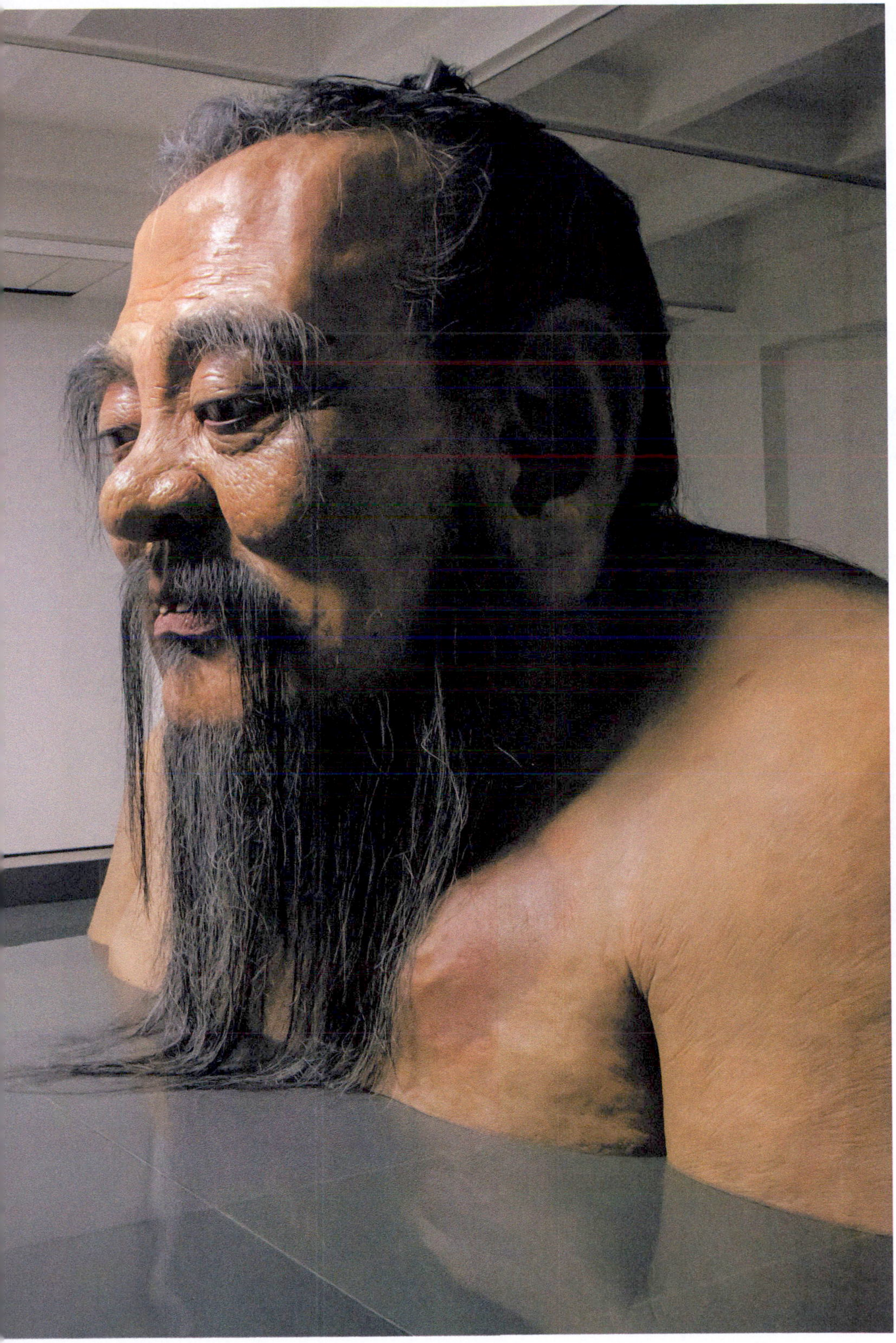

Zhang Huan and *Q-Confucius No.2* Installation. (2011), silicone, steel, carbon, fibre, acrylic 380 × 980 × 660 cm. Courtesy Zhang Huan Studio.

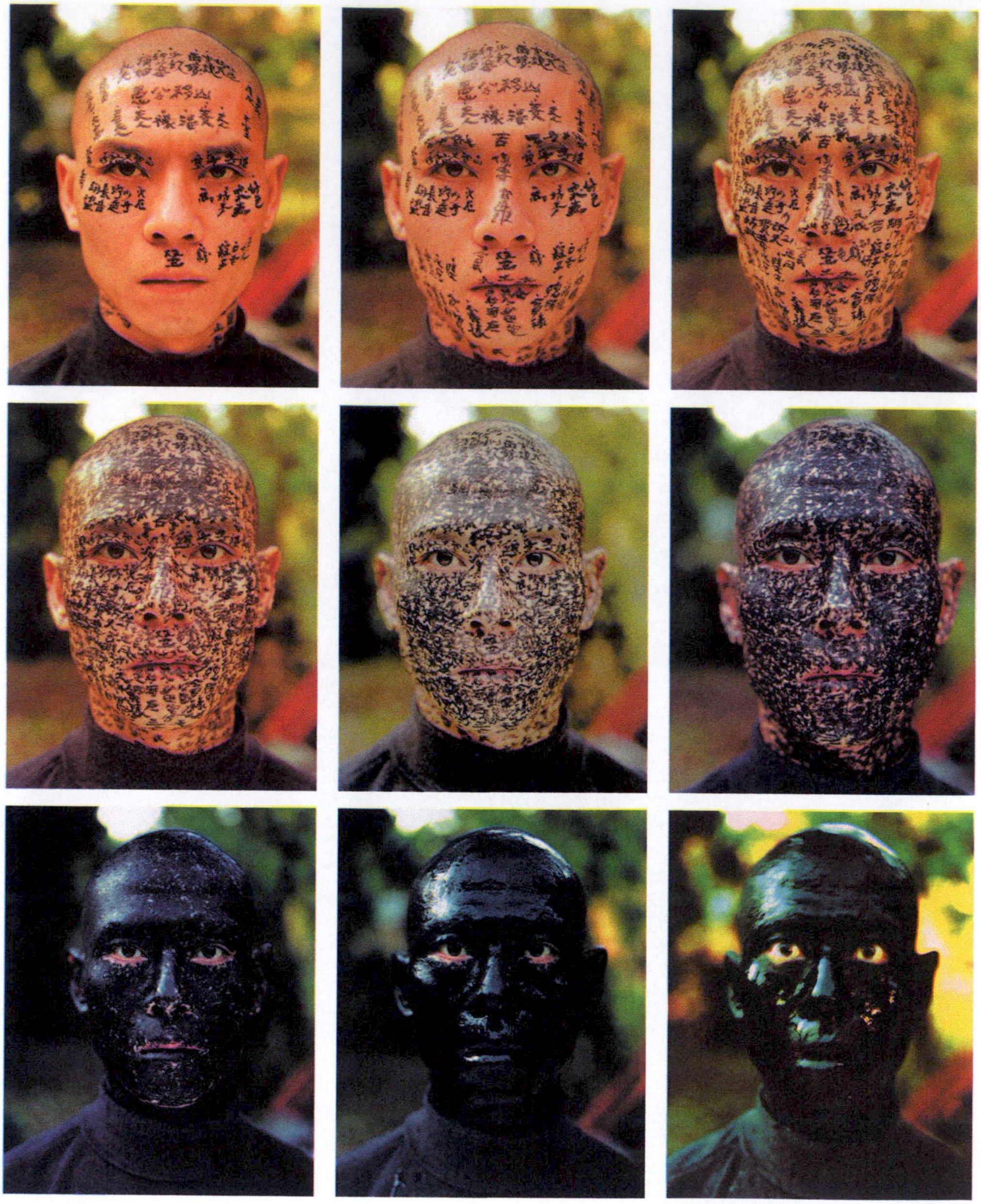

Zhang Huan, *Family Tree* (2000), New York, USA. Courtesy Zhang Huan Studio.

photo, it was altered only once. I then dedicate which parts to carve. It is actually really hard to decide which parts not to carve because it is so difficult to imagine what it will look like finished. So I actually really look forward to the end results.

Q4 The *Q-Confucius* series from 2011 introduced many, sometimes monumental, images of Confucius into your work. Why did you turn toward explicit references to Confucius at this time?

ZH

Zhang Huan, *Q-Confucius No.2 Installation*. (2011), silicone, steel, carbon, fibre, acrylic 380 × 980 × 660 cm. Courtesy Zhang Huan Studio.

The theme of the exhibition is "Q Confucius", and it discusses the religious loss of the present Chinese people who lose effective religion to support the reality in rapid social reforms. When human beings have to pay their debts to the earth, and when we have to pay the huge price for the destruction of the environment, when the end of day is coming, shall we copy everything from the West or return to our traditions? Or will there be a new spiritual religion that we can rely on? The project "Q Confucius" highlights its great significance in both the reality and also in the future.

I considered Master Confucius one of the common people. There is a soul hidden behind the images I made. I touched and communicated with the soul through the works.

One of the characteristics of contemporary art, in my understanding, is that if it doesn't present problems, it will lose its meaning and will run into problems itself. It presents its opinion, which can be destructive or narrative. Whatever it is, it needs to have its own position.

When preparing the exhibition, I studied the philosophy of Confucius again, among which I appreciated his saying that "At the age of 70, I have been able to do what I intend freely without breaking the rules." Except for the surface meaning of without transgressing the law. Which is you cannot transcend the law, nor the ethical principles or the common conventions of human beings. I always say that in the art world, you must transgress the law. For art, compromising means death, and rebelling means surviving.

I hope both my works and the audiences can raise some questions to ask themselves and make us think deeply.

Q5 Do you consider your current work to be in continuation of your earlier performance art?

ZH Naturally people will adopt corresponding ways to express their different ideas due to changing ages and living conditions. I do not like to repeat what I have done. My artworks can be considered as a whole piece, through which are my outlooks on life and the world. Now I use various media and skills in my works, so the patterns of manifestation seem different from the previous pieces. However, the kernel remains the same, because the DNA in me will not be changed.

Q6 Your work not only transforms objects and materials, but also traditional genres of work. Are there sources of inspiration that have been particularly important to you in challenging conventional forms of art?

ZH My inspiration is from the most trivial things in daily life such as eating, sleeping, working, and those which are always ignored in our ordinary life. I always discover and experience the nature of human from such things. Influenced by Tibetan Buddhism, in my works there are elements of life and death, reincarnation, meditation and so on. The development of my works is the outcome of my spiritual world. In my early works there were silence and meditation, which was more directly expressed in the form of Buddhist images after I became a Buddhist, and there were more meaning and thoughts in the works too.

I want to show in the form of contemporary art the quintessence of the Chinese culture and the world cultural heritage and all our good things. My artworks are the reflection of the current life and spiritual situation of the world.

Email interview by Nick Kaye, February 2017

The ghost time of transformation

Adrian Heathfield

> You do not run purposively through the world because you believe in it. The world, surprisingly, already runs through you. And that, really felt, *is* your belief in it. [...] We find ourselves 'invested' in the world's running through our lives because at every conscious moment our participation in it has just come to us newly enacted, already and again, defying disbelief with the unrefusable feeling of a life's momentum.
>
> Massumi 2011: 36–7

I will start in the middle of telling this story rather than at its beginning. In the thick of it, as they say. For we are always in the middle of things: in every performance; in every thought of performance; in every forging and meeting of words and things. I am watching a performance. I am in an experience, and an experience is being in the midst of things. The outside of this experience constitutes it. But for me there is only this inside experience, and other experiences, before and to come. I am not just being in it. For an experience is change, is changing, is a sensate flow of differentiations in which *I* and *it* are not that: not unitary, not resolved. I am distinct *and* inseparable from it, as I am in it. We are each and together becoming something else. I am being becoming. I cannot stand outside of it, this experience: there is no purely objective place from which I could write about it. I do try to know the experience, however, all the time. But I am not the knower of the performance as the known. The performance *is* knowing unknowing. And I am with and of this knowing unknowing even as we part from each other, in thinking and in being. We are this ongoing in and out of each other. Moreover, it will have been unknown to itself and to me. But a performance and I—in common—differently need to know how to know, differently. The event is a carrying together of our divergent needs and ways. I will try to write of it again, but where to start? I cannot tell where or when this story began/begins because it was/is an experience. Where am I now then? In a nowhen, where I am now experiencing writing this experience, which really happened and is happening in a space that is continually morphing and a time that is riven with other times. Being certain of beginnings in this context would be the last place to start.

These thoughts emerge from an experience situated within the exhibition 'Moments. A History of Performance in 10 Acts' at ZKM Karlsruhe (Germany, 8 March–29 April 2012) that brought together traces of significant performance works of the 1960s and 1970s from ten female artists. At a cursory glance this exhibition might have been mistaken for yet another retrospective of performance works from a now valorised period, following familiar coordinates of curatorial practice: the disclosure of buried dynamics of a formative epoch through the combination of recognised and less discussed works and artists, amounting to a form of historical re-narration. The exhibition carried some of the political rationale of this gesture: the work of well-known figures such as Marina Abramović, Adrian Piper and Yvonne Rainer was set against works of a cadre of less cited artists who were more geographically, culturally and aesthetically diverse. However, 'Moments'' conception and realisation shifted the act of exhibition into other radical trajectories of historiography, museological display, performance curation and public engagement. Borrowing a military and colonial term in naming these figures 'pioneers', the exhibition seemed nominally to have been following a revisionist logic that sought to shake off a particular history of dominant male figures of the performance avant-garde, re-gendering the movement's heroics. But what 'Moments' *did* with these artists and these works, sourcing and channelling dynamics of their force and ethos, went beyond historical revision and amounted to a systematic re-conception of the historicising gesture of the museological display of performance, its forms and potentials.

The temporal concept of the exhibition was its primary curatorial gesture: rather than being assembled privately and displayed publicly as a spatially static and consolidated entity, the exhibition was assembled, reconfigured and disassembled in public over a period of 52 days. This processual approach marked all of the works, and the frameworks of their display and interpretation, as subject to ongoing transformation. The 'moments' of this exhibition's title were an array of historically and culturally discrete performances, but rather than being held in a static constellation of a single exhibited duration, they were 'returned' through morphological display to conditions of relation, flow and multiplicity from which they had been extracted. Many of the contributing 'pioneer' artists were present at occasions of creative response throughout the exhibition and this relation further complicated and enriched its heteronomous nature. The open approach to the construction of the exhibit, as well as articulating curation and display as collaborative actions, generated a specific condition in the exhibited space: it became a kind of workshop, in which the unfinished nature of the displays reverberated with the particular contents and feel of the works. Some display walls remained unclad, exposing their fabrication; many pieces were laid on raised platforms rather than being hung; explanatory texts sat in piles in loose association with the works they addressed. Display was evidently in transition and awaiting further action. Aesthetic and ontological confusion ensued, since it was difficult to tell whether that handsaw left on a display platform was part of a work or not, whether that room with work desks, handwritten wall charts, and personal belongings was part of the exhibit or not, whether that artwork was finished and presented as it 'should have been'. There was a pervasive corruption of the unitary nature, completion, and sanctity of the artwork. Entering the space it was immediately and abundantly clear that one's time in the exhibit was a partial and limited slice of a volume of shifting time—the life of the exhibition—that far exceeded the spectators' or participants' capacity to witness it.

All of this was further complicated by an insistence on exhibition as an instantiation of durational collaborative relations with contemporary performance makers and specialist witnesses whose responses were serially integrated into the ongoing exhibit. The exhibition established periods of spatial transformation and creative response that radically reconfigured the nature of the showing: a group of performance makers led by co-curator Boris Charmatz researched, negotiated, and transformed aspects of the display (shifting materials into different spatial relations) and generated creative responses and performances that sat aside the exhibited works. A filmmaker—Ruti Sela—recorded and edited the many activations of the space within the space, eventually inserting her finished film into the exhibit. A group of commissioned 'witnesses'—early-career performance makers and thinkers—were present throughout all of these processes, absorbing its events and audience encounters, interpreting the exhibit's transformations and once more re-making it through material interventions in its final stages. These labours were open to the spectators encountering the exhibit so that the spectator did not simply view evidential registers of past performances, but witnessed their co-existence with instances of creative appropriation and live interpretation. This combination disallowed the institutionalisation of a representational documentary register, so that the representational was repeatedly folded into the presentational, the material objects repeatedly re-animated by their relations to embodied and spoken acts. In this regard the exhibition proposed performance as a primary medium of inter- and intra-generational response, but also as a self-replicating and self-differentiating force, situated within a fractured creative continuum that evolved organically in fits and starts, but could not be reduced to, characterised by, or defined by its instances or moments.

I write 'in the midst of things' too, because I was literally situated in the middle of the exhibition space, sitting on the floor and listening through headphones to a video recording of an interview with the artist, choreographer, and dancer Simone Forti. In the television image Forti is sitting beside her exhibited work, *Face Tunes* (1967), just as I was three weeks later, and she is discussing the influences and confluences that led to her to make this work 45 years earlier. *Face Tunes*, Forti explains, was made in a break, in the wake of a separation from her second husband Robert Whitman. The character of this passage of time is left unsaid, but instead Forti talks about the notion of imprinting: the biological and psychological mechanism of recognition and attraction through which the characteristics, behaviour, or movement of a primary figure are assumed by a dependent as a means of survival. The lover's face, Forti says, is also a kind of imprint; that face, she says, is '*the* face' and you carry it with you, amidst all the other faces that you encounter in life. Forti's invocation of the consequences of being touched by another, living with the impress of their face, was *moving* not just because of the figures involved and their historical distance. During the conversation Forti has occasionally broken off from words and from her seat, and started to move, always with the sense in which that movement is really just a continuation of thought, just another proposition or mode of discourse, with equal force, eloquence and consequence. For Forti it seems invention and articulation always *move* transversally, they cross means, materials, disciplines and bounds.

In her *Handbook in Motion* published in 1974 a slightly different account of the genesis of *Face Tunes* emerges:

> For two weeks I kept track of my perpendicular journey up and down buildings and subways. [...] At the end of the two weeks I drew up a musical staff and placed the different stations up and down the scale. [...] One day I handed the elevation tune to La Monte to hear what it sounded like. He whistled it to me, and in a palpable sense it had very much the feeling of those two weeks. It seemed to me that it was their ghost.
>
> Forti 1998: 71

Forti's *Handbook in Motion* presents several documents of this piece, and here she discusses performing early versions of the work in which she did not tell the audience that the tune they were listening to was derived from faces. Instead, she says, she wanted people to listen to the music. Linking the work to an intuition of an absent origin, and to a belief that arises from the tangibility of the invisible, she asserts:

> I had faith that, since the awareness of variations among similar events is so basic a life process, when they heard *Face Tunes* they would unconsciously sense a familiar kind of order. As form seemed to be the storage place for presence, I hoped that the act of translating a coherent aspect of a set of faces to a corresponding form might awaken a more primitive level of pattern or ghost recognition.
>
> Forti 1998: 76

It would seem important to note here Forti's language which links together matters of the spirit (faith and hope) with underlying physical or material conditions: a 'primitive level of pattern' may relate to the psychological imprinting of which Forti spoke in her talk some 38 years later, or perhaps orders of nature governing human animal behaviour. In either instance it would seem that what is at stake in Forti's *Face Tunes* is performance as a method of migration of forces across forms, planes, registers where the translation of one form to another manifests a disturbance of orders of sense, bringing to the fore a suppressed sensory dynamic. The feeling of this sense is a cause of faith and hope.

The curatorial sensibilities enacted in 'Moments' reflect and correspond with a growing shift in the practice of curation more broadly—beyond the many marked instances of museological performance curation in the last decade or so—where one might argue that, following Maria Lind's phraseology, the curatorial is being performed (Lind 2012). These key works of museal performance curation would include: Live Culture, Tate Modern, London, 2003; Marina Abramović, *Marina Abramović Presents*, Whitworth Gallery (Manchester International Festival), 2009; Tino Sehgal, *This Progress* (2006), Guggenheim Museum, New York, 2010; Marina Abramović, *The Artist is Present*, Museum of Modern Art, New York, 2010; Xavier Le Roy, *Retrospective*, Fundació Antoni Tàpies, Barcelona, 2012; Alexandra Pirici and Manuel Pelmuş, *An Immaterial Retrospective of the Venice Biennale*, Romanian Pavilion, Venice Biennale, 2013. Older notions of curation as a technocratic, neutral, non-creative activity have been supplanted in favour of curation as a self-questioning practice of mediation, translation and cultural production. Curatorial discourse accompanying this shift has moved away from its stress on the object, on arrangement, design, and display as orders of the visual, towards questions of the ethics and politics of relations between people and things, resistance to forms of institutional and discursive power, and the shaping and force of affective encounters in the experience of art. In the curation of 'Moments' these interests manifested in a radical commitment to experimental conditions for art objects and art history. As exhibition designer Johannes Porsch put it in the flyer accompanying the exhibition, this approach: 'opens up the possibility of testing: proto-typical display situations capable of transforming and promoting transformation (itself)—set-ups—emerge, which possess the ability to present the processual, the forever provisional, the moment of reconstruction in history.'

One might add that reconstruction here was seen as necessarily impossible and the history that reconstruction generates as necessarily non-linear and multi-vocal. The generativity invoked was not simply history forming, but a means to forge new works of art in explicit, free and attentive historicised relations. 'Moments'' approach to a slow transformation of the displayed artworks promoted a dynamic understanding of the artwork that is often lost in more static, precious, preservationist modes of exhibition. Instead the artwork here was seen through a vitalist perspective as a processual and relational formation subject to continuous social metamorphoses. There is much more that could be said about these tactics and the understanding they enact of curation as creative practice in an expanded field. A key question, for instance, is the readability and accessibility of these approaches: what kinds of ethical and political potentials and limitations reside in the nature of their broader public engagement? But for the moment I want to turn to the ways in which this sensibility of curation is not only contemporary, but itself re-activates a historical vitalist understanding of art making and reception.

In the mid-1930s the French art historian Henri Focillon wrote an influential but now somewhat overlooked treatise on *The Life of Forms in Art* (Focillon 1989). While this work is indeed absolute in its formalism, in its refusal of the significance of social and cultural contexts as determinants in art's meaning and force, there are many aspects of Focillon's thought that correspond with current sensibilities in the making and curation of art. Chief among these is his insistence that although artworks may appear static and resolved, they are in fact manifestations of movement. For Focillon an artwork is at once contemporary and untimely, and as such it exists in and manifests time's multiplicity, it is part of a ceaseless process of becoming (Focillon 1989: 152). As Jean Molino asserts, in Focillon's oeuvre 'forms are caught in perpetual metamorphosis [...] there is no form without change of form.' Focillon's writing also provides notions of influence and affinity that are not necessarily historically successive or linear between art movements and between artists; rather he anatomises the nature of their responsive generativity across forms and disciplines. Art '[s]ubstances,' he argues, 'are not interchangeable, but techniques penetrate one another, and at the moment of their doing so, interference tends to create new substances.' (Focillon 1989: 108)

Focillon's attentive readings of artworks as dynamic, complex, volatile sets of relations and interactions between a subject, action, matter and form, resonate with current new materialist sensibilities that think of matter (and objects) as active and affective, deconstruct the relation between form and formlessness, and are concerned with exposing the limitations of any philosophy that simply locates life as coterminous with the human. The interest here, whether in Focillon's critical writing or in current art curation, is in a phenomenological attention to the artwork as a field of affective relations and movements, which respects its life, its singularity: all the forces that are irreducible to the contexts of its happening. As Andrei Molotiu has noted, Focillon's conception of the life of forms was doubtless influenced by Henri Bergson, whose lectures he attended; and his notion of the artwork's singularity closely echoes Bergson's defence of the force of creativity from any retrospective contextual determination (Molotiu in Celeste 2000). The creative act, for Bergson, is one in which 'the concrete solution brings with it that unforeseeable nothing which is everything in a work of art. And it is this nothing that takes time. Nought as matter, it creates itself as form.' (Bergson 1928: 360) For Focillon, writing particularly on painting and drawing, it seems that this singularity is related to art's status as a sensate trace:

> form is not only incarnated, [...] it is invariably incarnation itself. It is not easy for us to admit this readily. Our minds are so filled with the recollection of forms that we tend to confuse them with the recollection itself [...] where they are as complete and as definite as on a public square or in a museum gallery.
>
> Focillon 1989: 101

The nature of this incarnation of art for Focillon is a moving tracery of gestures: in the multiple interactions between hand, tool, matter and form, there is a touching that may conceal itself, but will always nonetheless be felt. Touch here is crossing materialities and orders of the senses, from the tactile, through the visual, to the sensorium of the spectator: it is the nexus of art's vitality (Focillon 1989: 110).

It is the second day that I have spent in this exhibition and there is now some activity from performers in the space, some kind of set up is taking place. An event is emerging informally from the flow, spectators gather haphazardly around an action while others continue looking at the exhibits. Dancer and choreographer Meg Stuart is standing semi-naked in the exhibition space, close to Simone Forti's *Face Tunes*, and she seems to be opening her senses to the environment and the works within it. Burkhard Stangle, the musician and composer, is arranging some instruments and technology, and a flat tone, like a guitar note or just the buzz of electronics, is quietly reverberating in the space. Stuart looks like she is in a private reverie, but she has this thereness, this openness about her that makes her thinking-feeling present to us. She is dancing, but Claudia Hill, another performer, is cladding and costuming her in second-hand duvets, repeatedly interrupting her flow. Now there is music arriving hesitantly: iterated test melodies on the guitar, ascending and descending scales. And while the whole thing is layering and accumulating it feels like it has really not yet begun, it is in the condition of the warm-up, try out, or walk-through: a dance continually interrupted by its own preparation. Stuart is handed Forti's slide-whistle from the exhibit and now she is accompanying Stangle, while remaining somehow

Wamhof Franz-Josef, Photographs of the exhibition MOMENTS—EINE GESCHICHTE DER PERFORMANCE IN 10 AKTEN (2012). Meg Stuart, *Forti playing Face Tunes*, performance at ZKM, Karlsruhe. © DACS 2017.

in her separate world. She has taped up breasts and eyebrows, and mirrored sleeves. The duvets appear to have heavy weights sewn into their lining, and Stuart is now another body, inflated, cushioned, restricted, and weighted, but still trying out her moves. She is a softer, voluminous body, an older body perhaps. The thing that keeps her warm, clothed, protected, is also an impediment. She is dancing through the impediment into another way of being, of moving. She is a makeshift bedroom shaman: one third Meg Stuart, one third Michael Jackson, one third Simone Forti. Every gesture marks itself as preparatory: the rehearsal of another immanent dance. She hits her head repeatedly against the video monitor that plays Forti's interview, as if trying to climb inside the screen, and now she is channelling Forti literally through the monitor headphones: spin shaking herself into new life, an emanation, a glittering joy.

I am trying to think 'Moments'' reformation of the infrastructure of the museum, of its traditions of museological display, as one instance of an ungrounding of grounds, of the generation of a temporary space of inhabitation where embodied criticalities can emerge to interrogate the relation between what is given and what can be made afresh. There are of course many related vital spaces within and without institutions, zones of living encounter, where the question of what contains and poisons; what sustains and revives generative thought and action is tested out through ongoing relational experiences. This particular re-formation was one that designated and re-assembled the museum as an archival workshop or workshop archive. What a workshop might have meant in this context was perhaps closer to its ritualistic origins in early Medieval craftsmanship than the current dominant model of the workshop in creative economies, as an instrumental scene of skill acquisition and a networking opportunity. Richard Sennett has argued that the Medieval workshop was a surrogate familial structure housing sustained social experiences of making where questions of autonomy and authority in artful labour were dealt with face-to-face (Sennett 2009: 53–80) Perhaps Sennett somewhat romanticises what was most likely already a paternalist and hierarchised pre-industrial social structure, but nonetheless the workshop was a place in which a certain form of historical and ethical stewardship was conducted in relation to craft. One might think of 'Moments" convening of a community of affinity, action and thought around performance as a queer family workshop. Its figuring of performance pioneers in relation to a younger generation of artists posed the question of historical continuance within a context of sustained attention, sometimes to the 'pioneers' personally, sometimes to the products of their labour. It did so with a set of concerns that were insistently pre-modern: the process was slow, accumulative, collaboratively wrought, the products—if products they were—could not be judged primarily by their 'originality', but by their interrelations, by the qualities of their translation into other hands.

This workshop was archival in the sense that it took place within a container of historical knowledge, but one in which there was an interrogative relation to the 'house arrest' of the archive, the consignment that would have fixed and diminished performance's vitalities and potentials, its cultural, political and epistemological forces. As workshop archive 'Moments' staged 'technique(s) of repetition' that were willfully multiple, flighty and provisional, turning this archive self-consciously towards its outsides (Derrida 1996: 12). Here was a living archival instantiation where containment was questioned by its own evident durational fragmentation, by its presentation of the paradoxes of the record, by its subjection of its artifacts and artworks to contingency. The archival then, practised as a rigorous mode of re-invention, somewhat echoing Michel Foucault's thought: '[B]etween tradition and oblivion [the archive] reveals the rules of a practice that enables statements both to survive and to undergo regular modification. *It is the general system of the formation and transformation of statements.*' (Foucault 1972: 130) The paradox of the 'holding place' that was the 'Moments' exhibition, like the paradox of performance itself, is that it was both old and new, double and singular, a formation and a transformation, a conformation and a departure, an echoing and a propagation.

I am looking at Simone Forti's *Face Tunes* in the 'Moments' exhibition, and it is 45 years since she made it, and 38 years since she documented it in a book, and one year since she re-performed it to make the film that I am now watching, and three weeks since she sat in front of it in this very exhibition and discussed it with a public, and one day since I watched a film of this discussion, and two hours since I watched Meg Stuart try to press her flesh through all these screens, through all these years, to find the filament, to be in touch with 'the spirit of the thing', to take it elsewhere. These times are present here, just as time itself is immeasurable, in this enfolded and unfolding now. And I can't help thinking that the people whose photographs make the profiles, whose profiles make the score, the score that Forti touches and re-touches, that makes the music of *Face Tunes*, that moves me to make this writing, are somehow here-not-here in this very moment, in this tenderness: ethereal migrants carried across the waves of sound. Semblances of lives: uncanny feelings of their continuance after death. Because she wants him to remain, Pliny the Elder says, Butades' daughter draws around her lover's shadow on the wall of the cave to make a profile; the 'origin' of portraiture and of painting, we are told. A faint ephemeral line, appropriated and substantiated in clay by her father the *craftsman*. I am following the flatline on the scroll that gives Forti her zero tone, and I notice the iterated confluence of lines at the nasal bridge, that sensate zone that when touched induces letting go. For these are not re-iterated profiles of her lost lover Robert Whitman, whose face we have heard is imprinted on her eyes, but traces of a diverse community of friends and fellow artists. The parade of faces, semi-submerged: so many floating, bobbing Ophelias. Black line—white scroll. Some of the photographs from which the line of the profiles is drawn are of black faces, and I am thinking of the black face, of its near-invisibility in the history of Western contemporary art; of the black faces of the civil rights movement of 1967 when these lines were drawn, just before the assassination of Martin Luther King, Jr; of racial lines re-drawn in the present, of racial *profiling*: of the lures and traps of becoming visible, as a means of gaining some ground. Spinning out a line. And I realise that these horizontal faces are not portraits but landscapes, sketches at the horizon, the shape of the ground, the ground where bodies remain. Murmurs of the world: sounded but unworded. Spinning out a line: I am thinking about what it means to face things, not just the faces of other humans, but to face the natural non-human world, to face the matter that makes us, the matter we will once again become, our form transforming, dispersing. A shadow ethics, within and without all the mutual openings we make in the face of others, as a life courses through us with its undulating highs and lows, and we make of it a line, a lifeline. We are moved and removed by this movement of a life, whose semblance is the life of forms. To touch and to be touched by it: the sustaining force of art.

One of the difficulties of contemporary art curation *and* history in the wake of today's profound distrust of historical narrations is to find a meaningful response and mode of practice in which a kind of faith in the forces of historical works can be propagated. In the wake of so many authorial deaths there is a demand for an account of the forms and conditions required of historiography and its many cultural instantiations to sustain belief in the potentials of art. We are, it would seem, still trapped and lingering in postmodernity's much discussed condition of 'incredulity toward metanarratives' (Lyotard 1984). The pervading disbelief in the underlying organising logics of history leads an art theorist such as Jan Verwoert to declare:

> On a phenomenological level the experience of history in crisis is also the experience of a crisis of time [...] [I]n the time of crisis two different and essentially contradictory dimensions of temporality coincide: the time of empty duration and the time of absolute urgency.
>
> Verwoert 2005: 37–4

In Verwoert's analysis contemporary Western societies are still gripped by violent historical upheaval, but their cultures now lack the capacity and faith to tell of these changes; and so for those cultures' citizens the experience of time is marked by both an ongoing aimlessness and a quality of perpetual emergency, both of which are profoundly disempowering. Art may be one means through which this impasse can be surpassed, if it is able justly to imagine other 'potential historical realities' and thereby 'open up a different future' (Verwoert 2005: 38). Part of this reinvention of historical sense, I would assert, is the work of contemporary performance practices such as those initiated by the 'Moments' exhibition. Performance's capacity to activate and open the past within the present, its versatility in addressing and transforming the experience of time *as it is sensed and made into sense*, is its vital cultural and historical value. In the thinking-feeling of opened performance histories an impetus may be found: to continue the affective force of the techniques of survival and experiments in existence that make a creative life liveable.

References

1928 Bergson, H. *Creative Evolution*, London: MacMillan and Co.
1996 Derrida, J. *Archive Fever: A Freudian Impression*, Chicago: University of Chicago Press.
1989 [1934] Focillon, H. *The Life of Forms in Art*, New York: Zone Books.
1998 [1974] Forti, S. *Handbook in Motion: An Account of an Ongoing Personal Discourse and its Manifestations in Dance*, Northampton, MA: Contact Editions.
1972 Foucault, M. *The Archaeology of Knowledge*, trans. A.M. Sheridan Smith, London: Tavistock Publications.
2012 Lind, M. (ed.) *Performing the Curatorial: Within and Beyond Art*, Gothenberg: Sternberg Press.
1984 [1979] Lyotard, J.-F. *The Postmodern Condition: A Report on Knowledge*, Manchester: Manchester University Press.
2011 Massumi, B. *Semblance and Event*, Cambridge, MA: The MIT Press.
2000 Molotiu, A. 'Focillon's Bergsonian Rhetoric and the Possibility of Deconstruction'. *Invisible Culture: An Electronic Journal for Visual Studies*, 3, Winter, Visual and Cultural Studies Program, University of Rochester.
2009 Sennett, R. *The Craftsman*, London: Penguin.
2005 Verwoert, J. 'The Crisis of Time in Times of Crisis.' In A. Bangma, S. Rushton and F. Wüst (eds) *Experience, Memory, Re-enactment*, Rotterdam: Piet Zwart Institute and Revolver.

RETURN

2a Jog Shuttler
Blast Theory/John Hunter

2b Our 18 Beginnings
Lin Hixson and Matthew Goulish

2c Performing art history: non-linear, synchronous and syncopated times in Performance Re-enactment Society's Group Show (Arnolfini, Bristol 2012)
Paul Clarke/Performance Re-enactment Society

2d Re-enacting the archive: untimely meditations on the use and abuse of repetition
Pil and Galia Kollectiv

Archive, repertoire and embodied histories in Nao Bustamente's performative practice
Amelia Jones

The patina of performance: documentary practice and the search for origins in The Wooster Group's Fish Story
Andrew Quick

RETURN implies a more complex relation to the archive than REMAKE, because, in returning, there is both an acknowledgement of time having past, of the initial circumstances of the work's production and the production of its documentary remains having happened in a different time that is not now—with all the certainty and uncertainty that that entails; and an acknowledgement that the future of the artist who returns is somehow predicated on that past to which they now turn. All the artists in these pages explicitly open up this space-time between their archival sources and their new works through a range of strategies, from the use of retro-technology, creative constraints, institutional structures, and political philosophy, to explore the productivity of this impossible re-turn to both the past and the future: at the same time lost times and the host of potential futures.

The slippery and sometimes contested agency between artist and audience, and in the context of this volume—between artist and historian, the question—who finally makes the work?—is explored in Blast Theory's *Jog Shuttler*, an interactive installation at Arnolfini Gallery, Bristol UK, 2012. Using the defunct technology of VHS tapes, Blast Theory's Matt Adams and associate John Hunter returned to the Brighton-based artists' own extensive video archive to retro-transfer a range of formats on to VHS. Their sampling of over 20 years' work, renowned for its use of new technologies to produce ground-breaking interactive art, was playfully put in the hands of each visitor to the installation, who could select up to nine tapes to play on a bank of nine monitors, as well as mix the soundtrack from the nine sources. In this way, *Jog Shuttler* reminded us that the artwork is as much, if not more, a collective construction of its audiences, as it is the artist's; and what was once of value to the artist can be endlessly re-played and re-appropriated by those that follow. Furthermore, the retro technology points to the future obsolescence of all returns to the archive, that the very platforms, and in the case of the fragile VHS tapes themselves—the very substance, of the archive itself will (in Shakespeare's words) fade 'and leave not a rack behind' (*The Tempest*, 4.1.156).

The unfathomable abundance of the archive can daunt any artist's re-use of performances past. However, Lin Hixson and Matthew Goulish's aesthetic method of using constraints to focus creativity and produce novel constellations of material in their performance work with Chicago-based company Every house has a door was applied to *Our 18 Beginnings*, a project that began with visits to archives in two different cities, Bristol (UK) and Chicago (US) -The University of Bristol Theatre Collection and Arnolfini Archive, and the Randolph Street Gallery archives. By sourcing only the beginnings from nine works in each location, Every house has a door formulated a performative structure, described by Hixson as 'replay object image', within which the elements were allowed to (re-)appear in relation to each other as unique quasi-objects, somehow standing alone, absurd, splendid, of another time, happening now. This framing of the material was developed in Arnolfini (Bristol), then taken to the Randolph Street Gallery (Chicago), explicitly as a transferable methodology—an aesthetic investigation of the archive, as rigorous as the historian's, but very different in output. Counter-intuitively this focus on the beginnings of performances opens up in the two different versions of *9 Beginnings* a space which provokes a re-turn to what's to come, as Hixson writes 'The lack of middle and end allows the future to leak out.'

Performance Re-enactment Society's *Group Show* employs a range of interventions into the very structures of the arts institution itself, its architecture, its personnel hierarchies, structures which the institution often seeks to render invisible in favour of foregrounding the art it exhibits. In 2012, the Bristol-based artists collective, including Tom Marshman and Clare Thornton, occupied the galleries and backstage spaces of Arnolfini whilst it was 'in between' exhibitions, staging a series of performative interventions into these 'blank canvases' and 'dark stages'. Marshman invited visitors backstage into a dressing room to experience a montage of verbatim accounts of those who had performed at Arnolfini; and Thornton worked with dance artist Laura Dannequin to re-imagine sculptural works exhibited in the galleries. Clarke organised Arnolfini's team of invigilators to undertake tours in the empty galleries: aping audio-guides, they offered their own interpretations of works which had hung on those walls. In these various ways, Performance Re-enactment Society reminded us that any return to the archive should not ignore the architectural and institutional structures of the organisations that present art; and that those structures are themselves a crucial dimension in that art's production and its subsequent archiving: alongside the artists who make the work, the building and those who work in it are themselves a palimpsestuous living archive. Clarke's chapter 'Performing art history', reflecting on this three-part work, itself weaves in and out of PRS's artists' pages, each mode intervening in the other's realising of the 'now past' *Group Show.*

Pil and Galia Kollectiv's *Re-enacting the Archive: Untimely Meditations on the Use and Abuse of Repetition* is a piece of writing by the London-based artists that builds on Nietzsche's own meditations on how history continually irrupts into the present, haunting, sometimes violently, our lives. By comparing Nietzsche's lionisation of the historical figure of Frederich the Second, and the bizarre myths surrounding his death and 'reappearance', with the fictional heroine of the *Alien* films—Ellen Ripley, their text discloses the deadly drives of repetition structuring the culture industry's use of franchise films, to suggest that the critique of political philosophers, such as Adorno, Horkheimer and Debord, needs to be extended to imagine that 'repetition itself can become a critical tool against the totality of the spectacle'. And in this way, Pil and Galia Kollectiv's writing itself enacts a repetitive strategy similar to their installations and performance work, in which material from the historical avant-garde, political philosophy and the 'performances' of everyday labour are returned to and re-turned, as in—deconstructed to reveal the potential for resistance.

JOG SHUTTLER

1
Choose tapes from the pile.

2
Play the tapes on the VCRs using the Play (▷) button. Play up to nine at once.

3
There is a sound desk to the right of the VCRs. Use the sliders on the desk to control the volume of the TVs. Slider 1 controls the volume of TV 1, etc.

4
When you have finished watching a tape, rewind (◁◁) it and then eject (⏏) it.

NOTES

There is 15 minutes of video on each tape.

If you play a tape and the screen is blank, then it has reached the end and you need to rewind it back to the start.

Blast Theory, *Jog Shuttler*. Courtesy of the artist.

Blast Theory/John Hunter

> A bank of screens plays loops of unseen experiments, half-formed ideas and well-known work, in a large grid. What links the footage or the ideas behind it is not immediately clear, other than it has all been generated by the same artists' group over the last 21 years. Navigating through fragments of Blast Theory's archive, viewers impose their own edit by sifting, shuttling and looping, making sense of it for themselves.

Blast Theory's VHS archive contains over 200 tapes, featuring footage from 1994 to 2003. These tapes have been digitised and transferred to computer, and the resulting footage chopped up, edited and re-presented out of context in *Jog Shuttler*. The original tapes were for archival purposes—whatever could be recorded was recorded, because one day it might have been needed. In *Jog Shuttler*, users are invited to mix nine simultaneous loops visually and aurally to re-purpose these archives in a way never originally intended.

Referring back to the irreverent Hollywood-stunt-pop-compilation *Choreographic Cops in a Complicated World* (2000) and the intimately interactive *An Explicit Volume* (2001), the work gives one user at a time a remix kit for nine years of low-resolution experimentation, choreography, anxiety and loud music.

A note on process

Whilst I worked in Blast Theory's studio, it was my role to oversee the digitisation of these tapes. I saw tens of people spend hundreds of hours copying over footage, in what has become a comprehensive but extremely low-fidelity record of seemingly anything you could do in front of a camera. By the time I joined Blast Theory as artists' assistant in 2009, the company was already 18 years old. When the first of this footage was recorded, I was seven. *Jog Shuttler* is an 'outside eye' on a nine-year period that I and many others will only experience through crackly footage from a camera left in a corner of a room, dredged-up and redux-ed in a new context.

Reflection on the work

People wandered in and out of *Jog Shuttler*. They ignored the instructions a lot of the time, they chatted, they left without rewinding the tapes. They popped in for a look around and stayed for as long as it was interesting. That's what I'd do, too, I think. Before the show opened, painstakingly writing and re-writing those instructions, positioning and repositioning the bean bags and the labels, I imagined how people might interact with *Jog Shuttler*. Did I imagine that dream group, entering in silence, reading the instructions to the letter, sitting down for an hour, totally absorbed, working their way through every tape? Looking at the blurb I wrote before the show, it doesn't look like it. But for all of the intention around getting rid of reverence, of empowering the installation visitor to experience it and interpret it however they liked, there was still that slight pang of frustration when somebody sat on the instruction sheet, then fumbled about in confusion for the play button, later exiting with the tape still running. There's that tension between 'this is yours' and 'this is mine'—the tension of handing something over. If I was feeling it every time somebody ignored point 4 on the instructions, the people at Blast Theory must, as the public remixed these snapshots of them in their vulnerable, private and experimental moments, have been feeling it too. But it was handed over nonetheless, to see what might come out of it. And that's the point of letting someone else have a go, isn't it?

Blast Theory, *Jog Shuttler*. Courtesy of the artist.

Blast Theory, *Jog Shuttler*. Courtesy of the artist.

1
2
3
4
5

OUR 18 BEGINNINGS

Every house has a door. Photo by Katie Graves.

Lin Hixson and Matthew Goulish

Still young (Matthew)

I do not find it difficult to reconcile the young man in the sleeveless t-shirt on the video screen with the slightly stooped and graying man standing before me. With minimal effort, I can recognise the one in the other—eccentric confidence, grain of voice, speech pattern, hint of posture. It's March 1 2013, and we are in the Defibrillator Gallery, on Milwaukee Avenue, not unlike Randolph Street Gallery 24 years ago, long since closed, where the video documented the performance. Both situated on Milwaukee Avenue, one stop away from one another on the Blue Line train, once known as the O'Hare-Congress line. Do you remember those days? You probably don't—you're still young, and anyway one has trouble mixing these times with those, the relentless struggle with the beautiful fairy tale, or vice versa. Here is our dialogue, as I remember it.

MG: Chris, we want to restage the beginning of one of your performances for our *9 Beginnings: Chicago* project. It's a project that began in Bristol, England. We made a performance there last summer, drawn from four different UK video archives. We selected and re-staged the beginnings of nine different performances. We had two performers and two choreographed stagehands. We called it *9 Beginnings: Bristol*. We wove them together to make a new piece. Now the MacArthur Foundation funded us to continue the project, with *9 Beginnings: Chicago*, based on the Randolph Street Gallery archives. And if it's ok with you, we want to use a performance of yours for one of the beginnings.

CS: I would be very honored.

MG: It's from a performance called, I think, *Cavalcades in Learning*.

CS: I did do a piece called *Cavalcades in Learning*.

MG: The one with the creaky floorboards?

CS: Yes, that was it.

MG: Sometimes the videos are mislabeled. Anyway, we would restage the first two or three minutes.

CS: That one started with me lying in bed, listening to the radio, hoping for a snow day, waiting for the name of my school to be announced.

MG: Actually, no. That sequence came well into the performance.

CS: No, that's how it started. I always liked that beginning. No wait, you're right. It started with me coming out and singing that song I think.

MG: Um, no. It started with you talking to the audience.

CS: Really? I think I sang a song.

MG: I'm pretty sure. I just watched the video. You had a fake nose on, and made a speech over a light bulb. Mr. Sullivan cannot make it tonight, something like that.

CS: No, I don't think so.

MG: Mr. Sullivan has been in a terrible accident.

CS: Wait! That's right!

MG: An imposter has volunteered to go on in his place.

CS: That's right! That's right! Oh man!

Replay object distortion (Lin)

Matthew runs his finger along his transcription. With the volume turned up full, he tries again to grasp the phrase that the performer mumbles in his opening speech, that prompts a ripple of laughter in the audience. Matthew has the rest of the speech, but this phrase eludes him. It occurs to him that the laugh may have been his own, since the two of us attended that night, and maybe, with enough effort, he can recall the spoken words that the video does not capture; inaudible, unremembered. He closes his eyes. He reconstructs something of that room, its floor's texture, its ceiling's height, how it would contain the sound of a voice, how in quiet moments one could hear the train passing below; how young we were, and fearless, if not entirely innocent, with little concern of what the future would bring, of whom we would become. He imagines himself as he is now, standing in the room as it was then, only empty of people, chairs, lighting instruments, and he looks up, and turns in circles, and calls out to the emptiness:

> Do you remember? How have you been? Why did you never write to me?

He has kept this appointment in the archive, March 6 2013, to transcribe Chris Sullivan's opening speech. He asked me why we went to that performance in 1989. I remind him that when I was still in Los Angeles, about to move to Chicago, Mike Kelley told me about Chris, as somebody whose work he admired. I hesitate to mention Mike these days. Mike is gone, and his name casts a shadow on the present. Matthew takes the video back to start. He recalls January 1989 as a season of fewer distractions; concentration a state more readily achieved, time a quantity more spacious, and day and night volumes more forgiving. The speech overtakes him, and he tries to hear it as if for the first time, as if he is still young, with no memory of it. He knows that's how most of the audience will hear it, and how I will hear it as I direct it. I can shut off my memory more readily than he can. He claims that's what makes me a good director—the ability to see only what's in front of me, and nothing else. Not what it reminds me of, or what I want it to be. Freedom from the known, he says, to remind people what it means to pay attention. His words, not mine.

Pierre Huyghe writes:

> It is not the event anymore that is important. It is the replay. If artists in the 1960s and the 70s used to deal with this idea of event, performance, action—Kaprow, for instance—the representation of the event was not incorporated into the conception of the project. But now things have changed, and ultimately representation or images became more important than real events. Today, an event, its image, and its commentary have become one object.
> Huyghe 2012: 685

I break the last sentence apart into four separate words—commentary, image, event and object and combine these parts with the word 'replay'. To apply this word, 'replay' to performance, I separate it temporarily from its lodging in video or audiotape and use it as a stand-in for a live re-doing, re-performing, or re-constructing.
This triggers a pathway of thinking. I think of *9 Beginnings: Bristol* as a 'replay object commenting'. How the performance comments on the original performances by replaying only their beginnings, leaving a huge gap unperformed between the beginning of the original and its end. Another beginning of another performance fills the gap. And so we begin and begin and begin again. *9 Beginnings: Bristol* comments by the way it announces the years of the original performances, and accompanies those announcements with a reflection.

> *Inventing the Logic in Chaos*,
> Leicester Polytechnic Department of Performing Arts.
> '1. 1990. Begin again. Can we? Begin again. 1.'
>
> *Draft*, Lawrence Steger.'
> '2. 1998. It's a totally white room. 2.'
>
> *Saccades*, Nic Green.
> '3. 2006. I am I because my little dog knows me. 3.'

Grass, Javier De Frutos; *Chemical Wedding*, Blast Theory; *Unspeakable*, Kunst/Werk.
'4. 1997. 5. 1992. 6. 2006. People are grass. It still sounds fucking good. My heart was beating fast. 4. 5. 6.'

Walk With Me Walk With Me Will Somebody Please Walk With Me, Lone Twin.
'7. 2005. We cannot retrace our steps. Going forward may be the same as going backwards. We cannot retrace our steps. Retrace our steps. All my long life, all my life, we do not retrace our steps, all my long life, but. 7.'

Quartet (for Anna Akhmatova), Augusto Corrieri.
'8. 2008. Audience Participation. 8.'

White, Grace Surman.
'9. 2005. Without love, we are dead. Not dead like the dead, but dead like the living. 9.'

In our 2014 production we added an intermission after *9 Beginnings: Bristol* then continued with the second round, *9 Beginnings: Chicago*. These proceeded one to the next uninterrupted by the announcements.

1. *News Animations*, Simone Forti, 1989.

2. *O Klahoma! or The Farmer in the Astral Plains*, Robert Metrick, 1998.

3. *All Fall Down*, Jennifer Monson and Yvonne Meier, 1991.

4. *Collaborations*, Andy Soma and Alan Tollefson, 1989.

5. *The Dogs of Willow Street*, Example: None, 1992.

0. Mary Jo Schnell, pre-show announcement 1992.

6. *Shrimps*, 1988.

7. *Collaborations*, Mary Brogger and Brendan de Vallance, 1989.

8. *Cavalcades in Learning*, Chris Sullivan, 1989.

9. *An Epic Falling Between the Cracks*, Nancy Andrews, 1996.

I think of our 18 beginnings as a 'replay object image'. We watch archival video footage to compose each beginning, performed now by Selma Banich and/or Sebastián Calderón Bentin. They do not perform the original, but rather a document of that performance. We have remade a live replay of the videotape. The aura of the original experience is gone. I see the people surrounding the performance in the video. But I do not feel their breath. I cannot feel the breeze of that room. The roots of the word 'aura' come via Latin from Greek and denote breath or breeze. I can feel a new breath in the present when we perform *9 Beginnings* for others. Perhaps this present-day experience is the event in Huyghe's sentence *Today, an event, its image, and its commentary have become one*. Event joins with its image and its commentary in our performance to replay 18 beginnings. The nearness of these performances produces an unsettling effect in me. I know most of these artists and have seen their work. I have created performances alongside them during the same years. We have experienced time together but we have experienced that time with differences of age, history, and locale; a common ground travelled. Gertrude Stein wrote that 'a sentence means there is a future' (Stein 1975). I think each of our beginnings is a sentence in the Steinian sense. The present performance is simply a slight move of attention over a small distance. The lack of middle and end allows the future to leak out.

Cavalcades in Learning: Chris Sullivan, January 28 1989

(He applies a fake nose, then 'enters' by passing through a small curtain and over a step that separates the private stage right from the public stage left. The floor creaks as he walks on it.)

Hello. It's a pleasure to (inaudible.) (He huddles over a light bulb on the floor.)

I'm sorry to say there's a slight delay in the arrival of Mr. Sullivan. For the moment the program will have to be curtailed, and this is a, a, a mistake on my part and in no way reflects that of the vanity of part of this fine profession.

(He 'exits,' then 'enters'.)

Excuse me.

(He huddles over the light on the floor.)

Sorry to say it once again, there's, a small mistake has come up, a small lesion has opened as you might say in my ability to one might say cope or in a word troubleshoot certain situations that might arise in the planning of a production such as this. Please remain seated. I assure you that Mr. Sullivan will be on in just a moment. (He picks up a hand-crank pencil sharpener.) In the meantime I will sharpen any dull pencils in the audience.

(Pause.)

(He 'exits,' puts down the sharpener, 'enters.')

Excuse me, I'm sorry to be abundant, (huddles over light) I'm going to have to tell you that I'm afraid Mr. Sullivan has been injured in a terrible accident. He's not able to go on with the program, please go back to your homes, you'll get a partial refund at the door.

(He half 'exits' then turns back.)

Oh! An imposter has volunteered to go on in the place of the injured performer.

References

2012 [2004] Huyghe, P. 'Interview with George Baker'. In K. Stiles and P. Selz (eds) *Theories and Documents of Contemporary Art*, second edition, Berkeley and Los Angeles: University of California Press, p 685.

1975 [1931] Stein, G. *How to Write* (facsimile), New York: Dover Publications.

PERFORMING ART HISTORY: NON-LINEAR, SYNCHRONOUS AND SYNCOPATED TIMES IN PERFORMANCE RE-ENACTMENT SOCIETY'S GROUP SHOW (ARNOLFINI, BRISTOL 2012)

Paul Clarke/Performance Re-enactment Society

This essay interweaves what the book's Introduction calls *insider know-how and outsider knowledge*, juxtaposing artists' pages by the Performance Re-enactment Society (PRS) with critical-theoretical reflection, moving between the perspectives of arts practitioners and that of scholarly researcher. This structure troubles the distinction between creative and critical modes of practice, as the discursive framings transform the documents displayed on these pages, which also have the potential to make theoretical propositions. Curating the visual materials and writings from performance and restaging them in the context of this book has necessitated selection and transformation, which echoes archival practice; their dissemination in the form of this publication sees *Group Show* (2012) and the artworks cited in this Performance Re-enactment Society exhibition remediated again, passing from one medium to another.

Through theoretical reflection on and documentation of *Group Show*, I will explore the implications of Elizabeth Freeman's concept of 'temporal drag' (2010: 62) for the chronopolitics of art history, with specific reference to the embodiment of physical art objects through performance and the enactment of documents in gallery contexts. This addresses the potential of performance and such remakes to intervene in the conventional temporal practices and logics of exhibitions and art institutions, and to resist the 'developmental time' (66) of art history and the market. The chapter and case study explore agential interactions between bodies and objects across time, and performance, 'not only as that which passes away' (Lepecki 2010: 39), but as a mode of documentation, dissemination and gallery display. In *Group Show*, what is exhibited through performance are absent object-based artworks and this example will be used to trouble medial distinctions; to question the differentiations between immaterial or 'dematerialized art' (Lippard 1973) and material forms, like sculpture, which also have a temporality and produce ephemeral affects. The chapter will consider the economics of exchanges between artefacts and bodies; whether value can be placed in object-based artworks, in their immaterial reperformance, or in the event of their reception by gallery visitors and the affects that they then embody. That is, whether commodifiable qualities lie in the material or immaterial products of works of art. The text and its accompanying artists' pages raise questions around agency and authorship: who makes and signs the work, along with what and where the artwork is or happens. Finally I will touch upon issues of labour and its delegation in galleries and contemporary art.

Group Show was a work developed with PRS, the art collective of which I am a part, which was shown at Arnolfini, Bristol's contemporary art centre, in 2012. PRS is a collaboration between

Tom Marshman, Clare Thornton and myself, with occasional guests joining us for specific projects. It was founded with the intention of using documents and memories to revive past art experiences and create them anew. Its performance enactments, which often involve public participation, are both acts of conservation and transform past works into new events. Named in reference to the often derided and inauthentic practices of historical or battle re-enactment societies, the collective question the possibility and potential of re-enactment and instead prefer to use the term enactment in relation to their practice. Marshman and Thornton are solo artists and some of the projects they have produced in their individual practices have a close relationship to the work of PRS, responding to museum contexts, archival documents, combining art-making and curatorial practices, and incorporating oral histories or verbatim memories. For instance, Thornton's multimodal project, *Unfurl: A Work In Two Parts* (2011), was produced in residency at University of Bristol Theatre Collection, with Part 1 taking the form of a site-specific performance installation in The Red Lodge Museum and Part 2 comprising an exhibition and talks programme. The installation and tableau in The Red Lodge Museum was inspired by a costume piece from the Mander and Mitchenson Collection and the exhibition display was not structured chronologically or according to historical narratives, but rather by tracing depictions of pleats and folds. As Thornton writes, 'Through the production of performance, objects, garments and writing I explored [the museum as site], processes of display, concealment and transformation' (2011). An example from Marshman's practice is *Move Over Darling*, produced for Lesbian, Gay, Bisexual and Transgender history month in 2010. For this project, he collected older LGBT people's stories in Bristol, often linked to specific locations, like lost bars, clubs or hangouts. He wove together stories from this new oral history archive to produce a performance walk of Bristol, retelling personal and social histories from the LGBT community where they happened. *Kings Cross (Remix)* (2016) presented a London-specific version, transforming interviews with local LGBT communities about their memories of the Kings Cross area in the 1980s, into a performance monologue (Marshman 2017).

There is also a correlation with my work as a director with the theatre company Uninvited Guests, whose work often begins with documentary interviews from which performances-as-archives are compiled, in which the performers are intermediaries who speak others' words as though their own, use text to conjure visual images and reenact personal or cultural memories. For instance,

it is possible to trace the lineage of my practice-as-research with PRS back to touring performances such as *Film* (2000), in which Uninvited Guests imagined the end of cinema, a time when films have been lost or banned, the prints degraded or burned.
In a series of interviews, which took place in front of blank screens in cinemas, participants were asked to describe movie scenes, which they had retained as strong memories. In a theatre space, part studio, part cinema, Uninvited Guests restaged these fragmentary recollections and produced a live edit or mix, using performance and digital technology to try to piece the movies back together from fading cultural memories. *Memory of Theatre* (2012) also engaged with the idea of audience as archive, holding impressions of performances in their precarious, mobile or transformative bodies and memories. For this locative media app, we created a new archive of audiences' memories of performances. Bristol Old Vic Theatre, stories that were both recorded and listened back to in situ, with audio files accessed spatially, triggered by finding their location in the auditorium.

Turning to our collaborative work with PRS, which was founded in 2007, I will give an account of selected artworks and curatorial projects. *The Cover of a Book is the Beginning of a Journey* was co-curated by PRS from Arnolfini's collection of artists' books, which focused on instruction-based and interactive book works. First shown at Arnolfini in autumn 2009 the exhibition then toured to New Art Gallery, Walsall and Leeds Metropolitan University gallery. This type of book work is central to the recent tendency towards producing decentred and distributed artworks that take place across a number of forms and are re-mediated. The curators' interest was in performative books that went beyond conventions of reading, books that unsettle the distinction between writer and reader, which distribute and generate action and performance. As part of the show, PRS programmed *Things To Do With Books*, a series of four participatory events, which animated the archival exhibition. At each, visitors were invited to carry out a selection of instructions, sequenced and adapted for the contemporary context. The public produced new versions of the artists' works, which were then displayed in an exhibition the content of which accumulated and remained in process. Three of these participatory acts, inspired by works by Alison Knowles, Sophie Calle, and a montage of instructions from Yoko Ono's Grapefruit (1964), were later redone at Bristol's Spike Island, as part of *One Night Stand: Performance* (2012). Another selection from Things To Do With Books was also performed as a participatory intervention as part of *OPA 0.2 (on performance art)*: *Re-Think/Re-use/Re-make*, at Art-Athina, Athens international art fair in 2009. Alongside this I presented *Ghosting OPA 0.2*, a performance that appropriated the form of an exhibition tour and was based on interviews with the artists included in *OPA 0.2*. Rather than being a tour of the works exhibited, the guide in this performance described works that the artists exhibiting had been inspired or moved by, as though they were there.

In 2010 *Untitled Performance Stills* was commissioned for *The Pigs of Today are the Hams of Tomorrow*, a curatorial collaboration between Plymouth Arts Centre and the Marina Abramović Institute for the Preservation of Performance Art (MAI). For this project, the PRS collaborated with the performance photographer Hugo Glendinning. Over the course of three days, in a project space that was part archive, part photographic studio, audiences of live art recalled moments from performance events that had had a significant impact on them. Memories were accessioned into the Society's collection and audio recordings were made of their descriptions, along with associated feelings and personal recollections. Then participants worked with the PRS to perform their memory of the chosen event to camera and Glendinning captured a still image of the tableau they created. The photos of their re-enactments of performances from memory were exhibited alongside an audio montage composed from the oral history interviews. For the finissage, the Society performed an exhibition tour of these absent, remembered works, describing them verbally whilst taking down the photographs. Participants were given prints of the images they co-authored with us, which have Creative Commons non-commercial share-alike licences, so they can be downloaded and re-used. They have been disseminated in publications and circulated online, for example as Facebook profile images.

As part of its 50th anniversary, Arnolfini commissioned *Cover-ed* (2011), a series of curatorial and creative interventions into and around Ed Ruscha and Mason Williams' iconic 1969 photo novel *Crackers*, a copy of which is held in Arnolfini's archive. Over two months this bookwork became the inspiration for an installation and exhibition, an evening of talks and performative readings, an open photographic shoot, a new bookwork and a participatory performance event. A cover version of *Crackers* called *Salad Dressing* was made in collaboration with book artist Tom Sowden, which was shot publicly over three days in a hotel room installed in Arnolfini's reading room. *Crackers* was used as the script or score for re-enactments of Ruscha's stills, shot and designed in the style of a photo story and recontextualised in contemporary Bristol locations. Previous re-makes, rip-offs and re-creations of

Ed Ruscha bookworks were then displayed in the set of the PRS remake. The final chapter of the artists' book took the form of an intervention at the book launch, which was documented and published online. This participatory event performed an alternative ending to Ruscha's *Crackers*, which had a critical relationship with the gender politics of the original book.

PRS's work has taken place in the context of re-enactment becoming a prevalent strategy in contemporary visual art, dance and performance, along with the proliferation of performance as a mode of gallery display. I want to consider two identifiable strands to re-enactment as a curatorial and artistic methodology, firstly the reconstruction of 'classic' performance art works, particularly from the 1960s and 70s, by the artists themselves or others. For instance, *A Short History of Performance* (Whitechapel Gallery, London, 2002/3) and Marina Abramović's *Seven Easy Pieces* (Guggenheim, 2005), which attempted to preserve through performance canonical works by Abramović and her peers, an approach which Rebecca Schneider described as having a '*monumental* relationship to history' (2011: 132). The other distinctive strand of artistic re-enactments resists such drives to historicise or monumentalise performance, instead comprising creative interpretations, responses or cover versions, which do not aim to emulate, but rather to transform and critically remake past works for present contexts. PRS's work is aligned with this second strand of unauthorised, creative and critical return. What differentiates the approach taken in *Group Show* is that, rather than returning to archival documents of performance in order to redo or 'redocument' (Schneider 2009) them, the PRS has engaged with documents of exhibitions, some of which included performance art, but that predominantly displayed material art objects, which they have enacted or responded to through performance.

In addition to the context of re-enactment being taken up as a popular creative and curatorial strategy, the work of PRS also takes place in light of a performative turn in curating, with performance treated as a medium or mode of gallery display, live bodies and subjects staged in exhibitions and the transformation of performers or participants into moving sculpture. In particular I would note a turn towards curating dance in exhibitions and a range of critical interventions into museums and galleries by choreographers, for instance Boris Charmatz' *Musée de la Danse*, his dancing museum, which 'explore[s] the tensions' between the 'immutable and the ephemeral' (2009). But also, Siobhan Davies' *Table of Contents* (2014), 'a live movement installation', which used Davies' archive as its 'starting point' and also drew on the 'human body as an archive', to explore where her repertoire resides and 'how we remember and retain movement'. In galleries, including Arnolfini, Davies and dancers from the company drew on 'material from their past' and combined redoing movement sequences from their body memory with verbal commentary, descriptions or recollections. The choreographic situations enabled questions and dialogue between performers and spectators and, in addition, certain Siobhan Davies' movements were taught and passed on to gallery visitors through spoken instructions or shown and learnt through demonstration. At Fundació Antoni Tàpies, in *Retrospective* (2014), Xavier Le Roy explored the possibility of a gallery survey of his dance works, in which he worked with local performers to continuously reiterate, 'recycle and transform' motifs from his solos (2014). Although staged in museums or galleries, these retrospectives of dance works resist the 'museification' (Agamben 2007: 83), reification or canonisation of Davies or Le Roy's dances. Rather than being separated from the body of choreographic practices and dancers' bodies, put away and out of use in the museum or exhibited in the form of documents, they remain in the hands of dancers and choreographers, displayed and kept in embodied ways through ongoing processes of iteration, reuse and transformation. Finally, with *MoMA Dance Company* (2016), when invited to select his *Artist's Choice* from the collection, choreographer Jérôme Bel instead 'became interested in the relation of the Museum's employees to specific artworks [and] to the institution' and their labour in caring for and maintaining the art. Rather than selecting artworks to display he chose to curate and choreograph museum workers in a dance performance for the gallery.

***

Having outlined the broader context of performance, curatorial and choreographic practices, I will now turn to *Group Show* and propose some theoretical framings. With this work, PRS responded to Arnolfini's interest in exploring the relationship of its archive to the future after the art centre's 50th anniversary in 2011. The contemporary gallery is future facing and locates itself now, at the endpoint of a historical continuum. Arnolfini therefore tends not to exhibit historical shows or retrospectives and its curators attempt to innovate, to show new and emergent practices. Whilst it has an archive, there is no Arnolfini collection.

Group Show was an intangible exhibition, displayed through performance, with all four galleries empty of objects and the walls left white. The PRS curated *Group Show* from an imaginary permanent collection comprising all the visual art and performance that had been shown at Arnolfini since it was founded in 1961. *Group Show* brought together works from different periods in the institution's development and art history, by artists who were not originally shown together, in a new two-day event. This was an intervention into the art centre's modes of archiving and conventional strategies of exhibition display. Hayden White (1987) and Paul Ricoeur (1981: 257) have pointed out the exchange and interplay between history and fiction that take place when events are plotted chronologically or thematically, and that there is a close relationship between the way in which histories and fictions are told, historicised or narrativised. Whilst the research for *Group Show* drew on historical documents of exhibitions and archival evidence, the curation, selection, sequencing, and acts of telling or performing transformed the art centre's history and individual works into fictions.

Foucault calls museums and archives 'heterotopias of indefinitely accumulating time'; which attempt to enclose objects, documents, forms and styles from various times, eras and traditions in one 'immobile place', where they are put away beyond the ravages of time and human use, in an attempt to preserve them for perpetuity. For Foucault, museums and archives are founded on 'the idea of constituting a place of all times that is itself outside of time' (Foucault 1986: 26). *Group Show* is a form of living museum, a performed collection or queered archive, perhaps a temporary heterotopia in the gallery. But one that is aligned with 'the mode of the festival' and 'to time in its most fleeting, transitory, precarious aspect' (26). Bound by the time of the event, rather than being timeless or inaccessible, *Group Show* was constituted by close interactions with documents of art and human contact with visitors. This approach countered strategies of preservation, conservation and curation that separate art objects or documents behind glass, consecrate them and put them away in archival collections where they cannot easily be touched or handled by artists or public users (see Agamben 2007).

Schneider proposes that traces of the past persist in the present and percolate; that time is *'porous'*, *'given to rupture'* and return (Schneider 2011: 174). She describes labelling cultural practices and aesthetics as 'behind the times' as a way of excluding and othering them. Linear progress conflates the passing of time with accumulating value and this is certainly the case with the art market, along with curators' and artists' drive to innovate. Schneider has proposed 'crossing time', 'holding back' and 'detaining' as tactics for resisting the Enlightenment and capitalist projects. In this way, multiple temporalities can remain co-present and forms or styles of art—the potential of which was not exhausted—can be retained in an assemblage (174). Ways of making, thinking and looking that had been thought to be outmoded can come back, recur or be reiterated, gain currency and relevance again. Schneider is drawing on Freeman's notion of 'temporal drag' (Freeman 2010: 62), which in addition to practices of dragging up in queer contexts, has associations with 'retrogression, delay and the pull of the past on the present'. Rather than cross gender, temporal drag proposes performing in outdated modes, cross-dressed in the signs of other times. Freeman explains the 'way that periodicity relies on homogeneous time, as seamless, unified and forward-moving' (2010: 6). In line with Ricoeur on narrativisation and emplotment, she writes that, 'time becomes history through its organisation into a series of discrete units linked by cause and effect'. For Freeman, 'historical narrative organises various temporal schemes into consequential sequences'. For instance, we might think of the way in which art history tends to be narrated such that one artistic movement follows another in a sequence, one aesthetic or paradigm is the consequence of the previous, the ideas and approaches of which it counters. A new movement causes the disappearance of the preceding style, which is put out of cultural use in the museum or archive, rather than existing simultaneously or synchronously.

PRS imagined the galleries haunted by traces of past Arnolfini exhibits and modalities of art, selecting a collection of absent works to make present again. Like the figure of the spectre in Derrida, which comes back and no longer 'belongs to time', (Derrida 2006: xx) these acts of performing the archive had the potential to interrupt linear succession, temporal progress and art-historical periodicity, establishing new relations between 'present-past, present-present and present-future'. (39) As Schneider writes, 'In the syncopated time of reenactment, [...] then and now punctuate each other' and resonances take place across times (2011: 2).

***

There were three parts to *Group Show*: the first work was made by Tom Marshman and drew on interviews with Arnolfini staff and memories of performers who had toured work there. It revealed the workings of the art institution, taking you backstage to hear verbatim stories about late-night installations of exhibitions in the galleries and preparations for shows in the theatre. In the audio montage visitors heard the voices of gallery and theatre technicians, along with the buildings manager, who would generally not be visible to the public, labouring behind the scenes in the workshop, lighting booth or offices upstairs.

Part 1
Tom Marshman

An Audience with Dressing Room 2 took visitors through a staff door and behind the scenes, to revisit some past shows and previous versions of Arnolfini, before the building was redeveloped. Backstage, in the intimate context of one of the venue's dressing rooms, you heard the voices of past performers and gallery technicians, as they remembered preparing themselves, setting up spaces or getting into the zone.

I drew on interviews with Neil Bartlett, Polly Cole, Fiona Wright, Mark Hutley, Ewen Macleod, Darren Pritchard and Karen Christopher; past and present members of staff or performers who have shown work at Arnolfini over the last 30 years. Created and performed with Suzie Zara. Archive research and transcriptions by Cara Davies.

> You know, we would set up the space and umm we'd do a group warm up. We would mill around for a while then put our costumes on and make our hair stay, stay somewhere or something, and then would run, umm a few, through a few things in the show that would be likely to go wrong, umm things that were done in unison. There would always be something that we had chosen to be the thing we would use to repeat in whatever space. Usually it was a dance that we all did together or a sequence we had to do together; something we had to get right. So all these things will happen and they would have their amount of time and we would just work through them like soldiers or craftspeople. I don't even want to think about it, you know you have this procedure that you just have to follow. And so there always was this 10 or 15 minutes that we were spending right before the show, quietly backstage, kind of waiting in the back, waiting. Yeah, in the back, in the back area, either in the dressing room or the corridor and there is this kind of moment of suspension that takes over.
>
> Karen Christopher, Goat Island. Extract from audio track

Tom Marshman, *An Audience with Dressing Room 2*. Photos: Carl Newland.

The second was a series of performance interventions by Clare Thornton and Laura Dannequin, which took place in the galleries. They worked with paper-based documents of exhibitions and images from Arnolfini's archive as scores for choreography and movement, embodying past works, mostly sculpture. The performers maintained still poses and moved through a montage of movements scored by art objects, responding to slides of them in past exhibitions as performative, calling for exchanges between times in the gallery, and for interactions between their dancers' bodies and artists' objects, that had once been there in the same gallery spaces. Freeman might call this a 'queer archivalism, [which] turns bodies into living museums' (2010: xi) and animates the previously inanimate, disobeying object and subject distinctions: 'inter(in) animation', to use Schneider's term (2011: 163).

There is a relationship between this part and other recent uses of choreographic practice in galleries, like those named above, along with works in which performers impersonate object-based art. For instance: *An Immaterial Retrospective of the Venice Biennale* by Alexandra Pirici and Manuel Pelmuş, for the Romanian Pavilion at Venice in 2013, which staged works from throughout the Biennale's history as a series of tableaux; as well as their recent work, *Ongoing Perishable Objects* (2016), in which they performed works from the MMK and Tate collections through collective physical movement and figurative speech. In Tino Sehgal's *Kiss* (2003), titled after Rodin's sculpture, *The Kiss* (1901–4), two dancers move through a series of enactments of paintings and statues of 'kissing couples' from art history (Hantelmann 2010: 137). The MoMA Learning website states that Sehgal and the 'players' or 'interpreters' he employs 'transform the enduring, static forms and images depicted in these more traditional artistic mediums into two bodies in motion, and into a living, immediate, and, ultimately, impermanent experience' (n.d.). Dorothea von Hantelmann describes this as a 'reenactment of historical sculptures as choreographed movements' (2010: 137). For her, this performative work articulates an 'understanding of continuity', as the many art-historical actualisations of the motif of the kiss are repeated, take shape momentarily in the form of people, and are slowly transformed, one into the next. For Schneider (2011), *Kiss* is a work that works at passing from one medium to another: from 'statuary to dance' and from 'dance to statuary' (136). Sculpture attempts to 'transcend its own materiality' and performing bodies strive to become the sculptures they cite, inanimate or still: in their very failure to fully pass, there is possibility and the potential for 'social negotiation' (135) with viewers.

In Part Two of *Group Show*, live bodies 'trace sculpture', reiterating, memorising or documenting material art objects, rather than 'the other way around'. As Schneider points out, in *How To Do Things With Art*, von Hantelmann (2010) has suggested that 'all art is performative' (2011: 135), transmitting bodily affects and calling for response. Thornton and Dannequin think of artworks and documents as 'scriptive things' (Bernstein 2009: 69), which 'invite a person to dance' (70). There is a through-line here from PRS's public enactments of instruction-based bookworks, *Things To Do With Books* (2009), with descriptions in catalogues and exhibition slides here read as instructional. There is also a connection with Derrida's conception of the archive's relation to the future, that it is not only a place of origin or 'commencement', but also of 'commandment' (1998: 2). In *Group Show*, archival documents have 'animative power' (Bernstein 2009: 70) commanding reperformance, influencing, having agency or authority over Thornton and Dannequin's citational acts. For Robin Bernstein, things and images have the potential to 'shape human behaviours' and such interactions are destabilising, 'upset[ting] the boundary between person' (2009: 70) and thing. Below, in relation to performativity, I will return to questioning the differences between immaterial performance and material artforms, between human and nonhuman bodies, conceptual objects and things. Thornton writes that they tried 'to get to know' the sculptures and video works they selected by 'doing them'. Rather than this practice being mimetic or representative, through a process of becoming they explored affiliations between their bodies and these art objects, finding affinities with their affects. They attempted to do what these artworks were doing in order to approach understanding what it would be like to be them, to matter or materialise in the gallery in the ways that they did.

Part 2
Clare Thornton

I collaborated with movement artist Laura Dannequin to present a series of performance interventions in the galleries. During the research phase, we focused our attention on the Arnolfini Exhibitions Archive, in particular on sculptural works that had previously been exhibited in the building. We gravitated towards works that spoke to our interests in the body; the body itself as a sculptural object, inhabiting space, a material with which to explore our concerns around time, presentness and substance.

I began my research in Arnolfini's Reading Room, reviewing exhibition catalogues and then visiting Bristol Record Office where the exhibition slides were held. I presented a longlist to Laura and together we attempted to get to know these past sculptural works through 'doing them', re-imagining them through movement, gesture and text. Through our re-cursive reading, looking and physical testing, a selection of works began to cluster around the following four principal ideas, which helped shape the live work presented during *Group Show*. Our physical movements were punctuated by a collage of textual extracts from exhibition catalogues. These were mostly shared through speech, but occasionally as texts nailed to a gallery wall just before each new movement phase began.

Methods of containment & The Corner
Histoire des petites effigies,
Annette Messager, 1990
Twin Memories I-XI, Jaume Plensa, 1992

Anthropomorphic minimalism and the recognition of materiality
This Drinking Alone (The Deep Intoxication Series), Tom Burr, 2006 *Total Produce (morality)*, Cosima von Bonin, 2010
Loop, Margaret Organ, 1978
Scoops, Jane Simpson, 1993

Time, impermanence, the now, the now
Nine Perfect Minutes, Pierre Huyghe, 2000
Candle, Marine Hugonnier, 1998-2000

Getting to know a work by doing it
Military Figure, Kenny Hunter, 1998
Love Seat, Richard Hughes, 2005

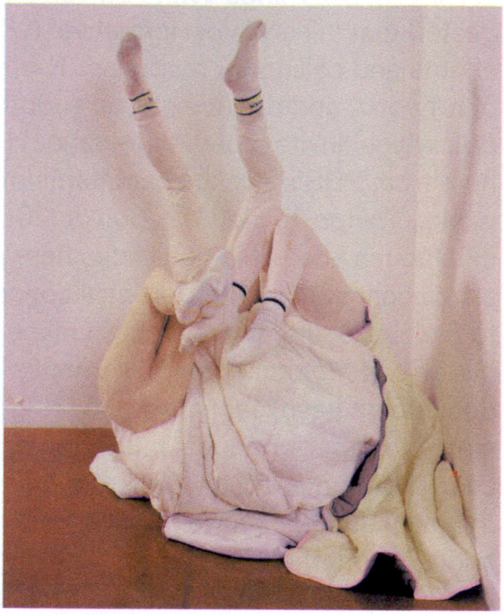

Richard Hughes, *Love Seat*, 2005, fibreglass, polyurethane foam, dyed clothing, bedding 188 x 87 x 86 cm, 74 x 34.3 x 33.9 ins.
Private Collection Paris. Photo: Ruth Clark.

Clare Thornton, *After, After Richard Hughes*, 2012, risograph print. Original photo: Carl Newland.

Getting to know a work by doing it, Clare Thornton and Laura Dannequin, 2012.

Kenny Hunter, *Military Figure*, 1998.
Courtesy of Kenny Hunter.

Anthropomorphic minimalism and the recognition of materiality, Clare Thornton and Laura Dannequin, 2012.
Photos: Carl Newland.

I curated Part 3, which was performed by Arnolfini's gallery invigilators: rather than fulfilling the conventional gallery steward's role, of offering explanations and interpreting the art on display, they described a series of works that had previously been shown at Arnolfini, but were now not there. Their acts of speaking the art were performative, making these absent works appear, remade differently as images in each listener's imagination, which they could project onto the white walls and bare concrete floors of the galleries. The dramaturgy of each invigilator's gallery tour was organised according to associative motifs, rather than a critical or chronological art-historical narrative. Part 3 ran concurrently with Part 2 and Thornton and Dannequin's choreographies intervened occasionally in the ongoing tours, appearing unannounced in different galleries.

This was an impossible exhibition of immaterial art objects and virtual performances, which accumulated in visitors' memories, overlaid in the gallery as palimpsest, like Foucault's heterochrony, a place in which times have built up (1986: 26). In the event, different moments in Arnolfini's institutional history became synchronous, works reverberated across periods, different points in time touched and encountered one another in the spoken text. Part 3 of *Group Show* undid the gallery's chronology and wove together fictional threads told by the stewards, whose visibility, agency and centrality to the work's realisation performed an implicit critique of their institutional position. Conventionally, the role of the invigilators is to be relatively invisible: to defer to the art objects, not distract attention from them and to watch over the inanimate work. However, here the invigilators were framed by and framed *Group Show*: they were central to its realisation as it was only manifested through their immaterial labour. The work would only appear if visitors spent time interacting with them, listening to and engaging with their words, as they performed their personal service.

For frequent Arnolfini visitors, certain descriptions would trigger memories of seeing exhibitions for themselves: so, from time to time, they interjected different recollections, their memories mingling with the invigilators' words. In this way, the describing was sometimes collaborative or conversational. The invigilators became keepers of an oral history archive, stewarding descriptions of past exhibitions and works, keeping them in circulation and use; countering their historicisation by speaking them and gesturing towards where they once were. Through these exchanges with the public the invigilators shared their caring for the past works, or at least the descriptions and mental images of them, passing this responsibility on to the community of visitors who attended, within whose memories the works might also remain or return. Potentially gallery-goers also retained embodied affects from the relational encounters with the invigilators and would recollect experiences of the tours they performed, which could be retold as oral stories or circulate further as rumour.

Part 3 of *Group Show* resisted time's passing, proposing passages of narrative that crossed times and citations between works from different periods, suggesting that chronologies of art are *'given to rupture'* (Schneider 2011: 174), as aesthetics and practices persist, are remembered, recognised again or come back. The co-presence of works from multiple times, both iconic and unknown, and from different fields of art, functioned as a critique of linear aesthetic progress as the overturning of preceding movements. Formal categories or taxonomies were also blurred as sculptures, paintings, photographs, video, installation and performance works were displayed alongside one another, in the same place and through the same form of words.

Part 3
Paul Clarke

On entering gallery 1, visitors were greeted by one of the invigilators, Jess Robins, who said, 'Hello. This is *Group Show* by Performance Re-enactment Society; would you like me to tell you about the work?' Further narratives unfolded upstairs in galleries 2, 3 and 4, performed by Fraisia Dunn, Katarina Complova and Stella Thompson, all regular gallery invigilators who had volunteered to participate.

I was inspired by browsing Arnolfini's slide collection, held by the Bristol Record Office, past brochures in the reading room and digital images of exhibitions found in folders on the institution's server. The 35mm slides were uncatalogued at the time and not yet digitised, whilst the raw jpegs were unedited and not always labelled with the names of the shows they documented. The text for this part was researched and curated with Cara Davies. Presented here are documentary photographs and an extract from the script for the invigilators' exhibition tour.

Extract from Gallery 1

This is the Museum of Eagles. And this is the Museum of Forgotten History.

There's a huge pile of rubble over there, which reaches to the ceiling; it's all broken concrete. Overnight, colourful graffiti has been written on the gallery walls. The Wild Bunch sound system is playing and there's a display of breakdancing. On the back wall, someone has spray-painted, 'English Go Home'. And here, by the entrance, there is vinyl lettering that says, 'Clifton Suspension Bridge 7th March 2003'; perhaps arranging or recording a meeting.

If you cast your eyes along the floor, you'll see deep cracks in the concrete surface, like there's been an earthquake. A series of short texts are marked in black and red ink. Near us are the words, 'Space Watcher'.

Behind the glass on this white plinth is what, to us, resembles a Greek urn, lying on its side. It has been painstakingly reconstructed by the museum's experts. It is mostly white plaster with only a few fragments of blue pottery here and there. It has a narrow neck with two blue handles, which to you look like they're from Ikea mugs. The exhibit is labelled, 'Ikea Vase', and the accompanying text explains that this was once a common object, used

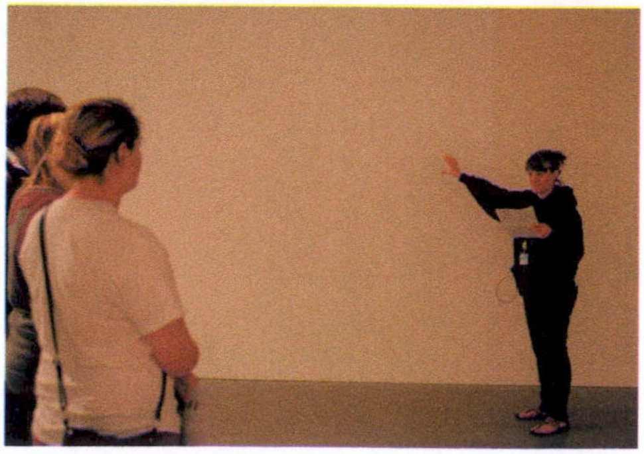

Photos: Carl Newland.

in the late 20th and early 21st century to hold flowers.

This is a plaster cast of the inside of the living room of an abandoned townhouse in London; 486 Archway Rd. The negative space is nine feet wide, ten feet deep and nearly 12 high; it comes close to the ceiling of the gallery. It is a ghost room: feel free to walk around it. You can't enter but you can see the trace of a door, and where a chimney-breast and Victorian fireplace must have been. There's the imprint of tiles, skirting boards, an indented light switch and door handle.

There is a white-painted room built in the gallery here. Two 16mm film projectors point through rectangular holes in the wall, with a few metres between them. The same film spools from one projector to the other. The two projections are side by side. On the left you see a black and white image of Yuri Gagarin, the first man in space, and on the right the date 1961. There's a 20-second delay between the projectors and after 20 seconds Gagarin appears on the right. He is replaced on the left by a headshot of an elderly man with grey hair brushed back, gold-rimmed glasses and a moustache. This is an interview with H.M., who had a large portion of his brain's temporal lobe removed in 1953, to control his epileptic seizures. After the operation he suffered severe amnesia, forgetting events almost as soon as they had happened. He could only recall things for around 20 seconds. If you were to leave the room and re-enter he would not remember you. The film is coming to an end and the voice-over says, 'What would it be like to live without recourse to the past? To lose the fourth dimension of time and live in the three dimensions of space alone?'

The next piece is a vast urban planner's model of an impossible city, which brings together some of the world's most iconic buildings. It is made entirely of sugar. The Clifton Suspension Bridge is represented alongside other landmarks like, Sydney Opera House, The Eiffel Tower, The Taj Mahal, the Empire State Building and the Gherkin.

The gallery is empty, except for an architect's model and a video. This shows a virtual tour of what was Arnolfini and is now being sold as real estate. In the 3D rendering of what is planned, the stone façade is all that remains and inside is a park, complete with deer. In the centre, raised on a single supporting column, is a new tower; a glass and steel skyscraper housing luxury apartments. A woman plays a grand piano in one of the penthouses. The upper floors disappear into the air and become less solid; an unfinished, skeletal framework.

The wall at the back of the gallery is now gold and made up of panels. Its glossy surface resembles that of a minimalist sculpture and you can see a trace of yourself and this room reflected in it. It looks like the foyer of a corporate lobby or hotel. It is an illusion, which occupies the same space as the thing it portrays. The title, *You Can't Touch This*, is borrowed from MC Hammer. There appear to be lift doors set into the wall and gold buttons. It is tempting to touch them to see if they work.

The exhibition continues upstairs, in the first-floor galleries.

My research process for *Group Show* shared some methodologies with that of a scholar searching the archives for evidence to support the writing of a historical narrative of the institution and its programme. But when browsing through Arnolfini's brochures, catalogues and the 35 mm slides that documented past exhibitions, I looked for visual motifs, recurrent materials or tropes and made collections organised according to thematics that emerged, such as water, crystals, rooms, architectural models and magic. Between the slides and other evidence of each exhibition kept in the archive, I tried to re-stage the show, to imagine being there among the objects displayed, how I might have been affected by the chosen work in its original context and what it may have meant to me. In the case of some recent exhibitions, which I had seen, I also drew on my own memories and those of the invigilators with whom I was collaborating, incorporating their experiences of protecting artworks and providing information to the public about them.

Where Thornton and Dannequin traced the documents spatially with their bodies, I traced them in writing and choreographed their speaking in the exhibition space and time. Firstly I transcribed the images of the artworks selected, translating them into written descriptions. This exercise in ekphrasis attempted to recreate works of art in words, to depict them in figurative language. Or, more precisely, these mimetic writings were responses to the slides and digital stills that documented these artworks as displayed in Arnolfini exhibitions. Ekphrasis was an anachronistic practice to apply in this context, more often used as an art-historical method when there are gaps in the record, in early periods, rather than when photographic reproductions survive. White has asked, 'how [...] can any past, which [is] by definition no longer perceivable, be represented [...] except in an "imaginary" way?' (1987: 57). Ekphrasis draws attention to the gap between text and its object, the difference between what words and images do; both how they represent and what they cause in terms of affect.

When described literally, many of the documentary images of works chosen for Part 3 of *Group Show* sounded impossible to exhibit or install; as if they were speculative fictions or still to be realised in some future show, rather than having already been seen at Arnolfini in the past. Ricoeur has noted the way that narrative is constructed metaphorically in both history and fiction: that there is 'fiction in history' (1981: 289) and historical documents and imaginative acts of narrating are entangled. In *Time and Narrative*, he aligns fiction with emotional affect and notes that fiction 'frees retrospectively certain possibilities that were not actualised in the historical past' (Ricoeur 1985: 191). The absence of an image necessitated a creative act on the visitor's part: they recreated each art-historical work from the interplay between the description, their memories and imagination, projecting their possible version onto the white wall indicated or into the empty space gestured toward. This relates closely to Andre Lepecki's proposal (2010), cited in the introduction to this book, that artists return to past works in order to release their latent possibilities and actualise virtual versions that the original artist or instance had yet to realise or kept in reserve. In this example, the art-historical fictions or versions generated out of the interactions between archival documents, artist, invigilators and gallery visitors were various and remained in the form of immaterial possibilisations.

During each tour a show built up, was collected and arranged in the visitor's memory—an exhibition that had never actually been seen. In the invigilators' spatial dramaturgies, you were periodically returned to the same locations in the gallery, where different works were described. In this dematerialised show, more than one thing could be in the same place, even monumental sculptures; for instance, a traditional Romanian wooden gate coated in gold leaf and embossed with a DNA pattern, a reconstruction of one of the Shah of Iran's tents from the tent city of Persepolis, and a plaster cast of the volume inside a room in a Victorian house. In the 'no-when' of *Group Show*, these absent art objects were made present by being spoken, becoming synchronous and occupying the same space.

The imagined exhibition was curated and the invigilators' tours were choreographed with the descriptions configured into distinct narratives for four of Arnolfini's galleries. Each absent piece was placed in the gallery space and arranged in relation to the other absent artworks that had been chosen to be part of the show. The curatorial arrangement was both topological and tropological, organised according to spatial logics and ordered by tropes or metaphorical relations. So that the gallery spaces could function mnemonically and walking through them might trigger the visitor's own recollections, cause their memories of other visits to intervene in the flow of the narration, I attempted to locate works where they had previously been shown, or in close proximity. In addition to attempting to position pieces according to their physical location in their original exhibition context, coherence also came from the recurrence and sequencing of tropes. Rather than telling a chronological or discursive story, associative threads were woven between different works and exhibitions.

As Ricoeur has noted, Part 3 attempted to 'make the pictures speak and the narrative show' (2004: 267). The artworks or their slides were read, interpreted and depicted in writing. These written texts were then spoken and transformed into oral history, transmitted aurally and disseminated face-to-face. The act of speaking the figurative writing tried to set something before the visitors' eyes, to give something to be seen. Whereas the artist Ed Ruscha—whose photo novel *Crackers* PRS remade—was interested in words becoming pictures, I was interested in pictures becoming words. Both Ruscha and Part 3 of *Group Show* explored ways in which 'each mode of representation [could find] its effect [...] in the domain of the other' (Ricoeur 2004: 267).

Paintings, sculptures, video, performance art and installations were recounted, not as absent, but as though present. The past artworks cited became contemporary through assemblage, through being recontextualised in the now of *Group Show*, collated and articulated as though part of a single exhibition or one complex collaborative installation. None of the artworks were named in the spoken descriptions, which were not discrete and flowed one into the next, such that the frames between works became porous. Artworks were folded together as the tours unfolded and motifs travelled between descriptions, generating ambiguity around where one appropriated work ended and another artist's began. Whilst a printed gallery, guide listed the sources, authorship was not accounted for in the spoken text and ownership became blurred, complicated and shared. As the visitor traversed the gallery, guided by the invigilator, the narration and choreography metaphorically traversed works, exhibitions and times, linking them together spatially and sequentially, conducting transactions between contexts and organising material lifted from the past into a new itinerary.

Each work was told in present tense, as though it were momentarily there or continuously present. There was a theatricality to the time-based interactions produced, which asked of viewers that they participate in realising the works, that they attempt to visualise them and perform or behave 'as if' they were there. In this way, the passing temporality of these interactions with the invigilators differed from the comparative presentness of experiencing material artworks: though visitors may have spent more time listening to them displayed through speech than they would have done if beholding them visually.

Consider each artwork described as a story, a spatio-temporal story in Michel de Certeau's terms (1984: 115). These found works were cited, quoted and summoned to appear, each from the time and context of a different exhibition or period in Arnolfini's history and from the last 50 years of art history. As Walter Benjamin has pointed out, to quote involves the 'interruption of [...] context' (1992: 148). *Group Show* was a montage, through which various borrowings, lifted from past exhibitions, were disseminated again in a new work, an original totality that was structured by a series of temporal and contextual ruptures or discontinuities. In the present time of the invigilators' tours and whilst walking with them through the contemporary gallery context, the visitor cut back and forth between other shows, which were curated at different art-historical moments. In the 'tissue of quotations' (Barthes 1977: 146) and appropriations woven by the invigilators, multiple times coexisted, various exhibitions took place concurrently in the same heterochronic gallery space. Prefigured times became configured into narratives and were refigured in the invigilators' poetic acts of mimesis, when spoken as if they were there now.

The stories of these works and their recitations functioned metaphorically, they opened up passages from the current scene to the past exhibitions referenced and they made present the art-works and their former contexts (Certeau 1984: 115). They opened up the contemporary to work and aesthetic modalities that had been consigned to the past, put away in the museum or archive: they reflected upon, intervened in or rewrote the historic contexts cross-referenced. Something was done *with* and *to* this material from previous shows: here re-use had a critical potential in relation both to the contemporary scene and the work's original visual art period or paradigm. As Freeman recommends of temporal drag, *Group Show*'s interest was in the belated and outmoded, in that which has been suppressed by periodicity, in asynchrony and in anachronisms that might interrupt or run counter to conventional genealogies of art.

***

In the last section of this essay I will address the 'labour of the live' (Schneider 2011: 131) that was delegated to the invigilators and to the gallery visitors with whom they interacted. I will also explore ways in which *Group Show* destabilised medial and ontological distinctions between object-based visual art and performance. This practice and thinking takes place in light of debates around performance disappearing and being an unreproducible art (Phelan 1993), and performance remaining or being characterised by reiteration (Schneider 2011). But the discursive tools I will apply here are performativity, affect and 'agential realism', Karen Barad's 'ontoepistemological framework' (2007: 45).

Part 3 of *Group Show* was made in collaboration with Arnolfini invigilators, who volunteered to participate and were paid appropriately for their time, had input into the curating of their narratives and the development of the dramaturgy of the tours. They selected some works for inclusion, which were not mute, but spoke to them, or that they remembered. As argued above, the invigilators acted as intermediaries, making connections between times and speaking for the absent visual or material art objects. Their performances were also intermedial. Like the 'players' in Sehgal's *Kiss*, who Schneider suggested 'labour at the pass between pasts and presents' (2011: 137), their immaterial labour was of passing; from one time to another and one medium to another. Historical visual artworks were remediated through performance, translated into text and repeated in speech: 'one medium recalls another medium' (Schneider 2011: 133). This was a performance that documented object-based works and photographic documents of exhibitions; it replaced material art with immaterial work, in this instance speech.

Visitors tend to pay attention to the inanimate works displayed rather than to the invigilators, who they turn to only if they require information about an exhibit or the gallery. Whilst they are the interface between Arnolfini's activities and the public, communicating with visitors and responding to enquiries, their position in the institution is minor and they have limited agency. In Part 3 attention was given to the invigilators, how they presented themselves and their interpretative services as commodities, and how they represented the art institution. Their labour and the way they performed their roles was theatricalised, along with the behaviours of the viewers, who the work also staged in Arnolfini's empty galleries. Rather than making physical objects, in *Group Show* the PRS produced relational exchanges and convivial interactions between invigilators and visitors, which occupied their time. Not only was the invigilators' time made more productive, as they carried out their service, produced and became the exhibition, but the gallery's past and its archive were also capitalised as useful resources, holding valuable materials from which to produce a new, contemporary art assemblage—an immaterial, experiential commodity.

Historically, performance, participatory and action art have their origins in resistance to an art scene founded on the production of commodity objects that are exchangeable in the art market and accrue capital in private and museum collections. Paolo Virno wrote that performance 'is an activity which finds its own [...] purpose [...] in itself, without objectifying itself into [...] a "finished product", or into an object which would survive the performance' (2004: 52). For him, performance, like personal services, *'requires the presence of others'* (52) and the product is not separable from the act of producing, or the producer with whom the client interacts. Our contemporary economic model is now one of 'general performance' (Sven Lütticken 2012), in which the common mode of labour is performance and workers are expected to perform themselves publicly and to produce immaterial goods, such as relationships with customers, positive feelings and affects. As Hardt and Negri write, contemporary labour 'from sales work to financial services, is fundamentally a performance: the product is the act itself' (2000: 200). In addition we might note that, in the context of what Pine and Gilmore have called the 'experience economy' (2001: 77), affects are new economic offerings or commodities, 'consumption is an experience' and the product is produced in the consumer: 'the *value* of the experience lingers in the memories' and as traces in the bodies 'of individuals engaged by the event' (2001: 80). In light of these shifts in what the contemporary economy values, which the art market has led or responded to, the affects and exchanges produced by performance are in line with the tendencies of the service or experience economy. Whilst resisting the contemporary art gallery's capitalist drive towards newness, *Group Show* took a timely dematerialised form, which could be criticised in relation to its alignment with immaterial labour and the economy of affects.

Tino Sehgal provides an exemplary example of this contemporary tendency to value ephemeral works, transient or relational art experiences, over or in addition to aesthetic things. His immaterial products sell well on the art market and are held in major international collections. They are valued precisely because of remaining immaterial and his signature concept that the works should not be transformed into documents. For instance, *Kiss* (2003) is held by MoMA, but unlike other pieces in the collection, there is no photograph online and the catalogue states, 'No image available'. This dematerialised, conceptual object is only evidenced by the title and the object number 592.2008. Its medium is listed as 'Constructed situation' and its 'Dimensions variable' (MoMA 2008). Whilst he stipulates that his works should not be recorded in any form and they are comprised of 'social encounters', intangible 'experiences' and the 'memories of engaging in' them, the 'situations' he makes can be bought and sold, loaned out, repeated and reproduced (MoMA Learning, n.d.).

It is worth noting that although they last longer than performances, with a few months between their beginning and end, gallery exhibitions of material artworks are still events with a limited timespan. Unless the exhibition is remounted or reenacted—which is becoming a trend—the works curated will only be arranged in the same way for the one duration. Exhibitions and installations are temporary and disappear. In Arnolfini's archive the slide collection documents 50 years of the gallery's visual-arts programme and, as with performances, these shows were only evidenced and accessible to me through photographic records. These documents are not fixed or immutable, but are also in a process of disappearing, as their colours fade, they require ongoing conservation, digitisation or migration to new media.

During exhibitions relational interactions take place, between visitors and artworks, and with those invigilating. The distinction between dematerialised art and material artworks is troubled, especially if we consider an artwork to be what it does or can do, its ability to affect. Visitors encounter sculptures, paintings, time-based media and installations in galleries, and these ephemeral encounters both disappear and remain like moments in performance. As Hantelmann (2010) has stated, all of these forms of art can be considered as performative since they act on us and produce affects, some of which stick in our memories or leave traces in our bodies; certain qualities that can return and that are valued.

The exhibition *Group Show* was composed of immaterial or conceptual art objects, but objects that mattered nonetheless. Barad's 'agential realist ontology' (2007: 33) offers a theoretical framework for rethinking the relationship between discursive practices and material phenomena and proposes a causal, rather than a representational, relationship between 'words and things' (34). This enables her to consider the material nature of practices, including discursive and immaterial practices, and how theoretical concepts matter. For Barad, 'matter is not a thing but a doing', it is not mute or passive, 'immutable or the exclusive property of physical things' (151). 'Materiality is discursive' and 'discursive practices are already material' because they are performative, acting to 'reconfigur[e] the world' (151–2). Agential realism enables us to think of art as a 'material-discursive practice', producing 'phenomena' (141) or 'things-in-phenomena' (140) rather than stable things. Barad cites Ian Hacking, to suggest that what 'count[s] as real' and matters is what 'intervene[s] in the world to affect something else' and 'what affect[s] us' (Hacking cited in Barad, 141). 'Agency is not an attribute' of any individual subject or object, but is the dynamism in relational 'intra-activity', in ongoing articulations and entanglements between human and non-human bodies and among material and discursive practices. *Group Show* was made of an 'entanglement of intra-acting agencies', which were inseparable and not discrete; documents, artists, invigilators and visitors, aesthetic practices and media, gallery architecture and conventions, institutional systems and structures, the economic context and apparatus of the art world and market. An artwork materialised through a particular 'congealing of [these] agenc[ies]' (151) and boundaries between forms; the artwork and other phenomena were reconfigured relationally in an ongoing way.

'Language matters' (132), performance matters and matter matters. Immaterial and object-based art matter, they affect us and reconfigure each other. In Part 3 of *Group Show* texts are performed, gestures are made and 'speech acts' (Austin 1962: 150) on the visitors, causing them to look, to recall absent artworks or imagine one of many possibilisations. These immaterial, imaginary and fictional works count as real in Hacking's terms as they intervene in the (art)world and 'affect us'; enact meanings, produce affects and generate discourse.

I will conclude with one of Group Show's inspirations, an inspiration that anachronistically I saw after Part 3 was made: Yves Klein's *Surfaces et blocs de sensibilité picturale—Intentions picturales* (1957), the short film of which was included in the exhibition 'Invisible: Art About the Unseen, 1957–2012', at London's Hayward Gallery in 2012. In it Klein:

1. looks at a blank wall, gestures as though to a painting and turns round
2. paper in hand, he stands back from the white wall and admires this invisible artwork
3. he sits, looks around the empty gallery and out at the viewer.

Klein might claim to make present 'the highest quality' of 'immaterial pictorial sensibility' (cited in Rugoff 2012: 33) on the wall and in the gallery, producing aesthetic value there with his intention, gaze and gesture. But where does the work of art take place in this instance and where does the value or commodity reside: on the wall, with the artist Klein, in the ephemeral gesture with which he expresses himself, or in the viewer, who imagines and actualises the work as art, and holds traces of its affects? With this work, Klein values the non-physical and art manifested through social encounters or intra-actions between artist, space and viewer; non-representational art that is only stabilised as phenomena or sensations, perceived and realised in the audience's imaginations and discursive conversations.

References

2007 Agamben, G. *Profanations*, trans. J. Fort, New York: Zone Books.

1962 Austin, J.L. *How To Do Things With Words*, Oxford: Oxford University Press.

2007 Barad, K. *Meeting the Universe Halfway: Quantum Physics and the Entanglement of Matter and Meaning*, Durham: Duke University Press.

1977 Barthes, R. *Image, Music, Text*, trans. S. Heath, London: Fontana.

2016 Bel, J. 'Artist's Choice: Jérôme Bel/MoMA Dance Company'. Available online. https://www.moma.org/calendar/performance/1669. Accessed 16 March 2017.

1992 Benjamin, W. *Illuminations*, ed. H. Arendt, trans. H. Zohn, London: Fontana Press.

2009 Bernstein, R. 'Dances with Things: Material Culture and the Performance of Race'. *Social Text*, 101: pp67–94.

1984 Certeau, M. de *The Practice of Everyday Life*, trans. S. Rendall, London: University of California Press.

2009 Charmatz, B. '*Musée de la Danse*: Museum's Manifesto'. Available online. http://www.museede-ladanse.org/en/articles/museum-s-manifesto. Accessed 15 March 2017.

2014 Davies, S., *Table of Contents*. Available online. http://www.siobhandavies.com/work/table-contents/. Accessed 15 March 2017.

1998 Derrida, J. *Archive Fever: A Freudian Impression*, Chicago: University of Chicago Press.

2006 *Spectres of Marx: The State of the Debt, the Work of Mourning and the New International*, London: Routledge Classics.

1986 Foucault, M. 'Of Other Spaces', trans. J. Miskowiec, *Diacritics*, 16(1) Spring: pp22–7.

2010 Freeman, E. *Time Binds: Queer Temporalities, Queer Histories*, Durham and London: Duke University Press.

2010 Hantelmann, D. *How To Do Things With Art*, Zurich: JRP, Ringier and Les Presse du Reel.

2000 Hardt, M. and Negri, A. *Empire*, London: Harvard University Press.

2010 Lepecki, A. 'The Body as Archive: Will to Re-enact and the Afterlives of Dances', *Dance Research Journal*, 42(2): pp28–48.

2008 MoMA Catalogue Entry for T. Sehgal, *Kiss*, 2003. Available online. https://www.moma.org/collection/works/117525?locale=en. Accessed 15 March 2017.

MoMA Learning (n.d.) 'Tino Sehgal, *Kiss*, 2003'. Available online. https://www.moma.org/learn/moma_learning/tino-sehgal-kiss-2003. Accessed October 2017.

2014 Le Roy, X. 'Retrospective by Xavier Le Roy'. Available online. http://press.moma.org/2014/08/retrospective-by-xavier-le-roy/. Accessed 15 March 2017.

1973 Lippard, L. R. (ed.) *Six Years: The Dematerialisation of the Art Object 1966 to 1972*, New York: Praeger.

2012 Lütticken, S. 'General Performance', *e-flux*, 31. Available online. http://www.e-flux.com/journal/general-performance/. Accessed 4 March 2015.

2017 Marshman, T. 'Inspiring Dialogues: Community and Cross-generational Projects'. Available online. http://tommarshman.com/inspiringdialogues.html. Accessed 15 March 2017.

2001 Pine, J. and Gilmore, J. 'All the World's a Stage!', *FUTURE—The Aventis Magazine*, January: pp76–81.

1981 Ricoeur, P. 'The Narrative Function'. In J. Thompson (ed.) *Paul Ricoeur: Hermeneutics and the Human Sciences*, Cambridge: Cambridge University Press, pp274–96.

1985 *Time and Narrative*, trans. K. Blamey and D. Pellauer, Chicago: University of Chicago Press.

2004 *Memory, History, Forgetting*, trans. K. Blamey and D. Pellauer, Chicago: University of Chicago Press.

2012 Rugoff, R. *Invisible: Art About the Unseen: 1957–2012*, London: Hayward Publishing.

2009 Schneider, R. 'Remimesis: Feminism, Theatricality, and Acts of Temporal Drag'. In cross links e.V. and Akademie der Künste, *Re.Act.Feminism*, Berlin, 22–25 January 2009.

2011 *Performing Remains: Art and War in Times of Theatrical Re-enactment*, London: Routledge.

2011 Thornton, C. 'Theatre Collection Inaugural Artist in Residence: *Unfurl: A Work in Two Parts*'. Available online. http://clarethornton.com/unfurl/. Accessed 15 March 2017.

2004 Virno, P. *A Grammar of the Multitude: For an Analysis of Contemporary Forms of Life*, trans. I. Bertoletti, J. Cascaito and A. Casson, Los Angeles: Semiotext(e).

1987 White, H. *The Content of the Form: Narrative Discourse and Historical Representation*, Baltimore: Johns Hopkins University Press.

RE-ENACTING THE ARCHIVE: UNTIMELY MEDITATIONS ON THE USE AND ABUSE OF REPETITION

Pil and Galia Kollectiv

Friedrich Nietzsche crowned thirteenth century German emperor, Friedrich the Second, 'the FIRST of Europeans according to my taste' and placed him alongside Caesar and Da Vinci in a special category of great men. In a very Nietzschean way, there is, of course, a twisted root to this greatness. Historical figures in periods of upheaval, he argues, or men belonging to 'an age of dissolution' tend to be weak. Since at these times, 'happiness' is defined negatively as the resolution of the destabilising conflict rather than as a goal to achieve in its own right, these historical periods are incapable of producing men of worth. The exception, to which Friedrich the Second belongs, are those who learn to live with their inner and external conflicts, to accept the fact that they embody a divided and conflicted time, to be at peace with being at war. Nietzsche does not really expound on why he finds Friedrich to be a good example of such an individual.

It is unsurprising that Nietzsche, as a self-proclaimed philosopher of decadence, had a lot of interesting things to say about history and the power it holds over the now. His essay 'Untimely Meditations: On the Use and Abuse of History for Life' is a detailed anatomy of the way in which the present is constructed from the dead moments of the past through repetition, identification and re-enactment. He considers the correct relationship between history and present life and the various ways in which one can attach or distance oneself from the past. Too much history can become a burden, weighing one down and thus preventing a fully realised present, but to live unhistorically, only in the now, on the other hand, can only buy one a 'dumb beastly happiness' without all the complexities of the past: memories, regrets, secrets etc., and without the bitter-sweet knowledge of the inexorable march towards death.

What is more surprising is that Nietzsche does not spend more time dealing with the myth of his first European, Friedrich the Second, and the way in which this myth created ripples in time and was repeated and reenacted many times over the centuries following the emperor's death. If we follow Nietzsche's logic, it is perhaps because of the violent tension that such men of conflict carry inside them, unresolved, that they reemerge again and again, haunting the centuries to come after their death like a Victorian ghost story.

In the mid-thirteenth century, several written works were in circulation promoting an eschatological narrative centered around the fall of the papacy, the division of its vast property amongst the poor and the establishment of God's true kingdom on earth. One of the most popular manifestos of this spirit by the Joachite Brother Arnold of Swabia not only calculated the exact time of apocalypse, in the year 1260, but cast emperor Friedrich as the main protagonist in bringing down the evil pope. Although these narratives were common enough in that period, the relative strength of the emperor, who indeed fell out with the pope, meant that in Friedrich many had a tangible figure onto which they could project their dreams of liberation. The only problem in the procession of the new age was that Friedrich the Second died in 1250, ten years before the promised date. His sudden death, however, proved to be quite contentious, and ultimately served only to strengthen Friedrich's myth. Rumours and stories started to appear according to which the emperor had not died but simply fled the pope to a foreign country. A monk in Sicily reported seeing the emperor leading an army of knights into the hissing sea in Etna—itself an echo of an Arthurian myth. Generations of Germans never stopped believing that Friedrich would one day return from his hiding place to strike a fatal blow to the papacy.

And indeed nearly 35 years after the emperor's death, a host of Friedrichs started to appear in various towns. In 1284 one set up a court in Neuss and, supported by some princes in the weakened and divided German state, set out to challenge the rule of the king. Having caused quite a bit of anarchic trouble for the Catholic church and the king, this pseudo-Friedrich ended up burnt at the stake but still utterly convinced that he would rise again to usher the end of all times. Soon after, a second (or third?) Friedrich was re-incarnated in Utrecht, claiming to have been reborn out of the flames, only to be executed next. A rich folklore emerged around these deaths and the promise of the return of Friedrich continued to echo through centuries of German history, still resonating strongly up until the sixteenth century.

The beauty of the myth of Friedrich the Second is that with every return, every echo of the original, its power was only enhanced. Rather than reveal the initial eschatological promise of another world as a hollow one, the repetition and reenactment of the martyr's death served to extend its appeal. The relationship here is not between an original and weak, faded, copies, but between many instantiations of the same story without an origin (as the thirteenth century Joachite narrative is already quite unoriginal). What enabled the myth to be carried into (and past) the period of the reformation, its source of power, is located exactly in the mechanism of repetition. This repetition, like a structural netherworld that erupts into particular historical configurations here and there, is a reminder that while the history of the victors is written as a series of unique moments led through historical characters who are the embodiment of their time, the historical narrative of the meek derives its force exactly from endless, non-original repetitions.

The reason why the pseudo-Friedrichs were suppressed quickly and with violence is that historical repetition can be dangerous. The original Friedrich was cast into his role of greatness by sheer luck, by inheriting a 'natural' right from birth. But the act of his many returns pulls the carpet from under claims of the neutrality and natural order of contingency. Still backed by a powerful religious myth, Friedrich can be de-historicised, taken out of a particular temporality and his divine right divided equally amongst many. Every madman in the German countryside with sufficient theatrical zeal is a legitimate king. This is a correction to the accusation levelled by Karl Marx against the European bourgeois revolutions that borrowed their theatrics and language from past epochs. Marx writes that:

> The social revolution of the nineteenth century cannot take its poetry from the past but only from the future. It cannot begin with itself before it has stripped away all superstition about the past. The former [bourgeois] revolutions required recollections of past world history in order to smother their own content. The revolution of the nineteenth century must let the dead bury their dead in order to arrive at its own content.

But what if one looks back not to 'past history' as what has been but as what has not, to historical non-events, to promises unfulfilled and unrealised? What if the dead have never been buried in the past but, like emperor Friedrich, are still, centuries after their presumed death, hovering between the living and the dead, a ghostly echo of what never happened?

Guy Debord's *The Society of the Spectacle* presents a more comprehensive philosophy of repetition. Itself stitched together from fragments of Western philosophy, it deals with the duplication and reverberation of ideas and experiences through a technique of duplication. Debord's thesis number 190 is almost a replica of Nietzsche's earlier quote, applied to the field of contemporary art:

> Art in the period of its dissolution, as a movement of negation in pursuit of its own transcendence in a historical society where history is not yet directly lived, is at once an art of change and a pure expression of the impossibility of change.

Nietzsche's dialectical problem is acutely felt by the contemporary artist. Art in its modern phase is defined as a revolutionary democratic force, and its explicit mission is to overcome the schism between the inherently privileged and undemocratic art institution and the everyday. Some, like Allan Kaprow, wish to flood the museum with the vital force of the everyday, to *un-art* art, while others want every moment in the world to be experienced as art. But ultimately both types of contemporary artist succumb to

Nietzsche's diagnosis that those who act to heal a rift will only serve to repeat and deepen it—that is Debord's 'negation in pursuit of its own transcendence'.

But Debord's historical dialectics goes deeper than that. In thesis 180, he writes:

> The end of the history of culture manifests itself in two opposing forms: the project of culture's self-transcendence within total history, and its preservation as a dead object for spectacular contemplation.

In a post-Hegelian or post-critical world, we have already internalised the knowledge that culture is a product of its time. Instead of acting as a mark of liberation, of an end to the separation between life (historical material conditions) and culture, this understanding only serves to reinforce the frozen and timeless dominion of the spectacle. History becomes a representation, removed from its material basis but unable to transcend the repetitive logic of the spectacle. Or, as Debord puts it in the famous first sentence of *Society of the Spectacle*: 'All that once was directly lived has become mere representation'.

This is similar to the argument put forward in Theodor Adorno and Max Horkheimer's essay 'The Culture Industry: Enlightenment as Mass Deception':

> But what is new is that the irreconcilable elements of culture, art and distraction, are subordinated to one end and subsumed under one false formula: the totality of the culture industry. It consists of repetition. That its characteristic innovations are never anything more than improvements of mass reproduction is not external to the system. It is with good reason that the interest of innumerable consumers is directed to the technique, and not to the contents—which are stubbornly repeated, outworn, and by now half-discredited.

Culture as an industrial product can only reflect the logic of mass production, an aliened endless repetition of forms separated from each other only by the deceiving veneer of packaging. Because of this dialectical structure in which pseudo differences are absorbed by the totality of the capitalist culture industry, the movements of cultural products and moments in opposing directions (the birth of the new in a market dictated by the logic of seasonal, ever-changing fashions) is experienced only as repetition and not as radical breaks with what already exists.

If we follow Adorno and Horkheimer or Debord, it would appear then that repetition as a cultural phenomenon is nothing more than the structural logic of Debord's 'bad dream of modern society in chains'—the infinite nightmarish loop from which one is unable to wake up, like the metaphor hammered home over and over by recent Hollywood blockbusters such as *Inception* and *Edge of Tomorrow*. But in some ways, the dialectical analysis of these authors has not gone deep enough to reveal the contradiction that lurks at its base, namely that repetition itself can become a critical tool against the totality of the spectacle. It is true that repetition is a structural feature of the culture industry, populated by bad remakes and cover versions. But if art is meant to sit at the top of the ideological superstructure, to invert and distort the alienated, repetitive conditions of production (and everyday consumption), by being itself the concretisation of these conditions and not their idealised mirror image, a strategy of repetition can open up some critical avenues for art.

This is not the same as repetition as an aesthetic motif or structural element in a composition like in serial music, techno or sixties minimalist sculpture. These forms of art, although a reflection of conditions of industrial production (and much has been said about the relationship between minimalism in sculpture or techno in music and factory manufacturing techniques), simply elevate this structural repetition to another level and transform it to an aesthetic experience of beauty, play and intrigue. This elevation dissolves the critical tension inherent in repetition since a new element—

that of aesthetic appreciation—is added to the repeated structure, which therefore preserves the dominance of the new over the repeated, a spectacle of a transcendental representation of repetition if you will.

By contrast, a final example, from the field of cinema, demonstrates how the image and practice of re-enactment can produce an excess to this structure of newness. In Jean-Pierre Jeunet's *Alien: Resurrection*, the fourth sequel in the sci-fi series, Ellen Ripley, the protagonist of the franchise, is resurrected in a lab from an amalgam of human DNA and the DNA of the alien with which she had been 'pregnant' at the time of her death in the previous sequel. This resurrection, exactly like Friedrich the Second's, occurs several hundreds of years after the initial death, and like the Emperor's return, it too carries with it some additional weight from beyond the grave. In the film's most gripping scene, Ripley wanders into one of the laboratories on board the spaceship she wakes up on to discover the mutant bodies of the many previous unsuccessful attempts to resurrect her and separate her DNA from the alien's, no doubt in order to exploit the alien as a new type of weapon. Half humanoid and half exoskeletal, these odd creatures, pickled in respectable looking formaldehyde jars, are a reminder of the grotesque work of historical repetition. This is obviously a smart comment on the tendency of the culture industry to repeat itself with the best Fordist predictability: an industry that would rather spend a large budget on the fourth reiteration of an already established brand because current manufacturing logic dictates that demand (i.e. brand loyalty to a classic cult film) precedes supply. But the scene offers an even stronger critique of industrial repetition. The horrific in the lab scene amounts to the excess carried forward in the act of industrial repetition, an accumulation of the corporeal misery embedded in productive labour. By the time the new is eventually produced in Ripley, and this is the very essence of newness—a new type of a hybrid human-alien—it already carries within it this horrific accumulation of capitalist torture. It is not surprising, therefore, that the last scene of the film sees the alien Ripley approaching earth as a vengeful harbinger of death. The Victorian looking space lab is the archival site that absorbs this grotesque accumulation of re-enacted histories. Confronted by this perverse catalogue of mutations, Ripley cannot but take upon herself the role of horrific violence, encapsulated in these many generations of exploited bodies and now finally unleashed upon the world. If repeated newness and novel repetition are, as Debord and Adorno both claim, structural features of capitalism, they carry within them a dialectical potential that explodes, like a newborn alien, directly from the soft belly of contradiction. In the accumulation of infinite reenacted historical moments we can eventually have the dialectical transformation of quantity into quality. When Ripley and the alien approach the fertile hunting grounds of earth we know that this time death will be quite final, not just for our heroine, but for the world that has given birth to her.

References

2016 Adorno, T. and Horkheimer, M. *Dialectic of Enlightenment*, London: Verso Classics.

1995 Debord, G. *The Society of the Spectacle*, trans. D. Nicholson-Smith., New York: Zone Books.

1986 Marx, K. *Karl Marx: A Reader*, ed. J. Elster, Cambridge: Cambridge University Press.

1997 Nietzsche, F. *Untimely Meditations*, second edition, ed. D. Breazeale, trans. R. J. Hollingdale. Cambridge: Cambridge University Press.

Archive, repertoire and embodied histories in Nao Bustamante's performance practice

Amelia Jones

> Modern memory is, above all, archival. It relies entirely on the materiality of the trace, the immediacy of the recording, the visibility of the image. [...] No society has ever produced archives as deliberately as our own, not only volume, not only by new technical means of reproduction and preservation but also by its superstitious esteem, by its veneration of the trace.
>
> Nora 1994: 290

If the 'modern' era is obsessed with the archive—building histories everywhere through accumulated traces—then it is no surprise that even the human subject can be and has been understood as articulated through reiterated traces as *archival*. There is, in fact, a rich genre of visual art in which the practice itself could be said to be a performative repetition of the self through representational traces as or into an archive: by artists from Yayoi Kusama, Ulay, Urs Lüthi, Martha Wilson, Eleanor Antin and Lynn Hershman Leeson, to Renée Cox and George Chakravarthi. The trick in apprehending and understanding these works is in engaging with each representational character with an openness to the range of identifications and psychic valences proffered through the image (is it being performed ironically? or as a 'sincere' alternative self?).

As such, we can engage with representations of embodied selves to access a range of possible embodied histories.

Lynn Hershman Leeson, Roberta Breitmore, *External Transformation A*. Manipulated photograph, c. 1975.

From 1974 to 1978 Hershman Leeson (at the time simply Lynn Hershman), in particular, was far ahead of her time in directly enacting and compiling an archive of the self—specifically an archive instantiating her alter ego Roberta Breitmore as a legal person and psychological subject in American society through an accumulation of biographical traces. The Roberta Breitmore archive or archives, as a number of different versions exist, including a virtual one established in 2006 on the Second Life website, consists of dozens of attributes: collaged or manipulated photographs, bottles of Roberta's prescription medication, psychiatric notes and documents on her various 'conditions', checks from her checking account, dental records and a provisional California driver's licence, a classified newspaper ad she took out to find a companion and roommate, and numerous other documentary elements.

I assisted in the acquisition of one version of the archive for the Whitworth Art Gallery at University of Manchester while I was teaching there in 2008. The items listed here are all in that version, along with many other objects and images; other versions of the archive include some of the same items, and it is never clear which is the 'original' and which are 'copies'. In Second Life, scanned elements from the material archive line the halls of a virtual 'Dante Hotel', the rooming house 'Breitmore' briefly occupied. In addition, working with robotics later, in the 1990s and following, Hershman Leeson produced 'CyberRoberta' dolls, which had camera eyes and followed gallery visitors with their gazes, sending live video images to Hershman's website (Hershman Leeson 2015). Through these versions, Hershman dramatically and brilliantly illustrated the way in which the self in contemporary, bureaucratised first-world cultures can be seen as orchestrated from a reiterative performance of legal, psychological, visual, sartorial and other elements. As well, the character functioned as a visual and embodied enactment: Hershman had to act as Breitmore to solicit and pull these archival elements together, including renting Breitmore an apartment at the Dante Hotel in San Francisco and inviting a bevy of other feminists to masquerade as multiple Robertas.

Here I want to extend this trope of performative self-display as reiterative self-production to art practices that function as commentary on the self-as-archive, in particular via the work of US performance artist Nao Bustamante. Invoking numerous characters and personae, Bustamante enacts these through live or taped performances, produced through a systematic raiding of various modes of representation and self-construction: from art installations to live performances to appearances on television talk shows to participation in a reality television show to, very recently, a direct engagement of the last survivor and archives of materials from the Mexican Revolution. The artist continually spins herself out across a range of new media formats in a fashion reminiscent of Hershman Leeson's strategic engagement of a range of technologies and media for staging the self. In Bustamante's case, however, there is a strong emphasis on emotional and psychological nuances, rendering her as a melodramatic, cagey, hilarious, or exaggeratedly ethnographic artistic subject—a trickster with multiple guises.

My goal here will be both to examine the complexities of Bustamante's work, which has not been fully addressed in histories of performance and installation art, and to use her practice as a means for understanding how performance can be, and perhaps always is, itself a way of working across the live and the archive. This is achieved through myriad media as ways of commenting on how, in Nora's terms, we obsessively compile images and remnants through an archival impulse in order to substantiate ourselves and others in the present. Bustamante's putting into play a range of emotional/psychological 'selves', often excessively emotional and directly engaging our feelings in response, functions to negotiate or question the self or the artistic subject as unified and a coherent origin for meaning.

In this way I will interpret the case of Bustamante as productively confusing, in fact, the distinction between the textual archive and the embodied performance made by performance theorist Diana Taylor. In her 2003 book *The Archive and the Repertoire*, Taylor compellingly argued that the 'archive' is a Western and colonising mode of knowledge production, wherein shreds of former activities are deposited and viewed as static representations of past actions. The archival mode contrasts to the performative, bodily forms of knowledge of colonised others. For Taylor, their performances can 'function as vital acts of transfer, transmitting social knowledge, memory, and a sense of identity through reiterated [behaviours]', serving as political acts to mobilise a concept of the 'repertoire' as a 'nonarchival system of transfer' through which the past persists into the present via embodied experience (Taylor 2003: 2–3). Western colonisers constructed the archive in opposition to embodied practice and knowledge, separating 'the source of "knowledge" from the knower' and erasing former forms of embodied knowledge to establish themselves as new forces of power. In this system, performance, she argues, is 'an episteme, a way of knowing' (ibid: xvi–xvii), and one that can function against the grain of the Western logic of the archive.

In contrast to Taylor's binary, which Taylor herself notes is never clear cut or fully oppositional, as it must be endlessly constructed by the efforts of colonial repression, Bustamante's performance practice deploys a range of media, sites, and venues in order to cross over the archival and the performative. In so doing she both adopts the power of the coloniser (in Taylor's terms), opening up ways to write or articulate her own 'archival' performance histories in relation to a clearly constructed 'self', while clearly sustaining a vital relationship to embodied experience, even when infiltrating mass media television. The irony and humour of her performance practice works against the idea that she is proffering herself through performance as 'a way of knowing'— or at least we question what it is we can know in engaging with her work. Each of her projects does this in a different way and here I will explore several of them, in roughly chronological order, before ending at her explicitly archival 2015 project, *La Soldadera*. This exhibition functions in relation to both the 'archive' and the 'repertoire,' resulting in a multi-part installation on the last surviving 'Soldadera' (woman soldier) of the Mexican Revolution, roughly 1910–1920.

Bustamante's reiterative self-imaging works through a kind of sometimes slapstick, sometimes ironic exhibitionism in a range of media, each of which is mined for its particular capacities to stage or produce the 'self'. Importantly, Bustamante's practice exploits each media and venue to solicit the attention, love, and/or loathing of her audience members. In so doing her practice foregrounds the way in which the self is—as sociologist Erving Goffman noted in his 1956 book *The Presentation of the Self in Everyday Life*—'a *product* of a scene that comes off, and is not a cause of it. The self [is] a performed character [...] a dramatic effect arising diffusely from a scene that is presented' through a mode of 'collaborative manufacture' with all of the other selves it engages on the stage of the social (Goffman: 245). Not only is the self contingent on social codes, in some cases stereotypes, and the modes through which it is enacted, whether the body itself or the more obviously mediated screens of video or television; it is also contingent on the others who engage and condition its manifestations. If anything, Goffman's model points to the self *as an archive* of sorts: a compendium of articulations that come to their full meaning and significance through the reciprocal engagement of others.

Bustamante stages and restages herself in set-ups, whether as a 'live' performer or through video or by engaging mass media formats such as talk shows, in such a way that we become hyper-aware of her contingency and thus of our own. Furthermore, we relate to each new performative staging in different ways that highlight the specificities of the medium through which Bustamante is enunciating herself. In this way, we also become aware of how different modes of media work in relation to the enunciation of the self. Ultimately her work is about history (how we know the past, even in relation to the self or ourselves) as much as it is about different modes of enunciation that articulate the self. It is about the relationality of how selves and thus of how histories are 'made'.

These relational circuits of meaning are foregrounded in her *Indig/urrito*, a live performance I have viewed in its video documentation from a version done in San Francisco in 1992: a piece that explicitly negotiates the colonial histories Taylor's model examines. Motivated by the swell of celebrations of Columbus's 'discovery' of 'America' going on in the USA that year, she stated: 'I was told this year, that any artist of color must complete a performance based on 500 years of oppression in order to get funded, so this is my version.' Standing on stage scantily clad in some sort of

Nao Bustamante, *Indig/urrito*, 1992 performance at The Women's Building, San Francisco. Photo: D. Oviedo.

vaguely S/M garb, Bustamante challenges all of the white men in the audience to apologise (one version of the work is available online at Hemispheric Digital Video Library: see Hemispheric Institute 2015). José Esteban Muñoz describes her in the piece as a 'post-modern Aztec Priestess/Dominatrix' (Muñoz: 196). She straps what she narrates as a 'vegetarian and [...] no dairy' burrito, 'ordered [...] without chili out of consideration for the white folk' onto her crotch like a dildo, then urges the 'white men' or 'anyone with an inner white man' to come and nibble off a piece to show their contrition. Once the participants come to the stage, she commands that they kneel one by one, introduce themselves, and take a bite in an amusing and campy yet pointed polemic, a playful version of post-colonial, feminist, and queer critiques, and a skewed version of Catholic ritual: 'I would like to offer you a bite of my burrito to absolve you of the sin [as a] ritual purification'.

Bustamante's burrito-dick is humorously, but also pointedly, 'forced' on audience members, but in this case by invitation and only to the white male participants, or those 'with an inner white man' presumably struggling to break free, one of whom, in San Francisco, announced: 'I am a girl [and] Hispanic'. White masculinity is both aggressively essentialised in Bustamante's enunciation of white men's presumptive guilt in relation to her objectification as a Latina ('I would like to ask any white men who would like to take the burden of the last 500 years of guilt to report to the stage now...') and exposed as a construction. It is blamed for possession of phallic feminist body while at the same time potentially detached from its privileges and its related guilt. It is, after all, Bustamante's gorgeously zaftig body, her face made up and sporting a black wig, which wields this ridiculous, edible prick, crumbling into pieces as the various kneeling 'men' chomp or nibble off pieces. And in a stroke of inspiration, the self-proclaimed 'Hispanic girl' tries unsuccessfully to apply a condom at the end to keep its remaining ingredients intact and in coherent penis formation.

The humour in *Indig/urrito* is dark, cutting, relentless: as Bustamante says at one point, after strapping on the burrito-dick, 'anyone who's offended by this, I really encourage you to leave your body'. Her performance of this burlesque, post-colonial, phallic body, no matter how excessive and over-the-top, places us in a position of responsibility for her objectification: in the abstract, we all become members of the white, male dominated, middle class art world. The audience laughs uproariously; but there is pathos as well in the kneeling bodies of the 'white men', who attempt to present themselves with varying degrees of contrition, cleverness, and just plain bravado. *Indig/urrito* relies as well on Bustamante's will to self-expose and perform: her exhibitionism enables her to make us laugh. Her joke makes several crucial points: most obviously about arts funding initiatives and the ongoing legacy of colonialism, but also about which bodies are expected to bear witness to this nefarious colonial past—certainly not usually those of so-called white men. While few today would point the finger at actual contemporary people identified as 'white men' to hold them solely responsible for colonialism, by taking this deliberately extreme and tongue-in-cheek essentialising position, Bustamante makes it difficult for anyone in the audience to avoid taking some responsibility.

The idea of performing extreme stereotypes linked to particular identifications—in this case an exhibitionist, Latina body, queerly voluptuous and sexualised—links as well to a key strategy in Latino/a culture in the Americas, and in Chicano/a body art. In particular, both are sites where the *trickster* figure is a common trope—a mythical character of great intelligence and cunning who thwarts expectations, breaks the rules, and undermines conventions with subversive humour. Bustamante updates the trickster for modern media culture, queering it by attaching it to feminist humour and sexual innuendo. The trickster enables the infiltration and undermining of normative structures of subjectivity connected to the form of culture at hand—here the early 1990s white-dominated art and performance worlds, as well as the quadricentennial frenzy of 1992. She allows us to join her in the humorous yet cutting retelling of the aftermath of colonialism, which at the time was manifesting in part as postcolonial guilt, making us complicit but also generously embracing us as part of the (and her) revisionist story.

Histrionics and the comic/tragic 'female' subject

Bustamante's work, which often consists of newly reiterated modes of self-imaging, addresses key aspects of late capitalist subjectivity itself through codes and strategies wielded across a range of media and modes of performative or theatrical self-presentation: from those of stand-up comedy, harrowingly violent body art, and feminist, queer and postcolonial critique, to those of burlesque theatre and the television talk shows, reality television and soap operas. The crossing of genres complements the crossing of identifications and emotional states in Bustamante's work. The emotions expressed are often extreme, for example, in the video included in the installation piece *Neapolitan* from 2003–4, where she sobs in response to a classic Cuban melodrama, repeatedly rewinding and repeatedly bursting into tears histrionically. *Neapolitan* points to the way in which Bustamante's performance work in general functions through the tropes of nineteenth- and twentieth-century melodrama, which relies on a tension between realism and emotional excess. Jennifer Doyle's beautiful reading of the emotional excess of *Neapolitan* informs my interpretation: the tension between the realism of live art—its obdurate presentation of a body doing something—and the romanticism of emotional histrionics is brought to an extreme in

Neapolitan, while *Indig/urrito* plays on the sexualised potential of the burlesque (see chapter three of *Hold It Against Me: Difficulty and Emotion in Contemporary Art*).

Nao Bustamante, *Neapolitan*, 2003–4; installation at Yerba Buena Center for the Arts, San Francisco.

Such extremes, along with the confusion of extreme emotional registers, not to mention her appearance via alternative personae on talk and reality television shows, beg the question of whether or not Bustamante is 'sincere': whether she is 'acting', 'faking it', or 'real' in her feelings and portrayed identifications. In this way, Bustamante's practice highlights our confusion about *agency* in the televisual and internet age. In the end what her work points out is that, perhaps particularly in late capitalism—the age of reality television, talk shows, and social media—these distinctions are irrelevant. But also that, far from cancelling out our fascination with the emotions (of others, of ourselves), this confusion of distinctions makes us even more frantically seek out encounters with ever more extreme and heightened—even *histrionic*—emotional expressions, accelerated and multiplied across these media. We become aware that we seek the 'authentic' subject all the more now that it is patently impossible to secure an emotionally or psychologically stable 'subject' who preexists her representation.

'Histrionic' signifies a theatricality and narcissism beyond containment, and this implication is deliberate in my choice of the word. Coded as feminine, the term is attached most often to women, like the word 'hysteric'; it is also often aligned with the other, in terms of class and ethnic identifications, say, linked to the hyperbole American Wasps might perceive in Mexican soap operas. Histrionics are seen as fake, overly theatrical, or insincere: the word developed etymologically from the Latin 'histrionicus', pertaining to an actor (for the etymology of 'histrionic', see: *Online Etymology Dictionary* 2015). The term histrionic has also now lent its negative weight to an official mental illness, sanctified in recent editions of the *Diagnostic and Statistical Manual of Mental Disorders* (American Psychiatric Association 2013). 'Histrionic personality disorder' implies, according to the *DSM IV* (American Psychiatric Association 2000), a pattern of disingenuousness, or excessive attention-seeking behaviours and emotional outbursts, including 'inappropriate sexually seductive or provocative behavior' (see Chapter 16, 'Personality Disorders, Cluster B').

Bingo! Nao Bustamante's performative strategies revealed in one nutshell diagnosis! But of course, the trick in the diagnosis is to identify the 'fake' part of histrionics, the acting part: notably, even referring to a diagnostic term in analysing her work makes it clear how the artist confuses the performative self with the 'actual' self, who might have a psychiatric problem. If the expression of emotion were taken as 'real' or 'sincere', the person expressing it would not be identified with a pathology. The conundrum with histrionic personality disorder is that, by definition, it is excessive and so must be pathologised as insincere, in order to ward off its effects, to repel and contain the person experiencing such difficult emotions, to keep these feelings away from he who interprets. A diagnosis of pathology thus relies on an interpretation, the authoritative claim on the part of the 'expert' that the person studied is dishonest or *manipulative* or *insincere* in her expression of feelings. Because of this dynamic, the very idea of histrionics creates an appropriate frame with which to understand the complexities of a practice that springs from extreme actions, whether violent and/or funny and/or sexual, actions that directly assert and/or indirectly solicit complex responses.

Crucially, Bustamante makes it clear in the ambiguity and complexity with which she mobilises feelings that ultimately their shape, meaning, and social, political, and aesthetic significance is *up to us*. We are implicated in, and responsible for, the determination of emotional valence in the circuit of meaning and desire that is set forth by her performing body across these different media—whether experienced by us as 'Bustamante', an actual person, or as 'Bustamante', a performative and open-ended portrayal of a performance artist as trickster. This is a queer and feminist performative structure, opening meaning always already to otherness and to the durationality of that process that involves an exchange between subjects. Bustamante's practice thus points to the fact that living, not to mention interpreting art, is a never-ending process of negotiating attitude, meaning, and making sense of where we stand in relation to the performed body of the other.

The real and the fake: 'reality' as spectacle

The complexity of Bustamante's work resides in her capacity to exaggerate tropes of Latina excess and feminine, or arguably *feminist*, histrionics and queer sexual innuendo through obvious 'acting', while conveying doubt as to whether, indeed, she means what she does. The self is articulated in embodied ways as an iterated archive of gestures: neither fully 'repertoire' nor fully 'archive'. The doubt puts us in motion, making us aware of the range of emotions she solicits over the time in which we engage the work. Notably, we may productively begin to doubt our own self-image as one of coherence and agential stability.

Bustamante persistently confuses the usual categories forged around identities both in mainstream culture and within the rights movements by activating a *range of identifications*—sexual/gender, racial/ethnic, class-related, religious or spiritual, all of which compete and confuse the tendency to fix bodies in terms of one category or another. Also in 1992, for example, Bustamante appeared as a pathological 'exhibitionist' on one of the most successful talk shows of the era, the Joan Rivers Show. Bustamante documented and editorialised on the intervention in a video entitled 'Rosa Does Joan'. We see Joan Rivers, per her habitual demeanour, enthusiastically expressing support and sympathy to the presumably disturbed Rosa.

Nao Bustamante (to Joan Rivers' left) as 'Rosa' on the *Joan Rivers Show*, 1992; television still.

Rivers' response makes clear that Bustamante's Rosa, a riff on the idea of the performance artist *as an exhibitionist*, functioned as an ambiguous character who could be taken as sincere only within the talk show's array of spectacularised and hyperbolic 'selves' paraded through each episode, each of whom is taken at face value as a 'real' or 'actual' person. In this case, Rivers seems patently duped, but only if we take Rosa as a manipulative fake, which in fact Bustamante's website clearly encourages us to do, describing this intervention:

> Sandwiched between a binocular-toting Manhattan voyeur and a naughty public access TV actress, 'Rosa' described her lifestyle as a 'stunt exhibitionist'. Unbeknownst to the audience, the 'Rosa' character was mostly a fabrication, allowing Nao to roll out a sex-positive spin, mindtripping Middle America while those in the know basked in the televised glow of her performance art prank (see Bustamente 2015).

Indeed, the most productive element of seeing the footage 20 years later might be the sense of empathy we have with Rivers' desire to be supportive of this 'freak' exhibitionist, as well as a blurring of the lines we might experience, informed by Bustamante's subsequent two decades of performative projects, between what would be defined as a 'fake' exhibitionist or a 'real' one.

Taking advantage of influential media of the moment to stage her exhibitionism and excessive body and emotions, Bustamante confuses the boundaries between an 'acted' self and a 'real' or 'authentic' self, fully aligned with her intentionality and knowable as an artistic origin for the meaning of the work. Expressions of self and of emotion, as well as modes of deportment, dress, gesture, and feeling, are not just body specific, but medium specific and particular to their time: in 2012 the television talk show is still around, but is hardly seen as a cutting-edge medium of entertainment. These expressions are also explicitly intersubjective in how they come to mean: watching the archival video, we find as much to react to in Rivers' responses to 'Rosa' as we do in 'Rosa's' self-presentation: both *affect us* as viewers, both *produce us* in specific ways.

Exhibitionism, after all, is in the mind of the beholder. One person's show-off is another person's retiring wallflower. One person's tormented exhibitionist is another person's 'fake'. Or an art historian's 'performance artist'.

We may think we know where the range of feeling and meaning lies in any performance, but in the end the very idea of 'sincerity' as proving a particular cultural valence and as securing the meaning as 'truthful' or 'ironic' or even 'abusive' (key questions in the talk show format) is thrown into question by the slipperiness of every Bustamante-an locution. She is careful to perform flamboyantly, emotionally, and excessively and across various media from the live and mediated to the digital or televisual and mediated, but never in ways that settle into a simple emotional or political register. The ambivalence forecloses any desire to fix aesthetic, political, or emotional value in relation to any one of her performative expressions; and it calls us forth as potential viewers and interpreters, making us aware of our role in securing the repertoire of gestures that constitutes 'Bustamante' and her work.

In sum, Bustamante's practice points to the way in which we participate in the constitution of Bustamante as artist. Perhaps this is the ultimate living archive, comprised of both the artist's performative expressions, archived in the televisual or other media, and our embodied engagements, memories, and interpretations, sparked by her live performances or these enlivened remains. As Taylor ends up acknowledging about the archive and the repertoire, they are never actually oppositional, but rather overlap and intertwine:

> In between and overlapping systems of knowledge and memory constitute a vast spectrum that might combine the workings of the 'permanent' and the 'ephemeral' in different ways. Each system of containing and transmitting knowledge exceeds the limitations of the other. The live can never be contained in the archive; the archive endures beyond the limits of the live.
>
> Taylor 2003: 173

Bustamante's use of her own embodied self and the range of new media formats speaks directly to this recognition. Her persona and agency are never fully contained by these formats, but her live self-presentations endure through them. This is our access to her iterative and never fully coherent performance of the self as art.

Sincerity is the new radical

Updating her use of mass media, Bustamante perfected the trickster, and brought the ambivalence necessarily introduced by claims of sincerity that are simultaneously histrionic, excessive, and explicitly exhibitionist, performative, and theatrical, to an extreme in her participation in the 2010 reality television show, *Work of Art: The Next Great Artist*. In this project, Bustamante infiltrated reality television as a new mode of self-portrayal, deploying the format and ultimately its offshoots as an extended artistic archive of a parodic version of the 'artist'. During the time in which the show was taking shape and being aired, I was concerned that her attempt to infiltrate such a debased medium with its claim to document 'reality' would be instantaneously incorporated into the circuits of late capital: the genre could not be farther from how people actually make art and interact with others off-camera. J. Paul Getty Research Institute consulting curator Glenn Phillips also expressed his trepidation on his blog post, 'Sincerity is the New Radical: Bravo's *Work of Art*', albeit using more traditional concepts of art practice than I would:

> For most artists and arts professionals, the show was a harrowing prospect—how can the artistic process and the complex world of contemporary art be reduced to a game show? Artists spend weeks, months, sometimes even years developing ideas for work, so how can we judge their abilities based on what they can do in twelve hours?
>
> Phillips 2010

Nao Bustamante on the Bravo website for *Work of Art: 'It's a pancake poodle party!'*, accessed 17 September 2012.

As I suspected, and not surprisingly, given the way in which her self-enactments confuse definitions of media, behaviour, and the boundaries between 'reality', 'art', and 'performance', once the show started airing, Bustamante was demonised as the 'oddball' and was one of the first to be dropped from the show.[1]

But to a large degree, I think my concern missed the point: I wanted to take care of the 'person' Bustamante, who by that time I knew, though not well, as a friend. But the Bustamante on *Work of Art* was a performative function, a repertoire of gestures pointing to something in me, in us, in the world that embraces 'reality television' as a delivery of 'actual' people. As all of the remnants and remains from Bustamante's participation in *Work of Art* attest, the artist's willingness to play the 'fool' in a classic, trickster role ultimately exposed the limits of those who 'rejected' her, rather than proving her own inability to make art or her vulnerability to the machinations of late-capitalist television. There are many traces of the artist's participation that can be accessed today—precisely, in fact, through the massive archive that is the internet. These have a disconcerting, potentially destabilising effect on our assumptions about difference or the compatibility between 'great art' and 'reality television'.

For example, the Bravo *Work of Art* website hosted some very intriguing images posted in Bustamante's scrapbook, all of which propose just the kind of confusion of categories, of emotional registers, and of the boundaries between 'archive' and 'repertoire' which I have identified here as key to her practice. The beginning image shows her blowing paint on a horizontal surface like a pre-school version of Jackson Pollock with the caption 'I love colour'. We move on to a picture where she holds a miniature poodle under each arm, holds a plate with pancakes, and wears a party hat with the caption 'It's a pancake poodle party!', and images of her actually looking at or showing works such as *Death Bed* (the self portrait work that 'put me in the competition', as the caption states). This is an archive of the 'self' orchestrated and captioned by the artist, but one proffered on the screen of the corporate staging of 'artist'.

And other remainders provide an ongoing intervention into the premises of the show, and of reality television in general. More dramatically funny in classic Bustamante style, a scrappy video posted on Youtube is described as having been 'prised' from Bustamante's presumably shy and unwilling hands and the caption further notes that the clips were taken from her audition for *Work of Art* (Bustamente 2015a). The video begins with voices singing 'Nao, Nao, Nao, Nao, Nao, Nao, Nao,' to the artist twirling in a white dress (a *quinceañera* debutante? a bride?). Then twirling in black chiffon saying to the cameraperson or us as later viewers, 'I want to make sure you get the swishing of my pantyhose'. We then see her seated on a bench outside, and she states to us (presumably the tape is aimed at those adjudicating the contestants for the show):

> I know what you're thinking. You're thinking, maybe Nao's a little too established for this show [...] a little too relatively well known [...] She'll try to turn this into the 'Nao show'; [...] she's going to try to control people, she's going to try to get other people to make her art for her. It's OK. I'm a team player. I'm a team player. I might be the team captain, but I'm a team player.

She then proceeds to eat a burrito, noting that she is starving because she just came off doing a serious workout with 'Heather the Hammer'.

There is a brief cut of her rolling on the floor in her black chiffon saying 'I'm an object', and then the video cuts to her standing next to a car in a park in the blazing sun. She is speaking to 'Heather the Hammer' (Cassils, formerly Heather Cassils, a genderqueer bodybuilder, trainer, and performance artist):

> Bustamante: I think I need to dial it down a little from camp [...] I want it to be our natural personalities, just dialled up, expanded a little, so that it reads on camera. I'm still trying to adjust my own dial.
>
> Cassils: Is this an ironic piece? Or is this genuine?
>
> Bustamante: Well, I think sincerity is the new radical, so—always genuine, always sincere.

A male voice, presumably the cameraperson, asks her to repeat the phrase and she does in several different versions.

The video cuts to Bustamante in a skintight lycra catsuit, ready to work out, talking to Cassils: 'I've heard that black is really slimming. [...] This is a way to keep my self-esteem up'.

After a pep talk from Cassils, the video cuts to Bustamante wincing, 'I'm getting a cramp', and then to her 'working out', which includes a segment of her doing an upward dog yoga movement, viewed from between Cassils' legs. Opening her mouth and extending her tongue in physical effort, the resulting

Nao Bustamante (with Cassils), 'audition tape' for Bravo *Work of Art* show, 2012; video still.

image implies she is giving her trainer a blow job. The last segment of the video shows her dancing up a hill behind her pied piper Cassils, who shouts inspirational instructions. Bustamante's beloved dog Fufurufu enters the frame, trotting behind her with a natural energy that makes Bustamante's efforts seem laboured and even more humorous.

In the video, Bustamante and her collaborators pre-stage the ridiculous, excessive character that Bustamante is to become on *Work of Art*. The studied fake sincerity Bustamante conveys in her dialogue with Cassils ('I think sincerity is the new radical. So—always genuine, always sincere') turns the notion of authenticity inside out. The statement directly challenges our desire to determine the artist's 'true' intentions and, by extension, our desire to discern who people 'really' are through late-capitalist media formats such as reality television.

In asserting to Cassils that *sincerity is the new radical*, Bustamante sums up the paradox of a claim that 'sincerity' is 'radical': for, don't we have to determine first whether she is being 'sincere' in her claim that to be 'sincere' is radical? Is her claim for sincerity 'sincere'? Is she making fun of us, art and performance critics who tend to validate works on the basis of whether they are 'radical' or not? Or is she making fun of the judges who determined the *Work of Art* contestants, supposedly headed by the executive producer, Sarah Jessica Parker, the actress who starred in the glamorous *Sex in the City* television series (1998 to 2004)? In the end, it is difficult to take at face value a gyrating figure in a catsuit dancing up a weed-covered hill behind an enthusiastic, apparently serious, and completely buff personal trainer, followed by a bouncing miniature poodle. And yet, maybe one of Bustamante's points is that a clearly theatrical enactment of a claim of sincerity in a culture of fakery (reality television) is what is radical. Fake sincerity is the most radical of all. Or sincere fakery. Far from proving she 'really is' sincere, Bustamante's claim of 'sincerity' implies a fakery or disingenuousness in the very statement. We become increasingly confused if we follow Bustamante deep into the rabbit hole of her 'logic'. The paradox is in the necessary statement of a positive that is a lie, which then becomes the 'truth'. Given the distorted fun-house of anti-logical claims of "fake news" currently being purveyed by the sham leadership of the Trump administration in the US to deflect the continual exposure of compromising facts being sent their way, such a gesture seems particularly radical in 2018.

'Sincerity is the new radical' as a statement points to the power of the marketplace of 'ideas', crystallised by the extreme consumerism of Bravo and its 'art' show, to determine meaning and value, whether aesthetic or political. 'Radical' after all has become a term of both aesthetic and political valence in art criticism since the early twentieth-century avant-gardes made their mark. This single claim, paired with the ludicrous yet also poignant imagery of the video, with Bustamante claiming her international fame, and willingly subjecting herself to workout procedures in the most ridiculous of outfits in a public space, exposes as patently absurd our desire to define value on the basis of 'beauty' or 'sincerity', on the basis of identifying the tone, attitude, and even the expressive and original *meaning* of the artist. *Deathbed* makes the ultimate charade of attempts to differentiate between sincerity or 'truth' and fakery. There is never a moment when we 'know' feeling, whether the artist's or our own. There is never a moment when we can 'know' meaning, or precisely pinpoint the tone of an expression (as 'sincere', 'fake', or otherwise). Or when we can 'know' the person or artist with whose expressions we engage.

No matter the medium, the archive and repertoire intertwine. All subjectivity is both embodied and representational, both always truthful and never coherent or fully knowable.

As the entire *Work of Art* project and its offshoots exemplify, the brilliance of Bustamante's practice is to reshape the very idea of self-imaging that has for so long been a key strategy among 'sincere' purveyors of identity politics as a way of becoming 'visible' or gaining a voice, but also among postmodern critics of representation: for example, Cindy Sherman's self-imaging strategy, which unhinges the idea of a preexisting 'true' self by endlessly masquerading as other. Bustamante reiterates herself as a kind of ongoing performative archive, joining the 'repertoire' of her lived self with the 'archive' of all of these means by which she is conveyed to us today, giving us at the same time the possibility of engaging her through a range of emotional and intellectual responses, while ultimately pointing to the impossibility of knowing artistic subjectivity or the meaning of a performance or of art, in part by confusing the 'ironic' and the 'sincere'. This is also the impossibility of knowing FINAL value, whether aesthetic or political in relation to any performance or any body/subject.

The person who engages Bustamante's body/self just has to be brave enough to accept confusion, and even to turn it into a sharp-edged sense of political and aesthetic possibility. To refuse the fixity of determinations, whether aesthetic or political. To embrace the openendedness of the performative self as the potential to make us think.

Conclusion: 'Serious' history—La Soldadera and the new medium of 'exploded cinema'

In 2015, Bustamante opened *La Soldadera*, an odd and wonderful show at the Vincent Price Art Museum in East Los Angeles. If Bustamante's practice up to this point has involved engaging live performance, video, installation, talk show and reality television formats, then *La Soldadera* explicitly engages the archive: both stemming from and creating archival experience. As such, *La Soldadera* epitomises what an artist can do in and with the archive. Through this show, Bustamante enacts herself in the role of artist as historian, artist as archivist and artist as curator, which is not to diminish the instrumental roles of the show's actual curator, Jennifer Doyle, and the Museum's Director and show facilitator, Karen Rapp, in working closely with Bustamante to make this complex exhibition happen.

Nao Bustamante, Kevlar © dresses and film in *La Soldadera* installation, 2015; Vincent Price Art Museum, Monterey Park, California.

Bustamante's installation is a hybrid between art and ethnography, brilliantly questioning the longstanding boundaries between the two, boundaries that normally serve to privilege male/European/'art' modes of production over female/non-European/'craft' modes. In Taylor's terms, it enacts the historical past through both explicitly archival means and explicitly embodied repertoires: those of the original historical actors in question, the artist, and we who engage the complex installation. Bustamante works as curator/filmmaker/artist in relation to several key archives of photographs and information relating to the Mexican Revolution (c. 1910–1920), in close collaboration with Doyle, who facilitates and creates the space, intellectual and creative, for Bustamante to implement her archivally-based multi-part installation, part exhibition, part work of art, as well as a teaching tool.

La Soldadera includes a number of hybrid works such as a film in which women dressed in Bustamante's designed Victorian-style Kevlar dresses enact a script from a Sergei Eisenstein film on the Mexican Revolution that was never made. Among other things, the film shows the role of women in both fighting and sustaining the army as a community. *La Soldadera* also includes several of the Kevlar dresses, one of which is riddled with bullets from a period gun; as well as a video of Bustamante working with a gun collector and shooting the dress to test its density; and photographs and archival elements in vitrines with commentary; and most astonishingly, *Chacmool*, a piece that incorporates a film of the oldest woman in the world, Leandra Becerra Lumbreras, a 127-year-old

Nao Bustamante, vitrine with peacock embroidery by Leandra Becerra Lumbreras and archival photographs from the University of California, Riverside Special Collections.

veteran soldadera from the Mexican Revolution, whom Bustamante met and filmed just before her death in March 2015.

It is *Chacmool* that most directly and productively merges the archive with the repertoire, presenting a historical figure on film, but in such a way that she can only be seen and understood when the viewer, in order to access the sound and visual components, actively engages with the structure of the piece. The film of Lumbreras banging on a drum and seated in a position reminiscent of the Mayan 'Chacmool' figure, hence the title of the piece, is presented in a set-up involving an antiquated embroidered stool, ad-hoc headphones with wooden earpieces and a small screen. The film can only be viewed by sitting on the stool to look through

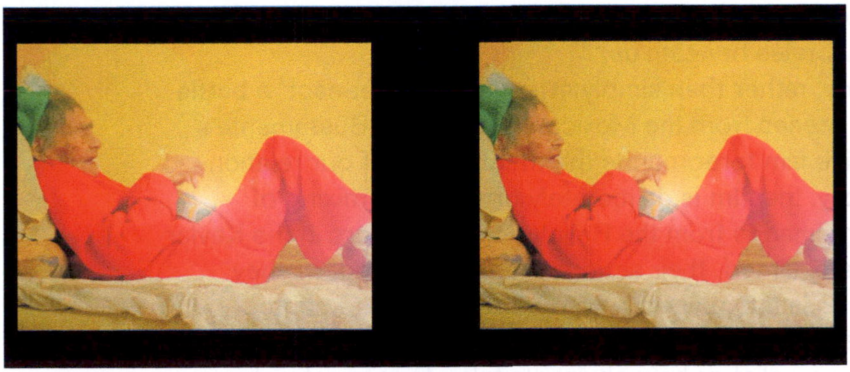

Nao Bustamante, still from film of Leandra Becerra Lumbreras, then the oldest woman in the world, 2015; installed in *Chacmool*, part of *La Soldadera*, Vincent Price Art Museum, Monterey Park, California.

a viewfinder, which necessitates wearing the headphones dangling in between. Two guavas fragrantly rot on a wire hanging just below one's head. The installation provides a multi-sensorial and fully embodied experience: the stool vibrates with Lumbreras's drumming and her lively but ancient figure, now indelibly gone, actively haunts our present. Through this haunting, we inhabit to some degree the distant event of the Mexican Revolution, relating to a historical figure who participated in it.

La Soldadera exemplifies the strategy of using history itself to open up queer, anti-colonialist, and feminist questions of the vulnerable yet strong body in a violent situation, and of using multi-media means to present a range of material relating to this epic historical event. Through its historical specificities, the work dramatically counters the currently fashionable tendency in art practice and discourse to trace broad connections across global cultures with little attention to local detail and historical particularities. If we call this trendy kind of work superficial and horizontal, as skimming the surface of a range of often unrelated cultural expressions, we have to say that *La Soldadera* is deep: Bustamante has delved vertically into a complex and specific historical moment in order to produce a highly sophisticated and performative commentary on the erasure of women in history and the role of women in wartime. The archive is not deployed to 'illustrate' pre-determined political or artistic points. The archive is both honoured (photographs of the war are in vitrines and provide background to the film) and brought to life as a multi-part situation in which the visitor immerses herself. This includes the Kevlar dresses, which are full-sized and stand before us, as if waiting to be inhabited. The *Chacmool* piece perhaps is the end point of our immersion: we are literally captivated by this ancient woman who drums out her stories of revolution and calls us into her visual, aural and odorous regime of camaraderie. Even our bodies feel it, as the seat vibrates beneath us.

Similarly, rather than simply attempting to 'reenact' a battle or series of scenes from the Mexican Revolution, Bustamante's semi-narrative film foregrounds the theatricality of our relationship to history: the film is deliberately crude in its mixing of documentary images from the Revolution and actors in the Kevlar dresses clearly filmed, their actions highly contrived, as they perform the Eisenstein script appropriated by Bustamante. As such, the film makes clear the constructedness of any effort, no matter how realist or how obviously fake, to reconstruct history through theatrical reenactments. Furthermore, Bustamante suggestively calls the installation 'exploded cinema', as it moves

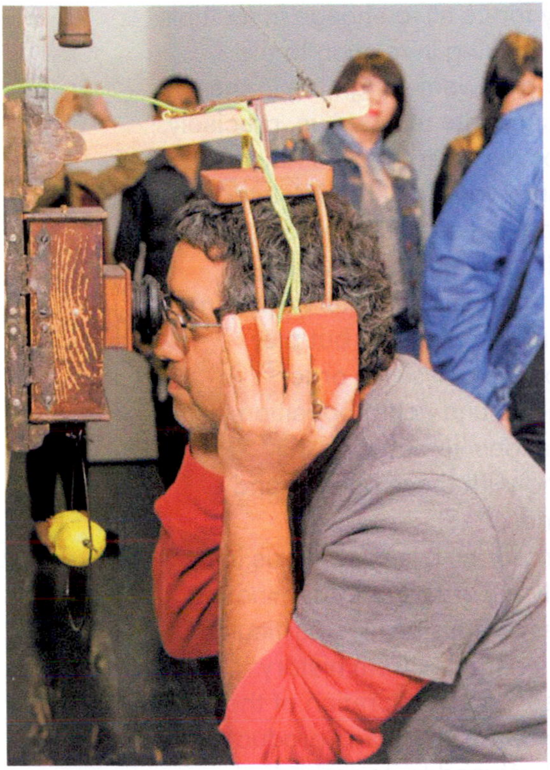

Nao Bustamante, *Chacmool* with viewer; installed in *La Soldadera*, Vincent Price Art Museum, Monterey Park, California.

abruptly and, in this case, with apparent crudeness of technique and some humour away from the seriousness and minimalist aesthetics of the Expanded Cinema movement of the 1970s (Bustamante explained this to me at the opening of the exhibition in May 2015). The entire show can be viewed in this way as 'exploding' beyond the frames of the film itself: it is as if the Kevlar dresses danced out of their role in the narrative, as did the elements in the vitrines.

As British historian R.G. Collingwood argued in his 1946 book *The Idea of History*, we can only 'do' history or understand the past by reenacting 'past thought'. He answers the question 'how does the historian discern the thoughts which he is trying to discover?' with the answer, 'by re-thinking them in his own mind' (Collingwood: 215). While Bustamante clearly does not propose to deliver the original thought of Lumbreras or anyone else from this historical period, she essentially re-does the history but through the means of a queer feminist anti-colonialist performance practice. Unlike Collingwood, she is not reenacting this history with the pretence that she can then deliver its truth to us. To the contrary, she is not presuming to inhabit or to theatrically render the body of Lumbreras or any other soldadera.

Rather, she provides the opportunity for us all to engage in multiple levels of meaning-making as history-making in relation to the complex multilayered histories relating to women fighting in the Mexican Revolution. In this way, Bustamante reminds us, precisely, that we are involved in these histories and that they are never static, final, or 'true'. Her method of interweaving archival, interview, and phenomenological elements nonetheless also reminds us that our historical reconstructions of the past should engage with the specificities, often archival, sometimes in interview form, of these histories. We must not just make things up but play imaginatively across what is given to us archivally in order to reconstruct the past. This is a thrilling and rich proposition, essentially performing a complex relationship between our embodied experience today, engaging with these objects and sounds and spaces, and these histories.

As such, Bustamante's endpoint for now is drawing us into a hugely poignant but also acerbically funny space for ruminating on how we relate ourselves to the past, in this case, a particular group of women who have largely been erased from history. *La Soldadera* and Bustamante's career-long exploration of the performative self as a whole instantiate the sharp and productive role the archival can play for an artist attuned to its embodied or 'repertoirial' resonances for the present.

Notes

1 See Jon Caramanica's rather unflattering account of Bustamante's stint on the show (Caramanica 2010 and 2010a).

2013 American Psychiatric Association *Diagnostic and Statistical Manual of Mental Disorders*, fifth edition, Arlington, VA: American Psychiatric Association.

2000 *Diagnostic and Statistical Manual of Mental Disorders*, fourth edition, Arlington, VA: American Psychiatric Association.

2015 Bustamente, N. 'Rosa Does Joan'. Available online. http://www.naobustamante.com/art_rosadoesjoan.html. Accessed 17 June 2015.

2015 nao_episode1.mov. Available online. http://www.youtube.com/watch?v=RZYpTIDfw8I&feature=endscreen&NR=1. Accessed 8 June 2015.

2010 Caramanica, J 'The Monitor: Performance Art Has its TV Moment'. *Los Angeles Times*. Available online. http://articles.latimes.com/2010/jul/18/entertainment/la-ca-monitor-20100718 Accessed 14 June 2015.

2010a 'Could Nao Bustamante be the "Villain" on Work of Art?' On *All Over Albany*, interview with Nao Bustamante. Available online: http://alloveralbany.com/archive/2010/06/10/could-nao-bustamante-be-the-villain-on-work-of-art. Accessed 8 June 2015.

1956 [1946] Collingwood, R. G. *The Idea of History*, Oxford: Oxford University Press.

2013 Doyle, J. *Hold It Against Me: Difficulty and Emotion in Contemporary Art*, Durham: Duke University Press.

1959 [1956] Goffman, E. *The Presentation of the Self in Everyday Life*, Garden City, NJ: Doubleday.

2015 *Hemispheric Institute Hemispheric Digital Video Library*. Available online. http://hidvl.nyu.edu/video/000509510.html. Accessed 17 June 2015.

2015 Hershman Leeson, L. 'Tillie and CyberRobereta'. Available online. http://www.lynnhershman.com/tillie-and-cyberroberta/. Accessed 17 June 2015.

2006 Muñoz, J. E. 'The Vulnerability Artist: Nao Bustamante and the Sad Beauty of Reparation'. *Women and Performance*, 16(2).

1994 Nora, P. 'Between Memory and History: *Les Lieux de Mémoire*', trans. M. Roudebush. In G. Fabre and R. O'Meally (eds) *History and Memory in African-American Culture*, New York: Oxford University Press, 284–300.

2015 *Online Etymology Dictionary*. Available online. http://www.etymonline.com/index.php?term=histrionic. (Accessed 14 June 2015).

2010 Phillips, G. 'Sincerity is the New Radical: Bravo's Work of Art'. Available online. http://blogs.getty.edu/iris/sincerity-is-the-new-radical-bravos-work-of-art/. Accessed 8 June 2012.

2003 Taylor, D. *The Archive and the Repertoire: Performing Cultural Memory in the Americas*, Durham: Duke University Press.

The patina of performance: documentary practice and the search for origins in The Wooster Group's Fish Story

Andrew Quick

> Origin is not [...] discovered by the examination of actual findings, but is related to their history and their subsequent development.
>
> Walter Benjamin 1998: 46

> When we saw the Geinin film it was just too good.
> It was very like us in our upstairs room at the garage. [...]
> It was like [...] God it was like looking into the future.
>
> Elizabeth LeCompte in Quick 2007: 58

Stage markings

I am looking at the floor of The Performing Garage in SoHo, New York, the home of The Wooster Group. The Group is rehearsing *Hamlet* and a recording of Richard Burton's voice booms in the theatre. Shakespeare's verse, here a staccato rhythm, seemingly whirls around the space, as words are wrestled with and sometimes wrecked in an attempt to master the text. The floor draws my eye because it is flecked with white lines and faintly coloured markings. Some of these marks appear to be much older than others as the striations are faded and broken, the dark floor, itself a texture of various shades of black, breaking apart the definition that the lines and marks once laid forth. Sometimes lines and marks overlap or run parallel to each other, creating textures and patterns that reveal how certain areas of the floor have been the object of much of the company's focus. Such patterning draws my attention to what appears to be the sites of frenetic activity, positions on the stage, that the company has returned to again and again across the history of their productions that began in 1975, some 40 years ago.

Hamlet (2007/2012) at The Performing Garage. Video still courtesy of The Wooster Group.

These marks, I surmise, are indicators of floor positions for parts of the set for a multitude of The Wooster Group's productions. What is fascinating is where the markings coalesce, reflecting the repeated patterning of placed scenography: walls, partitions, screens, raised platforms, spikes for performers, rakes and entrances and exits and so forth. Such marks, I propose, are archival. They signal the multiple scenographies that have populated The Group's working space across decades of performance making. I wish to discuss these remnants of a stage marking, a kind of stage writing or writing the stage, that, I suggest, form a key component of what might be considered the patina of their work.

The Wooster Group began by working within the organisational set up of The Performance Group in New York, which had been established by Richard Schechner in 1967. As has been well documented in other publications (Savran 1988, Aronson 2000, Callens 2004), The Group, under the leadership of director Elizabeth LeCompte, moved away from Schechner's focus on ritual and the emotional and psychological state of the performer as a mode of communication to situating the stage activity within what she later called an overarching 'architectonic structure' (Kaye 1996:

255). Within this structure material is encountered and negotiated, including the mediating mechanisms of performance itself (dramatic texts and scenographic components and technologies), as well as the wider mediums of communication experienced in everyday life (television, sound, video, digital images etc.). Equally significant, it also includes the performer and her/his biography and, crucially, the history of The Group's work (Quick 2007). Across the years, a series of iconic dramatic texts have consistently come under Group's scrutiny. These have included Arthur Miller's *The Crucible* (1953), Anton Chekhov's *Three Sisters* (1901), Eugene O'Neill's *The Emperor Jones* (1920) and *The Hairy Ape* (1922), Gertrude Stein's *Doctor Faustus Lights the Lights* (1938), Jean Racine's *Phèdre* (1677), William Shakespeare's *Hamlet* (1603) and *Troilus and Cressida* (1602), Tennessee Williams' *Vieux Carré* (1977) and most recently Harold Pinter's *The Room* (1957). There is not space here to do justice to the complexity and virtuosity of The Group's work although there are a number of publications that provide compelling accounts of the company's history, their methods of production and contextual analysis (see Savran 1988, Callens 2004, Quick 2007).

Anybody who has witnessed a number of The Wooster Group's performance works over the years can see how the company reuses particular scenographic components again and again (these include platforms, TVs (analogue and digital flat screens), rails, tables, rakes, moving partitions, the skeletal framework that seemingly ghosts the proscenium stage, etc.). Equally important is the company's repeated use of props and costumes across different performances: during the rehearsals of *Hamlet* I often witnessed cast members raiding the costume rails of past works for fabrics and garments as they built up the finely layered 'look' of the final production.

It is possible to see this raiding of the materials accumulated across past performance works solely as a pragmatic endeavour. Performance making at the scale that The Wooster Group pursue is undoubtedly a costly process and the recycling of scenographic elements is one obvious response to this challenge. This reusing of scenographic approaches and materials may also, a cynic might observe, be the result of a dearth of ideas: the company returns, obsessively, to the same themes, methodologies and scenographic solutions across the works that they produce because they inhabit a particular aesthetic and thematic prison. Consequently, The Group's use of scenography, as indicated in the patterns on the floor of the Performing Garage, becomes a signature that expresses limits as much as it allows for recognition. Indeed, companies that make work over a number of years, for example, Forced Entertainment in the UK, sometimes find that they are criticised for the ways in which their performances appear formulaic. Repetition in these instances would seem to reflect limitation rather than expression. The marks on The Performing Garage floor, looked at from this point of view, are seen as the consequence of a compulsive mining of the same ground, one that signals a stylistic replaying of ideas, now fading like the lines on the stage, that have lost their currency and originality.

Of course, any company or artist that makes work over a period of time develops tropes that become the signature of its/their work and it is perhaps inevitable that one slips into the error of interpreting such tropes solely as a form of stylistic recycling. However, in my staring at the floor during this rehearsal of *Hamlet* I am moved to consider that what might be at stake here is not a question of aesthetics embodied in the form of stylistic repetition, but rather that repetition itself might be part of The Group's larger enquiry. After all, what I am witnessing is The Group's response to an already existing performance of *Hamlet*, directed by John Gielgud in 1963, with Richard Burton taking the central role, which was recorded on film at the Lunt-Fontanne Theatre in New York in 1964. In the rehearsal room The Group are engaging with an already existing document of a past performance, in the form of digitally manipulated projected film, and incorporating it directly into the scenographic organisation of the piece they are developing before me. Burton's *Hamlet* appears to be a kind of ghost in the machine that haunts The Group's attempt to stage Shakespeare's text and I cannot help but speculate that this haunting of past performances of *Hamlet* probably affected Burton as well. He was, after all, being directed by Gielgud who had appeared in iconic versions of the play in the 1930s, one of which toured to New York in 1937. Equally significant, Burton's version was also the product of a drunken wager with Peter O'Toole who then performed *Hamlet*, directed by Lawrence Olivier, for The National Theatre's production in London in 1963, a year before Burton's endeavour. Olivier, of course, had played the role in a number of productions including the film version that he directed in 1948. In this way, it is impossible for any performance of *Hamlet* to be an isolated event: each exists in relation to past and future versions; each is in some way connected to the other. For an excellent analysis of the archival dynamics at play in *Hamlet*, see Callens (2009) and especially Worthen (2008).

The marks on The Performing Garage's floor also remind me of the interconnectedness of The Wooster Group's work, how each piece is built on the foundations of previous or earlier works. In this sense, as exemplified in their version of *Hamlet*, any piece created by The Group can be seen as a living document that incorporates crucial elements of past work. This not only includes the materials of set and costume that are recycled across different performances, but also the embodied practices that are pursued by The Group's performers and collaborators, many of whom perform and work across a number of pieces as members of its ensemble. Kate Valk, for example, has been with The Group since the late 1970s and has performed and collaborated on every work since. One enduring trope in her practice has been her use and engagement with blackface, first used in *Route 1 & 9* (1981), then in *L.S.D. (...Just the High Points...)* (1984) and finally in The Group's rendition of O'Neill's' *The Emperor Jones* (1993). Valk has observed how she uses blackface as a performance mask, one that allows a certain letting go of the actor's ego across a number of productions (Quick 2007: 158–62). Of course, these practices, which can be traced across the number of pieces any particular performer appears in, are marshalled by the director Elizabeth LeCompte, who has been in artistic control from the very beginning. Perhaps this interconnectivity and continuity of personnel, who have made up The Group at any one time, account for its focus on a particular form of documentation. Having worked in The Group's extensive archive in creating *The Wooster Group Work Book*, which was published in 2007, it became clear to me that documentation was primarily a pragmatic process and resource for LeCompte and her collaborators in terms of developing or restaging the work. In short, there was little evidence that the day-to-day process of documentation was being pursued to somehow provide The Group with a long term historical legacy. Documents always seemed to be a by-product of the process of making, developing and performing in works. An example of such archival practice can be found in the numerous actor scores that provide detailed accounts for performers to take on parts that are vacated as actors move on to other productions or leave The Group (Quick 2007: 50–2). See also the assistant director scores that give a documentary account of a complete performance work (Quick 2007: 174–7 and 122–57). Both are archival elements that are created to enable the restaging of work, which, in some cases, occurs many years after the original performances: for example, *Brace Up!*, first performed in 1991, was restaged in 2003; similarly, *North Atlantic* has been performed across three decades: in 1984, 1999 and in 2010.

What also became clear as I explored The Group's archive was how central documentation or an active negotiation with the document is as a core practice that shapes the work itself. This is perhaps most clearly seen in pieces such as *Poor Theatre* (2004) which opens with the company looking at archive footage and attempting to embody facial gestures and sounds from Jerzy Grotowski's Polish Laboratory's production of *Akropolis*, first performed in 1962 and staged in New York in 1969 (Dunkelberg 2005; Schneider 2011: 111–38). Indeed, one of the scenes that follows is a performed copy of The Group's filmed recording of a visit to the Laboratory in Poland. This engaging with documentary materials goes back to the earliest performances The Group created, the works that made up *Three Places In Rhode Island* (*Sakonnet Point* (1975), *Rumstick Road* (1977), *Nayatt School* (1978), *Point Judith (an epilog)* (1979), where key autobiographical elements of Spalding Gray's life were incorporated directly into the performances (see Savran 1988: 47–167). Another example is the ways in which The Group use documentation of performance works to organise choreographic sequences. In *To You, the Birdie! (Phèdre)* performers imitated and improvised their movements from recordings of Martha Graham's work such as *Cave of the Heart* (1946), *Seraphic Dialogue* (1955) and *Cortege of Eagles* (1967). These were played on monitors above the audience and used to score live movement created on the stage by the performers. Johan Callens provides an excellent analysis of *To You the Birdie! (Phèdre)* and the use of Martha Graham in his essay 'Reconfiguring the Text and the Self' (Friedmann 2009).

Documentary evidence and documentary practices, it would seem, are core components of The Group's creative practice. One piece, however, signals its explicit connection to documentary practice in its title and it is to this work that I wish to turn not only to tease out what might be at stake in The Group's active engagement with the practices of documentation, but also to explore how their approach to documentation might allow a rethinking of the status of the document and the archive in relation to theatre practice itself.

Creating plays from videotapes: Fish Story

The subtitle to *Fish Story*, first performed in 1994, is *A Documentary about Theatre Life in Eight Dances*. The piece is made up of three overlapping strands: lines taken from the final act of Chekhov's *Three Sisters* (the first three acts having made up the bulk of *Brace Up!*, created earlier by The Group in 1991); secondly extracts from Claude Gagnon's film *Geinin*, which is a documentary account of the day-to-day activities of the Sentaro Ichikawa Troupe from

Japan, made in 1976; and finally eight separate dance pieces that primarily draw and expand upon the Noh and Kabuki choreographies that had been engaged with in creating both the earlier *Brace Up!* and the more recently completed *Emperor Jones*, staged in 1993. Each of these three strands, in their own way, can be seen as documents: a play-text, a documentary of a theatre company, and existing documented Noh/Kabuki movement patterns available in book form. Interestingly, *Fish Story* is also performed on parts of the *Brace-Up!* stage, slightly foreshortened, with a video table replacing the ramp on the stage right side.

The Wooster Group, *Fish Story* (1994). Courtesy of Mary Gearhart.

Fish Story can be seen as a companion piece to *Brace Up!* because it presents the end section of the final act of *Three Sisters*, which had largely been omitted in *Brace-Up!* It brings to the fore the use of Noh and Kabuki techniques that had been one of the key textures and choreographic principles at play in the earlier work. However, despite plans to tour *Brace Up!* and *Fish Story* as a double bill the two pieces were rarely performed together and as LeCompte has remarked audiences, especially in Europe, found *Fish Story* somewhat abstract and difficult to relate to in comparison to the more accessible *Brace Up!* (see Quick 2007: 112). One of the elements that ghosted through *Brace-Up!*, the idea that the play is being performed by a travelling troupe of players, becomes one of the major features in *Fish Story* through the direct referencing to and quoting from the *Geinin* documentary. According to Kate Valk the documentary:

> [...] seemed such a good vehicle for our story—you know, a thinly veiled tale of a theatre troupe that was forced to reinvent itself in a modern world, where they didn't have access to the big theatres, where they weren't able to do the long shows they had once done, where they had to perform at hotels and tourist hot spots. [...] We had always thought of *Fish Story* as a sort of flash forward and Liz [LeCompte] always imagined what would happen if a troupe in the future, after the great days of theatre were long gone, found the last eight pages of Chekhov's *Three Sisters* and recreated a performance of the play from the video tapes.
>
> Quick 2007: 161

This creation of 'plays' 'from the video tapes' is one of the practices that The Wooster Group pursue in rehearsals and performances. This direct and close imitation of recordings can be seen across the whole trajectory of The Group's work. In Frank Dell's *The Temptation of St. Antony*, first performed in 1987, Ron Vawter's opening monologue is a performed live repetition of an already recorded video made by The Group, known as the 'Channel J' tape, in which Vawter enacts all the voices of the figures the audience see on the video monitors (see Marranca 1996: 269–75). In *Fish Story*, the audience have no visible access to the video of *Geinin*, but the words from the documentary are laced through the work's structure, its central characters doubling up with the main characters from the last act of Chekhov's play. The elegiac quality of Chekhov's text is delicately juxtaposed with the account of the Japanese theatre company adapting to new circumstances as their traditional approach to theatre making is having to make way for shorter and more accessible forms of performance. Consider the following exchange, extracted from the performance score created by Clay Hapaz, that takes place about 30 minutes into *Fish Story*:

> Rhode: Where's Maria Sergeyevna?
>
> Kulygin: Masha's somewhere out in the garden.
> Solyony and the barge are here in the rear,
> and all the rest of us go with the men.
>
> Sentaro: My shoes. Get my white shoes.
>
> In half an hour we'll be leaving here, and peace and
> quiet will return again...
> Just another picture...

> Narrator: Yukio's sister recently died of a kidney disease. Unfortunately, he is suffering from the same illness... In fact, he has lost both his kidneys. Still, he tries to join as many performances as possible even though he currently must spend five or six days a week in hospital.
>
> Quick 2007: 142–3

The sense of loss and resilience is felt across both textual strands. It is most obviously present in Chekhov's writing through his communication of the pain felt when friends and lovers part and leave a place forever. The sense of dedication and endurance in the Sentaro Ichikawa Troupe is captured in the brief account of Yukio's illness and his continuing attempt to perform when his dialysis allows him. Both strands explore how displacement profoundly affects, indeed, can traumatise, individuals: Sentaro's brief command for his shoes to be brought to him captures the urgency of getting ready for the stage and the inevitability that once the performance is over the troupe will have to move on to another place to perform again to another audience.

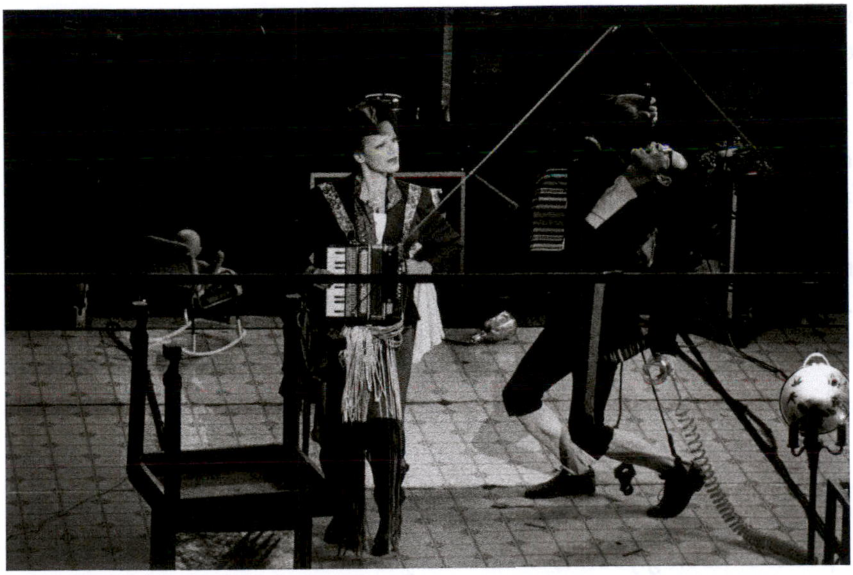

The Wooster Group, *Fish Story* (1994). Courtesy of Mary Gearhart.

Throughout the performance of *Fish Story*, it becomes increasingly difficult to differentiate between the two textual sources, however well one might know Chekhov's play, so much so that by the closing scenes the two become almost inseparable as textures. The elegiac tone of endurance that haunts *Geinin* is exquisitely juxtaposed with the sense of stoicism expressed by the three sisters, Olga, Masha and Irena, who, in their different ways, vow to carry on after the soldiers have left. As Olga puts it, 'Tomorrow there won't be a single military man left in town, it will be a memory. And of course for us it will be the beginning of a new life...' (Quick 2007: 124). This focus on being able to endure, to adapt to changing circumstances and to somehow productively negotiate the sometimes transient nature of human relationships is felt throughout *Fish Story* and, as I will discuss shortly, connects to the very essence of theatre itself, to theatre's relationship with the archive and the broader connection to the process of archiving in our daily lives.

Of course, one of the elements that drew The Group to *Geinin* was the way the documentary resonated with their own experience of being a theatre company. As LeCompte observed, 'it was just too good. It was like us in our upstairs room at the Garage, watching television all the time and only doing a play once in a while...' (Quick 2007: 58). This sense of connection also occurs in the last section of *Fish Story*, which is almost entirely dedicated to Vershinin's farewell to Olga. As the performers on the set of Fish Story begin to pack up and leave the stage, we watch the final interaction on a television monitor placed at the front and centre of the stage. What is significant about the video is that it is a recording of the dialogue that includes sections that would normally be cut out in performance: these include the off-camera assistance in lighting a cigarette and the putting of glycerine in the eye to simulate tears:

> Let's try, uh, some, uh, glycerine. Oh shit... Oooh -aaah... Yeah—all set. You, uh, you... I was what? Oh, I see. OK.
>
> My wife and my two little girls will stay on another month or so; if they need any help, do you think you could...
>
> I think I put too much glycerine in. Would you hand me... good ... thanks. Too much in one eye and none in the other... really... alright... yeah, here we go.
>
> Quick 2007: 155

Paralleling some of the tones and components of the *Geinin* documentary, what we witness here is the unedited preparation and delivery of the performance by Vawter as Vershinin. The scene is effective on a number of levels. It is a particularly moving account of departure and thwarted love: Vawter's delivery of Chekhov's writing brings this beautifully to the fore in these closing moments. Yet, the focus on the mechanics of stage/film production as a document, induced by the difficulty of getting the glycerine in the eye of the performer, undermines the sentimentality that appears to be a crucial part of the staged negotiation here. The real-time difficulty of dealing with the script and the glycerine brings a reality to the vulnerability that is an essential element of the scene's construction. What seems to be in play here is a subtle interaction of the prescribed emotion that exists somewhat melodramatically (and comically) in Chekhov's text with the reality of dealing with the mechanics of playing the scene. This results in a scene that, although mediated through the TV monitor, seems to be authentic and in turn comic as it progresses to the final long kiss with Masha before it is interrupted by Olga calling out—'Now, now, that's enough', lines that trigger the video fade-out of the two protagonists' image, marking the end of the performance.

The slow fade-out of Vawter's face is strangely poignant as *Fish Story* was to be his last performance with The Wooster Group. Again, echoing some of the elements in the *Geinin* documentary, the real-life experience of The Wooster Group makes its way into the performance as a kind of living document that is animated by becoming a key part of the dramatic action. LeCompte acknowledges that *Fish Story* was a kind of 'goodbye to Ron', a goodbye that was presaged by the fact that Vawter was making his own work 'outside of the group' and that 'he was very ill' (Quick 2007: 112). During the period that *Fish Story* was being performed Vawter created *Roy Cohn/Jack Smith*, which was first performed in 1992. Vawter's closing lines in *Fish Story* as a farewell to The Group are particularly moving: 'We must find a way to join love of work to love of higher things, mustn't we? Well, now I must go... I came to say goodbye' (Quick 2007: 156). Vawter died in 1994.

Performance as the originary document: re-thinking the archive

It would seem, then, that The Wooster Group engages with documents as a core practice in their theatre-making process and that most of the documents in their archive are the detritus left over from this creative interaction. Equally significant is the fact that each work exists in relation to those that came before and after: each contains documentary traces of previous pieces, traces that will inevitably contribute to future works. In this sense, as hinted at in the very title of *Fish Story* as a *Documentary about Theatre*

Life in Eight Dances, every piece produced by The Group can be defined by the term 'documentary' in that each is created in relationship to already existing material. This materiality is not limited to that which exists in their own archive, in the remnants (props, costumes) left over from previous works, in the embodied practices of their performers. It exists in the 'new' material, the texts, films, sources and new performers, that accrues around each new production and re-staging of already existing pieces.

A quick examination of the dictionary definition of documentary produces a number of nuanced meanings. On the one hand, and perhaps most obviously, documentary is 'pertaining to, consisting of, or derived from documents' (Brown 1993: 719). And, as I hope I have shown, it is clear how one might begin to identify The Group's work as being rooted in a form of documentary practice that matches this definition. The second definition of the term is very interesting as it begins to indicate the fact that the documentary act itself produces its own evidence and contains its own evidential materiality. Here the dictionary defines documentary as 'affording evidence, evidential' (Brown 1993: 719). Considering this second definition, it is possible to view the documentary act as one that creates evidence as a mode of production, that the bringing forth of evidential material is an event in itself. In this interpretation the key term here is 'afford' since the word is connected directly to the act of doing, of performance and, of course, to its dynamic of provision and production—Afford: 'Provide, furnish, grant; of things: be capable of yielding, yield naturally' (Brown 1993: 36). This, I would like to assert, comes close to locating performance as a documentary act, in that performance is always involved in a process of provision ('yielding') in the encounter that takes place between that which is created and those that witness (the audience) the product of this creation. Put another way, the documentary practice The Wooster Group engages with is not only based on the fact that they actively negotiate documents in the forms that I have outlined, but also because they appear to understand performance itself as a documentary act. This turn, that The Wooster Group makes towards the documentary, is not one solely concerned with their own individual and collective experience and history: it is a move that allows them to examine what constitutes performance itself.

Of course, a more obvious definition of documentary as a form (usually, radio, television or film) that attempts to unearth facts and the truth by looking at and presenting concrete evidence would seem to contradict the more ephemeral processes that are invoked when thinking about the constituent and ontological properties of performance. After all, as has been the subject of much discussion within the field of performance studies over the last 15 years or so, the ephemerality of the performance event has been seen as one of its defining features. Although there is not space to replay these discussions, The Wooster Group's engagement with documentary practice hints at how we might access an understanding of performance and its relationship to the search for truth and authenticity that is productively different from those articulated within the existing debates around performance's relationship to the document and documentation in general (for an excellent account of the discussions on liveness and mediatisation in performance, see Schneider 2011).

LeCompte and individual members of The Wooster Group have made numerous attempts to describe how their performances are constructed to somehow get at the truth of things or make contact with some authentic moment on the stage (Savran 1988, Quick 2007). Kate Valk, as a performer and collaborator, connects this pursuit of the authentic, the real, to the approach of the non-expert or the way a child might play without fear or inhibition. In an interview she asserts 'Liz always has this bottom line which is us encountering the material. I think that with any of the things we take on we keep, in the best sense, a beginner's mind, or, at least, the attitude of a divine amateur' (Quick 2007: 217). LeCompte has described that one of her roles as a director is to keep the room animated, to make the space kinetic, to keep things in play, in tension, that by 'relinquishing a certain kind of control there's an electricity in the whole room, because there are these things that are being played with that you can, in the best sense, channel and make a response to' (Quick 2007: 217). What seems to be articulated here is the fact that the truth or what feels like an original/real moment only occurs in the dealing with, the active moment-by-moment activity of doing, that performance always involves. Ron Vawter has described this process as a kind of 'figuring out' that takes place in front of the audience, that is based on discovering who he is before them, what he describes as 'ways of being myself, as best I could, publically' (Ibid: 274). LeCompte, in more abrupt terms, identifies this process as one that is a looking for, rather than a process of locating and learning: 'I don't learn, I search' (Champagne 1981: 28).

Performance in these terms can be seen as a truth-making practice, the 'figuring out' process that is variously described above. As such, performance becomes an originary activity in both senses of this word: originary in that it is the event that everything in its preparation bends towards *and also emanates* from, in terms of the residual elements that are left when it is over. Walter Benjamin's concept of origin, as expressed in his *The Origin of German Tragic Drama*, is helpful here. In one of his most memorable passages he describes the contingent nature of truth and how truth is susceptible to the operations of time and context: process as a tireless mode of contemplation. In his attempt to define origin in what is described as the 'Epistemo-Critical Prologue', he writes,

> Origin (*Ursprung*), although an entirely historical category, has, nevertheless, nothing to do with genesis (*Entstehung*). The term origin is not intended to describe a process by which the existent came into being, but rather to describe that which emerges from the process of becoming and disappearance. Origin is an eddy in the stream of becoming, and in its current it swallows the material involved in the process of genesis. That which is original is never revealed in the naked and manifest existence of the factual.
>
> Benjamin 1998: 45

Although Benjamin is not making any direct reference to performance, his attempt to describe and explain his concept of origin seems to parallel some of the defining features of performance. According to Benjamin, origin has no connection to genesis, it does not describe how things came to be. Rather, and this is where we get an uncanny parallel with performance, origin arises out of what he calls the 'process of becoming and disappearance'. What Benjamin appears to be signalling in the passage is a refusal to see origin as some sort of chronological starting point, nor spatially as a fixed form. Rather, as Howard Caygill analyses in his book *Walter Benjamin: The Colour of Experience*, 'origin is a patterning of the phenomena that changes over time' (ibid.: 57). According to Caygill, this patterning is 'rhythmic'. It is a patterning that is 'both concrete and a priori', one in which at any particular instance 'the pattern is both emerging and withdrawing, showing different aspects and concealing others' (Caygill 1998: 57). Crucially, it is temporality that permits the contingency (appearing and disappearing) that Benjamin locates as the crucial dynamic at work in his concept of origin ('the stream of becoming'). Thus the origin or the original is neither fact nor an object. Nor is it a product of abstract thinking (an idea). Rather, as Benjamin words it, the original is 'recognized as a process of restoration and re-establishment' which is also 'imperfect and incomplete' (Benjamin 1998: 45). Origin is an interruption, an 'eddy' in the stream of becoming and, perhaps more crucially, this eddy swallows up, muddies the materials that would somehow signify what an origin actually is.

Benjamin's concept of the contingency of truth and its resistance to being inscribed within a fixed order of knowledge resonates with my experience of watching and thinking about the performance work of The Wooster Group. This is not say that The Group somehow embodies the thinking of Benjamin nor, indeed, do I have any evidence that its members have ever considered Benjamin's writing in making their work. What is productive in this association of The Wooster Group with Benjamin is that it figures the materiality of performance as a mode of production, as a process of bringing things into *appearance*, rather than placing an undue emphasis on performance's transitory nature. The return to ideas and to the archival materials used in productions as seen in The Wooster Group's work can be viewed as a truth-seeking practice that understands that all searching for origins is built from negotiating what has constituted the past in the context of a present that is always allusive. Of course, this bringing into appearance is, as Benjamin alludes to, inevitably subject to disappearance. The facticity, the truth of things, can never be brought clearly into light, into knowledge, but it is in the process of dealing with them that origins might at least be critically explored. For Benjamin, truth resides in the process of contemplation itself and always resists being contained by the order of knowledge. He writes: 'Tirelessly the process of thinking makes new beginnings, returning in a roundabout way to its original object. This continual pausing for breath is the mode most proper for to the process of contemplation' (Ibid: 29). The pausing for breath signals the momentary dynamic of disappearance that such contemplation generates, but it is momentary, and certainly in the context of performance exists *within* the temporal frame of the performance event as much as outside it.

Fish Story's documentary energy is not focused solely on the performance's relationship to its two texts as source material: the *Geinin* film and the sections of *Three Sisters* that are referenced. It is important to remember that the work is structured around eight dances, as signalled in *Fish Story*'s subtitle. Dance, of course, operates as a repetitive act and The Group's allusion to the intricate movement patterns of Noh theatre emphasises the highly notated and archival dynamic of movement that is at work in certain forms of dance as a mode of expression. *Fish Story* is an intricately choreographed piece, but each choreographic section seems to operate as a temporal interruption in the flow of the piece as a whole. Indeed, interruption seems to be a motif that

The Wooster Group, *Fish Story* (1994). Courtesy of The Wooster Group.

occurs throughout the work until the very last section, which sees Vershinin and Olga's farewell scene played on a television monitor juxtaposed with the gradual emptying of the stage by the live performers. Of course, this scene is finally interrupted as Olga demands that their farewell kiss is halted (Quick 2007: 156). Interruption can also be located in the constant beeps, stamps and whacks that punctuate the piece. Indeed, Benjamin's concept of the eddy is an apposite analogy to describe the constant swirling out from the centre that is one of the central choreographic dynamics at play in this performance. Valk has described *Fish Story* as a piece with 'an empty centre, where there isn't really a play, but just its signs, the props, costumes, articles' (Quick 2007: 161). Because the centre does not hold, the effect is a kind of shattering of those components that would permit a moment to fully cohere into meaning, into the bringing into replete appearance that Benjamin seems so wary of. What we witness instead is a kind of spatio-temporal whirling, where the only resting places are the half-lit edges of the playing area: the reading table at the back and the ramps at either side. Played out in the centre is a form of constant furniture moving and placing; the slapstick battling to attain a core position to speak and to be able to present before the audience; and the highly ritualised dance routines that seem to have fetishised and distilled the dramaturgical components of the performance text to a point of almost complete abstraction.

What *Fish Story* playfully and, indeed, movingly acknowledges is that a performance work is always built from the tracery produced by all those who participate in its construction: a performance work always stands in some relation to the performances that came before and will come after it. Strangely paralleling Benjamin's observations on history, truth and origin, *Fish Story* seems to return again and again not only to the history of The Wooster Group, its performers, director and multiple and layered scenographic practices. It appears to return to the question of performance itself, what its constituent parts might be and what an interrogation of these parts might provoke. Following on from Benjamin, this performance can be thought of as an archival event in which the problem and potential of the document and the activity of dealing with documents (the documentary) is presented before us. The patina of performance, patterning. This would account for the work's exquisite choreographic ordering. Is not this patterning central to our experience of the temporal flow of performance, indeed, of life itself, where elements come before us through a process of appearance and disappearance, across and in time and in space? There, gone. There, gone. There in the memory, in the body, there in the faint lines on the floor.... There... There... There...

References

2000 Aronson, A. *The American Avant-Garde Theatre: A History*, London: Routledge.

1998 Benjamin, W. *The Origin of German Tragic Drama*, London: Verso.

1993 Brown, L. (ed.) *The New Shorter Oxford English Dictionary*, Oxford: Clarendon Press.

2004 Callens, J. (ed.) *The Wooster Group and its Traditions*, Brussels: Peter Lang.

2009 Callens, J. 'The Wooster Group's Hamlet, According to the True, Original Copies'. *Theatre Journal*, 61(4): pp539–61.

1998 Caygill, H., *Walter Benjamin: The Colour of Experience*, London: Routledge.

1981 Champagne, L. 'Always Starting New: Elizabeth LeCompte'. *The Drama Review*, 25(3): pp19–28.

2005 Dunkelberg, K. 'The Wooster Group's *Poor Theater*'. *The Drama Review*, 49(3): pp43–57.

2009 Friedman, S. (ed.) *Theatrical Revisions of Classic Works: Critical Essays*, Jefferson: McFarland and Company.

1996 Kaye, N. *Art into Theatre: Performance Interviews and Documents*, London: Routledge.

1996 Marranca, B. (ed.) *Plays for the End of the Century*, Baltimore: John Hopkins University Press.

2007 Quick, A. *The Wooster Group Work Book*, London: Routledge.

1988 Savran, D. *Breaking the Rules: The Wooster Group*, New York: Theatre Communications Group.

2011 Schneider, R., *Performing Remains*, London: Routledge.

2008 Worthen, W. B. '*Hamlet* at Ground Zero: The Wooster Group and the Archive of Performance'. *Shakespeare Quarterly*, 59(3): pp303–22.

REVIEW

This section brings together a series of reflective practices in the form of enactments and writings that are haunted by earlier performances. Yet the critical revision each of these contributions offers is emphatically 'future-facing': producing new work or readings of the differences between what was performed and what can be performed now; addressing what is elided in the coalescence of performance histories; revealing and extending the logic of 'original' rehearsal methods to produce new insights and forms for future archives. In the practices reflected upon here, the notion of REVIEW is elaborated in embodied historiographies and challenges to that which memory and re-telling elides or cannot capture. These processes implicitly use or anticipate the archive, but also challenge the legitimacy of what remains or is remembered, emphasising the lack or absences in which archives settle their limits or appear complete. As it is exemplified in these artists' contributions, REVIEW implies the knowing return to an original scene, whose critical recollection interrupts the emergent order of the archive.

Mike Pearson's *The Lesson of Anatomy* re-embodies the eponymous performance by Cardiff Laboratory for Theatrical Research from 1974, which comprised, in part, of two extended solos by Pearson animating texts by the French visionary and surrealist Antonin Artaud. Enacted, again, in 2014, at the performance's original theatrical site of the Sherman Arena, Pearson's exploration of his physical capacity, 40 years on, to stage *Flesh* and *Asylum* using contemporaneous photography, the return to the place of performance, and body memory, drives a recollection and writing over of his 'original' act. Memory, and differences of site, purpose and context, as well as performance styles 'now momentarily revenant', work with the differences in Pearson's physical capacity to articulate recurrence and loss through performance; the ephemerality of Pearson's 'original' performance appears to consign this repetition to an absolute difference, yet the event Pearson enacts again haunts everything he does. *The Lesson of Anatomy* is closely tied to Pearson's playing of archaeological ideas, practices and themes through performance (see Pearson and Shanks 2001). In his collaborative work with the company Brith Gof, from 1981 to 1993, Pearson explored the multiplicity of complex cultural sites for performance in Wales; sites known in their continuing occupation by previous and current narratives, in which found, created and hybrid narratives of place produced layered and multi-vocal site-specific performances. In one of Pearson's many solo works, *From Memory* (1999) he re-told the stories of the scars from these and other performances, pointing them out to his audience, revealing his work's traces and impacts on flesh and bone. *The Lesson of Anatomy* invites a reading of a similar layering of embodied times, as the present moment of performance unfolds in perceptions of physical absence and recurrence; where the body is a place to be performed. Fiona Templeton's 'Authority, authorship and authoring in The Theatre of Mistakes' transposes analogous themes and questions in which past events may be reviewed, towards the generation of performance histories, attending to the elisions in which such narratives garner textual authority. Focusing on the 'shared history' of the deeply influential performance art company she co-founded in the early 1970s, Templeton speculates over matters of voice, subjectivity, tense and position, in her own speaking—and in others speaking 'for her'—through various tactics; refusing the first person, reviewing and reflecting upon who speaks for who, in a layering of the voice and its implicit and explicit claims for authority and history. It is a questioning that Templeton also inscribes into the operation of The Theatre of Mistakes and its procedures for making work: in the dialogue between disciplines in which the group foregrounded 'a non-homogeneity of experience with a conceptual collectivity'; and in documentation that remains, much of which takes the form of instructions for future work. Templeton's critique calls for a 'dialogic' and 'future-facing' archive that reflects the complexities of such authorship and historiography, where 'history is always factual and constructed'.

Such concerns are also foregrounded, in these documents, in further embodied continuations of the practices and processes to which performance archives attend. For the UK performance company, Bodies in Flight, their return to *Do the Wild Thing!* (1996) extended the 'fractal' production and form of this performance as four of the original collaborators each made new works in reflection and extension of original acts and processes. Across these new events—the choreography *Still Moving: Moving Still*; the photographic series *Make the Fixed Volatile, and Make the Volatile Fixed*; the three-screen video installation *I'd Like to Call You Joe Tonight*; and the performance and book *Muse*—these responses can be read as realising one mode of the 'dialogic archive' to which Templeton alludes, where differing voices and practices speak to each other *through* the archive as medium. In each of their new works, Bodies in Flight amplify and carry forward the impulse towards disparate, dissonant voices in whose final meeting the earlier work is formed. Finally, in this section, Felix Gmelin documents a series of live and recorded performances, amongst them *Every Version is Part of the Myth* (2012), *Understanding Negative Dialectics* (2013), and *Utiphobia* (2013), in which children read philosophical and sociological texts they can only struggle to understand. Including, in *Negative Dialectics* (2010), Gmelin's young son reading a complex text by his grandfather, these presentations materialise gaps in time and understanding, using trans-generational exchange and performance to open questions over the continuities, sense and understanding of the archival text.

Mike Pearson, 1974. Photo Steve Allison.

1974

On 5 July 1974, the newly founded Cardiff Laboratory for Theatrical Research (later Cardiff Laboratory Theatre) premiered its first professional production in the Sherman Arena Theatre, Cardiff during the venue's opening season. *The Lesson of Anatomy: The Life, Obsessions and Fantasies of Antonin Artaud* was inspired by and included texts written by French theatre visionary Artaud in the final period of his life (1946–8), after his release from incarceration in various mental institutions. In these accusatory, incandescent and disturbing writings—part stinging indictment, part tirade, part reverie —Artaud rails against psychiatry and the injustices of his own personal suffering, whilst envisioning new worlds and devising new languages.

The Lesson of Anatomy was divided into four sections corresponding to Artaud's conceptions of the body: 'Flesh' —the body physical; 'Bardo'—the dream body of the *Tibetan Book of the Dead*; 'The Other Body' —the desire for an alternative body; and 'Asylum'—the social body. The work imagined the innovative shape of the Sherman Arena as an anatomy lecture theatre: Mike Pearson performed 'Flesh' and Asylum' as two extended solos.

Mike Pearson, 2014. Photo Russ Basford.

2014

On 5 July 2014, on the 40th anniversary to the day of their original staging and in the Arena (now Theatre 2), Sherman Cymru, Mike Pearson re-performed 'Flesh' and 'Asylum'. Drawing on a surviving series of 158 black and white photographs by Steve Allison and his own contemporary fragmentary notes—there is no video—the reconstitution suggests how period devised works might be performed again, to give a glimpse of styles long disappeared now momentarily revenant; how the site itself might help in the process of remembering and reimagining; and how additional dramatic affects might result from the impacts of aging on the performer, from the difficulty of performing the choreography and of recalling the text—the true 'lesson of anatomy'.

The Lesson of Anatomy was a contribution to Mike Pearson's Leverhulme Research Fellowship project *Marking Time: performance, archaeology and the city* (2012–14) in which his aim was to acknowledge, recover and evoke alternative theatre practices and related phenomena of the late 1960s/ early 1970s and subsequently, and to enhance appreciation and understanding of their historical, cultural and aesthetic significance, within both academic and popular contexts; to do so by locating and examining such manifestations and their traces within particular social and geographical frameworks, and in relation to one city—Cardiff.

On these pages, Steve Allison's photographs from 1974 are juxtaposed with a series from 2014 by Russ Basford.

1974

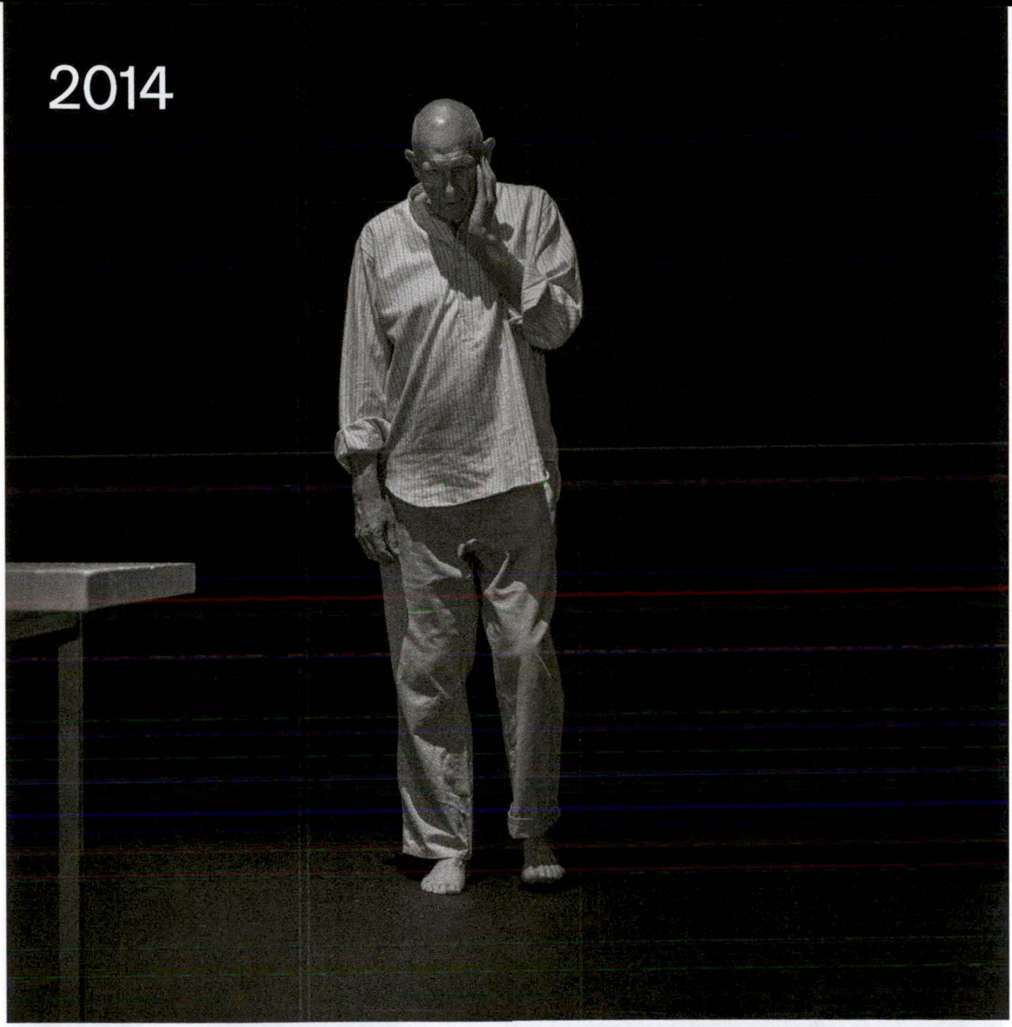
2014

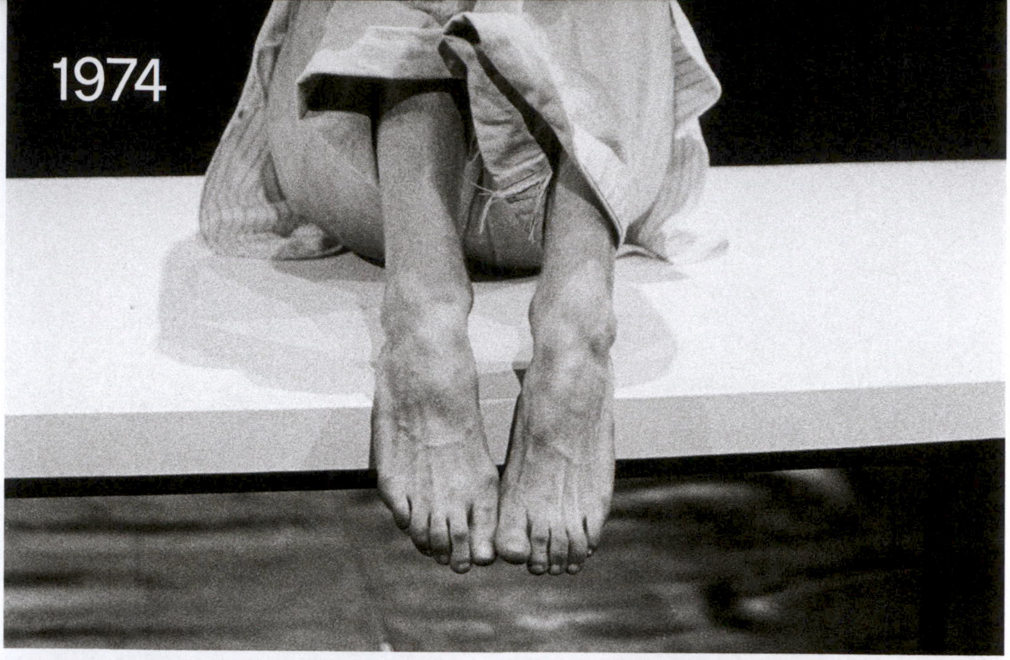
1974

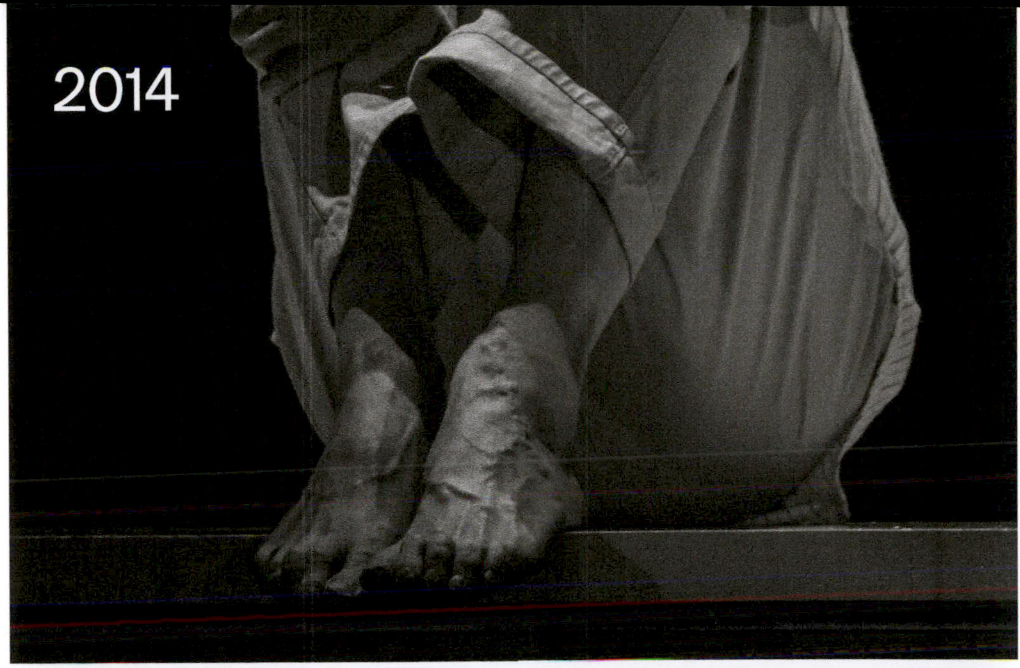
2014

AUTHORITY, AUTHORSHIP AND AUTHORING IN THE THEATRE OF MISTAKES

Fiona Templeton

1.

This paper has been slightly annotated (in italics) by the original speaker, in response to an editorial request to make more general the material that was specific to the context of the live talk. The original speaker notes the perhaps appropriateness of the further layer of authoring. However, in interrogating the fixing dynamic of documentation of performance, the original talk asked also how to embody the interrogation. How to represent the ephemeral or context-specific, the voice in place, the subject in voices, the supposed illegitimacy of speech, in the later document. Some of that original material is therefore here presented as quotation.

> Is it going to be possible, for the duration of the present talk, to avoid using the first person pronoun? And that specifically when addressing a personally lived and professional history, in conversation and dialogue and no doubt occasional contradiction, with intertwined histories where unless by some fabulous coincidence there is a similar strategy, the first person pronoun will no doubt be used by another person on this panel speaking of the ostensibly shared history?

The position will not be useful to take unless it also refuses and interrogates disguised first-person, such as the royal *we*, or that *we* which assumes agreement with the speaker by the listener, or that *we* which ascribes a common subjecthood to a group rather than at least attempting to use the *we* for the group or the name for the person only in terms of factual history, whatever that means.

Nor is this an academic objectivity, that speaks through the authority of 'knowledge', 'knowledge' as used academically being a legal term, the authority to speak ventriloquially for and as such 'knowledge' conferred by participation in its so called body by its de facto legal authority. That would be inappropriate for a conceptual strategy which wishes to foreground a non-homogeneity of experience with a conceptual collectivity.

Will the refusal of the first person by one party be an unintended lending of mastery to the user of the first person pronoun? Can an actualised investigation of alternatives to the first-person authoritative subject *not* constitute self-erasure? And yet, can subjecthood-s and subjectivities within contested historie-s be really addressed without such an attempted radical positioning?

The word *attempt* has been used twice already. This is not a tentativeness, a lack of the assumption of authority—it is an embracing of the present-ness of the enterprise, the rigour of the experimental.

There might need to be use of the first person within quotation. Templeton's 2009 article, 'Acting Brackets—Notes on Directing the Extra-lexical Aspects of Leslie Scalapino's *Flow*[1] '(a production by The Relationship, Artistic Director Fiona Templeton) considers how in Scalapino's written text, such punctuational symmetries as the quotes, the brackets etc are portals that frame the subject, the actors voicing not only a single subjectivity each but also giving voice to other subjects, an again ventriloquial enterprise that is sometimes, on the one hand, voluntary and authorial, and on the other sometimes an involuntary possession *by* authority 'man in black robes', voice crossing the portal in the other direction. The difference is important, and the ventriloquism is examined.

So this talk must be understood as a performance in time, in the sense that the time of posing the question did not yet know the answer.

2.

In Marie-Anne Mancio's recent investigation of The Theatre of Mistakes archive, in collaboration with Jason Bowman's curatorial approach to the collection of the company's documents, her talk on the subject concludes that the facts of the company's work are unknowable, since versions of it are contradictory. (Ironically, she was to read this talk at Psi15 as part of a Shift on The Theatre of Mistakes organised by Fiona Templeton, but as Mancio could not be present, the talk was read by a conference attendee[2]; Mancio had asked that it be read by Fiona Templeton as her representative, but as the talk questioned the veracity of Templeton's voice, for Templeton to speak it would have been equivalent to calling herself a liar or at best dissociative.) But was this talk in fact written by Marie Anne Mancio *and* Jason Bowman? How did it just feel, for Jason Bowman 'here present' to have it described as a talk *by* Marie-Anne Mancio, and what indeed does by mean? If real memories were being recounted, were the speakers then no-one? Must there be agreement, consensus, for a person's knowledge of their own experience to be validated? If there are differing authors, is there no such thing as authority? Is authority always exclusive?

The Theatre of Mistakes' core group's final ensemble work, *Going*, enacted what the group called *being each other*.

In the post-Theatre of Mistakes work *Against Agreement*[3], a collaboration between former Theatre of Mistakes members Fiona Templeton and Peter Stickland, a key sentence spoken by Templeton was 'I wasn't disagreeing, I was talking about something else.' Does disagreement not always posit a primary position, a first voice, disagreed with?

3.

Jason Bowman has remarked on the unusual (for those days) wealth of documentation produced by The Theatre of Mistakes. There are various discrete reasons for that.

First, many of these documents were not documentation. The company saw itself as art-makers. The subtitle to 'The Theatre of Mistakes' was 'a performance art group'. The Antigravity series of photographs represent what was perhaps never really a performance, though it was done in public; it was a photoshoot by company member Mike Evans. We were also conceptual art-makers, and much conceptual art that was the context for the work took written form, for example Douglas Huebler's instructional performance works. Moreover,

The Theatre of Mistakes, *Going*. Courtesy of Fiona Templeton.

company members were from different disciplines, so our question was, how do architecture, dance, writing, sculpture etc, speak with each other? This was a primary conceptual project of the company.

And further: the 1977 *Manifesto of Mutual Art* by The Theatre of Mistakes was not only collective, it was also not itself a statement, but a set of instructions as to how you, you too, could follow the company's mutually agreed procedures for arriving at a mutually agreed set of statements. The crucial factor in the procedures was the use of choice by chance such as the roll of a dice, between differing possibilities that were nevertheless unanimously agreed to be equal.

The Manifesto of Mutual Art is a document. However, is it a document of something? Are instructions towards a future a document of a past? The instructional mode of the 1976 *Elements of Performance Art* by Anthony Howell and Fiona Templeton was a refinement of the extensive *Gymnasium*, a weighty file-folder of instructions created over a few years by members of the larger Ting. That refinement was towards less given content, more *possible* content. The written nature of these exercises, each on an A4 sheet of paper, was practical. At the company's weekly open Free Sessions, new exercises or instructions would be pinned to the wall for that session. They could be followed, or not. Exercises included 'Exercise Exercise': 'Create an exercise'. An exercise was not towards a skill, but generated a doing in itself.

The Ting, the larger group which preceded the core group of The Theatre of Mistakes, was the Norse parliament, where weapons were left outside the door. This was the utopian project. The Manifesto of Mutual Art, a document with no single author and written to provoke further multiple authorship, was a utopian project. It was a manifesto in the form of instruction, not statement, not single truth.

Making the art was not about being right, but about being in the present.

In *Shattered Anatomies*[4] (UK editors Adrian Heathfield and Andrew Quick, US editor Fiona Templeton), the thesis for the US curating was that the emergence of the trace could occur at any point along the temporal trajectory from conception to remains, and to invite the artists to contribute their preferred trace of a work. Beyond that, perhaps an artwork too can occur at any point along the trajectory, or at more than one. For The Theatre of Mistakes,

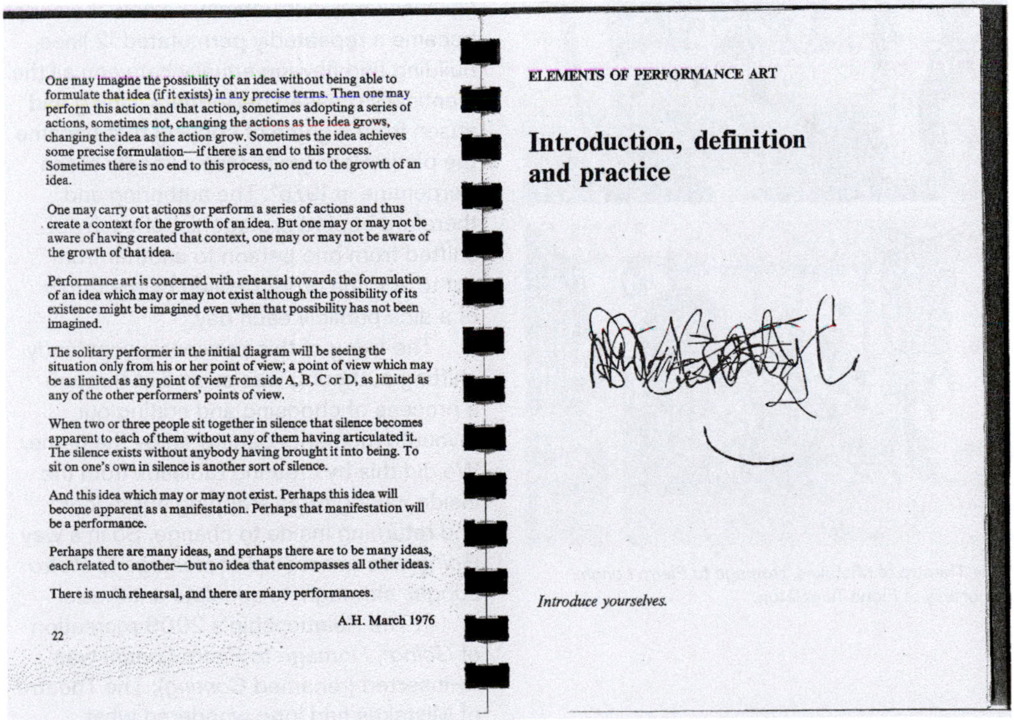

One may imagine the possibility of an idea without being able to formulate that idea (if it exists) in any precise terms. Then one may perform this action and that action, sometimes adopting a series of actions, sometimes not, changing the actions as the idea grows, changing the idea as the action grow. Sometimes the idea achieves some precise formulation—if there is an end to this process. Sometimes there is no end to this process, no end to the growth of an idea.

One may carry out actions or perform a series of actions and thus create a context for the growth of an idea. But one may or may not be aware of having created that context, one may or may not be aware of the growth of that idea.

Performance art is concerned with rehearsal towards the formulation of an idea which may or may not exist although the possibility of its existence might be imagined even when that possibility has not been imagined.

The solitary performer in the initial diagram will be seeing the situation only from his or her point of view; a point of view which may be as limited as any point of view from side A, B, C or D, as limited as any of the other performers' points of view.

When two or three people sit together in silence that silence becomes apparent to each of them without any of them having articulated it. The silence exists without anybody having brought it into being. To sit on one's own in silence is another sort of silence.

And this idea which may or may not exist. Perhaps this idea will become apparent as a manifestation. Perhaps that manifestation will be a performance.

Perhaps there are many ideas, and perhaps there are to be many ideas, each related to another—but no idea that encompasses all other ideas.

There is much rehearsal, and there are many performances.

A.H. March 1976

22

ELEMENTS OF PERFORMANCE ART

Introduction, definition and practice

Introduce yourselves.

Mutual Signature (1976) by Mickey Greenall, Anthony Howell and Fiona Templeton. Courtesy of Fiona Templeton.

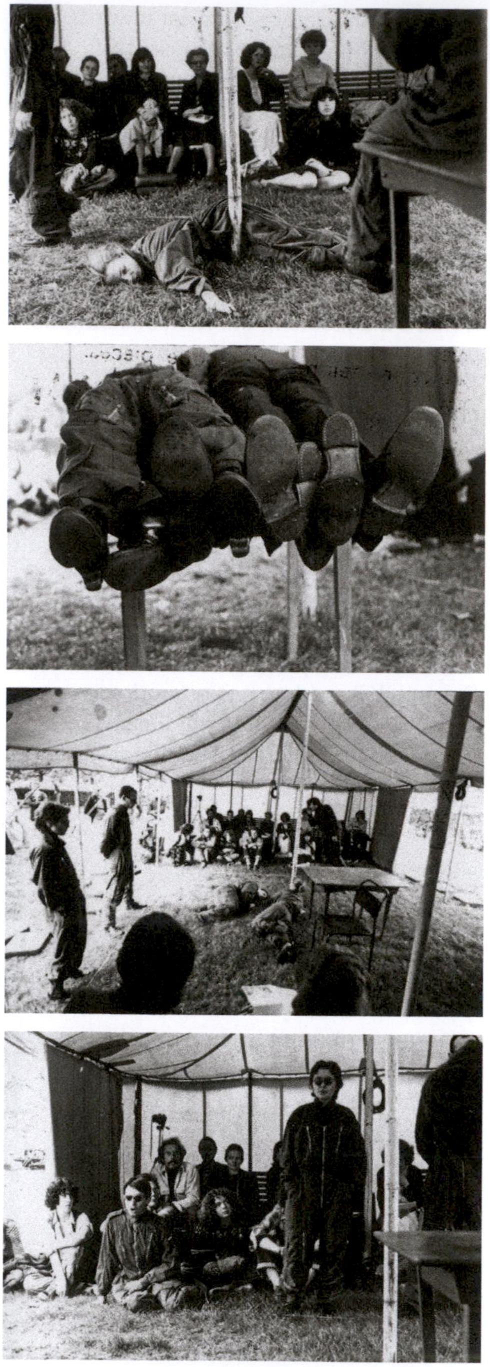
The Theatre of Mistakes, *Homage to Pietro Longhi*.
Courtesy of Fiona Templeton.

the piece was not the same as the performance. The necessary impossibility of repeating the event was already contained in the substitution of a script, as in conventional theatre, with instructions that were game-like. So not instructions to complete a given set of actions, but instructions that would generate multiple possibilities of action. The unknown outcome, the unknowable content. And on these trajectories, where might authorship lie? The signature of the Theatre of Mistakes was a stamp made from a signature made by Fiona Templeton, Micky Greenall and Anthony Howell all holding the same pen and each writing their own name at the same time. Another utopian project.

Going[5], the final piece by The Theatre of Mistakes core group of Micky Greenall, Fiona Templeton, Anthony Howell, Peter Stickland, Miranda Payne and Glenys Johnson, was scripted. A script of never ending, never leaving, where we became too good to make mistakes and had to invent rehearsed ones. As with the previous work of refining by a stylistic *emptying* of the *Gymnasium*'s instructions, so now the script became a repeatedly permutated 12 lines, building and flowing equally between all the identically dressed performers. Going had arisen from a game of copying that became the piece *Homage to Pietro Longhi* at the Serpentine in 1976[6]. The authoring and therefore copied protagonist of each act shifted from one person to another from act to act, the order chosen by the throw of a dice publicly each day.

The fixing of this previously constantly shifting authoring was arrived at through a process of choosing and editing our favourite moments generated by the game. We did this by creating tableaux from the inside, taking turns stepping out to look and returning inside to change. So in a way *Going* was our record of *Homage to Pietro Longhi*, although its absolute antithesis.

In The Relationship's 2009 recreation of *Going*[7], *Homage to Pietro Longhi* was re-inserted (renamed *Coming*); The Theatre of Mistakes had long wondered what *Coming*, the opposite of *Going*, might be,

but *Going* was already in fact an opposite and so *Coming* was *Homage to Pietro Longhi* without the visual reference).
In *Going with Coming*, the fixed Acts 1, 3, and 5 were interleaved once more with the game, reimprovised by and giving authorship to the twenty-first century performers, as young as we were then. The memory or the photographic document may be the trace of the content of the event. The apparent content-emptiness of the instruction is the content of the game. The content of the game *Homage to Pietro Longhi*, or *Coming, is* the repeated and polysubjective re-authoring.

This was, at a utopian level, also the content of The Theatre of Mistakes.

4.

The question of representation of voice is not only abstract, but a reality with legitimacy at stake. This is a feminist issue, among other struggles. It is as true of the present as of the past, of documentation and record as of what is lived.

Yesterday the phrase 'Anthony Howell's work' reactivated the memory of a discussion with Man A in the leadup to the publication of his Book Z on seeing drawings from 1977 in the book's proofs credited (and thus documented) as 'drawings by Anthony Howell', and returning the drawings to Man A with the request that they be ascribed 'drawings by Fiona Templeton' because of a lived memory of their painstaking execution, and some months later having the proofs returned by Man A with the credit 'drawings by The Theatre of Mistakes', a more conceptually accurate credit; and yet seeing other diagrams in the proofs by analogy then also by The Theatre of Mistakes nevertheless still ascribed to Anthony Howell. In this exchange where had the slippage occurred? In the error, in the deferral, in the untruth, in the assumption? Or in someone's easy elision from the first person singular to the first person plural and an easy slippage back from the whole of the collective to the first person singular. That being what this short paper wishes to interrogate. Yesterday Anthony Howell, in referring to specific copies of the same drawings, used the phrase *Micky Greenall's drawings*. Indeed this version of the drawing had been beautifully overpainted by Mickey Greenall. Today, Man X enumerated the achievements of Anthony Howell past and present and the achievements past and present of Jason Bowman, and introduced Fiona Templeton as a lecturer at Brunel University. Man A and Man X remain un-named here, naming and intention or otherwise being less the point than the lapsus and the gender.

Fiona Templeton in the UK is not the same as Fiona Templeton in the US. This naming is not that of a person but of a conglomerate record. Fiona Templeton in the UK, apparently, has worked in the 70s and the 80s, and for some time now, according to a recent description, has a concern with the archive, performed or of performance. Fiona Templeton in the US is the director of the group The Relationship, and created previous solo and large-scale work in the 80s and 90s; she is also a poet.

The use of the name here is not simply equivalent to a use of the first person singular here but refers to naming, to the issue of naming.

If the purpose of an archive is to capture a history before the disappearance of evidence, it must be inclusive. Inclusive not only of parallel and differing histories, but of the richness of their argument. History is always both factual and constructed. A dialogic archive rather than a nostalgic archive is a future-facing one.

Will the present difference between the continuity Theatre of Mistakes-Fiona Templeton-The Relationship and the continuity Theatre of Mistakes-Anthony Howell still be true after the artists' deaths?

I am still alive.

Notes

1 Templeton, F. (2011). 'Acting Brackets: Notes on Directing the Extra-lexical Aspects of Leslie Scalapino's *Flow*', Philadelphia: Jacket2. Available online. www.jacket2.org. Accessed 28 February 2017.
2 Mancio, A.M. (2009) 'MISPERFORMANCE: Misfiring, Misfitting, Misreading'. Conference paper, Psi15 Conference, Zagreb.
3 Stickland, P. and Templeton, F. (1982) *Against Agreement*. Performance, The Red Bar, New York.
4 Heathfield, A., Quick, A., Templeton F. (eds) (1997) *Shattered Anatomies*, Bristol: Arnolfini and Arts Council of England.
5 The Theatre of Mistakes (1997) *Going*. Performance, Cambridge Festival of Contemporary Poetry, Cambridge (UK).
6 The Theatre of Mistakes (1976) *Homage to Pietro Longhi*. Performance, Serpentine Gallery, London.
7 The Relationship (2009) *Going with Coming*. Performance, Chashama Theater, New York.

DO THE WILD THING! REDUX

Bodies in Flight, *Do the Wild Thing!* performance, Jane Devoy and Dan Elloway. Photo: Edward Dimsdale, 1996, courtesy of Bodies in Flight.

Bodies in Flight

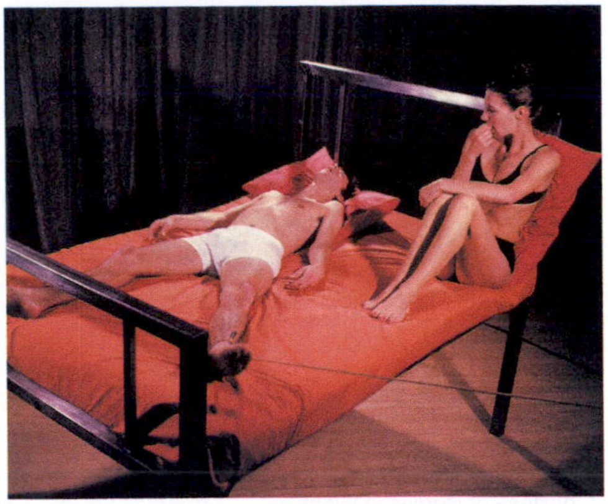

Bodies in Flight formed in 1990 to make work about the encounter between flesh and text. Our eighth project *Do the Wild Thing!* (1996) was the first to be led by a specific research concern: to explore this encounter between discursive and embodied practices by separating what is heard and what is seen. For four weeks we worked in separate rooms, choreographer Sara Giddens with performers Jane Devoy and Dan Elloway; writer Simon Jones with performer Jon Carnall, only sharing our work for two hours every Friday. Alongside this, composer Christopher Austin wrote a score for string trio, to be played live; and designer Bridget Mazzey physicalised this processual separation by dividing the stage-space into three. From this non-collaboration, the dualities of a genuine complementarity could begin to find their own modes of engagement: solitarinesses from which a collaborating could emerge.

In 2012, for Performing Documents' *Do the Wild Thing!* Redux (Arnolfini, Bristol), four of the original collaborators extended the show's ideas of non-collaboration by working independently until the day of installing the work. Returning to the archival remains of this peepshow about desire and voyeurism, each produced a separate new work in their own medium—dance, photography, text and video. Our collective brief was that each non-collaborator would take their own inspiration from their first involvement in *Do the Wild Thing!* and, where possible, pay particular attention to those elements of the archive each produced.

We found ourselves each looking askance anew at the quasi-object that had been the show. Like a hologram, shattered, we offered a set of different perspectives, (literally) through-seeings on to the object that was no longer there. The show, which now appeared through the perspectives of each work making up the installation, existed in between the media as an expression of inbetweenness 'itself'. The illusionary centre, the real of the work-object, was evacuated to the edges of multiple viewpoints, expressions of each non-collaborator's journey between the non-communicable parts, the aspects of the re-dux/re-turn. The performance's single point of view, its proscenium-arch set-up was re-placed by the fugacious affect of the choices made by each non-collaborator, disentangling media as they crisscrossed in between and across the work's archival remains. From this dispersed periphery, we looked back at, re-turned to face the primal scene we had fled 16 years earlier.

Bodies in Flight, *Do the Wild Thing!* Redux installation, Arnolfini (Bristol). Photo: Carl Newland, 2012. Courtesy of Bodies in Flight.

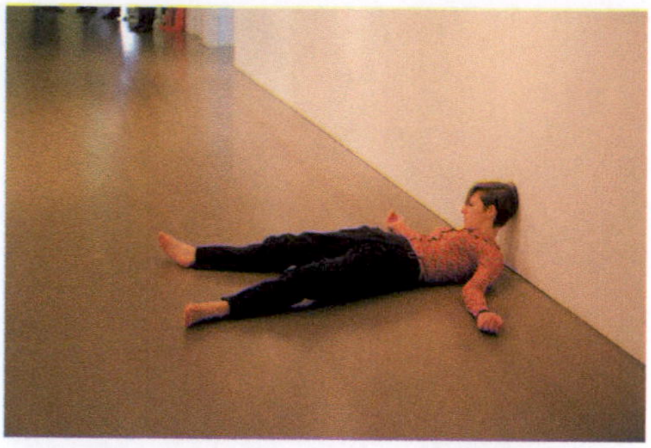

Sara Giddens, *Still Moving: Moving Still* dance, Martha King. Photo: Carl Newland, 2012. Courtesy of Bodies in Flight.

Sara Giddens, *Still Moving: Moving Still* dance, Tom Bailey and Martha King. Photo: Carl Newland, 2012. Courtesy of Bodies in Flight.

Choreographer Sara Giddens worked for two weeks with performers Tom Bailey and Martha King exploring the micro-choreography of exchanged looks and minute gestures she had first developed with Dan and Jane. *Still Moving: Moving Still* was a durational dance duet, performed a number of times over *Redux*'s opening weekend. Over a two-hour period, the dancers moved through the installation and out into other gallery spaces, ending up in Arnolfini's Reading Room where some of the archival remains Sara used in the reinvention were being exhibited.

Photographer Edward Dimsdale decided to respond to his archive of negatives from his documentation of *Do the Wild Thing!*, as well as super-8 footage he had taken of the show's final dance sequence. In *Make the Fixed Volatile, and Make the Volatile Fixed*, he wanted to explore his current research interest in the re-working of one photographic technology through the frame of another, specifically re-figuring old photogravure techniques with the digital, and so foregrounding both the processes of producing the image and the materiality of the print itself. To do this, he re-printed the negatives in a variety of formats, including frame-by-frame reprints of the film footage. These large and small images in both black-and-white and colour were then distressed and pinned to the long wall of the gallery to produce a bricolage glimpsing a fragmented timeline of the show's languid, interrupted primal scene.

With *I'd Like to Call You Joe Tonight*, video-maker Tony Judge decided to explode the single perspective of his 1996 multi-camera record, taken from the audience's point of view, by harnessing the potential of high-resolution imaging and hard-drive synchronisation. He worked with cinematographer Terry Flaxton to produce a three-screen video-work that reinvented the show from each of its actors' points-of-view—Grace, Joe and the Man. The three screens were installed on three different walls of the gallery, so that it was impossible to view all three without turning one's head. Each

Edward Dimsdale, *Make the Fixed Volatile, and Make the Volatile Fixed* photography. Photo: Carl Newland, 2012. Courtesy of Bodies in Flight.

screen had its own separate soundtrack that was only audible if one approached the monitor. Tony wanted to use his medium to accentuate the voyeurism that drove the first work by representing each actor from the point of view of the others: a triangle of gazes that implicated even more intimately the spectator in the erotic play of its primal scene.

For *Muse*, Simon Jones explored his central concern as a writer: the relationship of text to flesh in the performance-event, of the spoken or heard word to the physical presence of the performer. Inspired by a rehearsal photograph he took, he made a limited-edition book musing upon his relation to Dan during those original rehearsals. For two days, Dan read extracts from Muse to gallery visitors. In comparing the text's imaginings of flesh with the person lying on the mattress, the visitor could see how Dan's body had aged over the intervening 16 years. This gap between representation and flesh ghosted the imaginative space in the writing between two kinds of desire: first, the desire to know, to be able to own the person *thoughtfully through* words as symbols; and secondly, the desire to have, to be able to own the person *feelingly through flesh* as sensation. The writing attempted to achieve both these impossibilities, and knowingly failed.

Each non-collaborator's work became an *approaching*, a touching without ever reaching: to begin again towards the emptied scene. So, *Redux* did not provide a more complete version of *Do the Wild Thing!*, as film directors might like to think their reduxs do—a version more original than the original. It actually opened up more gaps, exposing the show's auratic mask of originality, its documents' claim to be *the* work, by pointing to multiple, possible future works. In this way, our stepping aside and disentangling resonated with the 'original' process of both making and documenting, disclosing the incompletenesses in between and within media—the middles of middles. Furthermore, the installation itself attempted to re-enact for the visitor the experience of transitioning between material and media,

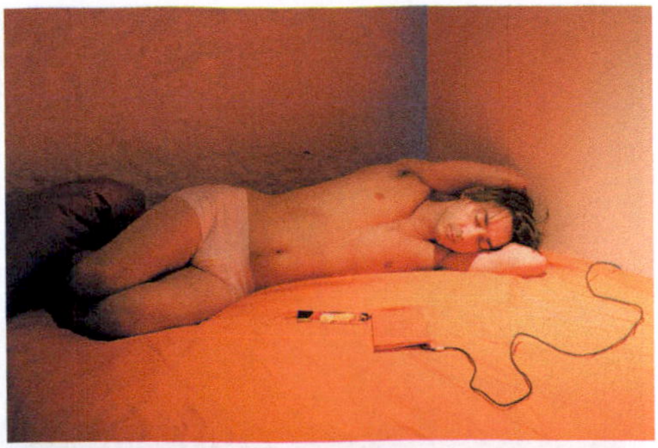

Simon Jones, *Muse* print and installation, Dan Elloway. Photo: Carl Newland, 2012. Courtesy of Bodies in Flight.

techniques and perspectives, which we as makers experienced in making the 'original' work and auditor-spectators experienced in its performing. For Bodies in Flight, the archive's very productivity emerged from crossing these gaps, and so experiencing the impossibility of completeness, of realising an origin. The artist's indirect relation to the archive, thence to all technologies, says something more about performance: that at its heart is collaboration as indirectness. The Redux exercise brought these two kinds of indirectness together: the first, in relation to technology and thence performance's relation to liveness—livingness; and the second, a fundamental mood to artists working together, not predicated upon common ground, nor agreed terms, but upon revealing impossibly from out of unspeakable and non-communicable complementarities what the work can do amongst the wills of its makers.

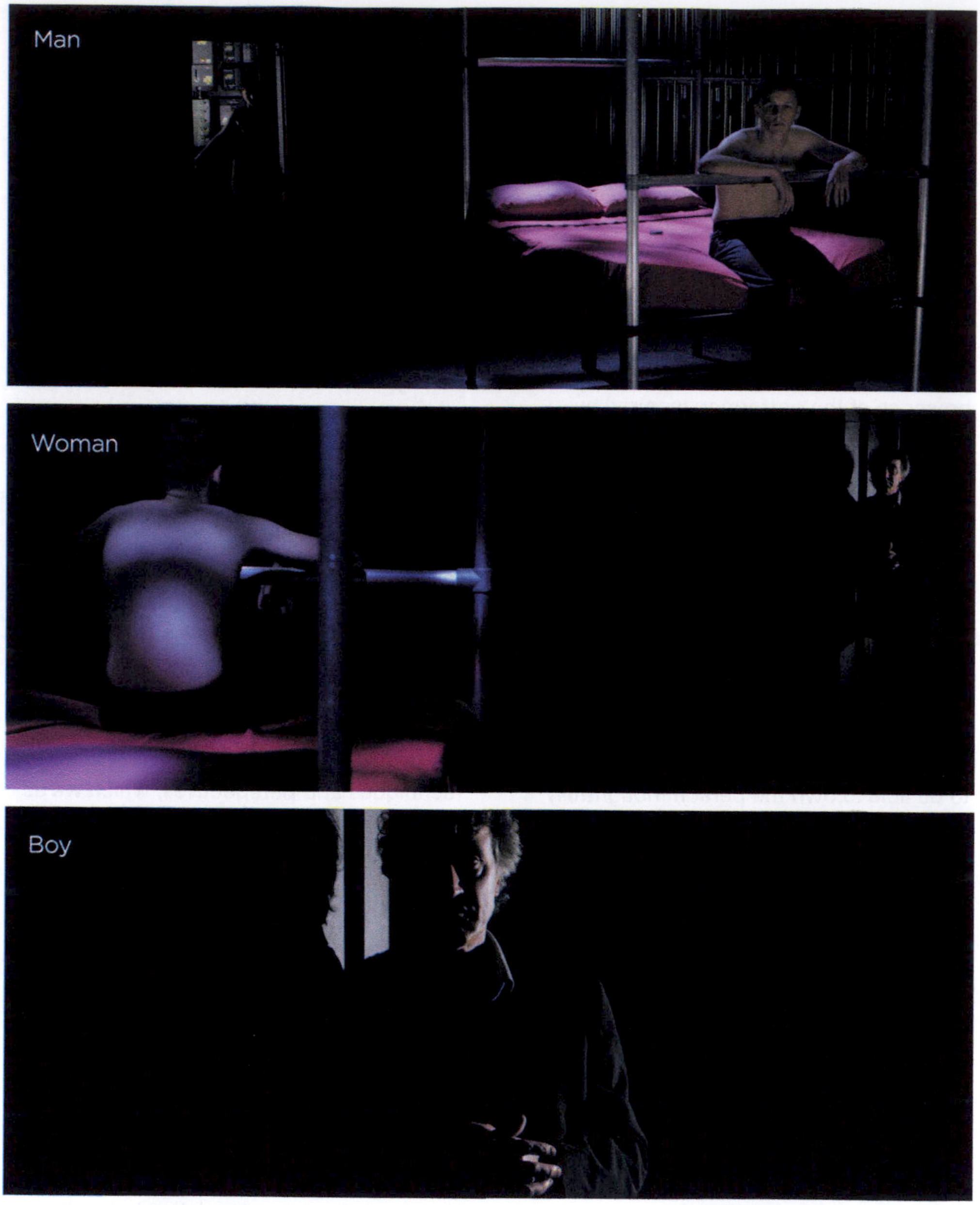

Tony Judge, *I'd Like to Call You Joe Tonight* multi-screen video, Chris Bianchi, Polly Frame, James D. Kent. Video-still Tony Judge, 2012. Courtesy of Bodies in Flight.

Man

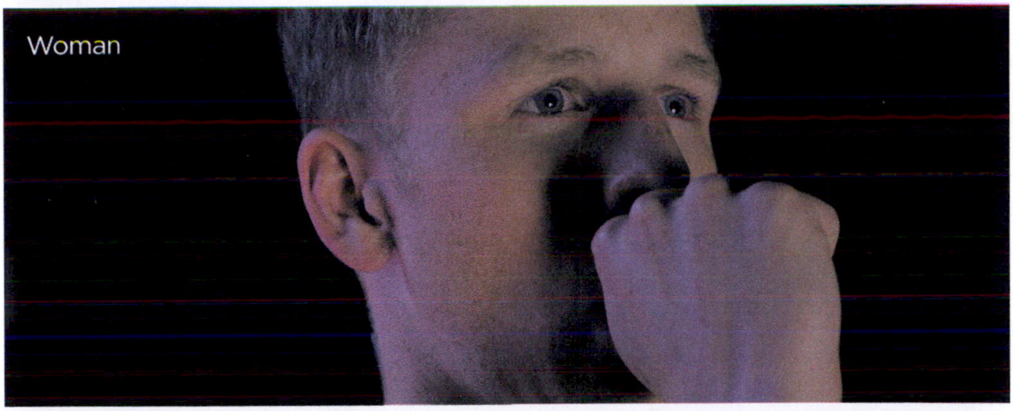
Woman

Boy

UNDERSTANDING NEGATIVE DIALECTICS

Felix Gmelin

As in Gary Hill's work *Remarks on Colour* from 1994, where he makes his 12-year-old daughter Anastasia read from Ludwig Wittgenstein's 1950 book *Remarks on Colour* at an age where she cannot understand what she reads, my son and the children in Bristol also struggle with a text that is far too transcendental and abstract for them to understand at that age. The difference between Gary Hill's daughter Anastasia and my son David, Gracie, Jayden and William from Bristol is that Anastasia within her father's staging is talking about her own presence while my son and the children from Bristol are talking about the future they will inherit. In both cases these works talk about how strange it is to address and plan your future before you know what you want and desire.

> The better organised the means of the individual, and thus the possibilities of resistance, the more obliged are public affairs, as a societal rule, and for self-preservatory reasons, to integrate whatever the individual is, in order to prevent its neurotisation of public affairs, and thus to prevent accidents or catastrophes. The claim for totality must sustain the individual even if it does not reveal it, or, from its standpoint, is unable to reveal itself to it. The contents of the collective rest with the individuals. If it is not conscious of the tensions of the extreme, as a correlation, it is simply padding without an engine, an emasculated patriarchal-collective ego in the veiled twilight of an infantilised alienating animal. Its cultural effigies are the symbols of the death-chambers of waiting in one-dimensional mass-communication. It would strengthen the collective ego's power to anticipate itself in concrete utopias and in its images, and send packing the eternal animal's revelations, which seeks the end of the world with consternation, ascension and panic.
> trans. from Gmelin 1969

Felix Gmelin, *Negative Dialectics*, one channel video with sound in 03,16 min. loop, filmed in Weimar, Germany, June 25 2010. Excerpt and translation from German to English: the artist. Courtesy Vilma Gold, London.

Felix Gmelin, *Left and Right and Right and Wrong*, one channel video in 16,52 min. loop, filmed in Bristol, UK, July 4 2013 depicting two children reading two texts: John Sutherland's praise of capitalism from his 1948 film 'Make Mine Freedom' juxtaposed with an excerpt from Sven Wernström's 1971 book 'Kamrat Jesus', (Comrade Jesus) explaining Jesus was a Communist.

Reference

1969 Gmelin, O.F. 'Die neue Linke nach Adorno'. In W. F. Schoeller (ed.) *Negative Dialektik—Schaltsystem der Utopie*, Munich: Kindler Verlag.

Felix Gmelin, *Understanding Negative Dialectics*, performance staged at Arnolfini, Bristol, April 13 2013. Commissioned by Tom Trevor and Axel Wieder for Arnolfini. Production: Lucy Badrocke / Arnolfini. Courtesy Vilma Gold, London.

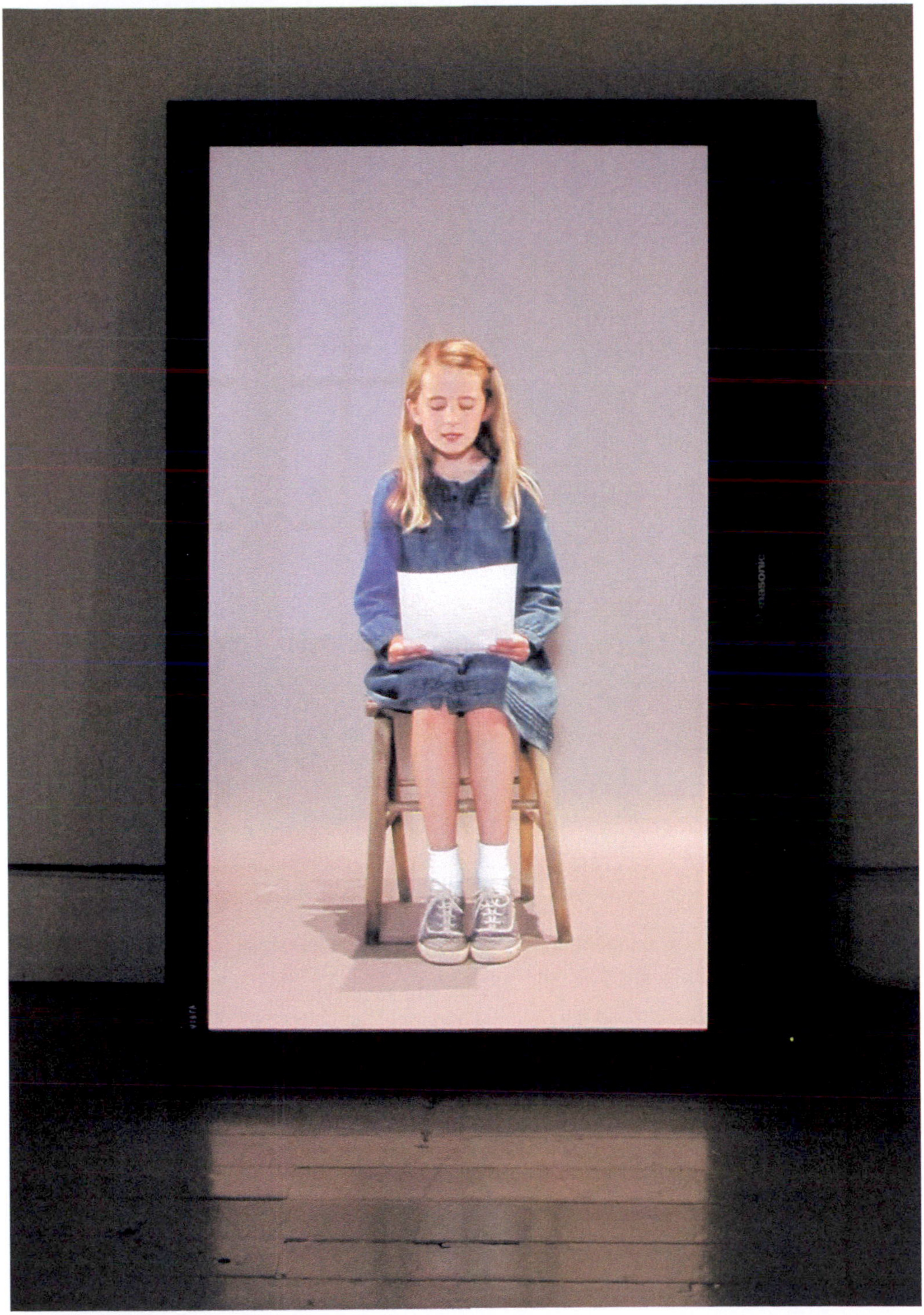

Felix Gmelin, *Utiphobia*, one channel video with sound on a tilted flat screen monitor in 19 min. loop. Filmed in Bristol, UK, July 5 2013 depicting a young girl reading 'Negative Dialektik—Schaltsystem der Utopie', written by my father Otto F. Gmelin and originally published in: 'Die neue Linke nach Adorno', (The new left after Adorno). Edited by Wilfried F. Schoeller, Kindler Verlag, München 1969. Production: Lucy Badrocke / Arnolfini. Cinematography: Rhiannon Chaloner. Courtesy Vilma Gold, London.

9 Beginnings: sonic theatrical possibilities and potentialities in the performance archive

Johanna Linsley

'Good evening. I love you.'

A performer stands centre stage in a black-box theatre and says these words. Elsewhere onstage, a banner made of white A4 paper reading 'I Love You' flutters. Nothing particular is made of this repetition. There is a shared space and time, and a collection of perceptions: the rustle of paper, the sound of a voice, the modest placement of text, the presence of two people in a theatre space facing an audience. From this, it is the possibility of and potential for relationships that suggests itself.

'I love you' is a declaration that has been made before, elsewhere, obviously. Specifically, the first declaration is lifted from a performance by British performance duo Lone Twin, titled *Walk With Me Walk With Me Will Somebody Please Walk With Me*, and the second from a piece called *Saccades* by Glasgow-based artist Nic Green. These re-utterances, spoken and printed, share a stage as part of a third performance, *9 Beginnings*, by the international, Chicago-based company Every house has a door. *9 Beginnings* is composed entirely of beginnings of other performances, all drawn from specific performance archives in the UK and USA (the Live Art Archives at the University of Bristol and the Randolph Street Gallery Archives at the School of the Art Institute of Chicago).

The institutional connection between the source material is attended by other, less predictable connections between the pieces, what dramaturge Matthew Goulish calls 'unexpected echoes [that] presented themselves to us. We did not set out to look for them' (Goulish, 2011). The act of declaring love to strangers is one of these unexpected echoes.

The sonic term 'echo' captures well what is happening in *9 Beginnings*. Echoes disorient. The repetition of the echo (echo… echo…) as it is experienced depends on the listener's position in relationship to the trajectory of sound. Echoes suggest an origin, but in the event of reverberation, linear sequence can be disrupted as sounds bounce on surfaces and return, and in this disruption, the possibility of other sequences or orders are present. In the echoed 'I love you', the repetition of the words combines with the unique tone of the voice (what Roland Barthes calls its 'grain' [Barthes 1978]), its accent, its pitch, its tempo, the flimsiness and flutter of paper, the architecture of the theatre space, the modes of attention in the audience (who may not even register the repetition). These all resonate with the physically absent historical performances, but the trajectory, and thus meaning, of that resonance is not fixed.

In recent years, sound has received increased attention from theatre and performance scholars: see, for example, the collection *Theatre Noise: The Sound of Performance* (Kendrick and Roesner, 2011). While questions about, for instance, the voice have long been addressed from a training perspective, there is a renewed interest in theatre and performance in theorising the sonic as such. This is conditioned by a rising interest in aurality among theorists from further afield, including a consolidation of the field of sound studies. Of particular interest for this chapter is the way sonic theory has addressed the key terms of possibility and potentiality, driven by a sense that aurality has some purchase on these ideas. Jean-Luc Nancy describes listening as 'straining toward a possible meaning', as opposed to the more linear analysis that hearing, framed by Nancy as understanding the sense of something, provides (2007: 6). Other thinkers whom I engage later in this chapter also draw on sound to suggest a kind of material immateriality, something located in the here and now that also suggests, as in José Muñoz's understanding of critical utopian thinking, a 'then and there' (2009). I draw on these thinkers and others, in relation to *9 Beginnings*, to explore how sonic concepts and sonic theatrical techniques (some of which might have sonorous qualities without being necessarily or only audible) help with understanding the documentation and archiving of performance in terms of possibility and potentiality.

In spite of the recent surge of interest in sound in the arts and humanities broadly and within performance more specifically, still the work of theorising sound in relation to performance documentation is largely undone. Whether this is because, as Ross Brown argues, sound poses material and logistical challenges for institutional imperatives around documentation and evidencing (Brown 2010), or because the terms of debate around performance documentation have so often circulated around disappearance, thus reinscribing appearance as the central—if negative—concept, still the sonic has much to offer theorising of performance documentation. In Salomé Voegelin's reading of sonic representations of space in contrast to visual mapping, for instance, she finds 'a contingent geography between the self and the world in which we live, without insisting on a central or determining authority, neither divine nor scientific' (Voegelin 2014: 24). While it is important not to overstate the purchase of sound on openness and indeterminacy—not least because of the deeply ableist consequences of any statements on the inherent or essential qualities of a particular mode of sensing—as a way into thinking possibility and potentiality, the sonic offers a range of theoretical avenues.

How and why we turn and return to performance archives is still so often a question of complicating the notion of origin, which over the past few decades within performance studies has been approached through a dizzying range of conceptual frameworks. The terms of these debates shift, cede ground and return, transformed—terms like liveness, or presence, or remains, or repertoire, or redoing '*not as before* but *once again*' (Lepecki 2012: 156, original emphasis). Issues posed by poststructuralist literary and cultural theory of textual authority and authorial intent have long been explored in this context—some might say exhaustingly, if not exhaustively. In this chapter, however, I argue that aural concepts—like the echo or, as I discuss later, voice or rhythm or amplification—can refresh this complex work. The sonic theatricality I propose is grounded in the materiality of the past, for which archives are privileged sites, and opens up these materials' contingencies to flux and change.

In this, I intend something akin to what Voegelin calls 'sonic sensibility'. For Voegelin, this means a mode of attention to the sonic, or a way of using sonic material to develop a type of attention that can:

> reveal what this world is made of, to question its singular actuality and to hear other possibilities that are probably present too, but which, for reasons of ideology, power and

> coincidence do not take equal part in the production of knowledge, reality, value and truth.
>
> Voegelin 2014: 3

This is not to make a universalist claim for sound as more radical, or even ultimately separable from other modes of perception. Rather, a sonic sensibility informs a situated practice which proposes that in a world dominated by a visual paradigm, aurality is one powerful tool for challenging the configuration of the possible.

Every house has a door is a performance company known for challenging such configurations, and I argue in what follows that attention to the sonic offers new ways of thinking about their methodologies. Further, such focus on the sonic dimensions of this methodology leads to greater understanding of the possibilities and potentialities of performance archives more broadly. *9 Beginnings* is a particularly valuable example for exploring sonic possibility, located as it is entirely in the set-up for other pieces—the period in a performance right before the point of no return, when everything could still go another way. The echoes and reverberations and resonances and rhythms and imitations and, indeed, silences to be found in this work gesture to a horizon that is unfixed, whilst emanating from and referring back to material bodies and spaces in the here and now. Dee Heddon figures the horizon of sound as a necessarily intersubjective geography, which can be extended and modified in relationship between listener and listened-to (2010). It is this kind of complex horizon that *9 Beginnings* gestures towards.

Performance documentation: possibilities and potentialities

For the sake of this present work, it is worthwhile considering a distinction between the terms possibility and potentiality, whilst acknowledging that any attempt to chart conditions of possibility and fields of potentiality as such, would, within the scope of this chapter, come up against the limits of impossibility (not to say absurdity) quite quickly. I am interested, rather, to study these terms in relation to performance documentation, and to show how sonic perspectives open them up. The phrase 'conditions of possibility' recalls Michel Foucault's development of the 'episteme' in his early work, or the underlying discursive order of any given historical period which makes certain types of knowledge possible (1971). For many performance scholars working on documentation, the contingency of the conditions of possibility, and their processual nature and openness to change, have been key to the work's potency.

Carolyn Steedman notes that the writing of history 'depends on the unsettling knowledge that nothing need have been said or written in the way it was... nothing at all' (2001: 108). In this sense, then, all archives are less the authoritative records of historical stability, and are instead collections of traces from events that could have turned out otherwise, produced in ways that could have been done differently. This is not to over-emphasise individual choice in the course of history, but rather to attend to the multiple contingencies that are continuously in process in any cultural formation. This contingency does not end when documents are accessioned by the institution. Steedman also writes that '[y]ou find nothing in the Archive but stories caught half way through: the middle of things; discontinuities' (2001: 45). The discontinuity of the archive signals an indeterminate future. Much of the wide and diverse scholarship around performance, documentation and archives is engaged with exactly this 'unsettling knowledge'.

Muñoz, for example, declares that performance scholarship has value as a 'queer world-making project' in part because it refigures the status of evidence. Re-working how we approach the historical record, and the practices of documentation and archiving that produce it, in turn offers alternative ways of thinking the past and ultimately the future. Queer lives have historically revealed themselves 'covertly', through things like 'innuendo, gossip, fleeting moments, and performances that are meant to be interacted with by those within its epistemological sphere' (Muñoz 1996: 6). When evidence of queerness can attract attack, the ephemeral, performative act is an important way of signalling one's existence without drawing unwelcome or dangerous attention. Muñoz argues further, however, for the ephemeral itself *as* evidence. Performance scholarship, and the tools it has developed to understand 'what a queer act does' more than 'what it might *mean*' (Muñoz 1996: 12), might be able to shift the focus of research from the interpretation of a fixed evidence-base to a critical practice of making and re-making the world.

Amelia Jones has also influentially made the case for the political value of highlighting the indeterminacy of documentation. For example, in her well-known article '"Presence" in Absentia: Experiencing Performance as Documentation' she counters claims for the unmediated, un-documentable presence of 1970s body art and also rejects ideas about the photograph as stable proof of an act occurring. She emphasises instead the multiple and intersubjective qualities that body art highlights, tracing a dynamic relation between acts of the body, documents of these acts, and modes of perceiving the work by audience members or critics. She analyses the historicity and ideological investments in notions of both unmediated presence and stable evidence, which she argues signals an oppressive modernist ideal. On the other hand, for Jones, body art—particularly feminist body art—with its dispersed subjectivities, effects 'the dislocation of the fantasy of the fixed, normative, centred modernist subject'. Such a dislocation 'provides a radical challenge to the masculinism, racism, colonialism, classism, and heterosexism built into this fantasy'. Jones emphasises how the body art she considers is fundamentally conditioned by historical constructions of subjectivity—'late capitalist, postcolonial, postmodern'—at the same time that it intervenes in these constructions (Jones 1997: 12).

In both of these cases, what is at stake is an understanding that the world is not fixed, that the conditions which circumscribe possibility may themselves be subject to change, and that how we understand documentation and/as evidence in relation to the making of history is connected to how change might occur. A whole range of performance scholars have wrestled with similar stakes—from Diana Taylor's argument for a decolonising understanding of the transmission of knowledge through embodied rather than textual practices (2003), to Rebecca Schneider's investigation of historical re-enactment as a performative mode of historiography (2011), to the debates around Peggy Phelan's analysis of 'liveness' as the ontological condition of performance (1993). Performance studies is hardly the only discipline to be concerned with historical contingency, a defining question of postmodern thinking and beyond. However, debates about the configurations of performance act, document, perception or encounter, in relation to the production of knowledge have underscored foundational work in the field. Further, much of this work proceeds from the idea that the practice of theatre and performance itself offers valuable methods for staging, as it were, the possibilities of historical contingency and alternative ways of doing history.

Within sound studies, too, the relationship between recording, reproduction and contingency has proved fruitful for analysis. Jonathon Sterne, for instance, has undertaken the historicisation of sound reproduction (recording, broadcast, amplification, etc.) alongside the development of ideas of 'original' and 'copy' themselves. His social constructivist analysis traces how the conceptual shifts that attended sound reproduction technologies, like the idea that recording 'separated sounds from their sources', reflect historically conditioned attitudes which in turn influenced how technologies developed (Sterne 2003: 8). The idea of hi-fidelity, for example, first depends on the invention of the idea of a pure 'original' sound, which was neither an obvious nor inevitable cultural concept before the modern period. Innovations in technology aimed at reproducing an original sound with fidelity are, Sterne argues, part of the larger process of the development of modernity, and rely as much on cultural attitudes towards unity, wholeness and a universalised subject as they do on advances in technology. Indeed, Sterne argues that cultural practices are the conditions of possibility for these advances. As with Jones and Muñoz, the stakes of the analysis lie in its ability to articulate the multiple, in-process contingencies surrounding the production of representation, which in turn leaves open the possibility of political action and change.

If contingency has been a key mode for understanding possibility in relation to both performance documentation and sound reproduction, there are other modes of analysis, particularly associated with the sonic, which might be better understood as addressing potentiality. Eleni Ikoniadou, for instance, develops the concept of rhythm in relation to a kind of potentiality that is non-linear, and functions in gaps, excesses and intensities. She writes:

> Our stock market tools, insurance policies, entertainment industries, preemptive tactics of war, and the constant imminence of 'the next' potential pandemic—all unveil a human fascination with (and fear of) the future and what it may hold. In these examples, what might come to be but does not yet exist is widely assumed to be subject to prediction, accountable to a set of probabilities, and capable of being quantified, modelled, managed, or even escaped. In other words, futurity and contingency in the event, which may or may not be actualised, are commonly understood according to the metaphysics of possibility.
>
> Ikoniadou 2014: 18

The work of prediction involves constructing a totality of possible outcomes and weighing them against each other to identify the most likely one, or to mitigate the risks associated with them. The limitations of this approach, Ikoniadou's 'metaphysics of possibility', is not only that the construction of a totality might be incomplete, or miss factors out, or even that it might affect the outcome of an event by legitimising or prioritising certain factors over others. For Ikoniadou, this metaphysics is oppressive because the idea of a transcendent totality cannot account for 'heterogenous processes that are irreducible to units and hierarchies' (2014: 7). She argues instead (drawing on Deleuze's reading of Nietzsche) for a philosophy of 'pure becoming', which is not teleological, or aimed at a single or bounded set of outcomes, but rather immanent to the material situation. As I will explore further later in this chapter, the concept of rhythm helps Ikoniadou articulate this philosophy. This work in turn helps with an understanding of performance archives as in rhythm with past, present and future.

If potentiality may be useful for thinking of the future in terms of immanence and heterogeneity, it can also be figured in relation to impotentiality, to what doesn't or won't happen. As Giorgio Agamben develops it, the potential to do is necessarily wrapped up with the potential *not* to do (2000). Alice Lagaay has taken Agamben's work on impotentiality as an entry point to consideration of the voice in relation to silence. Here, to think about the potential of the voice is to think about the not-spoken as inextricable from what is said. Lagaay's reading of Agamben turns on the insight that the process of learning to understand language instills in humans the experience of the voice in an intermediary position between meaning and meaninglessness. From here, it can be recognised that the 'experience of potentiality is not only to be interpreted as an experience of the possibility of speaking. More profoundly at stake here is the experience of a fundamentally human *in*ability' (Lagaay 2011: 66). This experience of inability lingers even when we are able to understand speech. Indeed, for Lagaay, the silence that surrounds a voice is necessary for this understanding, for 'a voice that were only ever in an active mode of actual speaking performance, a voice that knew no silence, could not be a real voice nor even identified as an hallucination' (2011: 65). Using this thinking to approach the potentiality of performance archives allows not just recognition of the paths untaken which haunt any history, as valuable as this is. It also allows for listening to the silences at the very heart of what *did* happen, what *has* taken place.

In the following reading of the work of Every house has a door, these different modes of possibility and potentiality are all at play. The work evokes a sense of contingency, particularly the idea that history could have happened differently, and is also keenly aware of the conditions of its possibility. Indeed, as I discuss below, *9 Beginnings* makes some of the conditions of its own theatrical mechanism part of the material of the work, resonating with the conditions of the archival performances it draws from. The piece also plays on modes of potentiality I have discussed, including rhythmic heterogeneity and vocal silence, along with other sonic theatrical techniques and textures. However, *9 Beginnings* produces these possibilities and potentialities under a series of limits and constraints, complicating notions of openness and indeterminacy, and connecting 'then' (both the past and the future) with the now of theatrical time. I will consider how some of these constraints function, and then address how a sonic sensibility helps sound out the vibrations between possible and impossible, potential and impotential, that are found in the work.

Sounding out constraint

Every house has a door, like Goat Island (the company Lin Hixson and Matthew Goulish worked with previously), uses limits as a key methodology, both self-imposed aesthetic and conceptual constraints, and the external constraints that come with working in non-commercial and experimental ways. Stephen Bottoms locates an ethics in Goat Island's concern with *possibility in impossibility*, which is applicable here. He argues that 'any honest attempt at taking responsibility for one's place in the world (with all the contradiction and blind spots that implies), must bring us face to face with the impossible' (Bottoms and Goulish 2007: 25). Bottoms is drawing, in turn, on Jacques Derrida's assertion that 'the condition of possibility of this thing called responsibility is a certain experience and experiment of the possibility of the impossible' (Derrida 1992: 41). This work with constraint, then, offers an understanding about the very real limitations of individual reach in the world. It is within these limitations, or rather in response to or negotiation with limits, that a form of potentiality emerges, which dodges determinism while also rejecting ideas of total, seamless openness.

The format of *9 Beginnings* is clearly the product of a series of constraints. First, Hixson and Goulish set themselves the task of identifying nine beginnings from historical performances. Given the make-up of the cast (there are two main performers and two choreographed stagehands), beginnings were chosen which could be performed as solos or duets. The beginnings were also broken down into three types. First, there are beginnings that, as Goulish writes, 'set the stage'. These beginnings are concerned with 'preparing the audience as a precondition of the performance'. The second type of beginning is ritualistic, a beginning that 'harnesses duration as an energy, and seems to gather the many rhythms of the audience into the single, directed rhythm of the performance'. Finally there are beginnings that drop an audience into action that is already in progress. These 'in medias res' beginnings construct the fiction that the world of the performance was in operation before the audience arrived (which also may imply the possibility that this fictional work persists after the audience leaves) (Goulish 2011).

The content and status of the historical performances was also considered. There is work by both younger and older artists, well known and hardly known at all. Unlike many performance re-enactment projects, a sense of the iconic is strictly avoided. Goulish writes, 'we avoided work that seemed too signature, that might suggest that if you do not recognize the source artist, that you are missing out on something' (2011). This is supported by the printed programmes that are distributed to audiences, with the source material clearly referenced, along with the archive or collection from which it was selected (this use of printed material that goes beyond traditional production credits is common for Every house has a door, as it was for Goat Island).

While the format of *9 Beginnings* is clearly highly structured, there are also deviations. The most obvious of these to an audience is that the piece actually includes ten beginnings. I look at this tenth beginning in a later section, but it is worth pointing out here that it is precisely because *9 Beginnings* has such a rigorous framework that variations like this stand out.

Two more constraints, or categories of constraint, are key to the piece: the specific archives Every house has a door draws from, and the theatricality of both the source material and the techniques the company uses to respond to this material. *9 Beginnings* does not function as a representation of the archives it draws from, nor does it summarise the type of work collected there. Rather, the documentation is the occasion for the piece. However, the framework of *9 Beginnings* is also not simply a replicable franchise. Instead, the framework arises from a deep and long-term engagement on the part of Hixson and Goulish with many of the artists and organisations represented in both the Live Art Archives at the University of Bristol (UK) (an institution with which Hixson and Goulish have a long association through, among other things, Goat Island summer schools held in Bristol) and the Randolph Street Gallery archives at the School of the Art Institute of Chicago (where Goulish and Hixson are both professors).

The two contexts may have more in common than not—both the Bristol and Chicago selections include experimental, sometimes playful, intellectually adventurous performance. Hints of institutional discontinuity can be found, however. Randolph Street Gallery was a not-for-profit, artist-run space (it closed in 1998), which was dramatically affected by the so-called culture wars in the USA in the 1990s, during which federal funding for the arts, and particularly practices which were seen as controversial or provocative, was slashed. (For a contemporaneous look at the factors which forced Randolph Street Gallery to close, see Obejas

1998). The precarious condition of this is subtly highlighted in one of the beginnings Every house performs: Goulish enacts a pre-show announcement by the gallery's director which includes an appeal for donations from the audience. The selections from the Live Art archives, on the other hand, reflect that the 1990s and early 2000s were a time when experimental, interdisciplinary performance began to receive institutional acknowledgement and support in the UK, and the term 'Live Art' itself gained wider visibility and traction. (For an in-depth analysis of the development of Live Art in the 1990s, see Klein 2012.) Relatively greater access to public resources affected the type of work that was being produced in institutions in the USA and UK around roughly the same time. A very blunt difference can be seen in the fact that all of the artists in the 'Chicago' iteration of 9 Beginnings have or had direct institutional connections to the School of the Art Institute of Chicago, whereas the 'Bristol' iteration includes both international artists and artists from regions in the UK outside of London, where cultural resources are often based, indicating the effect of cultural investment in Live Art on the range of artists represented in the Live Art archives.

On the other hand, it is important not to overstate the discrepancy between the US and UK contexts. Both the 'Bristol' and 'Chicago' iterations show individuals and organisations attempting to make space for art that might not have other outlets. It is also worth pointing out that Live Art in the UK has certainly experienced significant levels of precarity, and that the New Labour-style rhetoric around the creative economy, which advocates of Live Art were able to use for the advantage of otherwise marginalised practices (Klein 2012), has largely dissipated since at least 2010 with the rise of the austerity policy paradigm. While *9 Beginnings* does not explicitly address these contexts, outside of a few sly references such as the appeal for donations mentioned above, there is a subtle advocacy for artists who are working at the limits of what is possible within external, material constraints.

9 Beginnings also works explicitly within, or rather at, the limits of theatre. In choosing the beginnings, Hixson and Goulish focused on work that is 'set in theatres, with an audience that enters and finds their seats, and lights that dim to start the show' (Goulish 2011). The kind of work held by both the Randolph Street Gallery and the Live Art Archives often occupies an uneasy disciplinary position between theatre and visual art. Beth Hoffman notes a sort of defensiveness particularly in the UK context in the positioning of Live Art against theatre by its practitioners, stating that 'Live art has long spent a great deal of time citing its "visual base"' (2009: 102) as a way to distance itself or break with theatre. Lara Shalson, on the other hand, accepts that practices associated with Live Art may indeed turn to the visual, but argues that the 'breaking' of theatre here may be a less a negation of theatre and more a way to 'push theatre to its limits, to separate it into pieces, to scrutinise its components' (2009: 107). In focusing on work that happens in theatres, Every house has a door are not denying the legacy of work that happens outside of these spaces, but rather continuing this scrutiny, and putting the limits of theatre to work as a kind of resonating chamber for possibility. While the visual is important in this work, attention to its sonic elements may offer a way of thinking about performance in relation to history and potentiality that does not involve an opposition between the theatrical and the visual. Here, then, I want to turn to thinking about the sonic theatricality of *9 Beginnings*.

Whose voice am I this time? Theatrical decisions and the possibilities of vocal imitation

The beginning of *9 Beginnings* is actually a tenth beginning, placed before the nine beginnings that are to come. In this beginning that is also not a beginning (because not included in the counting of nine beginnings), Goulish enters centre stage and faces the audience. Dressed in a black shirt and jeans, he stands behind a music stand. He announces the title of the show, and names the archives from which the show is generated. Then he begins to describe a film scene. He removes his glasses, steps back from the music stand and speaks with a subtle Texan accent, relaxing his own clipped Midwestern American pronunciation, and producing an altogether different pattern of emphasis from his previous precise delivery. He is performing the opening of Richard Linklater's 1991 film *Slacker*, and he is doing an impression of Linklater delivering a monologue to an unseen cab driver. The monologue is an account of a dream about a book about an idea. The idea is that every thought that anyone has in turn creates its own reality. 'It's like every choice and decision you make—the thing you choose not to do fractions off and becomes its own reality and it goes on from there...forever', he says (Linklater 1991). This stoner logic is the premise of *Slacker*, and it also in a sense describes the structure of *9 Beginnings*, though even this is somehow provisional. Goulish is playing a character, which we understand through the subtle shifts in his voicing, and in that character—in that voice—he offers the *Slacker* interpretation of *9 Beginnings* as one possibility.

This balance between the provisional and the decisive is characteristic of *9 Beginnings*. As Goulish says, '[e]ach moment seems to demand its own set of rules, or constraints, with no uniform measure, and disciplined adherence to those constraints gives the performance its authority' (2011). Each decision is adopted rigorously, but every shift in archival material and theatrical situation demands a new decision, and a new rigorous adherence. This makes for a heterogenous theatrical texture, where task-based acts give way to postmodern, self-reflexive monologues which themselves give way to surreal images and to choreographed dance, and on and on. Holding this together is a precise structure. There are two performers and two choreographed stagehands who keep the piece moving. There are limited props. The nine sections of the piece move forward in a linear order, and there are programme notes which audience members can follow to orient themselves. Yet within that structure, the host of other possible decisions, other possible beginnings, everything that could have happened but has not, are somehow present in relief.

Importantly, the structure of the show is not commented upon by the performers, but simply undertaken. Goulish's opening—and particularly the choices he makes in his vocal delivery—set the precedent for this. He starts the piece seemingly as a narrator, someone who stands outside of the action and interprets. However, as he slides into his vocal impression of Linklater, the assurance of a stable mediator fades and is replaced by the sense that we are inside the theatrical mechanism already, and that here, anything could happen. Decisions around voicing—and re-voicing, particularly—continue throughout the piece to call into question the position of the performers in relation to the audience, to the archival material, and to the theatrical structure itself.

For instance, each 'beginning' in the show is preceded by an announcement made by one of the performers. These announcements are generally quotations, whose sources are listed in the programme—the sources include Gertrude Stein, Lawrence Steger, Gregory Bateson, Matt Adams, John Lennon and Arnold I. Davidson. The eighth announcement is not obviously a quotation but perhaps more of a warning: 'Audience participation'. This announcement is made by all of the performers, who line up and speak the text, one by one, into a microphone. Each performer speaks the text in their own 'native' language—these include Spanish, Serbian and Italian, as well as English. The performers then distribute a printed piece of text, which is in English, to the audience, and then performer Sebastián Calderón performs a translation of that text in Spanish. This is a recreation of the beginning of Augusto Corrieri's *Quartet (For Anna Akhmatova)* as presented at the National Review of Live Art in Glasgow in 2008. When Corrieri performed this piece in Glasgow, he spoke the text in English.

A number of questions arise. Is the decision to use Spanish made because Corrieri plays 'himself' in the piece, and if Calderón were 'himself' he'd speak Spanish? If so, this decision is not consistent throughout *9 Beginnings*. For instance, when Calderón and the other main performer, Selma Banich (who is Serbian), perform the piece by Lone Twin they use English, though they refer to each other in their own names in place of the original performers' names, signalling that the question of 'whose voice is this?' was considered. So is the language decision more closely related to the 'audience participation' announcement? Some audience members were surely relieved to discover that their participation did not involve leaving their seats. Did the participation lie, then, in listening while they read? Was this, in a sense, a theatrical machine producing an encounter between voice and text powered by audience members' attention? An encounter which could also be understood as a separation of voice from text? The individual experience of this depends, of course, on whether an audience member understands Spanish or English or both, and how they choose to direct their attention. Do they read or listen for textual meaning? Do they attempt to experience language without meaning, or voice without language? Are these last impossible tasks? All of these questions—which might be framed as questions about 'aural attention' (Home-Cook 2015)—are present in many types of theatrical encounters. None of these questions are answered, or even made explicit in this sequence. Rather, the sequence unfolds with a matter-of-factness which characterises much of the piece so that while it is not exactly clear *why* the theatrical decision to perform this text in Spanish has been made, the fact that it *is* a theatrical decision is more than evident. This has the effect of placing the dramaturgical emphasis on the possibility of performance archives—the underlying sense that within the precise and rigorous theatrical structure, and given a certain number of material constraints, nevertheless things could go another way. This sense of possibility frames the historical performance as a starting place, a point of departure.

Other theatrical decisions around voicing and re-voicing arise throughout the performance. When Banich sings 'Thunder Road', is she 'covering' Bruce Springsteen, or is it an imitation of Gregg Whelan from Lone Twin when he sings the Springsteen song? Whelan is clear in the Lone Twin piece how much he loves the song. What are Banich's feelings? Does it matter? Does it matter that Banich's voice is 'stronger'—more in key, better breath control—than Whelan's? On the one hand, these questions may be exactly the point of *9 Beginnings*. The company approaches material with a set of questions and makes theatrical decisions which do not exactly answer the questions but stage new questions for an audience to pick up (or not). On the other hand, all of these questions could be answered differently, or replaced by other questions.

I am not suggesting, however, that the decisions Every house make are simply arbitrary or unconstrained. As Daphne Brooks reminds us in her study of the 'sonic blue(s)face' of Amy Winehouse, vocal imitation is never culturally neutral. For Brooks, the vocality of someone like Winehouse is a complex intersection of racial and gender mimicry and (dis)identifications with early female blues pioneers, as well as contemporary male hip-hop bravado. The value of these vocal moves, notwithstanding their often troubled associations and appropriations, lies for Brooks in 'exposing the cross-pollinated aesthetics of gendered musical gestures in popular music culture' (Brooks 2010:55). In *9 Beginnings*, far away from the world of popular music, still the particularities of the performers on stage, their histories, their physical bodies, their voices and the languages they speak, and innumerable other materialities interact with archival documentation of previous performances and the absent presence of other performers. In these interactions there are instances of theatrical potentiality.

Rhythm and time

From voice to feet, or rather, flippers. In the first beginning of the piece, after the non-beginning beginning of Goulish's Linklater impression, 'choreographed stagehands' Nik Wakefield and Annalaura Alifuoco recreate the beginning of *Inventing the Logic in Chaos*, a work by students at the Leicester Polytechnic Department of Performing Arts, performed in Glasgow in 1990. They are both wearing swimming flippers, and holding a cardboard cut-out of a cloud which hides their heads and upper bodies. They perform a simple routine in unison with their flippers making plastic tapping sounds on the stage floor. Then they lower the cloud, and begin to rearrange the stage set-up for the next beginning. The unison tapping sound disperses into the sounds of walking with purpose but no pre-determined route—while wearing plastic flippers. The sounds transform from patterned to unpredictable.

This simple sonic sequence calls to mind Elena Ikoniadou's work on rhythm. She points out two, seemingly contradictory, connotations of the term: rhythm as both discrete and quantitative measurement, and as indeterminate 'flow'. The historical development of the concept of rhythm partakes of both order and fluidity, and has stuck as a concept precisely because of this dual function. 'Rhythm is thought to determine form', Ikoniadou writes, 'albeit in a fluid, mobile, changeable way' (2014:11). Further, she draws on Deleuzian thought to connect rhythm with potentiality, as a mode of analysis for 'the event-yet-to-come' (Ikoniadou 2014: 19). Rhythm is part of the virtual background against which the actual is perceived (an idea indebted, as well, to Michel Serres's understanding of 'noise' as the background to the 'event' (1995)). It is both abstract and material, 'the vibration prior to becoming sensed sensory action' (Ikoniadou 2014: 13). The rhythms of two sets of plastic flippers slapping the floor, sometimes with easily measurable regularity, sometimes with stochastic variability, gently draws the attention to this oscillation or overlapping between order and potential.

These rhythmic flippers may also suggest a way of thinking about relationships between the bodies on stage and with the other pairs of flippers slapping the stage 25 years ago. There is a sense throughout *9 Beginnings: Bristol* of being in rhythm both in a particular moment and across longer durations of time than the hour-long performance. Roland Barthes' notion of 'idiorrhythmy' is useful here. Like Ikoniadou, Barthes connects historical understandings of rhythm with form, here particularly with forms of life or living, 'subtle forms [...] moods, unstable configurations, phases of depression or elation [...] The exact opposite of an inflexible, implacably regular cadence' (Barthes 2013: 8). Barthes develops the notion of 'idiorrhythmy' as a way to think about forms of communal living in which individuals maintain their own rhythms which in aggregate are the rhythms of the community—a sort of being-alone-together. The materiality of the flippers—their awkwardness and their striking visual appearance (again, this investigation of the sonic is not separate from the visual or the somatic)—help construct just such a sense of being-alone-together. The performers gently struggle with the effect of the flippers on their movements, and they have this struggle in common even as it leads to asynchronous rhythms. These asynchronous rhythms are also useful figures for the connection with the source material—the work by the Leicester Polytechnic students and the other pieces represented in *9 Beginnings*. The recreations by Every house are not set to a recurring, repeatable beat but rather the rhythms of the earlier work are given space and time for their own idiosyncrasies to play out in relationship to the present moment.

Amplification and silence

In a show with minimal tech, the one significant piece of equipment onstage is a microphone. This microphone becomes a sort of recurring character, and it is connected as much with silence and struggle as with amplification. In the Corrieri piece described above, the microphone is set up, but ignored. In the final beginning, a recreation of a piece called *White* by Grace Surman, Banich stretches to reach a microphone that Wakefield holds just out of her reach, until she finally places a large, stuffed manatee underneath it, upon which she stands to speak the final words of the show—a greeting: 'good evening, good evening, good evening, good evening…'. (The show ends by returning us, again, to the beginning).

The second beginning of *9 Beginnings* is a recreation of Lawrence Steger's 1998 performance *Draft*. Calderón begins this beginning by facing the audience, leaning forward with his palms on a table and shaking his head and shoulders. Goulish approaches him with a microphone stand and tilts it so the microphone is at Calderón's mouth. 'It's a totally white room', Calderón says. (The theatre is, in fact, completely black both in *Draft*, as performed in Manchester, and *9 Beginnings: Bristol* as performed at Arnolfini). He tells the audience how pristine the current situation is: 'no setbacks, no contradictions'. Then he looks up and asks for the music to start over. As Calderón moves around the stage, precisely re-performing Steger's staging as captured on grainy VHS, Goulish shadows him, keeping the microphone near his mouth without obscuring his face.

Steger's piece is a wild deconstruction of the archetypical American road trip story, drawing on both *Huckleberry Finn* and the media furore surrounding serial killer Andrew Cunanan, who murdered five people in 1997, including fashion designer Gianni Versace. Steger focuses, as well, on the rumours, amplified by media at the time, that the murders were motivated by an HIV diagnosis. Cunanan was not HIV-positive. *Draft* is a performance that doubles back on itself, over and over, a perpetual rough draft, referring to, without ever becoming, a narrative. Steger is, reviewer Justin Hayford says, 'more intrigued by the potential for a story than with the story itself' (Hayford 1998), and this focus on potential is also a dismantling of the hateful, and seemingly fixed, narratives around HIV and gay men constructed and supported by the mass media.

Calderón's recreation does not get into this context, or ends before it gets a chance to. After the seeming false start of the opening lines, the text switches into third person, as Calderón/Steger describes a person's movements that also, as if by coincidence, match the movements he makes. The description is punctuated by instructions to this person (Calderón says, 'shake it off'; Calderón shakes his upper body and arms). Then the perspective shifts again, and Calderón/Steger starts an argument with himself: 'What are you trying to say?' 'I think you know what I'm trying to say' 'I think we know different things'. Through all of this Goulish follows, pivoting at corners, dodging the microphone cord, and adjusting the height as needed. Finally, Calderón/Steger decides that what is needed is characters, characters he does not know and has not met, but who are constructed through the media. As he lists the sources for these soon-to-be characters ('literature, tabloids, radio, television') Goulish begins to step away, creating a manual slow fade so that Calderón's voice is finally only heard unamplified until he stops speaking. He drops his shoulders and his face assumes a blank expression, then he moves upstage right to deliver the final lines of this sequence, including a paraphrased line from an essay by philosopher Arnold I. Davidson: 'Without love we are dead. Not dead like the dead, but dead like the living'. The actual quote refers to both music and 'love toward another person. Without one, without the other, we are dead, not dead like the dead, but dead like the living' (Davison 2003: xii).

Lagaay writes that the voice traverses binaries. It is 'individual *and* communal', 'linguistic *and* non-linguistic', 'temporal *and* transcendent', 'sounding resonance *and* silent potential'. From this, she concludes that:

> [W]hat distinguishes voice from noise is its intrinsic relation to the possibility of silence. For, inasmuch as silence can be considered as a mode of vocal expression, voice cannot be defined in clear opposition to silence (nor *vice versa*). It follows from this that the philosophy of voice is not exhausted in a philosophy of human performance qua activity but must also take into account and articulate itself as a philosophy of human *potentiality*.
>
> Lagaay 2011: 65

As I discuss above, Lagaay's understanding of potentiality and the voice is influenced by Giorgio Agamben's work on the subject. For Agamben, humans' capacity to do is fundamentally connected to their ability to *not do*. 'Beings that exist in the mode of potentiality *are capable of their own impotentiality*', he writes (Agamben 2000: 182). Impotentiality is a capacity which attends every other capacity.

The capacity for impotentiality can be found in the seemingly simple interactions between bodies and microphone in the recreation of *Draft*. An audience member unfamiliar with Goulish and Steger would not know that they were friends before Steger's death in 1999 of complications from AIDS. Goulish wrote about Steger's death in 'Not Eulogizing Lawrence Steger'; it is at once an expression of grief, and a struggle with the impossibility of such expression. Goulish speaks of this writing which happens 'in haphazard fashion, page after page, the memories that poison us'. Yet this incessant writing is also not-writing:

> We do not know the names of sickness, and when we look at our memories we see they have a hole. We don't write about that. We think we choose avoidance, but even when we write about it, we don't write about it. How can you write about an absence? We circle it, describe the edges. This absence is your absence.
>
> Goulish 2000: 118

Absence is irreconcilable, though it exists alongside the inexorable going-on of life. Lagaay's reading of Agamben figures potentiality as residing in the space between ability to understand voice as speech, and inability to do so. Here, not-eulogizing is an absence of language that is also an excess of it.

Again, an audience member not familiar with Steger or Goulish would not learn of their friendship, nor of Goulish's loss, from the sequence in *9 Beginnings*. However, as Goulish backs away from Calderón and his voice fades, there is a sense of describing the edges of an absence. The microphone, a tool which promises the possibility of amplification becomes a tool for potentiality as it draws attention to silence. The potentialities of absence are in no way a consolation for loss, but rather the space to approach this loss. The persistence of the archive is stark against the backdrop of what has gone.

(Not) another beginning

Imitation, rhythm and amplification are only a few of the ways that the sonic might be thought with *9 Beginnings*. Other examples, other techniques, and other modes could certainly have been addressed here. Every house makes very specific choices about music, for instance. In the development process, it became important to track down a limited edition recording of acid house track 'It's Grim Up North' by KLF to accompany the recreation of Blast

Theory's *Chemical Wedding*. What are the potentialities of nostalgia and attachment found in the announcement preceding this section of the piece ('It still sounds fucking good')?

I mention the other possible avenues this chapter might have taken partly because one broad impulse for this study is to argue for the value of thinking about performance and live art, and their archival remains, from a sonic perspective. Attention to sound can draw interdisciplinary connections—as diverse as music hall, punk, sound art, field recording or experimental poetics—through a set of practices that is significantly defined by its approach to interdisciplinarity. It can also expand how we think about practices that might not automatically call to mind aurality, and for that reason, lend a different dimension.

However, the examples above require not just attention to sound, but the kind of 'sonic sensibility' I described at the outset of this chapter. Salomé Voegelin's proposal for the sonic as a method for thinking beyond 'singular actuality' (2014) chimes with the efforts here to bring together sound and archival material to think in complex ways about possibility and potentiality. The aim has been to consider how performance history and performance creation resonate with each other, and how performance can be understood as something that reverberates over time and returns in unpredictable ways—ways that are full of potential.

At the same time, it is worth ringing a note of caution. It is not just that in a world full of potential, disaster can also happen (which is nevertheless worth keeping in mind), but that openness and indeterminacy are not guarantee of emancipation. As Luc Boltanski and Eve Chiapello have argued, the impulse towards flexibility and openness in experimental arts practices maps onto and, at least since the late 1960s, has been co-opted by the neoliberal, Post-Fordist model of labour (Boltanski and Chiapello 2007). Bojana Kunst specifically frames this argument as a question about how contemporary arts practice, and particularly performance, is orientated towards the future, writing that 'art and the creative professions have never before placed so much emphasis upon future projects [...] as well as upon encouraging and practicing the ability to conceive of *what is yet to happen*' (2015: 154). This orientation towards possibility can have the result, not of liberation or subversive alternatives, but of openness to exploitation, and experiences of indebtedness to a promised future which is forever out of reach. For Kunst, an answer to this problematic investment in speculation and communication is 'to return back to the material aspect of work, to the sensuous and material base of any activity' (2015: 146).

Importantly, *9 Beginnings* is not about speculating on a set direction for the future any more than it is about preserving a codified version of the past, though it does have space for approaching both history and the future. In thinking about this work with a sonic sensibility, the aim has been to foreground the 'sensuous and material base' of the piece, drawn from performance archives, as the place from which to perform potentiality. In the broader scope of contemporary life, it seems fair to say that now is a period of dramatic uncertainty with profound anxieties underlying our approach to the future. There is a sense that conventional tools for analysing the future—tools from political polling to economic forecasting—which have long been the subject of critique, are now in fact breaking down. This has consequences for how we think about the archive as a key site from which data for modelling the future is drawn. Other ways of thinking and performing possibility and potentiality in relation to the archive seem increasingly necessary. Performance can feel like a frail method for advocacy or change, but the value that can be found in a piece of work like *9 Beginnings* is a sustained investigation not within limits but of limits, as such.

I began this chapter thinking about echoes. There is, of course, the troubling association with echoes of the echo chamber, or the practice of mistaking one's own voice for the voice of the world. However, in this instance, the echoes are polyvocal and suggest, instead, a non-fixity based in relationality. Goulish writes about the structure of the piece that '[w]hile the sequence is linear, the echoes are multidirectional' (2011). Listening to *9 Beginnings*, the echoes of historical performances reverberate in the very present bodies of performers and audiences and throughout the theatre space. Paying attention to the sonic in the techniques Every house use, and to the theatricality of these sonic techniques, helps strike a balance between the possible and the potential, the ground and the horizon, the here and now and the there and then (both of the past and the possible, potential future).

References

2000 Agamben, G. *Potentialities: Collected Essays in Philosophy*, ed. and trans. D. Heller-Roazen, Stanford: Stanford University Press.

1978 Barthes, R. 'The Grain of the Voice'. In *Image—Music—Text*, ed. and trans. Stephen Heath, London: Fontana Press, pp179–89.

2013 *How to Live Together: Novelistic Simulations of Some Everyday Spaces*, trans. K. Briggs. New York: Columbia University Press.

2007 Boltanski, L. and Chiapello, E. *The New Spirit of Capitalism*, trans. G. Elliott, London and New York: Verso.

2007 Bottoms, S. and Goulish, M. (eds) *Small Acts of Repair: Performance, Ecology and Goat Island*, London and New York: Routledge.

2010 Brooks, D. '"This Voice Which Is Not One": Amy Winehouse Sings the Ballad of Sonic Blue(s)face Culture'. *Women and Performance: A Journal of Feminist Theory*, 20(1): pp37–60.

2010 Brown, R. *Sound: A Reader in Theatre Practice*, New York: Palgrave Macmillan.

2003 Davison, A.I. 'The *Charme* of Jankélévitch'. In V. Jankélévitch *Music and the Ineffable*, trans. C. Abbate, Princeton: Princeton University Press.

1992 Derrida, J. *The Other Heading: Reflections on Today's Europe*, trans. P.-A. Brault and M.B. Nass, Bloomington and Indianapolis: Indiana University Press.

1971 Foucault, M. *The Order of Things: An Archaeology of the Human Sciences*, New York: Pantheon.

2000 Goulish, M. *39 Microlectures*, London: Routledge.

2011 'Interview by Sedated by a Brick'. Available online. http://www.arnolfini.org.uk/blog/every-house-has-a-door-2013-9-beginnings. Accessed 17 January 2016.

1998 Hayford, J. 'Plumbing the Unfathomable'. *Chicago Reader*. Available online. http://www.chicagoreader.com/chicago/plumbing-the-unfathomable/Content?oid=895586. Accessed 3 March 2014.

2010 Heddon, D. 'The Horizon of Sound: Soliciting the Earwitness'. *Performance Research*, 15(3): pp36–42.

2009 Hoffman, B. 'Radicalism and the Theatre in Genealogies of Live Art'. *Performance Research*, 14(1): pp95–105.

2015 Home-Cook, G. *Theatre and Aural Attention: Stretching Ourselves*, Basingstoke and New York: Palgrave Macmillan.

2014 Ikoniadou, E. *The Rhythmic Event: Art, Media and the Sonic*, Cambridge: MIT Press

1997 Jones, A. '"Presence" in Absentia: Experiencing Performance as Documentation'. *Art Journal*, 56(4): pp11–18.

1998 *Body Art: Performing the Subject*, Minneapolis: University of Minnesota.

2011 Kendrick, L. and Roesner, D. (eds) *Theatre Noise*, Newcastle upon Tyne: Cambridge Scholars Publishing.

2012 Klein, J. 'Developing Live Art'. In D. Heddon and J. Klein (eds) *Histories and Practices of Live Art*, Basingstoke and New York: Palgrave Macmillan.

2015 Kunst, B. *Artist at Work: Proximity of Art and Capitalism*, Winchester, UK and Washington DC: Zero Books.

2011 Lagaay, A. 'Towards a (Negative) Philosophy of Voice'. In L. Kendrick and D. Roesner (eds) *Theatre Noise*, Newcastle upon Tyne: Cambridge Scholars Publishing, pp57–69.

2012 Lepecki, A. 'Not as Before, but Simply: Again'. In A. Jones and A. Heathfield (eds) *Perform, Repeat, Record: Live Art in History, Bristol*: Intellect, pp151–70.

1991 Linklater, R. (director) *Slacker*. Film: Orion Classics.

1996 Muñoz, J. 'Ephemera as Evidence: Introductory Notes to Queer Acts'. *Women and Performance*, 8(2): pp5–17.

2009 *Cruising Utopia: The Then and There of Queer Futurity*, New York: NYU Press.

2007 Nancy, J-L. *Listening*, trans. C. Mandell, New York: Fordham University Press.

1998 Obejas, A. 'A Requiem for Chicago's Incubator of Performance Art'. *Chicago Tribune*, 23 February 1998. Available online. (http://articles.chicagotribune.com/1998-02-23/features/9802230110_1_art-institute-artists-and-arts-professionals-performance-art). Accessed 16 November 2016.

1993 Phelan, P. *Unmarked: The Politics of Performance*, New York: Routledge.

2011 Schneider, R. *Performing Remains: Art and War in Times of Theatrical Reenactment*, New York: Routledge.

1995 Serres, M. *Genesis*, trans. G. James and J. Nielson. Ann Arbor: University of Michigan Press.

2009 Shalson, L. 'On the Endurance of Theatre in Live Art'. *Contemporary Theatre Review*, 22(1): pp106–19.
2001 Steedman, C. *Dust*, Manchester: Manchester University Press.
2003 Sterne, J. *The Audible Past: Cultural Origins of Sound Reproduction*, Durham and London: Duke University Press.
2003 Taylor, D. *The Archive and the Repertoire: Performing Cultural Memory in the Americas*, Durham and London: Duke University Press.
2014 Voegelin, S. *Sonic Possible Worlds: Hearing the Continuum of Sound*, London: Bloomsbury.

Resistance to representation and the fabrication of truth: performance as thought-apparatus

Maaike Bleeker

Who's Afraid of Representation? (2005) by Rabih Mroué and Lina Saneh consists of a series of short monologues, many of them based on documentary material of artistic happenings and performances by Chris Burden, Marina Abramović, Gunter Brus, Gina Pane, Hermann Nitsch and other artists, and some others describing in detail how the speaker violently killed eight of his former colleagues and wounded four others at an office in Beirut. Many of the artistic performances described in the monologues are well known, yet most people who know about them will probably only know them via documentation. The title *Who's Afraid of Representation?* brings to mind a reluctance towards representation often associated with these kinds of artistic happenings and performances: they were not intended to represent something else but as events taking place here and now, and they were events that supposedly could not be adequately documented because documentation would never be able to accurately represent the experience of being there in the flesh. Yet at the same time, Amelia Jones observes, these works depend on documentation to attain symbolic status in the realm of culture. In her '"Presence" in Absentia: Experiencing Performance in Documentation' (1997), Jones distances herself from this resistance to representation and argues that although certainly differences exist between witnessing a performance live and knowing it through documentation, 'neither has a privileged relationship to the historical "truth" of the performance' (Jones 1997: 11). The fabrication of this truth is the subject of *Who's Afraid of Representation?*, as well as of much of Mroué's other work.

Many of Mroué's performances are about images: images found in archives, books, newspapers, on the street or online. This fascination for images is reflected in the title of the book that presents an overview of his work: *Image(s) Mon Amour. Fabrications* (Mroué 2013). The '(s)' in *Image(s), Mon Amour* causes an oscillation between images as objects and the verb 'to image'; an oscillation between a description ("images, mon amour") and an address ("image, mon amour") ordering, or seducing, the addressee. This duplicity is important to what his performances show images to be and do. The title also echoes that of Alain Resnais' *Hiroshima Mon Amour* (1959), a film about the (im)possibility of knowing what the event of Hiroshima was if you were not there when it happened. Or perhaps, following Jones, we might say, about the difference between knowing Hiroshima from first person experience and knowing it through documentation.

Mroué shows images to be complex entities that do much more than (accurately or not) depict things, people or events. Images are places where truths are fabricated, which come into being in and through them. These 'truths' are not only a matter of how well or not images represent a reality supposedly preceding them, but of how images, as simultaneously objects showing something and an address to the viewer's imagination, set the stage for ways of knowing. They propose modes of perceiving that which they supposedly merely depict, and these modes of perceiving resonate with practices of knowing and understanding that are constitutive of our apprehension of 'how it is' in the world as we encounter it. With his performances, Mroué shows this knowing to be conceptual in the sense described by Deleuze and Guattari in *What is Philosophy?*, namely in how images present a heterogenesis, an ordering of components that through this ordering proposes a particular understanding. The concept of a bird, for example, Deleuze and Guattari write, is found 'in the composition of its postures, colours and songs: something indiscernible that is not so much synesthetic as syneidetic'. Understanding what a bird is arises in apprehending the logic of connections between these aspects. Grasping the composition is getting the concept: they call the concept 'an act of thought' (Deleuze and Guattari 1996: 20–1).

Mroué investigates how images present such acts of thought and how they mediate the performance of thinking. He demonstrates the potential of performance and the theatrical apparatus as what I propose to term a 'thought-apparatus'. His works explore performance as a practice of materially thinking-through the fabrication of truth in images, in line with how Walter Benjamin and others in the 1930s and 40s experimented with new kinds of texts they called thought-images. Thought-images are short prose texts that do not offer explanations or interpretations but set up constellations of elements that evoke an image of the point the text wants to make, and evoke it as *image*, that is, not as a linear narrative explanation but in ways that a linear explanation cannot. Thought-images are 'philosophical miniatures' that offer 'conceptual engagements with the aesthetic and aesthetic engagements with the conceptual' (Richter 2007: 2). The thought-image encodes a poetic form of condensed epigrammatic writing in textual snapshots, flashing up as poignant meditations that typically fasten upon a seemingly peripheral detail or marginal topic, usually without a developed plot or a prescribed narrative agenda, yet charged with theoretical insight (Richter 2007: 2).

Probably the most famous example of this type of writing is Walter Benjamin's ninth thesis on the philosophy of history, the 'Angelus Novus', (Benjamin 1968) which describes a painting by Paul Klee (titled *Angelus Novus*): the eponymous angel is being forcefully blown backwards into the future by a storm coming from paradise while staring in horror at a pile of debris growing skyward out of so-called progress. The image evoked by the text and title questions assumptions about a teleological, linear understanding of history by suggesting a set of connections between historical development, progress, destruction and lack of control and direction. The text does not explain the understanding of history suggested by these connections but evokes an image that embodies these connections. Similarly, Mroué's performances take their audiences along in acts of thinking that cross over between the conceptual and the aesthetic. His performances do not evoke images by means of writing (as thought-images do) but take images as starting points and use performance and the theatrical apparatus to unpack how images embody connections between constellations of elements and how, in doing so, they perform modes of knowing, understanding, thinking. In this respect, we might say, his works present an inverse of the thought-image. Whereas thought-images aim to evoke an image that embodies a particular constellation of elements by means of writing, Mroué's performances use performance and the theatrical apparatus to unpack the logic embodied in images.

Mroué and the authors of the thought-image share a sensitivity to mediality and materiality as part of how things can be known and transmitted. The thought-image is a mode of writing that does not try to pass for a transparent representation of ideas existing independently from the medium in which they are expressed. Rather, shared by Benjamin, Adorno, Bloch, Kracauer and other authors of the thought-image, is the view that '*what* they say cannot be thought in isolation from how they say it; that any philosophical truth-content their writing may contain invariably is tied to and mediated by its specific and potentially unstable figures of presentation' (Richter 2007: 2). In our current, increasingly media-saturated culture, this insight has gained critical urgency, and relevance beyond the medium of writing. Media are not merely means to represent ideas, knowledge, understanding, or a reality existing independently from them, but are themselves co-constitutive of how knowledge, understanding, thinking, as well as reality, take shape. They are co-constitutive of the fabrication of truth.

Fabrication of truth

Mroué introduces the expression 'fabrication of the truth' in his reflections about his performance *Three Posters* (co-created with Elias Khoury in 2000). *Three Posters* is a performance based on video recordings of the final testimony of a Lebanese resistance fighter named Jamal El Sati. This final testimony was recorded a couple of hours before his suicide mission in 1985. Mroué encountered the video recordings of El Sati in 1999, 14 years after his suicide mission took place. Mroué was familiar with this kind of video message because creating video testimonies before leaving on a suicide mission had become common practice for resistance fighters in Lebanon at that time. After the successful completion of their mission, the videos would be broadcast on national television. However, what was different was that what Mroué encountered in 1999 was not the final document as it had been shown on TV in 1985, but the three takes in which the statement had been recorded. The material trace of the past embodied in the three takes took Mroué back to the moment of recording, to the moment when the man on the tape had not yet performed his mission. A moment before that is nevertheless crucial to the fabrication of the truth of what happened afterwards.

'The video challenged us', Mroué observes, 'it demanded that we consider the limits of truth and its representations' (Mroué 2013: 304). He is referring in particular to one sentence, spoken by El Sati, saying: 'I am the martyr'. This is an impossible statement, Mroué observes, because he will become a martyr only after completion of his mission. Therefore he can never speak to us as the martyr that he will become only after he dies. The statement is true, however, now, after his death. As a result, the video recording has become a truthful representation of something that did not exist at the time it was recorded. The truthfulness of the video document cannot be understood in terms of how the document presents what Philip Auslander calls 'an indexical access point to a past event' (Auslander 2006: 9) and truthfully documents what was there in front of the camera, but requires that we acknowledge the document itself as part of the space in which the performance occurs and its truth comes into being. Auslander makes his observations in the context of reflections about performance documentation and his point is that performance documentation cannot be understood to document an event preceding the documentation. Actually, documentation is co-constitutive of what will become the performance, even in the case of performance documentation that is supposedly a recording of an event that took place independently of the act of recording, as, for example, Chris Burden's action *Shoot* (1971). Auslander points out that a closer look at the practice of performance art shows that, even such archetypal works of body art and performance as Burden's were not autonomous performances, the documentation of which supplements and provides access to an originary event, but staged to be documented at least as much as to be seen by a live audience. He refers to Gina Pane describing how the role of the photographer in her work, and how the work will appear in the documentation, is not a matter of the documentation being a mere recording of an event existing independent of it: it is part of how the work is conceived. Auslander also quotes Jones explaining that Burden:

> carefully staged each performance and had it photographed and sometimes also filmed; he selected usually one or two photographs of each event for display in exhibitions and catalogues [...] In this way, Burden produced himself for posterity through meticulously orchestrated textual and visual representations.
>
> Auslander 2006: 3

Who's Afraid of Representation? makes a similar point by having 'Chris Burden' describe his action *Shoot* as follows:

> I entered with two friends, one carrying a camera, the other carrying a gun. The three of us stood there, the audience watched. I screamed out: 'Shoot!' And one friend filmed

> as the other shot me in the hand. [...] The second the bullet entered my hand the image entered history.
>
> Mroué 2013: 237

Who's Afraid of Representation? plays with the double meaning of 'shoot' to draw attention to the role of the media in what would become the work *Shoot*. Elsewhere I have elaborated how accounting for this role of recording also involves taking into account the order that mirrors that of 'shoot', namely 'cut' (Bleeker 2014). Cut marks the end of the recording and the separation between the recording and the event. The cut does not deny the relationship between the historical moment and its recording, but it is the moment that marks a shift in relationships between them. Accounting for such processes of renegotiation, I argued, is crucial for understanding the circulation of signs and images in global digital culture in which, as Jon McKenzie observes, 'Highly localized ensembles of words and gestures can now be broken apart, recombined and hyperlinked to different ensembles in ways unlike anything in the past at speeds incredible from all perspectives except those of the future' (McKenzie 2001: 22). Accounting for the impact of these processes and how they are part and parcel of the fabrication of truth requires an approach that acknowledges the power of technology, not only to capture what was in front of the camera but actually, after Heidegger, to *challenge forth* the world: the power of the camera to 'challenge forth' Jamal El Sati the martyr and the power of the camera to challenge forth the work known as *Shoot*.

Accounting for this power of the camera requires an approach that, instead of focusing on images as an adequate or inadequate representation *of* a reality preceding them, helps to understand the role of images *in* reality: how images are part of reality, how they are part of how reality takes shape. Mroué's performances point to the importance of taking images seriously as being of the world (and not only a more or less accurate depiction of the world) and in certain ways also being our world. His unpacking of images and what they do suggests that placing the focus of attention on the differences between images and the so called real world obscures that the boundary between them is porous, and that rejecting images for being unable to capture the real world in its fullness is also a means to claim the existence of a real world outside of images. In this respect, *Who's Afraid of Representation?* is a key work in Mroué's oeuvre for how it not only engages with images by means of performance but also draws attention to resistance to representation as part of our complex relationship to images, and how body art and performance of the 60s and 70s, including its complicated relationship to documentation, might be symptomatic of this resistance. His work also shows how the critical reworking of these assumptions by Jones (1997), Auslander (2006), Groys (2005) and others, has a relevance that extends beyond the field of art.

Who's Afraid of Representation?

The title *Who's Afraid of Representation?* redirects attention from representation as itself being a (or the) problem, towards the question of who is the subject of such resistance and what is at stake in it. This question is addressed by means of a performance that, like thought-images, does not explain but unfolds through juxtapositions of a relatively small set of elements and that, as a result of the way these elements are combined, triggers associations, points to connections and evokes thoughts rather than offering a narrative explanation. This begins already with the flyer announcing the performance. The flyer shows a large part of a famous painting by Manet, titled *Olympia*. Exhibited for the first time at the 1865 Paris Salon, this painting caused a lot of resistance because of what it represents. The problem was not that it shows a naked female body displayed for the eye of the viewer. The painting continues a long tradition of depicting naked women in comparable ways and is modelled after Titian's *Venus of Urbino* (1538), which in its turn is a variation on Giorgione's *Sleeping Venus* (c. 1510), both much respected works of art, also at that time. What is different, however, is that Manet's painting does not frame his representation of a naked female body displayed for the viewer by means of a title that presents the painting as the image of a goddess, but uses a title that, in combination with some of the details in the image, suggests the woman shown in the painting is a prostitute and a contemporary. The painting was criticised for being vulgar and distasteful both for what it represented and how. The female body is not idealised according to artistic conventions and shown in harsh light. And, whereas the curled hands of the Venuses of Titian and Urbino, directing the viewer to their sex, seem to signal their desire for the viewer, the hand of Olympia firmly blocks their view and access, thus contradicting the suggestion the painting (and by extension, the practice of the one represented) is about her desire. Her confrontational gaze redirects attention to the viewer as the subject of the desire she represents for this viewer. Naturalist writer Emile Zola observed that, 'When our artists give us Venuses, they correct nature, they lie. Édouard

Manet asked himself why lie, why not tell the truth; he introduced us to Olympia, this *fille* of our time, whom you meet on the side-walks' (cited in Andersen 2004: 79). Manet's painting, Zola points out, might be considered a more truthful depiction, yet it is rejected for what it more truthfully represents.

In combination with the title, *Who's Afraid of Representation?*, the reproduction of this famous painting invites a shift in focus with regard to resistance to representation, away from what is represented and whether this is an accurate depiction of a world outside the image, towards who is resisting representation and what is at stake in this resistance. The title, *Who's Afraid of Representation?*, echoes that of Edward Albee's well known play, *Who's Afraid of Virginia Woolf?* (1962), a title that in its turn is a version of that of the nursery rhyme, *Who's Afraid of the Big Bad Wolf?* The play depicts an evening at the house of a middle-aged couple, named Martha and George, who have a younger couple, Nick and Honey, over for late-night drinks. During the evening they discuss various details of their lives; sometimes all four are present, sometimes one or two of them are off-stage. From the very beginning Martha and George are humiliating each other and, as the evening progresses and they get more and more drunk, they also become more and more aggressive towards their guests. It also becomes increasingly clear that the image they present of their lives is a fabrication and that its continuous upkeep is the truth about their lives. The play critiques the idea of the perfect American family and challenges social expectations about life and love, and confronts the audience with images of life, love and family that, like Manet's *Olympia*, were considered distasteful and vulgar. The play was selected for the Pulitzer Prize in 1963, but the nomination was cancelled because of the indecent language and representation of sexuality.

On Mroué's flyer the title, *Who's Afraid of Representation?*, is added to Manet's painting but also a wound, a cut in Olympia's side. The way the painting has been cropped, in combination with how the bright red wound is framed between Olympia's hands, turns this wound into the centre of attention and suggests she is showing it to us. Did she cut herself like many of the body art and performance artists whose work is the subject of *Who's Afraid of Representation?* Like Manet with his *Olympia*, many of these artists confronted their audiences with indecent and overtly direct ways of showing the body and, like *Who's Afraid of Virginia Woolf?*, this often involved humiliation and aggressive behaviour, albeit not directed towards others but towards their own bodies. The image of the cut in a painting in combination with the title,

Who's Afraid of Representation?, brings to mind Barnett Newman's *Who's Afraid of Red, Yellow and Blue?*, a series of large-scale paintings famous for their bold act of not representing anything. Famous also for how the painting in Amsterdam's Stedelijk Museum was violently attacked and cut with a knife. And then again, famous for the scandal around its restoration. On display for the first time after a restoration that took years, it was observed that the painting had been repainted with a paint roller rather than restored with a brush, as it had originally been painted by Newman. This resulted in heated debates, not only about whether this was indeed the case (it turned out to be so), but also about whether it mattered if it was restored one way or the other. Is the painting essentially a representation of a bold idea or is its 'truth' to be found in its materiality, in something that is 'beyond representation'?

The juxtaposition of image, cut and title on the flyer announcing the performance thus opens up a field of associations and reflections. This is continued in the performance itself. The performance is constructed according to a task-based logic and using (the suggestion of) chance procedures reminiscent of 1960s performance practices. Mroué and Saneh enter an almost empty stage and set up a screen. They play 'head or tails' which seems to determine that Saneh opens the book she is holding at a seemingly random page and says: 'VALIE EXPORT, page 57.' Mroué answers: 'Page 57 means you have 57 seconds.' Saneh steps behind the screen and the audience sees her image on screen as if facing them. Mroué sets a timer and says 'Top' to indicate the time has started. Saneh starts talking:

> My name is VALIE EXPORT [...] I have created a lot of performance art during my life, for example: In one of my pieces I built a box and hung it around my neck so that it dangled over my breasts [...] a box like a little peep show booth, open in the back and closed in the front with a black curtain.
>
> Mroué 2013: 217

The text turns the description of VALIE EXPORT's work in the book into a first-person monologue, a dramaturgical strategy that brings to mind Auslander's observation that documentation should be understood as analogous to speech acts. Like speech acts, documentation is performative in that it brings into being that which it supposedly merely describes. *Who's Afraid of Representation?* turns the performance documentation in the book literally into a first-person speech act. The way in which 'VALIE EXPORT' recounts how she cut out part of her jeans and, wearing no panties, exposed herself to people in a movie theatre, brings to mind the image of Olympia on the flyer, challenging her viewers, with the difference that 'EXPORT' describes how she also carried a machine gun in her hands.

After 57 seconds Mroué shouts, 'time out!', Saneh steps from behind the screen and walks towards him and the entire process is repeated. And then again, and again. When Saneh opens the book for the sixth time she says, 'picture', instead of the name of an artist. She moves behind the screen to hold the book up to the camera and on screen the audience sees a picture from a theatre play. Mroué moves to the screen, but before he is there, she closes the book. However, the second time that a picture of a play comes up instead of the name of an artist, he steps in front of the screen and also speaks a monologue, not as if it is from one of the artists in the book, but one that describes in detail how the speaker violently killed several employees of the office in which he used to work. During the rest of the performance this pattern is repeated, alternating between performance artists' statements, and the testimonies of the man who violently killed his colleagues in combination with images of theatre. Hearing one testimony after another about violent actions, humiliation and indecent exposure, one starts to wonder: What is at stake here? Why these violent actions? Who are these people doing this and why?

From the fourth artist's 'testimony' on, another element is added. Every now and then the descriptions of the artists start to include references to the war in Lebanon. Kim Jones states that 'this piece could have another name, "In memory of Ashoura," but this was unthinkable at that time' (Mroué 2013: 220). A few monologues later, 'Marina Abramović' remembers:

> When the 'Battle of the Hotels' began in downtown Beirut, I laid out a table and placed 72 items on it, like scissors, a saw, a razor, a fork, knives, glass bottles, a tube of lipstick, a whip, pins, bread, an axe, a bottle of perfume, paint, matches, candles, nails, a comb, a newspaper, a mirror, needles, honey, grapes, tape, a real gun and a real bullet. And I put up a big sign which read: On this table are 72 items you may use on my body as you see fit.
>
> Mroué 2013: 222

What 'Marina Abramović' describes will probably be recognised by at least part of the audience as one of her most famous performances, *Rhythm 0* (1974). *Rhythm 0*, like *Olympia*, presented a challenge to its participants. In *Rhythm 0* it is a real female body, not a painted representation, that offers itself to the desires of the spectators. She challenges them to do whatever they want, suggesting that, unlike Olympia, she is not going to stop them. A lot has been said about how the performance had to be stopped when spectators threatened to go too far.

Boris Groys observes that the relationship between art and violence is a complicated and ambivalent one. There is a tradition, at least since the beginning of modernity, of art and artists wanting to be radical, daring, taboo breaking, going beyond all the limitations and borders. Art uses the language of the military to describe itself as avant-garde, aiming to destroy traditions, violate taboos, explode norms, and attack institutions. And, he observes, 'to this very day this criterion of radicalness has lost nothing of its relevance to our evaluation of art. The worst thing that can be said of an artist continues to be that his or her art is "harmless"' (Groys 2008: 122). In this sense, Groys points out, a connection can be observed between the artist and the warrior or the terrorist in how both strive for bold, radical and violent gestures. Yet, however much realness and truth art like body art and performance may strive to achieve, violence in art is of course not the same as violence in real life. When 'Abramović' begins to include references to Beirut in her description of *Rhythm O* and ends her monologue with 'I stopped the performance. Not too long after that, the massacre in Damour took place' (Mroué 2013: 222), this similarity and difference is precisely what is evoked.

When it comes to violence, Groys observes, art can never be as extreme as terrorism and war can be, and for this reason, art today is left far behind by terrorism and war when it comes to the production of extreme images of real violence. What art can do today is to help us engage critically with the representations of such violence as *representations*. When it comes to the images of terror, violence and war that circulate in contemporary media there is a strong tendency to recognise these images as being true, that is, to look at them as an index of the horror performed to produce the document, rather than as an image, a representation, of this horror. These images, he argues, play into our fear of denying their realness and thus that of the real horror performed to create them:

> After so many decades of modern and post-modern criticism of the image, of the mimesis, of the representation we feel ourselves somewhat ashamed by saying that the images of terror or torture are not true, not real. We cannot say that these images are not true, because we know that these images are paid for by a real loss of life—a loss of life that is

documented by these images. Magritte could easily say that a painted apple is not a real apple or that a painted pipe is not a real pipe. But how can we say that a videotaped beheading is not a real beheading? Or that a videotaped ritual of humiliation in the Abu-Ghraib prison is not a real ritual? After so many decades of the critique of representation directed against the naive belief in photographic and cinematic truth we are now ready to accept certain photographed and videotaped images as unquestionably true, again.
Groys 2008:124

Groys observes that such resistance to an understanding of the image as representation gets in the way of critical engagement with what these images perform and how they perform in the circulation of mass media. This is not to deny the horror of the deeds performed to produce the images, but rather to point to the importance of distinguishing between the individual, empirical event that is documented by a certain image, and the image as a representation that can be analysed for how it represents what it represents, and what it does as it begins to circulate in media networks 'and acquires the symbolic value of being a representation of the political sublime' (Groys 2008: 126). For, as Groys rightfully remarks, many of the images of terror and counter-terror that circulate in media networks are not shown primarily in the context of an empirical, criminal investigation, but have a function of showing or producing something else: 'the universally valid images of the political sublime' (Groys 2008: 126). In this context Groys sees an important role for art. For 'a terrifying, sublime image of violence is still merely an image' and, as image, it can be analysed and criticised in terms of critiques of representation (Groys 2008: 126). He also observes that such criticism already seems to be taking place, but refrains from mentioning names. Here Mroué's work presents an example, because of how it engages with images, and also how it does so from a position informed by a history of critiques of the production of sublime images of real violence in art.

Who's Afraid of Representation? draws attention to these aesthetics as they are part of both the performances and the ways in which these are documented. Including references to Beirut and Damour in 'Abramović's' description of *Rhythm O, Who's Afraid of Representation?* draws attention to how documentation of this and similar performances do not usually foreground the connections with such concrete places and events outside the arts. Although performance art and the discourse around it often highlight the eventhood of performance—its here and now-ness at a particular place and time where one has to be in order to understand the work—this connection to time and place is usually not foregrounded in documentation. Auslander observes that, 'In that sense, performance art documentation participates in the fine art tradition of the reproduction of works rather than the ethnographic tradition of capturing events' (Auslander 2006: 6). How this presence of performance distinguishes itself from the actual here and now is demonstrated by a beautiful moment in the documentation of Abramović's *The Artist is Present* at MoMA in 2010. At one point her former partner Ulay comes to visit the show. He is filmed while looking at the relics of the many works exhibited there. He seems impressed but not overwhelmed. Instead, his responses relate what is present in the museum to concrete moments of there and then: 'oh yes, that was there. Oh see, this is what we did then.' When he encounters Marina Abramović at the centre of the exhibition, she starts to cry. He shows emotions too but in a light, nostalgic, friendly and sentimental way. He seems touched but not shaken. He sits there for a while. She reaches out to grasp his hands and they exchange a few words. And then he goes, again with a certain lightness, into the real world, here and now, leaving her behind, present in the museum as a relic existing outside the actual here and now. A presence that is already indicated by the title of the exhibition, framing her presence at this specific place and time in terms that precisely disconnect her presence from who she is and from where this here and now is. The title is not Marina Abramović is present at the MoMA in New York, but *The Artist is Present*.

The inclusion of references to Beirut and Damour in 'Abramović's' recalling of her *Rhythm O* in *Who's Afraid of Representation?* subverts such presence and raises the question of how the absence of references to actual place and time affects the understanding of what the work is. A little later, the inclusion of references to the war in Lebanon in 'Orlan's' description of one of her works draws attention to how such references may actually change what the work is about, thus pointing to the role of documentation in the fabrication of the truth of artistic actions 'beyond representation', that is, to the role of representation in the fabrication of what their 'truth' is.

> They could see how my body was transformed, how I was sculpting myself, inside and out. Pay close attention: these operations are against God and his party, and not at all against cosmetic surgery. Against nature, sure. They are

> a salute to morphine and a celebration of the defeat of pain. A defeat akin to the one suffered by Israel in South Lebanon.
>
> Mroué 2013: 231

What the work is, as Auslander points out in 'The Performativity of Performance Documentation', takes shape in and through the way it is represented in documentation. And, as he explains, this can go as far as documents showing performances that never took place outside documentation. His example is Yves Klein's *Leap into the Void* (1960), a work that shows the artist in the midst of a jump, caught horizontally in mid-air. Although the artist did jump to create the photograph, several times, 'attempting to get the desired transcendent expression on his face' (Auslander 2006: 2), what he did in front of the camera was not the leap into the void that is the work. A tarpaulin was held for him that does not appear in the photograph and the photograph is actually a composite of two different shots. The photograph thus shows a performance that takes shape within the medium: 'The image we see thus records an event that never took place except in the photograph itself' (Auslander 2006: 2).

Such performances that exist only in the documentation are not necessarily always intended. Jones reminds us of the mythical tale of Rudolf Schwarzkogler's suicidal self-mutilation, based on the circulation of a number of photographs showing a male torso with bandaged penis and a razor blade lying nearby. She refers to Kristine Stiles' critique of Henry Sayre's *The Object of Performance* (1992), that opens with a discussion of Schwarzkogler's performance, arguing that:

> Sayre's desire for this photograph to entail some previous 'real' event [...] leads him to ignore what Stiles describes as 'the contingency of the document not only to a former action but also to the construction of a wholly fictive space'.
>
> Jones 1997: 16

Jones argues that Sayre's fixation on 'presence', even while he acknowledges its new destabilised siting in reception, informs his unquestioning belief in the photograph of performance as 'truth' (Jones 1997: 16). Such a fixation is symptomatic of what Jones describes as the mutual supplementarity of performance art and photographic document: the performance needs the photograph to confirm its having happened; the photograph needs the performance as an ontological 'anchor' of its indexicality (Jones 1997: 16). This supplementarity turns the pictures of a torso with bandaged penis into a photograph of a performance by Schwartzkogler that never took place outside documentation. In fact, the photograph does not even show Schwarzkogler but another artist, Heinz Cibulka.

'Schwarzkogler's' 'own' description of how the myth of his self-mutilation-suicide came into being in *Who's Afraid of Representation?* suggests that this myth is a denial of the connection between his art and the social-political context:

> In any case, it is unimportant whether I killed myself or fell by accident. In the end they found me in 1969, having fallen out of a window and died. That was at the height of the student and popular movements in Beirut, the rise of the leftist tide, the Palestinian struggle and of course the national democratic plan that was supposed to provide an alternative to political sectarianism. And my friends have, until now, not made the connection between what I was doing and the failure of the national movement at the beginning of the civil war and the consequent death of the Lebanese left and the demise of its dream for change. They were associating my death with the war of the mountain and the April 17 accord. This is what they wrote to all the newspapers, to dispel the rumours that surfaced after my death, even though at that time, I was not opposed to any of them. These rumours say that I pulled my dick out onto a chopping board and started to cut it into little pieces with a sharp knife. That I bled profusely and died.
>
> Mroué 2013: 234-235

According to 'Schwarzkogler' 'himself', the mythical story of his self-mutilation is a denial of the relationship between what he was doing and actual political developments at that time. His monologue does not specify who his friends are who made up this story but, if we take 'my friends' to refer very generally to the art context in which he operated, 'Schwarzkogler's' testimony in *Who's Afraid of Representation?* suggests that the myth results from how the art world was invested in an understanding of the extremities performed in body art in terms quite similar to how Barnett Newman describes the sublime he aimed for with works like *Who's Afraid of Red, Yellow and Blue?* In his text 'The Sublime is Now' (1948), Newman observes:

> We are freeing ourselves of the impediments of memory, association, nostalgia, legend, myth, or what have you, that have been the devices of Western European painting.

> Instead of making cathedrals out of Christ, man or 'life,' we are making [them] out of ourselves, out of our own feelings. The image we produce is the self-evident one of revelation, real and concrete, that can be understood by everyone who will look at it without the nostalgic glasses of history.
>
> Newman 1992: 173

Image wars

Who's Afraid of Representation? does not present a historical or theoretical argument, rather it is a speculative exploration of possible connections, relations and associations between a diversity of materials. This speculative character was also important to Benjamin, Adorno and other authors of thought-images. They were looking for ways of writing that would not take the past for granted—as something that can be known and described as it was and that carries its truth within itself so to say—but instead take readers along in thinking through how our image of the past and our understanding of historical truth emerges from traces, documents and memories; how these documents are not merely passive carriers of information about the past, but actively participate in how the past can be understood. A well-known example of the kind of writing of history they aimed for is Walter Benjamin's *Passagenwerk* (Benjamin 2002), an extensive and never finished project about the nineteenth-century shopping arcades in Paris, arcades that were already in decay at the time of his research in the late 1930s and early 1940s. Benjamin's arcades project is not a history of the arcades in the traditional sense. He does not offer us a linear, chronological description that describes what arcades are, explain when and why they came into being, or how they functioned. Rather his extensive writings are a kind of composition or constellation of pieces of information about various elements of the historical arcades. In Benjamin's text these pieces of information are placed side by side in such a way as to invite a thinking-through of relationships between these elements and what this may tell us about what the arcades once may have been, and also about the logic of the larger culture of which they were a part.

Similarly, Mroué's performances as thought-apparatuses draw attention to the relationship between images and elements of the larger cultural logic of which they are part. They show images to be not merely depictions or documentation of what happened, but themselves co-constitutive of modes of understanding. His performances are speculative explorations of how images themselves set the stage for performances that take shape in and through them. In some cases these performances, like Yves Klein's *Leap into the Void* analysed by Auslander, have no existence outside the image. For example, in the image that is the subject of *The Inhabitants of Images* (2008) which shows former Egyptian president Gamal Abdel Nasser (1918–70) and former Lebanese Prime Minister Rafik Hariri (1944–2005) standing next to each other, yet the two could never have met during their lifetimes. The easy explanation, as Mroué points out, would be that this image is a photomontage or a photo-manipulation. Yet, such an explanation can only account for how the picture has been produced, not for what the image does. The technique of photomontage allows for an explanation of the picture as a material object, and for how this object is constructed to represent something (Nasser and Hariri standing next to each other), but it cannot account for how this construction appears to a beholder, nor for the acts of imagination evoked by the image. Furthermore, what the image does is not a matter of deceiving the viewer that this encounter did actually take place, by attempting to pass for a truthful documentation of a real-life encounter to which the image provides an indexical point of access. Rather, the image proposed by the photomontage in *The Inhabitants of Images* sets the stage for a performance that only happens within the medium. The viewers it addresses know very well the event did not happen. Yet, like Klein's *Leap into the Void*, it invites them or compels them to imagine:

> Was it an attempt to mobilize the Sunnite faction in support of Hariri's son, in front of the increasing Shiite expansion in the region, but far from religious fanaticism? What a contradiction! The father, a liberal, modern, Pan-Arab Sunnite Muslim, invites Nasser, also a Sunnite Muslim, also modern, also Pan-Arab, to meet with him. Nasser responds to this meeting, and comes to pledge allegiance to Hariri's son, the heir of the true Arab line. Together they declare that their 'Arabism is the true Arabism'. This Arabism stands in opposition with the Shiite Islamic project, which shows loyalty to Iran. From another angle, Hariri is welcoming Nasser in order to reassure him that his Arabism is not dead, and that Nasserism is still alive within us; it will remain alive as long as the Hariri son is carrying its flag, and fighting any outsiders, whether the outsider is represented by the Shiite Iranian Islamic project or the Zionist Israeli-American project, or the new colonialist western project.
>
> Mroué 2013: 344

Mroué shows images to be much more than (accurate or inaccurate) representations of a reality supposedly existing elsewhere. His performances show images to be themselves the site where conflicts are being fought out and negotiations happen. Interesting in this respect are also observations by Mroué about *Three Posters* (2000), and the struggle with how to engage with the recordings of the testimony in a performance. Mroué describes how initially he and collaborator Elias Khoury struggled with questions like:

> Should we allow a public 'foreign to the party and the family' to witness a martyr's emotions before his death? Could we present a tape that did not belong to us? Would he have wanted this video to be seen with all its rehearsals? Were we exploiting this tape to make an 'art work' from which we would draw both moral and financial profit? Were we, in a sense, violating the sacred space of the martyr in order to critique the concept of martyrdom and by extension the powers that nourish and encourage such ideologies, official or otherwise?
>
> Mroué 2013: 305

That is, at first they struggled with questions related to the tape as an index of a past event, yet the longer they debated these questions, the more they became convinced that the real issue was something else: questions not about the video as document, but about what is being played out through how it shows what it shows. These questions include:

> the Civil War and the role the Lebanese Left played in this civil strife. The question of how the resistance against the Israeli Occupation began as secular and ended as fundamental and fundamentally Islamic, that is, under the aegis of Hezbollah. The question why the left failed. The question of the use of media in politics and their relationship to, or correlation with, death. The questions of the medium itself: how does video relate to an action that is going to happen but that we have not witnessed yet, particularly when we are accustomed to thinking of video as the recording of something that has happened? How does such 'documentation' represent or deceive reality?
>
> Mroué 2013: 305–6

Mroué and Khoury aimed to address these with their performance *Three Posters* that, like *Who's Afraid of Representation?*, traced this complex web of connections and relations by means of a very simple dramaturgical construction consisting of the juxtaposition of a limited set of elements without narrative framing. The performance begins with Mroué performing a martyr-to-be who is recording his final testimony in three takes. This happens in the presence of the audience, yet behind closed doors. The audience sees the performance on a video screen above the closed door. When finished, Mroué opens the door, shows the place of recording and joins the audience in watching the three original tapes, Maaike originally recommended that the illustration came after ' ... the time of the interview still active as a politician.' If this layout does not work, could the image be laid out before 'When finished, ' rather than interrupting the sentence? which show the three takes of Jamal El Sati's statements on the same television. This is then followed by an interview, also on video, with Elias Attallah, who was the party leader responsible for El Sati's suicide mission and who was at the time of the interview still active as a politician.

With his reenactment of the three takes in the here and now shared with the audience, Mroué invites the audience to look at the recordings of El Sati that follow his performance from the same perspective, that is, to look at these historical documents not from the perspective of what happened afterwards, but from a position

Video still of Rabih Mroué's *Three Posters*, 2000. Courtesy the artist.

before. The audience sees El Sati struggling with how to phrase his motivation, how to frame his deed, how to explain what he is going to do. All quite different from the final cut that was shown on TV, which suggested a clear statement without hesitations and revisions, an unequivocal truth. This is then followed by the video interview with the politician, who has to relate it from the perspective of today and to negotiate between his perspective back then, as the one responsible for El Sati's deed. This constellation of elements making up *Three Posters* draws attention to the historical truth of what happened as the product of a struggle, a complex negotiation, and to the fabrication of truth as an ongoing process played out in and through documentation.[1]

In his reflections on *Three Posters*, Mroué provocatively proposes that perhaps we should conceive of the video testimonies of the martyrs as the first local and Arabic productions of video art, since no one had been working in this medium before. He quotes Jalal Toufic, film theorist and video artist, stating that:

> I consider Sana' Muhadli, who introduced the new genre of videotaped testimonies of soon-to-be martyrs and a new kind of utterance 'I am the martyr (name of speaker)', as the first Lebanese video artist. Prior to her martyrdom, Sana' worked in a video store in the al-Musatbi area of West Beirut. During this time, she recorded 36 videotapes of the martyr Wajdi as-Sayigh, who performed his operation against enemy forces in an area close to that where Sana' carried out her martyring operation. It is in that video store that Sana' videotaped her testimony using a VHS camera.
>
> Mroué 2013: 311–12

Mroué's provocation, after Toufic, brings to mind Groys' observation that in today's media society terrorists and warriors themselves begin to act as artists and that video is the medium of choice for contemporary warriors. Video was the medium with which Bin Laden communicated with the outside world. Therefore, Groys argues, we know Bin Laden first of all as a video artist, and '[t]he same can be said about the videos representing beheadings, confessions of the terrorists etc. In all these cases we have to deal with the consciously and artistically staged events that have their own easily recognizable aesthetics' (Groys 2008: 121). This situation, Groys observes, implies a fundamental change with regard to the relationship between warriors and artists. Once upon a time warriors needed artists to represent them, to bestow fame on the warrior and to secure this fame for the generations to come. Today's warrior does not need an artist any more to get fame and inscribe his action into universal memory. In words that bring to mind the testimony of 'Chris Burden' in *Who's Afraid of Representation?*, Groys observes:

> For this purpose the contemporary warrior has all the contemporary media at his immediate disposal. Every act of terror, every act of war is immediately registered, represented, described, depicted, narrated and interpreted by the media. This machine of the media coverage is working almost automatically. It does not need any individual artistic intervention, any individual artistic decision to be put into motion. By pushing the button that led a bomb to explode a contemporary warrior or terrorist pushes a button that starts the media machine.
>
> Groys 2008: 120

He also points to an important difference between the terrorist and the contemporary artist: the terrorist wants us to believe in the image whereas Western art has a history of criticising the image. Art is iconoclastic whereas terrorism is iconophilic. 'The terrorist's or the warrior's image production has the goal to produce the strong images—the images that we would tend to accept as being "real", as being "true", as being the "icons" of the hidden, terrible reality that is for us the global political reality of our time' (Groys 2008: 124).

Yet, this iconoclastic attitude, which has been so important to art, is also what is challenged now in the face of the strong images produced by terrorists. Images which, Groys observes, we cannot say are not true, 'because we know that these images are paid for by a real loss of life—a loss of life that is documented by these images' (Groys 2008: 124). It is this knowledge, that means, after many decades of the critique of representation, 'we are now ready to accept certain photographed and videotaped images as unquestionably true, again' (Groys 2008: 124). Therefore this problem is not merely a matter of visualisation, of images, but also of documentation and how what Jones analyses as the mutual supplementarity of performance and photographic document, prevents a critical reading of the document as image. The knowledge that the images were paid for by a real loss of life serves as an ontological 'anchor' of the photograph's indexicality, which places photograph and event in the condition of mutual supplementarity observed by Jones and prevents a critical reading of the document in terms of how it represents what it represents. What is needed in this context, therefore, is not only a critique of the image, of images, but also more broadly, an unpacking of what is at stake in our resistance to engaging with the image as representation and how such resistance is part of the fabrication of truth. *Who's Afraid of Representation?* questions this resistance and draws attention to how such resistance is supported by the supplementarity observed by Jones, by means of a dramaturgy that juxtaposes representations of violence in the arts with non-artistic violence and places the audience in the position of a jury judging how to read and assess the truth of these representations. The audience finds itself confronted with a long series of confessions about violent deeds by artists and by the man having killed his former colleagues. The point is not to compare their deeds. What the parallel shows is how the supplementarity of performance and documentation operates differently in each case. At the very end, the man concludes his last confession with: 'Dawn of January 1988, my death sentence is carried out by hanging. During this whole time, they never once asked me to re-enact my crime, as they usually ask of all the other accused. My name is Hassan Ma'moum' (Mroué, 2013: 241). 'The other accused' could refer to other criminals. In the context of the performance it also refers to the artists who, in the performance, appeared in 'court' with him. The staging of their 'testimonies' highlights these being representations. The 'artists' speak to us via Lina Saneh whose presence is mediated by the camera. Although she seems to be speaking directly to us, in fact she is standing with her back towards the audience behind the screen facing a camera directed at her from upstage. And, although she speaks in first person, her 'confessions' are performed representations of documentation in the book. And all of this is explicitly demonstrated by the construction of the performance. The man on the other hand speaks directly to the audience, standing in front of the screen. In his testimonies he describes the same crimes time and again, in different ways: as carefully planned revenge, a moment of rage out of control, out of shame for a financial problem, as revenge upon those who insulted Islam and Muslims, and as a result of psychological problems caused by the violence committed by Israeli commandos. However, in the end, how he represents them appears not to matter. And indeed, when it comes to punishment, it may perhaps not matter that much how he represents what he did. But, when it comes to how representations of his crime will find their way into the circulation of signs and images in global digital culture, it does.

Note

1 This was also addressed in the video lecture about *Three Posters* in which Mroué explains why they had decided to stop performing this work. El Sati's suicide mission, he explains, took place in 1985, that is, before suicide bombing would become a trade mark of Islamic terrorism. Jamal El Sati and other Lebanese suicide bombers were secular, left-wing resistance fighters of the National Resistance Front fighting the army of a foreign nation, Israel, occupying their country. They were not terrorists threatening civilians in order to destabilise other nations. Yet in the early 2000s this image of suicide bombing started to dominate public imagination to such an extent that it also became part of the perception of El Sati's deed and Mroué's performance about it. At this moment Mroué decided to stop performing *Three Posters*.

References

2001 [1962] Albee, E. *Who's Afraid of Virginia Woolf?* London: Vintage Publishing.

2004 Andersen, F. 'Corpus Delicti: Zola's *Nana*, Breton's *Nadja*—Siamese Twins in the Body of the Novel'. In K. Simonsen, M. Huang, M. and M. Thomsen (eds) *Reinventions of the Novel*, Amsterdam: Rodopi, pp73–94.

2006 Auslander, P. 'The Performativity of Performance Documentation'. *PAJ: A Journal of Performance and Art*, 84: pp1-10.

1968 Benjamin, W. 'Theses on the Philosophy of History.' In Walter Benjamin, *Illuminations*, trans. Harry Zohn, New York: Schochen Books, pp253–64.

2014 Bleeker, M. 'Challenging Forth the Truth: Rabih Mroué's *On Three Posters*'. In M. Blazević and L.C. Feldman (eds) *Misperformance. Essays in Shifting Perspectives*, Ljubljana: Maska, pp171–82.

1996 Deleuze, G. and Guattari F. *What is Philosophy?* New York: Columbia University Press.

2008 Groys, B. *Art Power*, London: MIT Press.

2005 Groys, B. 'The Fate of Art in the Age of Terror'. In B. Latour and P. Weibel (eds) *Making Things Public: Atmospheres of Democracy*, London: MIT Press, pp970–7.

1997 Jones, A. '"Presence" in Absentia: Experiencing Performance in Documentation'. *Art Journal*, 56(4): 11–18.

2001 McKenzie, J. *Perform or Else: From Discipline to Performance*, London: Routledge.

2013 Mroué, R. *Image(s), Mon Amour: Fabrications*, Madrid: CA2M.

1992 [1948] Newman, B. 'The Sublime Is Now'. In B. Newman *Selected Writings and Interviews*, ed. J.P. O'Neill, Berkeley: University of California Press, pp170–3.

2007 Richter, G. *Thought Images: Frankfurt School Writers' Reflections from Damaged Life*, Stanford: Stanford University Press, 2007.

1992 Sayre, H. *The Object of Performance: The American Avant-Garde since 1970*, Chicago: University of Chicago Press.

ARCHIVE

In assembling *Artists in the Archive*, it became evident that its trajectory might imply a kind of deadly logic, in which dynamic practices of remaking, reviewing and returning all lead to their own final resting place in the static archive. By designating this final section ARCHIVE, however, the aim is to upend this logic, to foreground archiving not only as a repository, but as a practice, full of indeterminacies and potentialities. This move is in line with other projects which figure the archive (or better, archives) as historically specific, as in progress and as potent tools for social or cultural intervention. As Kate Eichorn notes in her work on archives and recent grassroots feminism in the United States, 'the archive is not necessarily either a destination or an impenetrable barrier to be breached, but rather a site and practice integral to knowledge making, cultural production and activism' (2013: 3). In the following section, it is this framework of *both* site *and* practice that comes through.

Artists have, of course, been drawing on archives, archival logic and archival aesthetics for decades. Hal Foster draws a genealogy between pre- and post-World War II visual practices (conditioned, respectively, by expanded access to image-making technologies and by rising interest in appropriation and seriality), and with the 'archival impulse' in artists such as Thomas Hirschhorn, Tacita Dean and Sam Durant in the early 2000s, for whom artistic practice could be understood 'as an idiosyncratic probing into particular figures, objects, and events in modern art, philosophy, and history' (Foster 2004: 3).

The artists included in the following section have made works that do not necessarily partake in archival aesthetics—the works may not *look* like archives. Rather, these works all in some way propose that archiving can be thought as a performance practice, or that the performance space can be understood as a kind of archive. Indeed, in Simon Jones' concluding chapter following this section, the very question of what performance is, now, can be thought in relation to archives and the technologies that produce them. This question of mediality—what makes performance performance?—is also posed by Jones as an epistemological question: what kinds of knowledge are produced by performance *as* performance?

In Giles Bailey's series of performance and visual works pulled together under the title *Talker Catalogue*, the artist proposes performance as a methodology for creating performance history. The performance strategies he develops include various modes of public address and the use of the monologue, mining film and television archives for minor characters and footnotes, and ultimately foregrounding the subjective experience that threads through the construction of any history.

For Terry O'Connor, too, the seemingly minor and subjective are key connections between archives and performance. Her contribution is prompted by a series of photographs taken by Hugo Glendinning of the influential UK theatre company Forced Entertainment (of which O'Connor is a member, and with which Glendinning has a long association). The photos had never been used until now, when they become the motivation for a reflection on performance devising as a process of documenting and selecting, and the theatre space as archive of this process, connecting to the idea (found articulated on a sign in an industrial conservation area in Sheffield) that 'nothing goes to waste'.

Koh Nguang How's *The Singapore Art Archive Project* is an archive that 'pretends/acts' as an archive, as the artist puts it. Comprising now more than a million items, the project began with a personal basis, with newspaper clippings Koh collected as a student, and documentation produced through administrative tasks as a curatorial assistant. This developed into a self-assigned project of documenting the history of arts practices in Singapore that may be in danger of disappearing, with particular attention to gaps, mistakes and discontinuities.

The duo hancock and kelly reflect on a multi-year collaborative archiving project titled *Lone Duets*. The artists individually created a series of performances, each a 're-make' of the others' previous performance, so that a chain of performance reactions developed over an extended period. In framing this process as a fleshy archive, the artists also figure the archive as leaky, and capable of contamination and infection.

Finally, writer and performer Claire MacDonald extends this consideration of the body as an archive, particularly aging bodies and women's bodies. The piece emerges from a collaboration with Charlotte Vincent, who had, in 1999, recreated a performance of MacDonald's from 1984 (in *Carrier Frequency*, originally a collaboration between Impact Theatre and novelist Russell Hoban, and recreated by Stan's Cafe). Nearly a decade later, in 2008, Vincent and MacDonald found a quick and close connection which MacDonald attributes, in part, to a shared gestural vocabulary based on Vincent's efforts to reproduce and inhabit MacDonald's physicality.

References

2013 Eichorn, K. *The Archival Turn in Feminism: Outrage in Order*, Philadelphia: Temple University Press.

2004 Foster, H. 'An Archival Impulse'. *October*, 110: pp3–22.

TALKER CATALOGUE

Giles Bailey

Giles Bailey, *Tom/Lutz: Two Scenes in 1983* (2011). Courtesy of Giles Bailey.

Statement

Talker Catalogue is a project that proposes alternative strategies for assembling and recounting a history of performance practice.

It aims to challenge the orthodoxies, conventions and methods of documenting performances, and also to challenge the ways that these become incorporated into traditional, linear historiographical models. Using performance itself as a methodological tool, it responds critically to the limited nature of, for example photographic documentation, and its failure to convey the nuances and complexities of time-based work. The research's originality lies in its use of performance itself to become an active participant in its own history, rather than a dispassionate authority commenting on it from the outside. Attendant to this work are broader implications for historiographical practices in other fields and how they might be critically reappraised.

Each of the four performances that constitute the research, (*Exit THE AZTEC, The Nineteen Sixties, Tom/Lutz: Two Scenes in 1983* and *All Whirlwind, Heat and Flash*), address details, fragments, documents or footnotes of what could be considered as 'the history of performance'. By experimenting with a combination of modes of public address (explicatory, academic, dramatic, discursive, anecdotal) texts were appropriated or elaborated from this material to be delivered as monologues. Through repetition, collage and speech, a new descriptive mode was developed emphasising the subjectivity of a singular, speaking subject. The performances thus interrogated the particularities of key historic visual material by integrating it into the live scenario. This introduced and problematised questions of appropriation, image reproduction and authorship for the audience.

The Performances

Tom/Lutz: Two Scenes in 1983 (2011)

...These are just ordinary eyedrops and what I do is simply remove the cap and place it in my mouth, tilt my head back and tug the flesh above my cheekbone to expose the eyeball and ease the application of the liquid. The head is tilted forward again, the eyes blink to displace any excess, I remove the cap from my mouth, replace it on the bottle and screw it tightly. I'm aware it might seem a little strange at first but my hope is that through repetition it will become normalised and habitual...

In *Tom/Lutz: Two Scenes in 1983* accounts of two ostensibly unconnected incidents concerning male protagonists are told simultaneously. The death of Tennessee Williams by choking on the cap of a bottle eyedrops and the filming of a scene from Chantal Akerman's documentary *Un jour Pina à demandé* in which the dancer Lutz Förster performs George Gershwin's song *The Man I Love* in American sign language are footnotes in the history of performance that become paired in order to inflect and contaminate each other.

Exit THE AZTEC (2010)

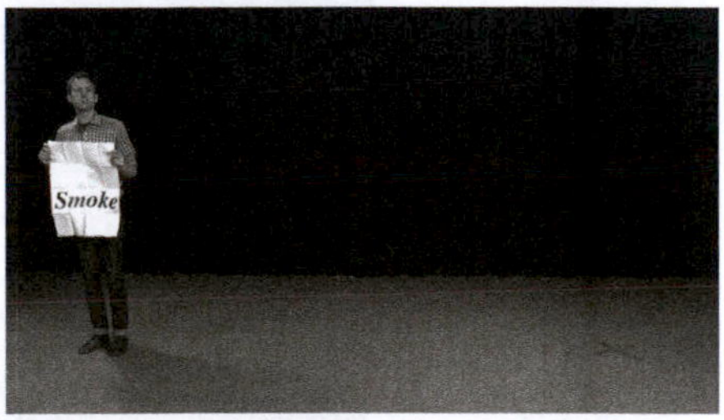

Giles Bailey, *Exit THE AZTEC* (2010). Courtesy of Giles Bailey.

The stage is bare except for two xs on the floor made from coloured adhesive tape. There is a space of approximately three meters between them. On one x stands a male performer in nondescript attire: jeans, shirt, sweater. He begins.

Preliminary choreography for the magic trick:

1. The performer lifts each arm and tugging the cuff of his sweater demonstrates to the audience he has nothing up his sleeves.
2. In a workmanlike fashion he roles his sleeves.
3. Holding up both hands in the attitude of surrender he rotates his wrists to show his hands back and front.

He stops abruptly and speaks.

'Actually, I'm going to begin with this, by showing you something.'
He draws a folded piece of paper from a back pocket and unfolding it displays a poster baring the stage direction 'Smoke'.

The performance is a re-staging of a minor character in François Truffaut's 1962 film *Jules et Jim*. Barely speaking, appearing on screen for less than a minute and mysteriously dubbed THE AZTEC in the director's screenplay, he steps from the movie to become a site inhabited by a number of characters and voices and the nexus of various narrative threads. He presents a speculative tool to question the motions on and off a stage or on and off camera.

All Whirlwind, Heat and Flash (Undertone) (2011)

Drunk at the wheel they laugh together as the foam from another beer explodes across the windscreen as she pulls the ring from the can. Sweet suds are in his hair as he idly spins the chamber of the revolver between his knees while she drives. They are intoxicated as much by the hot wind and the velocity as they are by fatigue and when the car drifts to the shoulder of the desert highway, the front fender clips a heap of rocks and the car flips, rolls and eventually comes to rest on its roof the wheels still spinning round they crawl from the wreck unharmed. Passionately they kiss

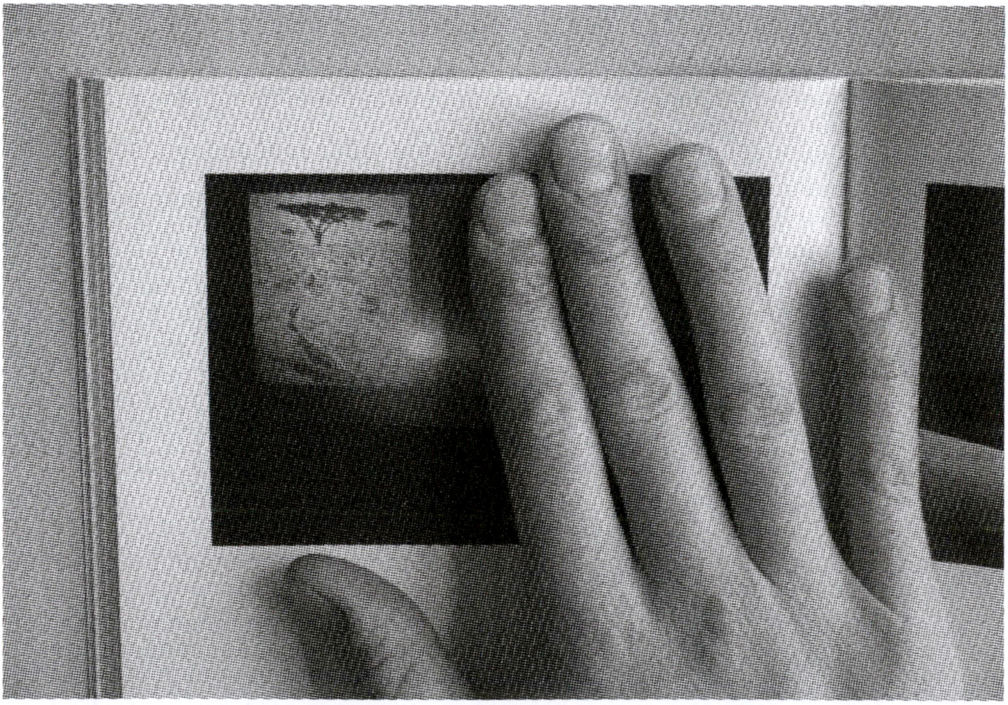

Giles Bailey, *The Nineteen Sixties* (2011). Courtesy of Giles Bailey.

Giles Bailey, *All Whirlwind, Heat and Flash (Undertone)* (2011). Courtesy of Giles Bailey.

in the dust by the roadside. Her blouse is ripped so that you can see her shoulder and her hair is mussed so that it falls down the side of her face, dark and lovely. Very becoming...

All Whirlwind, Heat and Flash (Undertone) is a performance with an extract of Vito Acconci's video *Undertone* (1972) that has been widely circulated on the internet. In the original video Acconci details a masturbation fantasy while apparently caressing himself under the table. In my performance the sound of Acconci's fantasy is faded out and I deliver a monologue that constructs an alternative narrative, a counterpoint redolent with the clichés of a cinematic love story and replete with car chases and betrayal. I become a vicarious counterpart to Acconci's narcissism, living a fantasy through the structure of his video rather than the vivid sexual act he describes.

The Nineteen Sixties (2011)

...He rises and stretches. Seated on the wide, flat expanse of the wooden floor he grips one foot then the other, arcs his spine rolls his neck and thinks:

Antimony, arsenic, aluminium, selenium, hydrogen, oxygen, nitrogen, rhenium, nickel, neodymium, neptunium, germanium, iron, americium, ruthenium, uranium

Then there's breakfast which he drinks and eats...

The Nineteen Sixties is a ten-minute monologue and photographic series that responds to the distance created by documentation of Yvonne Rainer's evening length work *The Mind is A Muscle*. Selectively working from the incongruous records that exist of the event, the performance entangles disparate elements of autobiography and other cultural residue to propose an subjective historiographic process that negotiates a defining moment in the history of performance art.

NOTHING GOES TO WASTE

Terry O'Connor

Forced Entertainment. Courtesy of Hugo Glendinning.

1.

These images are photographs of Forced Entertainment's work, taken over the years by our friend and collaborator Hugo Glendinning. It's an extraordinary archive of our work together and could make its own claims to be the truest. I asked Hugo to spend a little time picking some photos from his collection that had not been released for press or general use, photos that may not really have been seen by anyone else.

2.

By thinking about archives I found myself thinking about process and how process could be considered a continuous archiving of sorts. In the case of Forced Entertainment it often feels as though our process is a long conversation (not entirely verbal) about what 'works', a sifting of moments that we like, or don't like, a fixing of moments that are either 'in it' or not.

Just the day before this writing, at the University of Sheffield, I was working with a group of Theatre MA students on a project that seemed to extend this approach to the making process. It was a project that was very busy with its own documentation, busy recording the moments of its making and looking out for opportunities to turn those records into another kind of material. Walks were planned and drawn or captured, walked and photographed. Photographs were ordered into slide shows in minutes, decisions left here or right there turned into routes on maps projected and used as lighting sources for a whole room. The theatre space we met in became a growing archive of these recordings, simultaneously elements of the decision process and also, always potential parts of the final piece. Alongside this, statements of intent and written contributions in many forms were printed and pinned to the drapes. The empty black studio acquired its own careful archival order, a layered collection of thought and capture and selection.

Outside, beyond the studio space where we might originally have expected our performance to take place, we found ourselves planning to stage our event in a derelict and abandoned industrial conservation area north east of the university. The site was an area called Well Meadows, home, long ago and still today, to the rag and bone trade and the waste disposal business around steel production. Behind walls and gates, sorted piles of wood and metal waste were visible. This shifting assortment of waste product sat amongst a further, less organised collection of evidence, condoms and needles, and the crumbling remains of derelict nineteenth century back to back terraces. In amongst all this stands the UK's only remaining Cementation Furnace, beneath which is written:

> By this process blister steel was manufactured and in the true Sheffield tradition nothing goes to waste

Performing in this outside space, the students used phone apps to throw dice so that they could follow in the tradition of chance construction, they googled texts to throw into the performance, they played a song on the weedy speakers from their many phones held aloft all playing the same song, all set to play at the same time.

The whole process seemed an easy and continuous approach to archiving, an inevitable questioning of where documentation ends and the art begins, a pretty constant exchange or interplay between archives, documents, records and websites: material provided and provoked and appropriated and re-ordered.

3.

Brian Eno claimed that modern art is 'as much about curation as it is about creation' (Eno in Kelly 1995). The grand narrative of the 'absolutely new' fractured and split a long time back and in consequence, perhaps, art is another site where the records of the past are brought back to visibility and where the present is re-ordered into visibility. Through that process you could imagine whole great stacks from past and present sifted into

Forced Entertainment. Courtesy of Hugo Glendinning.

useful/useless, interesting/not interesting 'in it/not in it'. Artists perform and keep a different kind of public record.

In Forced Entertainment, when we are trying to make a new piece, we often find ourselves trying to name what we like, trawling a detritus of memory and impulse.

These are our starting points:

this is good it feels a bit like...
or...this is good it feels quite different to...
long collection of moments that are like or unalike, real or imagined.

The 'ghost dance' in *The Coming Storm* (2012), uses the same piece of flimsy gauze, the same floaty moves as Jerry's 'Dance of Peace' in *The World in Pictures* (2006), also a recurrent performance costume motif for the cardboard sign 'Banquo's Ghost' in *12AM Awake and Looking Down* (1993), like some quasi-mythical 'dance of veils', like Marilyn in the last sittings, like Salome, like a kid in a sheet, like playing afterlife, playing dead, like a skeleton costume, like the skeleton dance in *Who Can Sing a Song to Unfrighten Me?* (1999), the skeleton in *Spectacular* (2008), like Claire dying a death of constant movement behind the skeleton, like play dying, like Richard's onstage 'heart attack' in *The Thrill of it All* (2010), like Phil's heart attack behind Richard's in the *Thrill of it All* (2010), like Rob's spaghetti death in *Showtime* (1996), like the white faced ghost of dead Elvis in *Some Confusions in the Law about Love* (1989), like the white faced showgirls in *Some Confusions*, making speeches about love, like the skeletons in *Some Confusions*, their trembling tale of love and on.

(I remembered, just now, just in writing this, an incident, another dance, 1985, I was doing an MA in Leeds. A friend from a band called Dorothy's Cottage asked me to dance beside the band in a full body pink lycra triangle, at a fundraising gig at the 1 in 12 club in Bradford. I wasn't keen but didn't want to say no. I hadn't remembered this experience before. Not in the weeks of making *The Coming Storm*, not in the

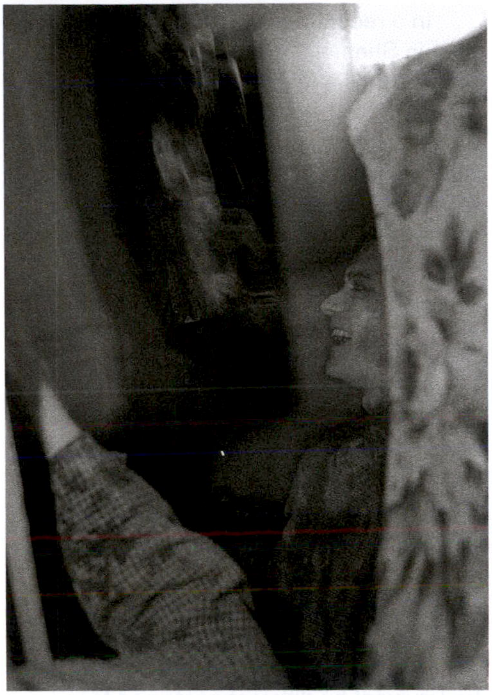

months of performing it, but now, in the moments of writing it, memory is not a reliable archive.)

Then, also, the synchronous threads of other people's work, other ghosts, other dances, the things we've seen like this moment, like that device, like that great look, that thing they did with language, with soundtrack, like the way they didn't move, like the way they talked, like the way they looked at the audience, like other words we've read or heard, like moments felt in cinemas, moments in exhibitions and solo performances or the first encounter with a particular photograph, never seen before.

This process is a sort of conversation in which the seen and known is described, (inevitably reworked in the telling), to reach for the unseen, the unknown. Derrida writes that the same is not the identical. In his work on 'differance' (with an a), he discusses an equivocal passage from one difference to another, from one term of slight or qualifying opposition to the other (Derrida 1968). There is something of this construction within philosophy, as a systematic ordering of the same. There is also this kind of ambivalent differentiating in the making process, an identification of formal elements needed for performance and a teasing out of difference for each iteration. What can we do with the stage, the curtains, the address to the audience, the edges, the pretense, the game, the faltering and failure, the gaps between ourselves and our enactment... this time? Teasing out the difference from previous work, ours and others'.

4.

I was thinking about the selectivity of archive as I trawled London, looking for a copy of Can's *The Lost Tapes* (December 2013). In this edit of 30 hours of forgotten recordings of their experimental methodology, the offstage of their process becomes the exclusive product, the rare and costly collector's item. Like these photos of Hugo's, which must at one stage have been rejected in favour of others, interesting and selected now because they have never been seen before.

In a recent posting as part of a reading loop in Sheffield, a colleague at the university describes a feeling of discomfort when having traced what he thought would be a rare collection of vinyl in the Kelvin flats to the north of the city, he found, on picking them up, that he wanted very few of them and was then left with the emotional complications of discarding them: somebody else's selection dismantled, the greater part re-catalogued as surplus to requirement, as waste. The acts of selection running through archival processes are inevitably political and the field of performance has very particular questions in relation to this politics of methodology and knowledge and its relation to ephemeral event. The nature of our evidence, the remains or traces of performance are often contestable, posing questions around live work that remains resistant to archive. Traditionally in performance, the script or score survived to be 'revived' by different casts and teams. The text is the thing. Outside of dramatic literature or representation through text, works may find themselves occupying a marginal or problematic shelf in the archive. Photographic or recorded representation of some work in this field is also sometimes difficult or impossible. But since the explosion of performance art in the 70s, artists have found ironic and inquisitorial ways to play the gap between the event and the document. In *Selected Works 71–74* Chris Burden (1975) talks us through a playfully edited selection of grainy footage and faltering camera work, teasing us with the suggestion that this/all representation is inadequate, weaving a testimonial voiceover based on memory and hindsight and ultimately spinning mystique around the unrepeatable original event. It is a very beautiful piece.

5.

My friend, the artist Penny McCarthy has spent a lot of time in archives, actual and virtual ones. A part of her work is concerned with hand drawn copies of particular, chosen archival sources, pages of the languages and beauty of knowledge from the past. *Book (Art History)* is part of a series of drawings taken from details of Leonardo Da Vinci's work as found in assorted tomes. For another piece, she made exact copies of all of the pages from a Borges short story, *Pierre Menard, Author of the Quixote*, a story that is itself about copying and authorship. All of the drawings are precise size for size pencil-drawn copies of the real thing.

She describes archival searching as: 'an odd, lonely activity' saying that 'much of the time you are talking to ghosts. The best moments are of discovery, when you come across a scribble or scrap of marginalia, the trace of something never meant for you to see that seems to bring you closer to the ordinary humanity of the author' (McCarthy and O'Connor 2010).

Here, again is the notion of the chance encounter with the never seen: the archive as a place to lose a sense of your own direction and follow the trail of ghosts, or to follow a trail of the archive itself. You can think about closeness, about bringing to life or bringing back to life as ideas that flicker between theatre and archive.

Some time ago I led a project in which theatre students in Sheffield worked with colleagues at The National Fairground Archive at the university, using their documents and accounts as a starting point for new work. They worked with the story of the last *Sleeping Beauty Birmingham* 1966, a traditional fairground show where you are invited to look at a scantily clad woman lying down with her eyes closed. They looked at the gimp, the lowest form of employment in the fairground, a guy who was employed to eat live animals.

In traditional theatre the actor fills and interprets the written role. For makers of new work confronting an archive as a starting point, the question in the process might be: so now in response... what do we do? The process obliges us to take a position that looks forwards and back, to account for our work both ways, to ask basic questions about the live form we choose to work with, how it might best bear testimony to both past and present, creating a feeling of urgency and charge, how it might work the understanding that comes through doing.

Written into the idea of archive, is the sense that what may be important to a future researcher, maker or thinker cannot be predicted, that the nugatory and the crucial are categories we cannot determine for future sensibilities. But whilst there is always an aspiration to completion in the idea of archive, the complete collection or the Borgesian library and its promise of an infinitely open and generative store shifting kaleidoscopically moment by moment, endlessly re-ordering, there may also be the suggestion of the small and random point of contact, a handwritten question that fires across new synaptic gaps: so, now, what shall we do?

References

1975 Burden, C *Documentation of Selected Works* 1971–74, New York: Electronic Arts Intermix.

1968 Derrida, J. 'Difference'. Available online. https://projectlamar.com/media/Derrida-Differance.pdf. Accessed 27 February 2017.

1995 Kelly, K. 'Gossip is Philosophy'. Available online. https://archive.wired.com/wired/archive/3.05/eno_pr.html. Accessed 27 February 2017.

2010 McCarthy, P. and O'Connor, T. *Stealing Voices. The Mediating Effects of Spoken and Autographic Utterances*, London: Artwords Press.

THE SINGAPORE ART ARCHIVE PROJECT

Signage for The Artists Village and Tang Da Wu at the road junction of Lorong Gambas, Singapore, 1989. Photo: Koh Nguang How. Reproduced courtesy of the artist.

The Singapore Art Archive Project (SAAP) is a work in progress (site-specific) first conceptualised in 1999 at my home and only given its name in 2005 at p-10 (an artist-run space). As the term 'archive' usually refers to a place or institution and 'archives' would be the materials in its collection, the SAAP pretends/acts as an archive related to art in Singapore and its wider international connections.

Collection and photography

My collection for The Singapore Art Archive Project began with newspaper cuttings (English and Chinese) when I was a student in junior college in 1980. I was also doing art as a subject, so naturally my focus was more on art related articles. I continue to collect the newspaper cuttings till this day.

My first occupation was a Museum Assistant (curatorial) at the National Museum Art Gallery, Singapore (NMAG), from October 1985 to January 1992. The environment allowed me to meet and work with artists, curators and other people in the art world. The NMAG was a common and central place for local artists and art societies to have their shows; and with a range of events such as exhibitions, lectures,

Koh Nguang How

workshops and competitions. As such, my experience of art and related issues grew progressively along with my collection of related materials. The new materials in my collection expanded to include exhibition invite cards, catalogues, posters, flyers, photographs, videos and sound recordings.

Photography was not a designated duty for me at the National Museum Art Gallery but an essential process of artefact registration and exhibition preparation; I developed my basic knowledge of photography and started to record events such as exhibitions, opening ceremonies, press conferences, lectures, workshops, studio visits and performance art.

Coordination and research jobs

In early 1992, I left the National Museum Art Gallery to become a full-time artist. I was associated with the newly registered art group 'The Artists Village'. I travelled occasionally as an artist and collected materials for the archive project from the events and places I visited.

In 1996, I had the opportunity to act as a coordinator for Fukuoka Art Museum in Japan, for its exhibition project 'The Birth of Modern Art in South East Asia: Artists and Movements'. My involvement in the project allowed me to learn more about some older and forgotten artists, their works and the early history of Singapore art. After that Fukuoka project, I decided that my collection and documentation priority should be on the fast-disappearing old artists' works and their experiences. Thereafter, older materials were collected through the old artists themselves and unexpected sources like antique shops, flea markets, second-hand bookstores, books sale, vacating buildings and garbage sites.

Soon, the amount of materials on the older art history of Singapore grew; the task of preserving the materials became a serious concern for me. By then, I realised that it was impossible for me to document and research into two different areas: the future and the past art histories. I decided to spend less of my time and resources on younger artists and future events, especially with the arrival of the internet and digital recording devices in Singapore.

Archives as content and medium of art

Koh Nguang How at *Performance Week*, Gallery 21, Singapore, 1992.

My first exhibition of photographic records of art events was in a group exhibition called 'Performance Week' at Gallery 21, Singapore, in August 1992. I put together photographs which I have taken of performance art in Singapore from 1987 to 1992 against some newspapers in the background.

In 2004, I was invited to have a solo show by a new curatorial initiative 'p-10', situated near Little India in Singapore, where some young artists created their studios from apartment spaces. I decided to present some of my archival materials for the new artists' community, which resulted in the p-10 curated show 'ERRATA: Page 71, Plate 47. Image caption. Change Year: 1950 to Year: 1959; Reported September 2004 by Koh Nguang How'. The 'ERRATA show' was based on the wrong dating of a 1959 painting of Malay language as the new national language of the new self-governed state of Singapore, by artist Chua Mia Tee, in the book *Channels and Confluences: A History of Singapore Art*, written by the Director of the Singapore Art Museum Kwok Kian Chow in 1996. I presented different groups of old publications from my collection to provide clues and answers for the audiences to find the correct answer to the date of the painting.

The 'ERRATA show' became the start of a series of works in which I would present archival materials to the audience so that they could view them as archival resources as well as installation artwork.

Naming of Singapore Art Archive Project

After the rather well received 'ERRATA show', p-10 invited me for a residency in 2005.

From the residency room at p-10, I started the name 'Singapore Art Archive Project' (SAAP).

In 2011, I was invited to make a work for 'Open House'—The third Singapore Biennale at 8Q at Singapore Art Museum (8Q-SAM). I took the opportunity to show my 30 years of newspaper cuttings including many uncut issues. I named the installation work 'Artists in the News' (also known as SAAP@8Q-SAM) featuring the English and Chinese morning papers mainly from 1980 to 2011. The newspapers were presented in various subjects on the walls like large pin-boards and in smaller installation pieces. I highlighted a news article of the 'groundbreaking' installation work by Tang Da Wu from April 1980 called *Earthworks*, however, as a reference to the 30 years later developments of the arts in Singapore and the world. This *Earthworks*, however, was prematurely terminated by the Director of the National Museum in 1980.

'Singapore Art Archive Project @CCA', NTU Centre for Contemporary Art, Gillman Barracks, Singapore, 2014-2015. Photo: Koh Nguang How. Reproduced courtesy of the artist.

'ERRATA: Page 71, Plate 47. Image caption. Change Year: 1950 to Year: 1959; Reported September 2004 by Koh Nguang How', p-10, Singapore, 2004. Photo: Koh Nguang How. Reproduced courtesy of the artist.

'Artists in the News' (SAAP@8Q-SAM), Open House-Singapore Biennale 2011, 8Q at Singapore Art Museum, 2011. Photo: Koh Nguang How. Reproduced courtesy of the artist.

In 2013, the NTU Centre for Contemporary Art, Singapore (CCA) was officially announced for the new Gillman Barracks, a contemporary arts cluster in Singapore. It was followed by an invitation to me to do a residency at Gillman Barracks starting 1 July 2014 to 31 Jan 2015.
I presented my archives under the name 'Singapore Art Archive Project @CCA' (SAAP@CCA) in four different exhibitions during the residency. The SAAP@CCA would also facilitate research and collaboration between the different artists-in-residence, CCA curators, visiting curators and research fellows.

Future of Singapore Art Archive Project

The Singapore Art Archive Project now comprises over one million items. Most of my archive materials are in a rented storage and in my own and parents' flats in Singapore. The strategy to curate and present the archives in different ways and themes will continue as long as possible.

PLAYING WITH SHADOWS AND SPEAKING IN ECHOES

Richard Hancock and Traci Kelly

Archive as call to remain

The archive is predated by events; things, stuff, occurrences in muscle tissue, text and imagination, chemical balances, that remain, and will (to) not be forgotten. An acceleration of matter, a material shift, that exhales and spores. A deceleration of molecules, a slow, absent duet, that inhales and ripples across years.

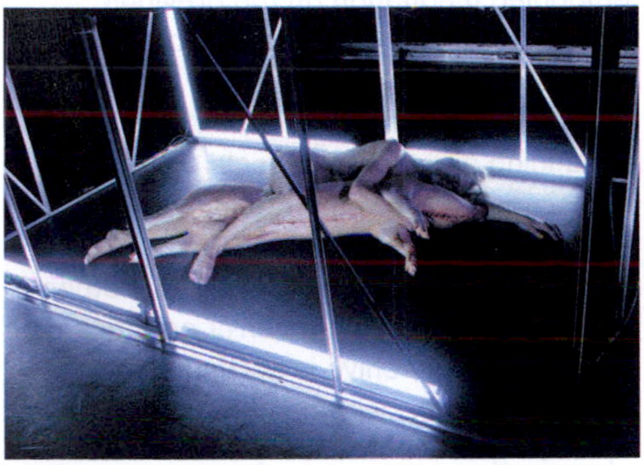

Dermographia, from *Lone Duets* (2005–8), hancock and kelly. Photo: Luke Warda.

Archive as energy

A de-territorialisation of self, one artist gives their work to be the source of the other's. The archival body-as-source is a place from where things are gotten. Performance as issue is an eruptive boundary, a flux-line emitting radiation in the advent of real time subject formation.

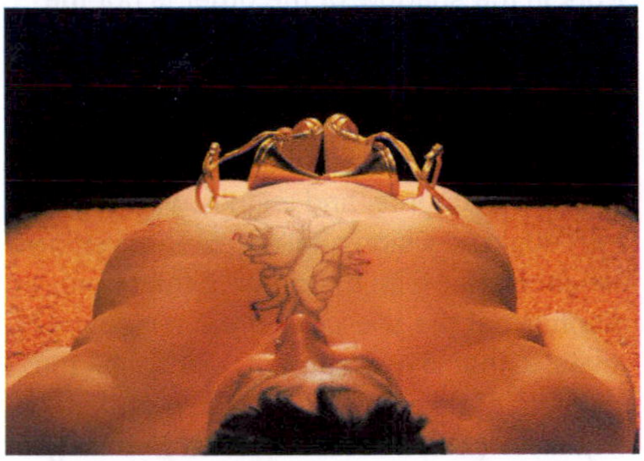

Rupture, from *Lone Duets* (2005–8), hancock and kelly. Photo: Lisa Urwin.

Archive as mark

The things that we touch, also touch us; the archive marks. It creates a frame of reference that accumulates, builds and shifts its points of focus and power. Its desires run deep, but its course remains divergent and open to coercion.

Postures A-to-M, from *Lone Duets* (2005–8), hancock and kelly. Photo: Luke Warda.

Archive as critical point

Reply performances made by the performer-in-waiting offer a counterpoint, introducing imbalances with cellular archiving and the de/coding of corporeal indexes. Tipping point, a moment of crisis. Unfaithful accounts. Falling. Fallen.

The Mirror Pool, from *Lone Duets* (2005–8), hancock and kelly. Photo: Sian Stammers.

Archive as lack

Defined as much by what is absent, as what is present, the archival body struggles to articulate itself around its gaps, holes and borders. Militant and transgressive tunnels open up and take us to unexpected ends. Subjective, partial, and open to misinterpretation, these tunnels map endless invisible grids under the surface of the archive; just out of sight, they remain embedded in its visceral, structural architecture.

Open Wound, from *Lone Duets* (2005–8), hancock and kelly. Photo: Heidrun Löhr.

Archive as culture

The archive refuses to be bound, upon any disturbance it bleeds at the borders. Culture occurs as a cutting edge rupture at the end of leaves of paper. Polyvocal interjections, dissenting voices and the distortions of echoes cause it to be unsettled and re/generative, producing rather than cataloguing eventfulness. Shadows distort a singular reality.

In Season, from *Lone Duets* (2005–8), hancock and kelly. Photo: Luke Warda.

In *Lone Duets* (2005–2008), hancock and kelly employed contamination and infection as dramaturgical devices, cultivating a series of six solo performances. Each piece was made in response to the previous work, made by the other artist. Individual performances were founded in the experience, interpretation, and inevitable mis-reading of the other. Each response became a highly subjective, and deeply embodied meditation on the previous moment and an explicit invocation of the other as source material.

The body is inextricably archival, producing and storing muscle memory, protein pathways in the brain in order to recall, and sensate knowledges. In seeking to rearticulate the archive of the other, a sequence of embodied error emerges. The corporeal archive is particular to its keeper, but may become infectious, spreading its reach. Fleshy documents and cellular codes from visceral practices run contra to quarantined knowledge, they are unruly, unstable, at risk and full of potential. For all their trouble, fevers allow us to recognise that we tend to privilege the comfort of stability when presented with the body in revolt. Artists work feverishly.

In a state of uprising, we flicker between light and shade. A shadow is an occlusion and a distortion made variable by illumination and viewpoint. As subjects of enunciation, and of cultural specificity, making work in the shadow of the other is not the hierarchical event it suggests. It playfully and complexly acknowledges distinct bodies and their indexes. Acknowledging shifts in perspective within queer and feminist discourse, and wilfully working with doubtful vision challenges the fixation we encounter with the draw of the monument. What the source and the shadow reveal is that like documents we are all the subjects of time, and the shadow of the object will(s to) exist for that fraction longer than the thing itself.

Failure and doubt are the value systems of hancock and kelly's alternative archive; sought in the worn and inhabited performances of *Lone Duets* played out in the shadow of the existent amongst the echoes of the concrete and discrete body of the Other. An echo is a single reflection of sound source, a diversion and a split in time. A transmission medium is key. hancock and kelly do not look to the other for the clarity of sharp edges, which are to be found only in arrested states. Nor do they seek to be reliable witnesses; rather they declare the generous fallibility of the archive. They insert their physical bodies into the performance landscape, causing acoustic shadows in the terrain, troubling hearing over distance, through time and its splitting.

PERFORMING WITH GHOSTS: A TALK REMEMBERED

Claire MacDonald

Matthew Davison.

Isn't it the truth that when you are thinking about something—writing something, making something, even just musing on something—it appears everywhere, as if everyone else were suddenly preoccupied with it too? You find yourself at the nexus of a dialogue with the world. You switch on the radio, or pick up the paper, and every woman out there seems to be considering and reconsidering her body, her past work, her subjectivity, what she's going to do next. On a recent Monday night at a dinner in Brighton for twenty women artists (Anon. 2012), Becky Edmunds began to talk about the shape of creative practice across a long life, the life of the dancer Deborah Hay about whom she is making a film. On Tuesday I watched Jeannette Winterson on TV repeating the gestural language of her fire and brimstone adopted mother whose cautionary tales midwifed Winterson into becoming the writer she is (Winterson 2012). And that thing that I've been musing on? It's how the body is shaped by experience; how past and future play out, all the time, in one's own embodied sense of self.

Perhaps it's not *just* the prompt of coming here today that makes me think about the back and forth of body and language and performance—perhaps it's my age. Everywhere there are sightings of body weather in the high plateaus of later life: Charlotte Rampling talking about age and female experience in her new film *I, Anna* (Southcombe 2012); Vanessa Redgrave about to play Beatrice on stage, as an *older* woman; Emmanuelle Riva in Michael Haneke's extraordinary new film, *Amour* (Haneke 2012). I have a neighbour who is 88, a poet, still writing, older than my mother would have been if she had not died in her forties, and when we talk, which we do most days, I ask *her* to report from the front line, as it were. I tell her she should write a blog on sex, death and fashion and she laughs as she tells me about the exigencies of the ageing female body. We talk about clothes, and hair and nails and love, while we talk about writing. Sometimes when I touch her I am aware of her fragility, while I, at almost 59, still have the strength and solidity that I always did have, my mother's body, solid and muscular. The pleasure of it, the sheer pleasure of having lived with it so long, the pleasure even of its tribulations, the marks of history, all the things I have done and all the luck good and bad I inherited with red hair and physical impulsiveness. The weak shoulder and arm where the melonoma was excavated; the broken foot, an old injury where a piece of set fell on me, the deep cut in my vagina giving birth to my one child. To say 'I' is *never* abstract, subjectivity is always *written* on the body.

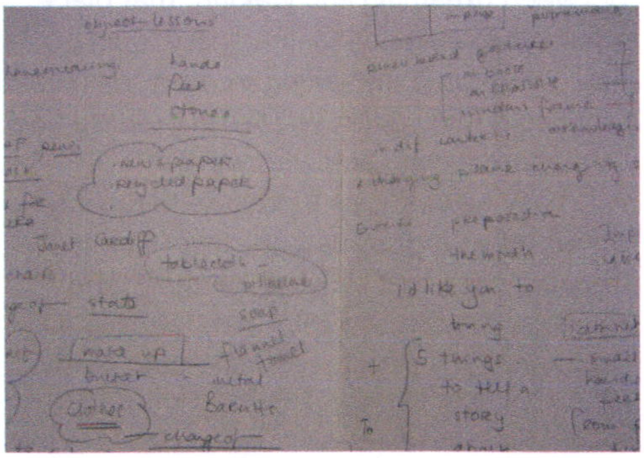

Courtesy of Claire MacDonald.

I am a writer who *was* a performer; who began writing as a performer and for whom writing opened up as a possibility *from* performance. Opened up, that is, as a territory, as another kind of space to be explored, and for whom writing has always had that strong sense of being *somewhere* rather than being *something*. Writing is a combination of activities whose material is language, an ongoing practice that I describe as multi-directional, promiscuous or rambling, sitting between the feckless and the driven. In practicing it I have excavated the same territory several times, most recently adding a third play to a trilogy I began in 1986 (MacDonald 2015). Each play is an enclosed, written world in which two people build, tend, grow, dig and destroy worlds through language. In the last and most recent piece, *Correspondence*, the speakers return to the scene after 20 years absence, and construct an imaginary encounter on a train passing through a landscape between dreaming and waking in which they tell a story full of holes.

As a title *Correspondence* suggests two things to me: an exchange of letters, and the corresponding spaces of a train, punning on the French *correspondance*. The book that haunts and drives the play is Alfred Kubin's 1908 novel *The Other Side*, one of the foundational texts of modernist experimental writing (Kubin 2014). It concerns a journey to an imaginary space on the border of the real, a place that holds the rational and irrational in tension. Fictionally framed, it is nevertheless experienced as real. The threshold between dreaming and waking, that place where the real and the imaginary touch, has constituted my writing territory, a fictional construct into which we step in order to find out where we are and who we are.

I say all of this as a prelude to talking about returning to one's past work because in every case that I have done that—and there have been several—that 'return' has been part of a private reconsidering of my own sense of self: who I am, what I am going to do next, who I was. Return always means returning to something embedded inside the scene of an older work. Returning unravels—in a way that is almost psychosomatic—the conditions under which I was operating at that time. If this just sounds solipsistic I should add that this isn't *all* that returning to one's work is about, but this is what I want to talk about, today, or just *now*, in my life. Today I'm thinking about this sense of return personally and selfishly, about how the archive of one's work—in its biggest, loosest sense, and including ephemeral as well as material elements—continues to structure and inform one's subjectivity—one's sense of who one is—even though one's apparent interests and direction may appear very different as one moves through one's life.

There are many models for the life of the artist, but there is no one prescriptive path. My own life is pretty emblematic of my own generation. After university I began making

Courtesy of Claire MacDonald.

ensemble theatre at the same time as having a child in a collective community. I had no plan for my life, I just put one foot in front of the other. I did things as they came up, shuttling back and forth between performing and making theatre, writing and editing, teaching and fellowships in universities, and, much later, a practice-based PhD. It's what I call a kit bag rather than a career, a high-level kit bag but a hold-all nevertheless.

That pattern—in which many different kinds of practice take place, feed off each other, interleave, disappear, return, are picked up as threads, go nowhere, go somewhere—is a common model, or was, for being an artist. It's driven by ongoing dialogue with one's peers, and as one gets older, it is carried in memory by colleagues and friends who one has known for one, two, three and now four decades. For me it has also involved writing about other artists' work as a way of conversing with my own work. I have often written several times about the same artist over many years, as I have in the UK with Cornelia Parker (MacDonald 1988, 2005), or, in Greece, with Lizzie Calligas (MacDonald 1990, 2010). Returning to their work brings our pasts to our present and our future. It offers new possibilities for what happens next, throws light on neglected parts of the territory. It is an essential aspect of making.

I have always liked Joseph Kosuth's comment, about the painter Ad Reinhart, that an artist's work consists of their entire signifying practice: writing about work, making work, talking, teaching, living. The work is a constellation of events, objects and evidence. I came across his words when I was writing about the film maker and choreographer Yvonne Rainer, in an essay that I called 'All Over the Map' (MacDonald 1999). In my title I was imagining her practice as a territory. In her introduction to *A Woman Who ...*, Rainer's book of essays and scripts (Rainer 1999), Peggy Phelan recalls Rainer's work as a film maker, as a choreographer, as a writer, as a teacher, as an extended practice of 'graphing'—a lovely image of mark making. These practices exist together in a life, jostling one another for space at times. Together they constitute what I think of as a process of autography—the progressive *graphing* of oneself as a subject, as one continues to create one's identity, to invent who one is. It was this that Jeannette Winterson was talking about as she re-membered in her own body the threading together of her fantasy world with the prophetic utterances of her adopted mother. To return to her dead mother's doorstep and sit on its threshold, as she did in the TV programme, was to invoke body memory, to unsettle and therefore to re-settle a little bit of the territory.

Courtesy of Claire MacDonald.

In Leeds, earlier this year, I performed in *Traces of Her*, a two woman show devised with choreographer Charlotte Vincent (MacDonald and Vincent 2011). Our showing was the result of a dialogue that had started for me in a beguiling way. In around 2008 Charlotte wrote to me, since we had never met, and told me that she knew my 28-year-old body very well (Vincent 2015). She had learned, from video, my performance in *The Carrier Frequency*, one of the last shows I made with Impact Theatre in 1984. Impact was the Leeds based company I co-founded after university, and *The Carrier Frequency* was a collaboration with writer Russell Hoban, in which six of us performed in a large pool of dark cold shallow water (Impact Theatre 1984). The three-act one-hour performance unfolded as a series of tasks which became increasingly difficult to perform as we came colder and wetter. As it progressed the performance became more and more painful and frantic, scored to a soundtrack of industrial sound. It had been seen, both at the time and later, as a ground-breaking piece of theatre making, and was re-staged by the theatre company Stan's Cafe in 1999. Charlotte had performed 'me'. I had been living in America at the time. I hadn't spoken to her about it. I hadn't seen her do it, yet when she wrote to me I felt connected to her in a way that was—and still is—extremely intimate. She had performed *me*, not just a part written for an actor but me. She had copied my gestures, inhabited my space.

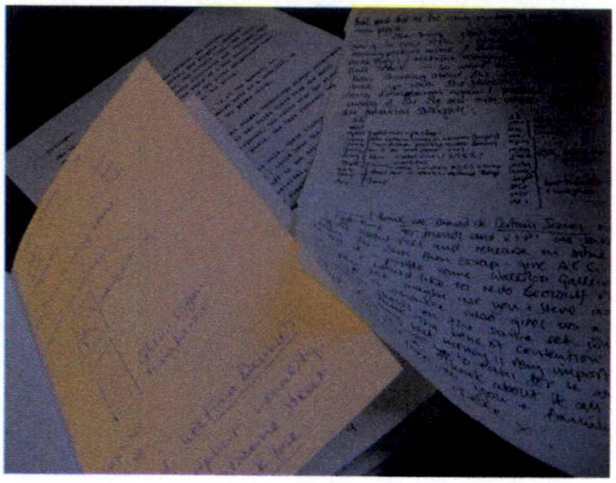

Courtesy of Claire MacDonald.

When Charlotte wrote that she knew my 28-year-old body very well, her letter flooded me with experiential memory—the *space* I had inhabited in that show as a *performer* had informed so much that I had later done as a *writer*. When she wrote to me I felt myself immediately connected to the psychic state in which I had performed that work. It had very little to do with any possible audience or viewer experience, and was more to do with remembering the internal logic which had enabled me to 'conduct' myself, to lead myself through the performance. It was as if Charlotte's hand had reached back and drawn that state into the present. So I agreed to work with her. Two of the many things that emerged from that work were these: the first is that my feelings meant *nothing* to her. They were not shared. She learned my gestures, precisely and with extremely accurate execution, to the extent that they were an exact mirror, as far as possible, of what I had done. They also had no back story, no psychic state, no meaning. They didn't influence or inform her, she had no powerful feeling about them. The second thing was that, despite this, I felt even before I met her that the sharing of a gestural language connected us very closely, and gave us a kind of bond. I became very close to her and very comforted by her presence as if she knows something about me that is beyond language.

What was it about my own psychic state in that show about which I felt so deeply? I was not playing a character. I was performing simple task-based actions—walking, carrying, praying, falling, wiping a table—but they were actions quite literally drenched with language and myth. *The Carrier Frequency* was a piece whose theatre making process was threaded through with the story of Orpheus and Eurydice, echoes of which make their way into the soundtrack, but which, for an audience, are never stated. That story, brought to us in Rilke's version by Russell Hoban, meditates on the point at which life and death, this world and underworld, meet. The state of death, or near death, as a psychic space, was at the time very close to me. My mother had died traumatically and young only five years previously, and my feelings about the female body, and about loss, were intensely bound into my performance, not consciously but experientially.

For me, as a performer, *The Carrier Frequency* was a performance that was double-layered with meanings about the female subject, haunted by the ghostly presence of a woman, albeit a mythical character, Eurydice, on the edge of death. My own performance experience hovered between narrative implication and reductive literalism. In 1982 we had all seen Pina Bausch's *1980* at Sadler's Wells, and my experience of performing in a viscerally physical piece, yet one deeply informed by literary and imaginative structures, echoed my memory of watching Bausch's work. In 1980 the performance space was stripped back to its bare walls; the stage a bright green field of grass; its smell filling the auditorium as water from a sprinkler soaked

Courtesy of Claire MacDonald.

into the soil. During the evening length piece, a female performer danced again and again under its spray, wet, tired, yet curiously transcendent; fully present as a performer, yet sketched in the lightest way as a character. She is not acting; she articulates energy and suggests narrative. She moves in a space in which the familiar co-ordinates of theatrical representation, its sense of make believe, its adherence to fictional time, have been replaced by real grass, real water, real exhaustion. Yet she remains otherworldly, the reality of her experience only underscoring the fictional framing.

It was in talking to Charlotte that I began to strip away the strands of meaning that informed my own performance experience, intimately connected to the history of my own earlier physicality, and still intensely felt to an extent that, to her, may have seemed incomprehensible. *The Carrier Frequency* was imbued—as all Impact's work and perhaps a great deal of work by a generation of performers who were children in the 1960s—with the collective energy of playground gestures: slapping, hitting, falling, shouting and jumping. All these movements were marked with a particular intensity for me, at least, as a formerly dirty, reckless girl, self-styled as brave. My own reckless child-self was always drawn to the highest tree, always jumping in rivers, always biking with no hands—often falling off, and going over the handle bars several times. To be that reckless girl was always to be against the grain of the prevailing culture. It meant being a questioning female subject, because one's body, and by implication one's mind, were always in question. My performance had evoked the gestural body of childhood with an overlay of myth that hinted at more complex images of female hesitation and loss. We have considered at length questions surrounding a performer's real presence and her subjective experience, and these have been a stimulus to the making of theatre and live art. We haven't yet (I don't think) thought very much about the ghostly, historically informed, bodies of our own recent performance history. I am thinking about them now, through my own experience, and I think I am only at the beginning of thinking about this.

When I gave a version of this essay at REDUX in Bristol in December 2012, I hadn't yet shown it to Charlotte, and when I did, quite recently, she shocked me by responding very strongly to the way I had written her into the piece. I had said that my gestures meant nothing to her. She just learned them from video. She knew nothing about the psychic background to the work, or about me. Then I received this from her:

> They meant a lot—but in translation not in a shared intention. I had very powerful feelings about them—just not the same ones as you, because we remade the work 'peripherally'—from the outside in, rather than how you made it, from the inside out, and without consulting you about where the gestures and images had come from. But I *felt* every one—made them my own whilst trying to honour you and your body—tried to make sense of them twenty years later, through committing to the physicality and force and muscularity of the movement. And that's what our bodies shared—the tomboy attack, the reckless indifference to whiplash injuries, the falling over and getting back up again. For me this is the connection—a robust, formidable, energy that was physical and is now more intellectualised out of necessity as our bodies break down. Up into the headspace away from the heart. But when I performed you the heart was really present there (and the feelings and the commitment) just my heart, not yours, with me mimicking, playing, searching for you.
>
> C xxx
>
> Vincent 2015

One returns to the past to find out who one is, not to settle biographical narrative but to resettle the terms under which one can go on, to remember that while life is linear, experience is a space, and, as an artist, also a space—a country, a field indeed—that holds all one's signifying practices, each available for return and repair, for restoration, for new collaboration and understanding. The act of returning to one's earlier work opens rather than closes. It is an act of touching, a hand reaching into the material, the fabric, the soil, the stuff of subjectivity in order to find out what to do—and who to be—next.

References

2012 Anon. The Brighton Table Dinner 27.11.2012. Available online. www.thetable.org.uk/activity/the-table-dinner-two. Accessed 27 February 2017.

2012 Haneke, M. (director) *Amour*. Film: Artificial Eye.

1984 Impact Theatre *The Carrier Frequency*. Performance. Text by Russell Hoban; designer Simon Vincenzi; music Graeme Miller and Steve Shill; director Pete Brooks; performers Heather Ackroyd, Niki Johnson, Claire MacDonald, Graeme Miller, Steve Shill, Richard Hawley.

2014 [1908] Kubin, A. *The Other Side*, London: Dedalus Press.

1988 MacDonald, C. 'Miraculous Order: On *Thirty Pieces of Silver*, a sculptural installation exhibition by Cornelia Parker'. Birmingham: Ikon Gallery.

1990 'Flesh Made Light: On *Stigma*, an installation by Lizzie Calligas'. Athens: Ileana Tounda Gallery.

1999 'All Over the Map, review essay: *A Woman Who ... Essays, Interviews, Scripts* by Yvonne Rainer'. *Performance Research*, 6(1): pp121–3.

2005 'Gloss'. In A. Jahn (ed.) *Perpetual Canon*, Stuttgart: Kunstverein, pp43–8.

2010 'Metoikesis'. In C. Petrinou and T. Syrago (eds) *Metoikesis: Lizzie Calligas*, Benaki, Athens: Cube Art Editions, Athens, pp15–24.

2015 'Correspondence'. In C. MacDonald (ed.) *Utopia: Three Plays for a Postdramatic Theatre*, Bristol: Intellect, pp51–68.

2011 MacDonald, C. and Vincent, C. *Traces of Her*. Performance: Juncture, Yorkshire Dance, Leeds, 24 March.

1999 Rainer, Y. *A Woman Who ... Essays, Interviews, Scripts*, Baltimore: Johns Hopkins University Press.

2012 Southcombe, B. (director) *I, Anna*. Film: Curzon Artificial Eye.

2012 Winterson, J. *My Monster and Me*. Available online. www.bbc.co.uk/programmes/b01p9b9c. Accessed 27 February 2017.

2015 Vincent, C. Personal email letter to Claire MacDonald, 5 May.

The future perfect of the archive: re-thinking performance in the age of third nature

Simon Jones

Artists in the Archive has focused upon the many ways in which artists working today are engaging with and using the remains of performance, the documents, records, ephemera and residual traces of the 'live' event of performance that make up the diverse media of its archives. Through a series of contributions, made by artists and scholars, the range of case studies has demonstrated how performance-makers and live-artists have continued to trouble notions of what constitutes the 'original' performance, how 'histories' of performance are written, and how both the archive and the 'idea' of the archive are used to inform and inflect practice and make new works. I want now to look prospectively towards the 'future' of the archive and offer some speculations on how performance-makers will have to come to respond to the fundamental shifts in our everyday use of new technologies. In part, I want to further the argument others have made that artists' engagement with the archive does not provide what the historian seeks—a *reflective* space in between now and then, which produces versions of what could have been and holds them up as 'equally', if not 'more', significant than the performance itself. Distinctively, the artist uses the archive as *recursive* space, informing what's to come; and more crucially for the future of the archive, offers a decisive resistance to the challenges of new technologies, which

I describe as 'third nature', and the hegemonic cultural and socio-political assemblages, within which both technology in general and the archive as fact and idea are embedded. Using the phenomenology of Martin Heidegger, I propose that the artist, by refusing to use up archive-technology as (in his terms) 'resource', by obliging it to appear as *itself*, re-minds us of this fundamental difference between ourselves as human beings and technology as non-human.

Even though I am driven as an artist-scholar to come to terms with the archive, because of its presence in my work, here I do not want to set the practitioner against the historian as I fully appreciate the role history plays in informing and enriching contemporary performance practices—the works at hand and yet to be done. However, I do intend to caution against what I see as the dangers of our archive culture inherent in this current phase of techno-capitalism, and in so doing, confront an unhelpful orthodoxy about the relation of the archive to practice, which ends up unintentionally colluding in performance's commodification and capitulation to those dangers.

> When the noise of mobile phone chat interrupted my understanding of the work before me, and numerous cameras obscured my view, my brain simply clamped shut.
>
> Helen Cole writing about the DaoDao Festival, Beijing, 2004 in Brine and Shu 2005

> These pieces' [by Qiu Zhijie, Yang Zhichao, Wang Chuyu and Wang Hong] original creative acts are so intertwined with their documentary records that we can hardly distinguish when the artists' performances end and their documentations begin.
>
> Cheng 2012: 174

Meiling Cheng's description of the synchronicity of performance and its documentation echoes Philip Auslander's polemic that the documents of performance themselves perform, that ontologically we cannot conceive of the performance without the document: indeed, in a reversal worthy of Derrida, to all intents and purposes the document stages the performance, in essence, is the performance: 'I am suggesting that performance documents are not analogous to constatives, but to performatives: in other words, *the act of documenting an event as a performance is what constitutes it as such*'. (Auslander 2006: 5, original emphasis). What Cheng sees as a necessary cultural-political tactic to ensure the preservation and dissemination of radical live-art in China—its documentation and circulation through documents (Cheng 2012: 182), Amelia Jones would understand as the necessary means by which we make sense of performance, herself reversing the hierarchy of 'being there' over 'reading' about it from its archival remains:

> As I know from my own experience of the 'real' in general and, in particular, live performances in recent years, these often become more meaningful when reappraised in later years; it is hard to identify patterns of history while one is embedded in them. We 'invent' these patterns, pulling the past together into a manageable picture, retrospectively.
> Jones 1997: 12

More about manageability later. But for the moment, for these writers, performance as an (efficacious) art-form is inaugurated in the instance of its documentation. Whilst it is acknowledged that the document cannot capture 'all' the performance may have entailed, it nevertheless takes priority, for either ontological (Auslander) or ideological (Jones) reasons, over whatever the performance might have been. As far as performance is concerned, there is nothing outside the document. I would contest that Auslander bases his argument on a false conflation of Austinian performatives with performance per se as an art-form: in short, to be performative is not the same as to perform; and to perform for the camera is not the same as to perform for an audience, as each kind of performing produces distinct art-forms—the photo-work and the performance (see Auslander's discussion of Acconci's *Photo-Piece*, 2006: 4–6)—a distinction he has more recently acknowledged in discussing performances made specifically for experiencing online (see 'The Liveness of Watching Online: Performance Room' in Wee 2016). And Jones, in my opinion, fails to consider the overwhelming logocentric force of the document when she argues that performances and their records are equally (if differently) informative, resulting in a flawed assertion that there is an 'equal' role for the historian in interpreting what the artist may have been doing (Jones 1997: 12): in short, paraphrasing Orwell, both performances and documents may well be equal, but some are more equal than others.

Nevertheless, these arguments about the primacy of documentation over performance as event have largely held sway and become the current orthodoxy. I intend to resist this orthodoxy by focusing on the archive *as technology*: I want to propose a counter-theory that the distinctiveness and efficacy of performance as an art-form are not inaugurated in the instant of its documentation and their subsequent interpretations by historians. This misrecognises performance's essential relation as *being with* the archive, resulting in its present being immediately taken up in its future perfect—what it will have been to future historians. It even goes beyond André Lepecki's idea of 'the will to archive' as that which identifies 'in a past work still non-exhausted creative fields of "impalpable possibilities"' (2010: 31), to figure performance's first relation as being with the technological: meaning, its present is immediately taken up with that which cannot be conjugated. By reversing Heidegger's insightful definition of technology, that it is 'no mere means. Technology is a way of revealing. [...] *Technē* belongs to bringing forth, to *poiēsis*; it is something poetic' (1978: 318), I intend to place performance essentially in relation to the archive as technology. This shifts the argument from 'liveness' versus record, 'presence' versus absence. I will then go on to speculate about the artists' role in the future of the archive, based on current developments in archiving technologies.

As a performance-maker, my practice over 20 years has been concerned with a repeated return to one basic question—why make performance in an increasingly mediatised age? In this digitised environment, what can account for the persistence of performance? As such there is an inevitable relationship to technology, but also to the archive as storehouse of performances past, and practice as research in the creating of performances present. This triangulation, within which performance as an art-form and its makers find themselves, is clearly a question of knowledge, more precisely how particular kinds of knowledge are produced, captured and disseminated. So, as a question of first principles, what is performance's claim to specialness amongst art-forms? It would not be that it is time-based or site-specific or contingent upon its participants, since other forms are arguably equally dependent upon their eventness. What performance offers us distinctively is the complexity and intensity, the multidimensionality and manifold temporalities of its bundling and intermingling of media, all gathered together and expressed by way of fleshes mixing, as Emmanuel Levinas succinctly expresses it: '*Esse* is *interesse*; essence is interest' (1998: 4).

Indeed, performance manifests this *being in-between (inter-esse)* in a particularly intense way, since it foregrounds not only its eventness, its happening in that time and in a certain place; but also the manner of this mixing of persons, their fleshes and histories, their desires and prospects. It does this through an intensification not of one particular relation between a material, its expressing by means of a single object, and the solitary viewer, as in our relationship to painting; but by compounding the sensations of the relation between relations. One fundamental in-between, that of different kinds of material, each with their own means and media, their own middles that meddle each in their own curious ways, is compounded furiously in the 'heat' of the event with another in-between, that of the gathering of persons, each aware of the others as persons in their own right. In performance, in putting my self into the middle of the event *as event*, its being both out of and in time, as I generally know it and then as I am experiencing it now, *entre-temps* as Deleuze and Guattari would have it (1994: 158); and its being both there and not there, as I generally position my body in space and there being potentially anywhere other than there, I put myself forth in a doubled sense: *into the midst of various middles amongst others*. This set-up and mix draws from Heidegger's definition of the art-work as essentially an event of participation, extended through time by those who engage with it:

> Preserving the work means standing within the openness of beings that happens in the work. This 'standing-within' of preservation, however, is a knowing. [...] He who truly knows beings knows what he wills to do in the midst of them. [...] [T]he essence of *Existenz* is out-standing standing-within the essential sunderance of the clearing of beings.
>
> Heidegger 1978: 192

From this putting forth, performance-makers seek out collaborators, working each in their own medium and skillset, each with their own discursivity—the choreographic, textual, sonic, musical, pictorial, fleshy. Each collaborator explicitly explores their own material in their own way, and in so doing sustains the open relations between different kinds of material and their composition in the performance: this is the out-standing standing-within unique to performance as an art-form (for more on this application of Heidegger, see Jones 2012). In encountering media in which they are not expert, each has to cross a void in between channels of communication in order to collaborate. This model of collaboration produces a kind of speaking without a common language, making these collaborative relationships endlessly productive and non-resolvable. Furthermore, to borrow a metaphor from quantum mechanics, they are complementary and compossible in that they produce worlds which cannot be equated the one with the other, and would, indeed, contradict one another, were it not that they somehow appear to work alongside each other in the 'same' space-time of the performance-event itself. In theory they should not work; but in practice, the work works precisely *at the point* where 'we' as collaborators cannot: impossible collaboration happens (see Giddens and Jones 2009 for further discussion of this idea and, in this volume, Bodies in Flight's *Do the Wild Thing! Redux* for a practical response to these speculations).

If this being in between the in-betweens is particularly heightened in performance—Derrida did call theatre 'the only art of life' (1978: 247) in critiquing Artaud's attempt to put himself outside of discourse, then how do I document this experience? How can I, if to attend to any specific discourse or practice would render the event's plenitude down to a single medium or text? No, to record in any one language, be it choreographic, musical, pictorial, verbal, would collapse the very specificity of the event's non-specificity, puncture the no-where of its now-here, evidenced only by the compulsively repeated failure of performance's documentary remains after the fact. I can only stalk the realness of the performance-event itself by way of metaphor, only approach it *indirectly* by way of forcing transitionings, crossings across from the representativeness of one kind of documentary remains to the representativeness of another, moving through one document's discursive field then phasing into another, facing another self then turning to a third. And in each phase-transition, the specific relation to the 'performance itself' is occasioned in its own way: it is disclosed as real, since momentarily apparent, observable, recognisable, navigable. This transitioning amongst any work's archival remains is as if I were pulling focus from one plane to another, from foreground to background: a zone of interest becoming a place of concern; and I feel this working-across the archive as movement, as a dynamic through (irreversible) time—*as an event of archiving.*

The document pulls focus from the blur of interest *in the performance* to the hard edge of a definable object of attention *in the record.* So here, by way of each document, the 'original' material's vagueness, which I feel haunting the work or exceeding in potential what the work could have possibly manifested, comes suddenly and always surprisingly into sharp relief. However, not as if I were experiencing the work through one lens alone, but as if suddenly recognising the concreteness of one specific material rendered all others unintelligible. Here is the peculiar clarity that strikes me about performance's documentary remains, each a glimpse in their own way that banishes all other remembrances. Whereas in the event of performance 'itself', I could say that interest dematerialises to the extent that any particular material materialises; and it is only when I sustain the materialising of interest, remain in between the betweens of the work, literally un-wording it, utterly un-phrasing it, patently blurring it, that interest can be properly opened out as new and progressive couplings of thought-sensations. This tension between sustaining the opening out of interest in the performance-event and the instances of clarity realised in performance's documentary remains becomes the productive catalyst at the heart of any encounter between performance-maker and archive.

If not uniquely, then decisively, this opens up questions about how artists work across archives and rehearsal spaces that are fundamentally *technological*, in that they tell us something about our relationship to all technologies. As a performance-maker, I experience two fundamentally different memories encountering one another in the archival remains of performances I have made: that of embodied practice, the experience of having made work over time; and that of the external record irrupting into practice from the outside. This interpolates what was felt with what could never have been felt—the image taken from the point of view I never occupied, the camera's; or even that of the page, since the word written down is never the same one that comes to mind. This struggle of lived memories with external records, the profoundly embodied, what drove the work, with the profoundly disembodied, as in—estranged, like something familiar taken from one and put at a distance, characterises the artist's relation to the archive. And this relating of two very different kinds of recall-retrieval produce significant consequences for performance's use of its archival remains in the age of the digitised record, as a kind of externalised memory, which I aim to theorise in this chapter.

For me, there is always a certain relief in being able to step away from the relentless issue of being together-alone out-standing-standing-within the work as it is being made. A relief in temporarily occupying the abstracted perspective of the document, looking from the outside at the quasi-object that is now the work at hand. Indeed, ironically, as Jones points out (1997: 12, quoted above), it may well be that only by means of the recording device's technological capacity, whether that be camera and computer or pen and paper, can any performance-maker actually realise their work as object, as some(quasi-)thing that can be pointed to and so commented upon. The relief of being able to separate clearly the outside from the inside of the making of the work, disentangling out-standing-standing-within, can provide this necessary refuge from the interminable issue of being in-between the making amongst collaborators. Temporally, this happens as a kind of rhythmic crossing-across from the rehearsal room to the archive, similar to those enacted within the making between media and collaborators. However, this time a transitioning happens from inside to outside that making: a stepping away that the artist temporarily makes in order *to look askance* at the work they have been in the midst of. The gap between these two different perspectives produces a *potentiality* between two profoundly different ways of knowing—insider know-how and critical knowledge. This potentiality becomes the gradient that drives the various crossings-across the artist makes back and forth inside-outside their return to and re-use of archives. It is also why the artist has to make these journeys into the archive *alone*, from their own embodied experience and memories towards these documents, by way of their own self and will amongst collaborators, as Tim Etchells remarked about the process of re-rehearsing Forced Entertainment's *Bloody Mess* (2004) seven years later:

> In many ways, the 'show', as we are rehearsing it in Toulouse, can only be understood as something caught perpetually in between our diverse and at times contradictory memories—what the show was, what it became—and the evidence provided by the numerous but not-quite-authoritative video records of the piece in different stages of rehearsal and presentation.
>
> Etchells 2015: 92

Using the archive in the making provokes a strategy of non-collaboration, designed to explore this solitariness: in an impossible dialogue between record and potential by way of memory and technique.

Furthermore, if insider know-how is always embodied, an intense bundling together of the experience of having made with the making now at hand, it can only be realised by way of specific technological assemblages of artist and equipment, techniques and conventions. Performance has a long history of early adoption of technologies, from *deus ex machina* to arc-light to holograms (see Baugh 2005)—a theme I do not have space to develop here. This fundamental relationship to technology is precisely in order to open up and test the relation between the performer's body as medium, *flesh as ur-technology*, and technology as medium: to explore what it is possible to do, say and feel with such equipment, which is as much as to say—what it is to *live in between such media*. So, with the same force, the performance-maker pushes archiving to reveal the limit-case uses of its technology by focusing precisely upon what cannot be captured by way of that equipment. Take The Wooster Group's 'version' of *Hamlet* (2006), which 'stages' the film-document of the 1964 televised version of Richard Burton's stage version of the iconic character. This complex assemblage of film and video technologies was an early method of broadcasting theatre on television—a forerunner of today's streaming of live events into cinemas. In 're-staging' the performance by way of its film-video document, shown 'simultaneously' as part of the new version, The Wooster Group used each framing to disclose different representative regimes, a relation of actual and virtual bodies and images, within which differences and similarities of performance mode constantly tessellated and interpolated the one with the others across a variety of media. Each had its own discursivity, spatiality and temporality, but all were experienced together by the auditor-spectator, whose attention flickered between the fleshiness of 'live' actors with their impossible task of 'reproducing' the (superhuman) screen-performances and the record's (inhuman) camera movements. Jones's two modes of experiencing slipped and slid alongside one another—'watching' the performance and 'viewing' the video (1997: 11) in an out-standing standing-within that precisely opened up that space outside the document but inside the performing. This space was where the non-human of the technological assemblage could be felt. Indeed and in action, here the impossible inherent in all technology, that which exceeds the human, was staged: a kind of science fiction which, in its logic, proposed the as-yet-unrealised future potential of that equipment. In the case of *Hamlet*, this was the 'streaming' experience of the 'live show' which, in its future perfect(ion), threatens to re-place going to the performance itself. At first, as in The Wooster Group's performance, this proposition is always experienced as fundamentally uncanny, actualised *in performance* as the now-here no-where between being (human) and the impossible (non-human) techno-archive.

The Wooster Group's strategy of incorporating the archive into the work suggests that, for a document of performance to work, it must be forced to fail entirely and completely on its own terms. For instance, it *makes sense* when documenting a performance with video to use multiple camera and microphone positions, to take advice from the camera-operator regarding what we should be looking at, to reshoot what they missed, to alter the theatrical lighting to accommodate the camera's sensitivity, to select shots in post-production and re-mix the sound. The archival document, whether audio-video, written-word or blog, is just such a device, which the performance-maker exposes for what it cannot do in comparison to the performance itself or the performers themselves. The partiality of each technological approach is necessarily disclosed, and in doing so reveals the gaps inherent within and between all media, however 'naturally' they have been embodied. In this way, each (non-)collaborator within any performance can only express in their own medium an aspect of 'the' work in its totality, which exists somewhere in between the photographs and video-screens, the printed page and dancers' moves: each 'document' necessarily pointing beyond itself towards its lost 'object'—the 'life' of the performance.

Therefore, the use of whatever recording technology, its techniques and skillset, inevitably provokes the performance-maker to *go beyond* what can be captured or known about performance, overflowing form and realising in each document a failure to do it all and say it all (see Reason 2006 for a comprehensive account of different forms of documentation; and Anderson 2015 for a compelling study of photography's relation to theatre). So that, despite all its craft and ingenuity, we, as both artists and audiences, still feel we need to *look beyond* what the document *as artefact* tells us about the quasi-object of performance it has realised in front of us. I believe this is why performance persists in a digital age: it is in an evolutionary race with technologies' zeal to capture and its processes of commodification, always running ahead of each new platform's claim to higher resolution and greater fidelity, towards that innovation's inadequacy in the face of performer as flesh, performance as event, as experienced, as lived. The current issue for performance-makers is that performance must now work *amongst* the readiness-to-hand of smart technology, which has foregrounded our relation to the archive in its step-change capacity to capture and replay ever greater instances of our lives, what I will now go on to define as 'third nature'.

I have argued that if an artist is genuinely open to collaborating with others working in different media, this inevitably leads to a deconstructive practice wherein that which each media cannot express effectively discloses the discontinuity in our everyday perception (see Giddens and Jones 2013). These 'gaps' are normally masked by the brain's desire to produce a continuous account (one might say—a fiction) of our being in the world; whereas, in fact, so much of how we experience is learnt through a combination of physical development and acculturation: in effect, what we inherit from the genome—our first nature, encountering what we acquire through interacting with the world—our second nature. Here, I understand 'nature' to be a general process whereby the individual acquires knowledge and techniques through establishing behaviours that are reinforced by exchanging information with the outside environment in ever more predictable circuits of feedback. Firstly, the child's own body is its environment, and instinctive, inherited systems encourage the learning of how to coordinate hand to mouth, to see, to walk and talk. Secondly, the world enlarges to include multifarious objects beyond what is simply 'there', and techniques develop which involve the body interacting with specific technologies external to the body, such as the bicycle or pen, mobile or PC. In each of these natures and in every acquisition, the first encounter is always profoundly disturbing: the knowledge always appears first as nonsense or the technique as ungraspable. Then we 'master' it; the trick is embodied; what was outside becomes part of the inside of being to such an extent that its strangeness is forgotten; it becomes as one with us: we incorporate the new knowledge or technique as second nature. Here, performance as an essentially mixed-media art-form has the potential to intervene in this general processing of how we acquire knowledge by using those very senses and technologies, upon which our techniques are grounded, against themselves, to reveal them as fundamentally strange. I called this deconstructive potential in performance—*de-second-naturing* (see Giddens and Jones 2009).

I want now to suggest that we are living through a profound transformation for the human which many scholars have described as the 'post-human' (see Braidotti 2013 and Hayles 1999 amongst others); but which I think is better understood as *third nature*. This paradigm shift in the human-event is occasioned by the development of complex, integrated and networked technologies, assemblages of robotic and digital machines, which have in effect wholly externalised what previously—in the realm of second nature—was experienced as *the relation between* embodied and disembodied knowledges. Firstly, robots do more accurately and enduringly what humans do; secondly, computers 'think' faster and more comprehensively than humans think; finally, digital archives 'remember' all that we have forgotten. Of course, my anthropomorphisation masks the actual non-congruence of these technological assemblages in the same way second-naturing internalises the fundamental strangeness of older technologies, their non-humanness. All technologies extend the capacity of the human, so second nature is already a move towards the non- (or post-)human, or rather, a troubling of the very notion of what it means to be human, as Steven Mulhall wrote of Heidegger's ontology of Dasein as *a being whose being is an issue for it* (1996: 14). What marks third nature as paradigmatic is the ubiquity and capacity of these techno-assemblages to store, exchange and correlate data. Through their ever-readiness-to-hand, their locative and interactive capacities, the so-called smart technologies of handheld devices, networked to big-data cloud-technology, have shifted the everyday ways in which we acquire and use knowledges and techniques. Not only do they offer us the experience of a ready-to-hand 'augmented' reality, but also their apparent 'instantaneous' 'reply' embeds the illusion of immediacy, that is, a knowledge apparently without a channel of communication—literally a new kind of 'embodied' knowing.

It is possible to trace the impact of third nature across a range of fields. Social media has been assessed as reshaping how individuals relate to their families, peer groups and the wider society, generating a new kind of politics alongside a 'post-truth' hystericisation of public debate: for example, see Marc Prensky's highly influential idea of the 'digital native', someone under 30 years old, born into a world of personal computers and smart devices (Prensky 2001). The increased interest in memory studies has been ascribed to profound transformations in individuals' relationship to the polis, the crisis in history emerging from post-modernism and the geopolitical forces of late capitalism: for example, illuminating studies by Joanne Garde-Hansen (2011), Nancy van House and Elizabeth Churchill (2008), Motti Neiger, Oren Meyers and Eyal Zanberg (2011) analyse the emerging relationship between personal, social and political forces with new media and its technologies, variously describing 'media memory', the impact of 'contextual computing', and the 'tangibility' of memory located in the handheld device. As online archives store ever greater amounts of data, emails, images, videos of individuals' lives (see Katie Day Good's locating of Facebook in a history of personal archives—2012, or Emily Keightley and Michael Pickering's comparison of analogue and digital photography—2014), so the anxiety around memory grows, including not only the fear of dementia, but also the acts of remembrance of culturally and politically significant events—'the history of a people': see Andreas Huyssen's (1995) and Alison Landsberg's (2004) compelling studies on the socio-political impacts of the techno-archive as producing 'prosthetic memories' and 'cultures of amnesia', or Anna Reading's critique of 'globital memory' (2014).

We could even say, in reference to Foucault's provocative history of the modern period (1979), that 'memory', however constructed and retrieved, has replaced sexuality as the primary aspect of individual identity: see Kerwin Lee Klein's critique of memory as a 'therapeutic alternative to historical discourse' (2000: 145). Scholars have speculated on the evolutionary effect 'big data' may have on the brain's capacity to remember, more specifically, what happens to forgetfulness, the brain's way of sorting useful information and avoiding the clutter of 'useless' memories, when everything we need to know is stored externally and there is no longer an evolutionary driver to remember: 'With such an abundance of cheap [online] storage, it is simply no longer economical *to even decide* whether to remember or forget' (Mayer-Schönberger 2011: 68, my emphasis). Victor Mayer-Schönberger calls for forgetfulness as a resistance to the techno-archive: 'As we forget, we regain the freedom to generalize, conceptualize, and *most importantly to act*' (2011: 118, my emphasis, more of this later). From the perspective of this paradigmatic anxiety, the increasing 'live streaming' of performances into cinemas and the increased use of online digital repositories for video documentation of shows, alongside the disciplinary contention between liveness and presence, look like performance studies' own version of this techno-fear: see Mark Poster's grim analysis—'The everyday life emerging in information society is a battleground over the nature of human identity' (2006: 230).

From a phenomenological as well as political perspective, the externalisation of these 'memories' in 'big data' archives, fulfils what Heidegger had predicted in the 1930s would be 'The Completion of Modernity'. This would be achieved when human life was rendered into that which is producible, that is, reproducible, representable, commodifiable, exchangeable. In *Mindfulness* (2006), Heidegger first makes the link to technology: 'The rational animal has become subject and has developed reason into "history", whose sway coincides with the sway of technicity' (2006: 21). Then he redefines 'Art in the Epoch of Completeness of Modernity' as that which leads to the producible: '[I]n its pleasantness, art is an unconditionally organized delivery of makability of beings unto machination' (2006: 23), where '*Machination* means the accordance of everything with *producibility*, indeed in such a way that the unceasing, unconditioned reckoning of everything is pre-directed' (2006: 12). So, for Heidegger, art's out-standing standing-within, its ability to actualise the issue/s of Being, will be replaced by a super-objective, already determined in advance, to render everything in life as representable, thence commodifiable:

> What art brings forth is [...] not works in being-historical sense that inaugurate a clearing of be-ing—the be-ing in which beings first have to be grounded. What art brings forth are 'installations' (form of *organizing* beings): 'poems' are 'declarations'; they are 'appeals' in the sense of *calling out* what already exists in the domain of the all-directing and all-securing public. Word, sound and image are means for

> structuring, stirring, rousing and assembling masses, in short, they are means of organizing.
> Heidegger 2006: 23–4, original emphasis

For Heidegger, this strips art of its decisive function: this producibility of images would inevitably lead to art which

> no longer search[es] 'behind' or 'above' beings, not even feeling 'emptiness', but searching and finding exclusively and maximally, what in the enactment of the machinational is 'liveable', and as such can be incorporated into one's 'own' 'life'—which is shaped by the masses—and thus to foster this as what is solely valid and assuring.
> Heidegger 2006: 26

So much so, that 'Sharing the sway of technicity and "history", art undertakes the organizing of beings whose being is decided upon in advance as machination' (2006: 27). The authenticity of each person's life is lost in the exchange of images of 'living', a bucket-list of 'experiences' that are subject to the 'experience economy' of current techno-capitalism. Heidegger predicted that the fundamental inter-relation of technology, capital and self in the modern age, what I would call this techno-capital assemblage, would pose a profound threat to the individual's capacity to (in everyday words) 'be her/himself':

> Metaphysically, the sway of 'culture' is the same as the sway of 'technicity'. Culture is the technicity of 'history'—culture is the manner in which 'historical' reckoning with values and 'historical' production of goods arrange themselves and so spread the forgottenness of being.
> Heidegger 2006: 147

The embodied memory of experiencing life disappears into the techno-archive's data, images, texts, recordings. These external quasi-objects appear to be prompts to memory (in the Proustian sense), but actually repress remembering in favour of reviewing, recalling in favour of retrieving, always images taken by means of the technology and from its point of view—a position no person ever occupied. Consider the 'selfie' as the ultimate personal archive: the self, seen from the point of view s/he could never occupy her/himself, that of the equipment. But not that of the Other, in Levinas's sense of the person whose otherness calls forth one's own humanity: the selfie de-selves the self into a non-human thingness, that which can be *re-presented rather than felt*. In Heidegger's terms, this set-up 'organizes' or 'pre-directs' us to see our self *as these lifeless images*: we 'perform' them. The apparently instant retrieval of the image appears to behave like a mirror, as if we were in the same time with our image: however, this image appears out of the techno-archive in an entirely different time, discontinuous with our own: the one thing the selfie cannot be is an image of the self. We repress this strangeness and uncanniness in our second-naturing of this techno-assemblage—smart device-selfie-stick-cloud-archive. Or rather, a terrible reversal of Heidegger's ontology of technology, whereby, instead of second-naturing the technology we use, *our nature disappears into 'its' uses of us*: the techno-archive, in 'remembering' us, 'forgets' our distinctive being.

This echoes the materialist analysis of Guy Debord's *The Society of the Spectacle* in its coupling of technology, mass production and cultural behaviour to forces of deathliness:

> The spectacle in its generality is a concrete inversion of life, and, as such, the autonomous movement of non-life. [...] The spectacle is not a collection of images; rather, it is a social relationship between people that is mediated by images.
>
> Debord 1995: 12

However, he did not predict that most of these images would be generated by individuals themselves, rather than cultural corporations and governing groups. The platform, enabling uploading and sharing of data, has become dominant over the channels or organisations, generating wealth for its owners indirectly through associated advertising and not directly through sales. 'Pro-suming' has replaced the Marxist horror of the (pacified and passive) consumer: see David Beer and Roger Burrow's comprehensive exploration of play and 'prosumption' in techno-archives (2013). So much so that the techno-archive irrupts into the making of an artwork, *re-places re-membering*, e-rases it through a foundational *superimposition*. In the facility with which the archi-byte is accessed and shared, the play between the actual and the possible, which has hitherto been the essential dynamic at work in the rehearsal room, is literally overwritten (e-rased): the archi-byte renders everything down to one field of discursivity, that of the document, or at best the negotiation between documents—the photograph versus the video. All becomes a question of 'organization', as Heidegger disparagingly labels art at the completion of modernity. Furthermore, the archi-byte is disentangled from the instant of its capture and endlessly replayed, paused, put into reverse, taken out of the flow of making. This desynchronicity brings the after-the-event-ness of the critical perspective into the making: the time of the historian interferes with the artist's time. I might say—the archi-byte's 'manageability' suppresses all other questions; and the interminable narrativising of one version of events set against another becomes the 'point' of the work, to which endlessly variable intelligibility the artist must be enslaved. In short, in third nature, the time of the historian supplants the time of making: Hal Foster has figured this as 'the archival impulse' of contemporary art, what he sees as 'the will to connect' (2004: 21). So, the autonomy of everyday lives is surrendered to 'smart technology' and 'big data' that feed back to us our 'likes' and 'preferences', and historicises our lives as 'time-lines'.

What then can performance as an art do amongst these techno-archives? How is it to respond to this third nature? In countering these hegemonic and deadening forces, I want to suggest that performance-makers' use of such archiving technologies can constitute a decisive resistance to these cultural and socio-economic assemblages. Because the performance-maker's relationship to the archive must expose the partialities inherent in each technological assemblage, it is essentially one of *de-second-naturing*. This mirrors their working across and in between both collaborators and each other's media in the making of the performance itself. The same fundamental approach carries over into the archive: archive-technology is incorporated into the working relations *as if it were another collaborator*. As such, it remains somehow outside, here somehow itself resistant to co-option, even as it elsewhere insinuates itself into our everyday lives apparently so 'naturally'. In this sense, the presence of the archi-byte in the making of a new work potentially works away at the gaps and aporia already in between the collaborators and their media, skillsets and technologies. The archive itself in its materiality adds an additional dimension to the forcing open of these media in the collaborative encounter, opening out the new work's out-standing-standing-within. It obliges a more explicit non-collaboration to happen—a non-collaboration that I have argued elsewhere emerges at the generative core, or better still—the in-between, of all collaboration in performance-making. This particular forcing of the archive and its technologies in relation to the artist in amongst the making of performance echoes Heidegger's description of the difference between our everyday use of technology and its use in any art-work:

> The more handy a piece of [everyday] equipment is, the more inconspicuous it remains. [...] [However,] the more essentially the [art]work opens itself, the more luminous becomes the uniqueness of the fact that it is rather than not. The more essentially this thrust comes into the open region, the more strange and solitary the work becomes.
>
> Heidegger 1978: 190–1

So, the art-work refuses to use up the archive-technology as resource, as we do our smartphones and cloud storage, by obliging it to appear as *itself* as non-human assemblage, as non-Being. In this way, the artist has the means to re-mind us of the fundamental gap between ourselves as beings and technology as equipment. Otherwise we would disappear in our everyday use into the archive-technology as it would disappear into us: we would not know where we ended and it began. The proof of the archive would replace the life of the event, and so, by extension, all those who participated in that event: 'I know I was there because the images are on Facebook'.

As with so many aspects of modernity and its completion, Samuel Beckett's work insightfully actualises in performance this *aporia-agora*: consider *Krapp's Last Tape* (1958) with its eponymous anti-hero sitting in his pool of light, bent over his tape-machine listening to recordings of his 'younger self'. The first line of the stage direction, which is not alluded to in the following dialogue between voice and recording, is—'A late evening in the future' (Beckett 1973: 9). It is as if Beckett understood the consequences of this then new recording technology, the impact it would have upon our ontology of Being, as well as how the theatre can actualise this uncomfortable and addictive slippage between embodied recollection and archival retrieval: between memory and recording technologies: for instance, Krapp's delight in the word 'Spool' (1973: 10); or his desire, having heard 'that stupid bastard [he] took [him]self for thirty years ago' (1973: 17) describe a sexual encounter, to 'be again in the dingle!' (1973: 19) And all this *played* by a 36-year old actor (Patrick Magee, born 1922, in the original 1958 production) pretending to be Krapp in his seventies listening to his thirty-something self. It is as if the performance were able to 'ravel up the time' of Krapp's life by confusing what we see on stage before us—a pretence of the ageing body, with what we hear on the tape—the actor speaking in his 'own' youthful voice. This places us in what Marcyrose Chvasta might well have described as 'a site of virtualisation, constituted by potentiality and heterogensis' (2005: 167), theatre as virtualisation machine, running ahead of the technology to its limit-case.

What Krapp's situation offers us is the experience of living *as one records*: we see Krapp perform a version of himself for the benefit of the tape-recorder: his topic is a commentary on his 'younger self': his 'life' has become the process of archiving his life. This differs significantly from the Listener in *Ohio Impromptu* (Beckett 1982) who has read to him an account of one listening to an account of his life: here, we cannot be certain that the prose recounts his life because we do not see him write it. It is not possible to write down the experience *as it happens*: the scriptural technology requires one step aside, sit down and write. However, Krapp with his tape-recorder is the equivalent of the modern tourist who views the places she visits through the screen of her smart device; or the concert-goer who holds his camera-phone aloft and peers at the stage by way of its tiny screen (one step further removed than Auslander envisaged in his encomium to mediatisation: see *Liveness*, chapter 3); or more politically in public-order incidents, the camera-on-camera contentions of differing perspectives, police-officer—demonstrator; or more pertinently to this discussion, the 'streaming' of theatre performances in cinemas. In all of these cases, projective looking—how we experience any event happening before us—is reduced to viewing the screen's two-dimensional plane. I am drawn into these 'performances' as would a historian be, deliberating between two documents, determining the truth as a variable between contesting data-sets. Here, life is replaced by the archi-byte; modernity is completed in the process of uploading the archive. This is because in Heidegger's terms the experience is reduced to that which is representable (the data-file). In rendering what I am experiencing as a record, its temporality is removed from the dynamic flow of living: it is, in effect, already done, already deadly. And in the uploading, life is produced as 'an experience' that *will have been lived in the future perfect of the archive*: the now is taken out of 'my' time, 'anyone's' embodied time, and becomes the only possible future through its 'production' as archive.

However, in Krapp's situation, Beckett leaves me suspended between recordings *as if* life were this silence in between, the blank between pictures, the affect the techno-archive cannot ' (re)produce'. He demonstrates that a response to the deadly logic of third nature only becomes possible in the deconstructive turn of opening up the space-time between archiving and the archive, between the making of the record and its production *as record*: take, for instance, Krapp's falling into a reverie as the tape-machine 'records' the silence; or the reverse, of Krapp launching into a prepared account before realising that the machine is not switched on; and then, hearing the 'younger' voice on the tape, sitting listening all together in the theatre—performer, character, recording, auditor-spectator. This goes beyond Rebecca Schneider's recuperation of the archive for performance where she 'resituates' knowing as 'body-to-body transmission', because her resistance is still predicated upon 'reading [...] the document as performative act, and as site of performance' (2001: 105). Beckett shows archiving *in process* alongside the archival *as product*: the capabilities and limitations specific to each are made apparent in their being actualised before us. Witnessing this process discloses an ethically indeterminate out-standing-standing-within in which all participants, Krapp-performer and auditor-spectators alike, can find delight or disturbance in the uncanny slippages between making the archi-byte and interpreting it, between one's embodied perception of the action (Krapp speaking) and what the document (tape) records. Within this archiving as event, we experience process and product as an undecidable in between thing and action, noun and verb.

Furthermore, this undecidedness is felt most keenly at the point the Krapp-performer decides to act (record). Here, performance as event as art-form interferes with or queers the archive's partiality, the very thing which Jones among other historians identifies as the engine of its endless productivity of histories (see Jones 1997: 12), and goes beyond the mere 'organising' of differing versions of reading the archi-byte, the what-ifs of writing a history. This act of deciding forces each archi-byte to appear in its material incompleteness, its solitariness, its inability to realise what is not within its purview, to capture 'it all'. So by participating in this decisiveness, each encounters the material's singularity disclosed there-then, as opposed to its producibility and exchangeability: in effect, we recognise human agency—*a will at work*. Heidegger attaches a crucial importance to this 'will' in resisting the fall into producibility and in expressing the individual's most authentic relation to her/his life:

> [T]he will to foundational knowing-awareness [...] [T]he 'will' 'unto' be-ing does not turn be-ing into an 'object' of striving so as to grasp be-ing representationally-explanatorily and to set be-ing aside as a possession. This 'will' is the will to be-ing, en-owned by be-ing itself unto what is ownmost to this will.
> Heidegger 2006: 52

It is as if each archi-byte awaits the Krapp-performer's decisiveness to bring it 'to life', to 'un-render' it, to give 'voice' to its sounds or 'flesh' to its images—Krapp's hand on the tape-machine's controls. And in acting in relation to the archi-byte, 'he' reminds us of our agency, re-sensitises us to our own unique relation to the archive, actualises how performance both reveals and overcomes the deadliness of the archive, in which everything will have been documented. The performer's decisiveness (will) is a call the performance-event obliges us to answer: we must take a stand in relation to the archive: and counter-intuitively, despite Krapp's endless night of documenting, we are empowered to redeem life from the 'representable' and experience from economy. Here, I am echoing Matthew Causey's plea for a deconstructive turn in performance to confront the hegemonic forces of the technologies of the virtual:

> If the theatre hopes to resist [...], it will have to be able to confront the field of the virtual, not through essentialized constructions of failed subjectivities and antiquated technologies, but rather through a strategic manipulation of the virtual, turning the system against itself.
>
> Causey 2006: 123

I have proposed that performance, because it is 'the only art of life', is an art-form capable of resisting the third nature of humanity when all knowledge will be externalised in massive, integrated techno-archives, achieving what Heidegger predicted would be the completion of modernity and the enslavement of individuals to the technologies they have created, the 'bare life' of 'experiences', 'life styles' and 'time-lines', the fundamental conjugation of which is the future perfect when life cannot be lived because it will already have been lived in the data yet to be archived. Performance's relationship to the archive and its documents cannot be other than an essentially technological one, a relationship to *techne*, technique and knowledge. So, the artist's relation to the archive, thence to all technologies, says something more about performance: that at its heart performance embodies *knowing* because *its very performing is an issue for it*. The relations disclosed in the performing, including those between its liveliness and its recordability as evidenced in the archive, the materialising of the in-between of in-betweens, the relation of relations, are what matters to performance, in the same way that Heidegger's Dasein is a being *whose being is an issue for it*. Indeed, this need or obligation to return to the archive is also a return to what it is that constitutes the performance or act or gesture as art. This recursiveness drives every performance tradition as it is itself driven by the crossings across between its making and its archiving *in and amongst fleshes*: every new generation of performers who must go back to those foundations, or rather, must re-build those foundations *as if for the first time and now amongst the techno-archives of our third nature*. Hence performance's challenge to knowledge as a progressive accumulation of data-sets, objects and reproducible procedures leading towards a 'better', (so say) more 'productive', future; and also performance's fundamental relationship to its archives—as perpetual reinvention in the promise of what's to come.

> Perhaps the point in any case is that repetition is never enough. You need to inhabit the structure, breathe differently in it; breathe a second time. You need to know it in order to forget it (partially). [...] You need to know and unknow.
>
> Etchells 2015: 93

References

2015 Anderson, J. *Theatre and Photography*, Basingstoke: Palgrave Macmillan.

1999 Auslander, P. *Liveness: Performance in a Mediatized Culture*, London: Routledge.

2006 'The Performativity of Performance Documentation'. *Performing Arts Journal*, 84: pp1–10.

2016 'The Liveness of Watching Online: Performance Room'. In C. Wee (ed.) *Perform, Experience, Re-Live*, London: Tate Public Programmes.

2005 Baugh, C. *Theatre, Performance and Technology: The Development of Scenography in the Twentieth Century*, Basingstoke: Palgrave Macmillan.

1973 [1959] Beckett, S. *Krapp's Last Tape and Embers*, London: Faber and Faber.

2013 Beer, D. and Burrows, R. 'Popular Culture, Digital Archives and the New Social Life of Data'. *Theory, Culture and Society*, 30(4): pp47–71.

2013 Braidotti, R. *The Posthuman*, Cambridge: Polity Press.

2005 Brine, D. and Shu, Y. (eds) *China Live*, London: Live Art Development Agency.

2006 Causey, M. *Theatre and Performance in Digital Culture*, London: Routledge.

2012 Cheng, M. 'The Prosthetic Present Tense: Documenting Chinese Time-based Art'. In A. Jones and A. Heathfield (eds) *Perform, Repeat, Record: Live Art in History*, Bristol: Intellect, pp173–86.

2005 Chvasta, M. 'Remembering Praxis: Performance in the Digital Age'. *Text and Performance Quarterly*, 25(2): pp156–70.

2012 Day Good, K. 'From Scrapbook to Facebook: A History of Personal Media Assemblage and Archives', *New Media and Society*, 15(4): pp557–73.

1995 [1967] Debord, G. *The Society of the Spectacle*, trans. D. Nicholson-Smith, New York: Zone Books.

1994 Deleuze, G. and Guattari, F. *What is Philosophy?* trans. H. Tomlinson and G. Burchill, London: Verso Books.

1978 Derrida, J. 'The Theatre of Cruelty and the Closure of Representation'. In *Writing and Difference*, trans. A. Bass, London: Routledge, Kegan and Paul, pp6–19.

2015 Etchells, T. 'Live Forever/ In Fragments, to Begin ...'. *Performance Research*, 20(5): pp87–95.

2004 Foster, H. 'An Archival Impulse'. *October*, 110: pp3–22.

1979 Foucault, M. *The History of Sexuality: An Introduction*, trans. R. Hurley, London: Penguin.

2011 Garde-Hansen, J. *Media and Memory*, Edinburgh: Edinburgh University Press.

2009 Giddens, S. and Jones, S. 'De-second Naturing: Word Unbecoming Flesh in the Work of Bodies in Flight'. In S. Broadhurst and J. Machon (eds) *Sensualities/Textualities and Technologies: Writings of the Body in 21st Century Performance*, Basingstoke: Palgrave Macmillan.

2013 'Working the Middle Ground: Making Bodies in Flight's Performance Walk, *Dream→Work*'. In N. Duxbury (ed.) *Animation of Public Space Through the Arts*, Coimbra: Almedina, pp140–60.

1999 Hayles, N.K. *How We Became Posthuman: Virtual Bodies in Cybernetics, Literature and Informatics*, Chicago: University of Chicago Press.

1978 [1936] Heidegger, M. 'The Origin of the Work of Art'. In D. Farrell Krell (ed.) *Basic Writings*, London: Routledge, Kegan and Paul.

1978 [1953] 'The Question Concerning Technology'. In D. Farrell Krell (ed.) *Basic Writings*, London: Routledge, Kegan and Paul.

2006 *Mindfulness*, trans. P. Emad and T. Kalary, London: Continuum.

2008 House, van, N. and Churchill, E.F. 'Technologies of Memory: Key Issues and Critical Perspectives'. *Memory Studies*, 1(3): pp295–310.

1995 Huyssen, A. *Twilight Memories—Marking Time in a Culture of Amnesia*, Abingdon: Routledge.

1997 Jones, A. '"Presence" in Absentia: Experiencing Performance as Documentation'. *Art Journal*, 56(4): pp11–18.

2012 Jones, S. 'Out-standing standing-within: being alone together in the work of Bodies in Flight'. In G. Giannachi, N. Kaye and M. Shanks (eds) *Archaeologies of Presence*, London: Routledge, pp153–71.

2014 Keightley, E. and Pickering, M. 'Technologies of Memory: Practices of Remembering in Analogue and Digital Photography'. *New Media and Society*, 16(4): pp576–93.

2004 Landsberg, A. *Prosthetic Memory: The Transformation of American Remembrance in the Age of Mass Culture*, New York: Columbia University Press.

2000 Lee Klein, K. 'On the Emergence of Memory in Historical Discourse'. *Representations*, 69: pp127–50.

2010 Lepecki, A. 'The Body as Archive: Will to Re-enact and the Afterlives of Dances'. *Dance Research Journal*, 42(2): pp28–48.

1998 [1974] Levinas, E. *Otherwise than Being*, trans. Alphonso Lingis, Pittsburgh: Duquesne University Press.

2011 [2009] Mayer-Schönberger, V. *Delete: The Virtue of Forgetting in the Digital Age*, Princeton: Princeton University Press.

1996 Mulhall, S. *Heidegger and Being and Time*, London: Routledge.

2011 Neiger, M., Meyers, O. and Zandberg, E. (eds) *On Media Memory: Collective Memory in a New Media Age*, Basingstoke: Palgrave Macmillan.

2006 Poster, M. *Information Please*, Durham: Duke University Press.

2001 Prensky, M. 'Digital Natives, Digital Immigrants'. *On the Horizon*, 9(5): pp1–6.

2014 Reading, A. 'Seeing Red: A Political Economy of Digital Memory'. *Media, Culture and Society*, 36(6): pp748–60.

2006 Reason, M. *Documentation, Disappearance and the Representation of Live Performance*, Basingstoke: Palgrave Macmillan.

2001 Schneider, R. 'Performance Remains'. *Performance Research*, 6(2): pp100–8.

CONTRIBUTORS

GILES BAILEY is an artist and lecturer based in London and Newcastle upon Tyne. Born in York in 1981, he works largely with performance, and uses texts, video fragments and choreographies—either composed or strategically plundered from elsewhere—to rethink conventional approaches to the assemblage and recounting of history. Solo exhibitions and performances have been hosted variously by CCA Glasgow, Kunsthalle Basel, The Hepworth (Wakefield), The Northern Charter (Newcastle), The Chisenhale Gallery (London), OUTPOST Gallery (Norwich) and Kunst Werke (Berlin).

BLAST THEORY is renowned internationally as one of the most adventurous artists' groups using interactive media, creating groundbreaking new forms of performance and interactive art that mix audiences across the internet, live performance and digital broadcasting. Led by Matt Adams, Ju Row Farr and Nick Tandavanitj, the group's work explores the social and political aspects of technology. Drawing on popular culture and games, the work often blurs the boundaries between the real and the fictional. Blast Theory is based in Brighton, UK. http://www.blasttheory.co.uk/

MAAIKE BLEEKER graduated in Art History, Philosophy and Theatre Studies at the University of Amsterdam and is currently Professor of Theatre Studies at Utrecht University. She taught at the Piet Zwart postgraduate program in Fine Arts and the School for New Dance Development, was an artist in residence at the Amsterdam School for the Arts (2006–7) and President of Performance Studies International (2011–16). Her monograph *Visuality in the Theatre* was published by Palgrave. She has co-edited several volumes including *Anatomy Live, Performance and the Operating Theatre* (AUP), *Performance and Phenomenology* (Routledge), *Transmission in Motion* and *The Technologizing of Dance* (Routledge).

BODIES IN FLIGHT is a long-term collaboration between writer-director Simon Jones and choreographer-director Sara Giddens. Founded in 1989 in Bristol (UK), the company has since produced 18 theatre works, gallery installations, site-specific performances and performance-walks, which have toured nationally and internationally. At the core of Bodies in Flight's work is the encounter between flesh and text in performance, where words move and flesh utters. Since 1997, this exploration of textuality and materiality has been articulated through a series of collaborations across media—video, sonic, musical, photographic, radio, sport, as well as more recently with communities across the UK. Alongside these artworks, Bodies in Flight have investigated the potential and limitations of documenting performance through a variety of media, including print publication and online archive, and *Flesh and Text* (2001)—one of the first uses of CD-ROM to archive performance. Bodies in Flight's work features in Josephine Machon's *(Syn)aesthetics? Towards a Definition of Visceral Performance* (2009).

ROSEMARY BUTCHER (1947–2016) was an independent British choreographer who has created over 50 works, toured internationally, and is regarded as one of Europe's most consistently radical and innovative practitioners. Over four decades she has made works that cross the disciplines of choreography and the visual arts. Continually enquiring into new forms and ways of making work, she collaborated with artists, filmmakers, musicians and architects throughout her professional life and influenced many creative practitioners through her choreographing, teaching and mentoring. She enjoyed strong recognition in Europe over many years and was awarded an MBE in 2014 for her contributions to dance in the UK. www.rosemarybutcher.com

PAUL CLARKE is Lecturer in Performance Studies at University of Bristol. He is the director of theatre company Uninvited Guests, whose work has toured nationally and internationally, and is a member of the art collective Performance Re-enactment Society (PRS). From 2008–10 he was the Research Fellow on *Performing the archive: the future of the past*, hosted by University of Bristol's Live Art Archives and Arnolfini archive. He was an investigator on the AHRC-funded project Performing Documents and has published and presented widely on performance and archives, including in *Performing Archives / Archives of Performance*, edited by Rune Gade and Gunhild Borggreen, Museum Tusculanum Press.

ROBIN DEACON is a British artist, writer, filmmaker, and educator. His interdisciplinary work has explored questions of memory, absence and fiction in performance practice, through a constant reconfiguration of his role as an artist—as a journalist and biographer, operator and technician, imposter and stooge. His recent research projects have explored histories of video documentation and outmoded media formats, as well as the practice and ethics of performance reenactment. His live and screen-based work has been extensively presented in Europe, the US, and Asia. He is an Associate Professor and Chair of Performance at the School of the Art Institute of Chicago.

TIM ETCHELLS is an artist and a writer based in the UK whose work shifts between performance, visual art and fiction. He has worked in a wide variety of contexts, notably as the leader of the world-renowned Sheffield-based performance group Forced Entertainment and is currently Professor of Performance at Lancaster University. www.timetchells.com www.forcedentertainment.com

FELIX GMELIN was born in Heidelberg in 1962 and lives and works in Oslo. He studied at The Royal Institute of Art in Stockholm from 1983 to 1988. He currently serves as Professor at the National Academy of the Arts, Oslo. He has had solo shows at PORTIKUS, Frankfurt a.M; Malmö Konstmuseum and Gasworks, London. Gmelin's work has been presented to wider audiences through exhibitions such as the 50th Venice Biennale curated by Francesco Bonami and Daniel Birnbaum; the 52nd Venice Biennale curated by Robert Storr and the berlin biennial 4 curated by Maurizio Cattelan, Massimiliano Gioni and Ali Subotnick.

RICHARD HANCOCK and TRACI KELLY have collaborated since 2001 on an internationally acclaimed body of work, which spans performance, video, installation, photography and text. Central to their research-driven practice are questions of intersubjectivity, materiality and identity. The resulting works have been a series of visceral and queer encounters, both moving and spectacular. Hancock and Kelly have performed, exhibited and lectured at events and venues such as the National Review of Live Art, UK (2005, 2007, 2009), Schwelle7, Germany (2008, 2009, 2010), Performance Space, Australia (2007), Critical Path, Australia (2007), the Museu de Évora, Portugal (2009), PSi, Denmark (2008), Nottdance, UK (2008), the SPILL Festival of Performance, UK (2007), The Granary, Ireland (2007), and the Arnolfini, UK (2007, 2010, 2011).

ADRIAN HEATHFIELD writes on, curates and creates performance. His books include *Out of Now*, a monograph on the Taiwanese-American artist Tehching Hsieh and the edited collections *Perform, Repeat, Record, Live: Art and Performance, Small Acts* and *Shattered Anatomies*. He is currently working on a creative research project—Curating the Ephemeral. He was co-director of Performance Matters, a four-year project exploring the cultural value of performance (2009-13). He co-curated the Live Culture events at Tate Modern, London (2003), was a curatorial adviser and attaché for the 20th Biennale of Sydney and an artistic director with the collective *freethought* of the 2016 Bergen Assembly, Norway. He is curator of Taiwan's exhibition at the 57th Venice Biennale 2017. He is Professor of Performance and Visual Culture at the University of Roehampton, London.

LIN HIXSON and MATTHEW GOULISH formed Every house has a door in 2008. Lin Hixson, director, and Matthew Goulish, dramaturge, formed the company to convene diverse, inter-generational project-specific teams of specialists, including emerging as well as internationally recognised artists. Drawn to historically or critically neglected subjects, Every house creates performance works and performance-related projects in many media. The company is based in Chicago.

JOHN HUNTER worked as artists' assistant at Blast Theory in 2009-12 on a number of ground-breaking interactive works including *A Machine To See With* (2010), *Ivy4Evr* (2011) and *I'd Hide You* (2012). He is now an associate artist with the company. Since 2009, John has been making work with non zero one, the artists' group he founded with friends at Royal Holloway, University of London. Their work has been shown at the Barbican, National Theatre, Roundhouse, BAC, Tate Britain, the Science Museum and others, as well as internationally. The company makes interactive work where you, the participant, are active and important. He also works as a freelance photographer and videographer under the moniker RULER.

JANEZ JANŠA is an artist, writer, performer and director of interdisciplinary performances as well as conceptual and visual artworks. His work contains a strong critical and political dimension and it is focused on the relation between art and social and political context. He is author of the book *JAN FABRE—La Discipline du chaos, le chaos de la discipline*, Armand Colin, Paris 1994) and has been editor in chief of MASKA, performing arts journal from 1999 to 2006. He is the director of Maska, institute for publishing, production and education based in Ljubljana, Slovenia. He is currently research fellow at the international research centre Interweaving Performance Culture in Berlin.

AMELIA JONES is the Robert A. Day Professor in Art and Design and Vice-Dean of Critical Studies at the Roski School of Art and Design, University of Southern California. Trained in art history, film theory, and performance studies, Jones is the author of numerous books, including *Seeing Differently: A History and Theory of Identification and the Visual Arts* (2012), *Self/Image: Technology, Representation, and the Contemporary Subject* (2006), *Irrational Modernism: A Neurasthenic History of New York Dada* (2004), and *Body Art/Performing the Subject* (1998), and the editor or co-editor of anthologies including the *Feminism and Visual Culture Reader* (new edition 2010), *Sexuality* (2014) in the Whitechapel "Documents" series, and, with Adrian Heathfield, *Perform Repeat Record: Live Art in History* (2012). She has also curated exhibitions including 'Sexual Politics: Judy Chicago's Dinner Party in Feminist Art History,' held at UCLA's Armand Hammer Museum of Art in 1996 and 'Material Traces: Time and the Gesture in Contemporary Art in Montreal' (2013).

SIMON JONES, Professor of Performance, University of Bristol, is a writer and scholar, founder and co-director of Bodies in Flight, which has to date produced 18 works and numerous documents of performance that have at their heart the encounter between flesh and text. He has been visiting scholar at Amsterdam University, a visiting artist at The School of the Art Institute of Chicago and Banff Arts Centre. He has published in *Contemporary Theatre Review, Liveartmagazine, Shattered Anatomies, The Cambridge History of British Theatre, Performance Research: on Beckett*, and *Performance Matters*, as well as co-edited *Practice as Research in Performance and Screen*. He recently led two major projects into the accessibility, preservation and creative re-use of live art archives—Into the Future and Performing Documents; and is currently collaborating with composer Michael Ellison on two new operas.

NICK KAYE is Professor of Performance Studies at the University of Exeter. His research focuses on relationships between performance and ideas and practices through distinct but related disciplines, including sculpture, architectural theory, conceptual and performance art, aspects of experimental music, installation, video art and video installation. His single-authored and collaborative books include: *Postmodernism and Performance* (1994), *Art into Theatre* (1996), *Site-Specific Art* (2000), *Staging the Post-Avant-Garde* (2002), *Multi-media* (2007), *Performing Presence: Between the Live and the Simulated* (2011), *Archaeologies of Presence* (2012) and *Dennis Oppenheim: Body to Performance, 1969-73*

(2016) as well as edited volumes of *Contemporary Theatre Review* and *Performance Research*. From 2005 to 2010 he was Principal Investigator for Performing Presence, a large-scale collaborative research project funded by the UK Arts and Humanities Research Council in collaboration with Exeter English, Stanford Archaeology and UCL Computer Science, and subsequently an Investigator for Performing Documents. His current projects include an authored book *Conceptual Performance: Conceptual Art and the Idea Of Performance*, for Routledge.

PIL and GALIA KOLLECTIV are artists, writers and curators working in collaboration. Their work addresses the legacy of modernism and explores the relationship between art and politics. They have had solo shows at Pump House Gallery, London, Te Tuhi Center for the Arts, New Zealand, S1 Artspace, Sheffield and The Showroom, London. They have also presented live work at the Stedelijk Museum, Amsterdam, Kunsthall Oslo and Arnolfini, Bristol. They are the directors of project space xero, kline & coma and work as lecturers in fine art at Reading University, the Royal College of Art and the CASS School of Art.

KOH NGUANG HOW, born in 1963 in Singapore, is an artist associated with the art collective The Artists Village and independent researcher on Singapore art. He worked as a curatorial assistant at the Singapore National Museum Art Gallery from 1985–91. He artistic practice encompasses photography, collage, installation, performance art, archiving and curating. He started exhibiting art archives as early as 1992 in 'Performance Week' at Gallery 21, Singapore. He created The Singapore Art Archive Project in 2005 and subsequently exhibited the project in parts and as a whole in several events including the third Singapore Biennale, the inaugural Singapore NTU CCA Residencies and the opening of Asia Culture Center, Gwangju, South Korea.

JOHANNA LINSLEY is an artist and researcher based in London whose work approaches questions of voice, language and the document. She has published in *Contemporary Theatre Review*, *Performance Research* and *Voice Studies: Critical Approaches to Process, Performance and Experience*. She is currently a post-doctoral researcher at the University of Roehampton, and is co-convener of the Documenting Performance working group for the Theatre and Performance Research Association. She is a founder of the performance/producing collaborative I'm With You (www.imwithyou.me), and a founding partner of UnionDocs, a centre for documentary arts in Brooklyn, New York. www.uniondocs.org. www.jhlinsley.com

CLAIRE MACDONALD is a writer, performer and Unitarian minister whose practice began in visual theatre and whose work now focuses on the practice of conversation. She has a PhD in Critical and Creative Writing from UEA, and is a Professorial Fellow at Central School of Speech and Drama. She co-founded Impact Theatre, the journal *Performance Research*, and, with choreographer Charlotte Vincent, co-directs the feminist network *The Table* (www.thetable.org.uk). She writes on interdisciplinary arts and performance history, and her recent book *Utopia: Three Plays for a Postdramatic Theatre* is published by Intellect. She is now writing a cultural history of Dartington, the modernist arts and education foundation.

TERRY O'CONNOR is a core member of and performer with Forced Entertainment, a collective practice of six artists based in Sheffield who have been making performances since 1984. The ensemble received the 2016 International Ibsen Prize for contribution to theatre. Terry is currently Creative Fellow at the University of Birmingham. In 2009, she was awarded an AHRC Creative Fellowship at Roehampton University and in 2011 she was made Professor of Contemporary Theatre and Performance Practice at the University of Sheffield. She has worked internationally as a mentor, dramaturge and performer, creating a body of her own work investigating exchange between creative and research practice.

MIKE PEARSON is Emeritus Professor of Performance Studies in the Department of Theatre, Film and Television Studies, Aberystwyth University, UK. He creates theatre as a solo artist; with artist/designer Mike Brookes in Pearson/Brookes; with National Theatre Wales; and with senior performers' group Good News From The Future. He is co-author with Michael Shanks of *Theatre/Archaeology* (2001) and author of *In Comes I: Performance, Memory and Landscape* (2006); *Site-Specific Performance* (2010); *The Mickery Theater: An Imperfect Archaeology* (2011); and *Marking Time: Performance, Archaeology and the City* (2013).

PERFORMANCE RE-ENACTMENT SOCIETY is an occasional collective of artists, archivists and researchers who use documents and memories to revive past art experiences and create them anew. Their collaborative performance re-enactments are acts of conservation and transform past works into new events. PRS are Paul Clarke, Clare Thornton and Tom Marshman, with guests. PRS have previously performed and curated projects for *The Pigs of Today are the Hams of Tomorrow*, Plymouth Arts Centre; Norwich Arts Centre; Art Athina, Athens; Arnolfini; Spike Island; South London Gallery; Walsall Art Gallery and Leeds Metropolitan University Gallery. Their bookwork, *Salad Dressing*, made with Tom Sowden and published by Arnolfini, was exhibited in *Ed Ruscha Books & Co.*, Gagosian, New York.

ANDREW QUICK studied English and philosophy at Newcastle University and trained as a theatre director at the Sherman Theatre in Cardiff in 1984. Having worked professionally in making and touring experimental performance, he returned to academic study in 1989, completing a PhD investigating the histories and languages of contemporary British experimental performance at Bristol University. He is currently Professor of Theatre and Performance at Lancaster University and is also a founder member of imitating the dog, an Arts Council funded performance company that tours nationally and internationally. His written academic work is closely bound up with contemporary art practices and much of his writing on performance, photography and installation investigates concepts of space, play, technology, documentation, scenography and performance ethics. He is the author of *The Wooster Group Work Book* (Routledge, 2007), and co-author of a number of performance texts including *Hotel Methuselah* in *Theatre in Pieces* (Methuen, 2011) and *Kellerman* (Presses Universitaires du Mirall, 2011).

STEFANIE SACHSENMAIER (PhD Middlesex University, DEA Sorbonne NIle, MA Goldsmiths College) is Senior Lecturer in Theatre Arts at Middlesex University, Programme Leader of BA Theatre Arts (Performance) and HEA Fellow. Her research interests and publications relate to the processual in creative practice. She has published several articles emerging from her long-term research with choreographer Rosemary Butcher including 'Just in Time: Rosemary Butcher, Making Memories and Marks', co-written with Susan Melrose and Rosemary Butcher, *Performance Research Journal On An/Notations*, 2015. She recently co-edited, together with Noyale Colin, *Collaboration in Performance Practice: Premises, Workings and Failures*, Palgrave Macmillan, 2016.

FIONA TEMPLETON is an internationally recognised innovator in writing and directing for theatre and performance. She is currently Artistic Director and founder of The Relationship, a performance group based in both New York and London; and in the 70s was co-founder of the influential Theatre of Mistakes. Her work is shown at venues as varied as the Tate Britain, the Tramway in Glasgow, the Vortex in Dalston, ODC Theatre in San Francisco, the Puerto Rico International Festival of Theatre, Fort Jay on Governor's Island in New York Harbor, and the abandoned Pennsylvania Eastern State Penitentiary. She has received awards and fellowships including from the Rockefeller Foundation, the US National Endowment for the Arts, the New York Foundation for the Arts, and has held a Senior Judith Wilson Fellowship in poetry and writing for performance at Cambridge.

ZHANG HUAN, born in Anyang Henan Province in 1965, currently works and lives in Shanghai. He focused on performance art in Beijing in the 1990s and was considered one of China's leading contemporary artists. In 1998 he relocated to New York where he gained international recognition. In 2005 he returned to Shanghai and established the Zhang Huan Studio. Zhang Huan expresses his thoughts on daily life, Buddhist doctrines, traditional culture and the current spiritual and physical environment. Besides oil painting, he adopts innovative media such as ash painting, ox-hide sculptures, door carvings, feather woodcuts and other new materials and forms.

ACKNOWLEDGEMENTS

The contributors and editors would like to acknowledge the following people and organisations who supported this publication and the artworks, exhibitions and events which contributed to it: firstly, the Arts and Humanities Research Council (AHRC) who generously funded Performing Documents, a three-year research project based at the University of Bristol and in collaboration with the University of Exeter and Arnolfini Gallery, Bristol, which commissioned the series of artworks, exhibitions and events which have led to this publication. At Arnolfini, we would particularly like to thank its then director Tom Trevor and visual arts curator Axel Wieder, Jamie Eastman Live Art curator and Lauren Jury Live Art coordinator; in addition, Helen Cole, artistic director of In Between Time Festival, Bristol, Susie Potts, administrator of Performing Documents, alongside Cara Davies project doctoral student, Bex Carrington curator of the Live Art Archives of the University of Bristol Theatre Collection and its director Jo Elsworth, who all contributed to the success of those artworks, exhibitions and events.

We would also like to extend special thanks to Zak Group, London, for their design of this volume, particularly Grégory Ambos and Julie Kim.

We are grateful to the following copyright holders for permission to reproduce the images in essays: Chris Burden Estate and Gagosian, Tom Marioni and Crown Point Press, Markus Tretter and Kunsthauz Bregenz, ZKM | Karlsruhe and DACS, Lynn Hershman Leeson, Nao Bustamente, Mary Gearhart, The Wooster Group and Rabih Mroué. Images in the REMAKE, RETURN, REVIEW and ARCHIVE sections of artists' pages are reproduced courtesy of the respective authors unless otherwise specified on the relevant page.

Nick Kaye is grateful to Professor David Houston Jones of the Department of Modern Languages, University of Exeter, for directing him to the artwork *An Incomplete History of Conceptual Art* by Silvia Kolbowski. Simon Jones is grateful to Peter Dickinson, editor of *Performance Matters*, for allowing an earlier version of part of his chapter to be reprinted here.

Thanks also to Clare Thornton and Carl Newland for kindly providing us with a fitting cover image emerging from one of the artworks specially commissioned for Performing Documents and this volume, entitled *After, After Richard Hughes*, risograph print (2012) Clare Thornton. Original photo: Carl Newland.

Lastly, the editors would like to thank our contributors for their commitment, imagination and patience throughout the process of completing this book.

INDEX

Unless stated otherwise, entries in italics indicate performances.

First edition published 2018
by Routledge
2 Park Square, Milton Park, Abingdon,
Oxon, OX14 4RN

and by Routledge
711 Third Avenue, New York, NY 10017

Routledge is an imprint of the Taylor & Francis Group, an informa business

British Library Cataloguing-in-Publication Data
A catalogue record for this book is available from the British Library

Library of Congress Cataloging-in-Publication Data
Names: Clarke, Paul H., editor of compilation.
Jones, Simon, (Academic) editor of compilation.
Kaye, Nick, editor of compilation.
Linsley, Johanna, editor of compilation.
Title: Artists in the Archive: Creative and Curatorial Engagements with Documents of Art and Performance.
Edited by Paul Clarke, Simon Jones, Nick Kaye and Johanna Linsley.
Description: Abingdon, Oxon; New York: Routledge, 2018. Includes index.
Identifiers: LCCN 2017050798
ISBN 9781138915381 (hbk)
ISBN 9781138929784 (pbk)
ISBN 9781315680972 (ebk)
Subjects: LCSH: Performing arts archives.
Arts—Philosophy.
Arts—Study and teaching—Philosophy.
Classification: LCC PN1575.5 .A75 2018
DDC 026/.792—dc23
LC record available at https://lccn.loc.gov/2017050798

ISBN: 978-1-138-91538-1 (hbk)
ISBN: 978-1-138-92978-4 (pbk)
ISBN: 978-1-315-68097-2 (ebk)

Graphic Design by Zak Group

9781138929784